Information Systems

Information Systems

The State of the Field

Edited by

John Leslie King
University of Michigan

Kalle Lyytinen
Case Western Reserve University

John Wiley & Sons, Ltd

Other Wiley Editorial Offices

John Wiley & Sons Inc., 111 River Street, Hoboken, NJ 07030, USA

Jossey-Bass, 989 Market Street, San Francisco, CA 94103-1741, USA

Wiley-VCH Verlag GmbH, Boschstr. 12, D-69469 Weinheim, Germany

John Wiley & Sons Australia Ltd, 42 McDougall Street, Milton, Queensland 4064, Australia

John Wiley & Sons (Asia) Pte Ltd, 2 Clementi Loop #02-01, Jin Xing Distripark, Singapore
129809

John Wiley & Sons Canada Ltd, 22 Worcester Road, Etobicoke, Ontario, Canada M9W 1L1

Wiley also publishes its books in a variety of electronic formats. Some content that appears in
print may not be available in electronic books

Library of Congress Cataloging in Publication Data

Information systems : the state of the field / edited by John Leslie King, Kalle Lyytinen.
    p.   cm.
  ISBN-13 978-0-470-01777-7 (alk. paper)
  ISBN-10 0-470-01777-5 (alk. paper)
  1. Management information systems.   2. Information technology.   I. King, John
  Leslie.   II. Lyytinen, Kalle, 1953–
  T58.6.I487 2006
  658.4′038′011—dc22   2005030101

British Library Cataloguing in Publication Data

A catalogue record for this book is available from the British Library

ISBN-13 978-0-470-01777-7
ISBN-10 0-470-01777-5

Typeset in 11/12.5pt Palatino by Integra Software Services Pvt. Ltd, Pondicherry, India
Printed and bound in Great Britain by T.J. International Ltd, Padstow, Cornwall.
This book is printed on acid-free paper responsibly manufactured from sustainable forestry in
which at least two trees are planted for each one used for paper production

Wiley Series in Information Systems

Wiley Series in Information Systems

To Gerry, who always looked up

Contents

List of Contributors

David Avison is Distinguished Professor of Information and Decision Systems at the ESSEC Business School in Paris, France. He has served previously on faculties at the University of Technology in Sydney, Australia, Brunel University in London, and the University of Southampton. His research on information systems has appeared in more than a dozen books and many academic journal articles. He has served as Co-editor of the *Information Systems Journal* as well as Co-editor of the Butterworth-Heinemann series in Information Systems, as well as in key editorial positions for journals such as *Information Technology and People*, the *Journal of Strategic Information Systems*, *Information Technology and Human Interaction*, the *International Journal of Business Research Methods*, and *Systèmes d'Information et Management*. He has served as President of the UK Academy of Information Systems, and Chair of IFIP 8.2. He holds an MSc from the Polytechnic of North London and a PhD from Aston University, and is a Fellow of the British Computer Society.

Izak Benbasat is CANADA Research Chair in Information Technology Management at the Sauder School of Business, University of British Columbia, Vancouver, Canada, and a Fellow of the Royal Society of Canada. His current research interests include evaluating user interfaces and web-based recommendation agents to facilitate business-to-consumer electronic commerce. He is the past editor-in-chief of *Information Systems Research* and currently is a Senior Editor of the *Journal of the Association for Information Systems*. He received his PhD (1974) in Management Information Systems from the University of Minnesota.

Gerardine DeSanctis was a Thomas F. Keller Professor of Business Administration, Duke University. She previously served on the faculty of the University of Minnesota. Her research focused on computer-mediated work and management of information technology, including the impacts of electronic communication systems on teams and organizations. She served in key editorial roles for *Management Science, Information Systems Research*, the *Journal of Organizational Behavior, Organization Science* and *MIS Quarterly*. She held a PhD from Texas Tech University.

Steve Elliot is Professor and Chair of Business Information Systems at the University of Sydney in Australia. He previously served as Professor of Business and Head of the Central Coast School of eBusiness and Management at the University of Newcastle and on the Faculty of Commerce and Economics at the University of New South Wales. His research work has been directed toward the development of theory in the strategic management of information systems-enabled innovation, particularly in electronic commerce, and has been published in books, international journals and refereed conference proceedings. He chairs the IFIP 8.4, and is a Fellow of the Australian Computer Society. He holds a PhD from the University of Warwick.

Robert D. Galliers is Professor and Provost of Bentley College. He has previously held faculty positions at the London School of Economics, Warwick Business School and Curtin University in Australia. He has published widely in many of the leading international journals on information systems and has also authored a number of books on information systems strategy and the management of change associated with the adoption and appropriation of ICT-based systems within and between organizations. He is editor-in-chief of the *Journal of Strategic Information Systems*, and has served as president of the Association for Information Systems. He holds a PhD in Information Systems from the London School of Economics, and has been awarded an Honorary Doctor of Science degree by Turku University of Economics and Business Administration, Finland.

Alan R. Hevner is an Eminent Scholar and Salomon Brothers/ Hidden River Corporate Park Chair of Distributed Technology Professor in the College of Business Administration at the University of South Florida. He served previously on the faculties at the University of Maryland at College Park and the University of Minnesota. He has published numerous research papers on information systems development, software engineering, distributed database systems and healthcare information systems. He holds a PhD in Computer Science from Purdue University.

Rudy A. Hirschheim is Ourso Family Distinguished Professor of Information Systems in the Information Systems and Decision Sciences Department of the E. J. Ourso College of Business Administration at

Louisiana State University. He served previously on the faculties at the University of Houston, McMaster University, the London School of Economics and Political Science, and Templeton College, Oxford. His research on the managerial and organizational aspects of new information technology has appeared in his books and in many academic journal articles. He currently serves as Consulting Editor of the Wiley Series in Information Systems, and has served on the editorial boards of many journals including the *Journal of the Association for Information Systems, Information and Organization, Information Systems Journal*, the *Journal of Strategic Information Systems*, the *Journal of Information Technology, the European Journal of Information Systems* and *MIS Quarterly*. He received his PhD in Information Systems from the University of London.

C. Suzanne Iacono is Program Director in the Division of Information and Intelligent Systems in the Directorate for Computer and Information Science and Engineering (CISE) at the US National Science Foundation (NSF). She previously served on the faculty in Information Systems at Boston University and as Visiting Scholar at the Sloan School, Massachusetts Institute of Technology. Her research has focused on the social and economic implications of information technology, and has appeared in academic journal articles, book chapters and conference papers. She holds a PhD in Information Systems from the University of Arizona.

John Leslie King is Dean and Professor in the School of Information at the University of Michigan. He previously served on the faculty of the University of California, Irvine. He has published many articles and five books on the relationship between technical and social change, and has served in key editorial positions for many academic journals, including *Information Systems Research, Information Infrastructure and Policy, Information Polity, Organization Science, Organizational Computing and Electronic Commerce, Information Systems Frontiers, ACM Computing Surveys*, the *Journal of Strategic IT, Computer Supported Cooperative Work*, and the *Journal of Information Systems Management*. He is currently a member of the National Science Foundation's Advisory Committees for the directorates of Computer and Information Science and Engineering and Social, Behavioral and Economic Sciences, and a member of the Board of Directors of the Computing Research Association. He holds a PhD in Administration from the University of California, Irvine.

Heinz K. Klein is Invited Chair at Salford University in greater Manchester (UK) and Adjunct Professor at the School of Management of the State University of New York at Binghamton. He has held teaching and research positions at Temple University in Philadelphia as well as in universities in Germany, Canada, Finland, Denmark, New Zealand and South Africa. His research on the philosophy of IS research, foundations of IS theory and methodologies of information systems development have appeared in *MISQ, ISR, Information and Organization, ISJ, CACM, JMIS, Decision Sciences* and other journals, as well as in research monographs and international conference proceedings. He serves on the editorial boards of several scholarly journals and the Wiley Series in Information Systems. He holds a PhD from the Faculty of Business Administration of the University of Munich, and has received an honorary doctorate by the University of Oulu.

Kalle Lyytinen is Iris S. Wolstein Professor at Case Western Reserve University. He has published books, articles and conference papers on his research, which includes system design, method engineering, implementation, software risk assessment, computer-supported cooperative work, standardization, ubiquitous computing, IT-induced innovation in architecture and the construction industry, design and use of ubiquitous applications in health care, high level requirements model for large scale systems, and the development and adoption of broadband wireless standards and services. He serves currently on the editorial boards of several leading IS journals including the *Journal of AIS* (Senior Editor), *Information Systems Research*, the *Journal of Strategic Information Systems, Information and Organization, Requirements Engineering Journal* and *Information Systems Journal* among others. He holds a PhD from the University of Jyväskylä, Finland.

Salvatore T. March is the David K. Wilson Professor of Management at the Owen Graduate School of Management, Vanderbilt University. His research interests are in information system development, distributed database design and electronic commerce. His research has appeared in journals such as *Communications of the ACM, IEEE Transactions on Knowledge and Data Engineering*, and *Information Systems Research*. He served as the Editor-in-Chief of *ACM Computing Surveys* and as an Associate Editor for *MIS Quarterly*. He is currently a Senior Editor for *Information Systems Research* and an associate editor for *Decision Sciences Journal*. He holds a PhD in Operations Research from Cornell University.

Wanda J. Orlikowski is Professor of Information Technologies and Organization Studies at MIT's Sloan School of Management, and the Eaton-Peabody Chair of Communication Sciences at MIT. Her research focuses on the relationship between information technologies and organizing structures, work practices, communication, culture, and control mechanisms, and has appeared in many academic journals and books. She is currently leading a major project on the social and economic implications of Internet technology use in organizations. She has served as a senior editor for *Organization Science*, and on the editorial boards of *Information and Organization*, *Information Technology and People*, and the *SoL Journal*, and is a Research Fellow of the Society of Organizational Learning. She holds a PhD from the Stern School of Business at New York University.

Jinsoo Park is an assistant professor of information systems in the College of Business Administration at Korea University. He was formerly on the faculty of the Carlson School of Management at the University of Minnesota. His research interests are in the areas of semantic interoperability and metadata management in inter-organizational information systems, heterogeneous information resource management and integration, knowledge sharing and coordination, and data modeling. His published research articles appear in *IEEE Computer*, *IEEE Transactions on Knowledge and Data Engineering* and *Information Systems Frontiers*. He currently serves on the editorial board of the *Journal of Database Management*. He holds a PhD in MIS from the University of Arizona.

Sudha Ram is the Eller Professor of MIS at the University of Arizona. Her research focuses on interoperability in heterogeneous databases, semantic modeling, data allocation, and intelligent agents for data management, and has been published in such journals as *Communications of the ACM, IEEE TKDE, ISR* and *Management Science*. She holds a PhD from the University of Illinois at Urbana-Champaign.

Daniel Robey is John B. Zellars Professor of Computer Information Systems at Georgia State University, with a joint appointment in the Department of Management. He previously served on the faculties of Marquette University, the University of Pittsburgh and Florida International University. His research deals with the consequences of information systems in organizations and the processes of system development and implementation, and his publications have appeared in many academic journals and conferences. Professor Robey is Editor-in-Chief of *Information and Organization*, and serves on the editorial boards of *Organization Science, Information Technology and Management*, and *Information Technology and People*. He holds a doctorate in Administrative Science (1973) from Kent State University.

Ron Weber is Professor and Dean in the Faculty of Information Technology at Monash University. He previously served on the faculty of Information Systems in the School of Business and at the University of Queensland, as well as visiting appointments in Canada, Hong Kong, Singapore and the USA. His main research interests are in ontology, modeling, and information systems management, audit and control. He has published extensively in both Australian and international journals, and is the author of the widely used textbook, *Information Systems Control and Audit*. He served as Editor-in-Chief of *MIS Quarterly*, and has held many other editorial positions on key journals in the field. He is a fellow of the Australian Computer Society and the Australian Academy of the Social Sciences, and a life-member of the Accounting and Finance Association of Australia and New Zealand. He holds a PhD in Management Information Systems from the University of Minnesota.

Robert W. Zmud is Professor, Michael F. Price Chair in MIS and Director, Division of MIS at the Michael F. Price College of Business, University of Oklahoma. He served previously on the faculties of Clarkson University, Auburn University, Georgia State University, University of North Carolina at Chapel Hill, and Florida State University. His research interests focus on the organizational impacts of information technology and on the management, implementation and diffusion of information technology. He is a Senior Editor with *Information Systems Research* and with the *Journal of AIS*, and he currently sits on the editorial boards of *Management Science, Academy of Management Review* and *Information and Organization*. He also serves as the Research Director for the Advanced Practices Council of SIM, International. He holds a PhD from the University of Arizona.

Foreword

I am honored to write the foreword to this book, both because of my interest in the collection of articles and essays but also because this book is dedicated to Gerardine DeSanctis. She spent much of her academic career at Minnesota, and I watched her development as a scholar and her unique contributions as a researcher. She was a valued colleague, a nice person, and an unusually fine mentor of doctoral students.

What does one write in a foreword to an interesting and important book of articles and essays? My approach to this book is to write about my reactions when reading it. Not everyone will have the same response, but I hope some of the thoughts I have with respect to the set of articles may assist readers in finding insights that they might otherwise overlook. Keeping in mind the way the field developed is helpful in understanding the discussion of the search for conceptual definition and identity. I therefore begin by giving my view of the development of computer-based information systems in organizations and the related academic field.

Information systems as an academic field did not spring forth full grown. It emerged slowly from the mid-1950s and through the 1960s. During this period, a relatively small number of professors at universities in different countries explored the use of computers for processing and storing data in organizations. These professors had a variety of academic backgrounds such as accounting, organizational behavior, management, operations, management science and economics. These diverse backgrounds, when focused on information systems in organizations, were brought together in forming a field of study in information systems (under a variety of names). Using the late 1960s as the starting point for the field, it is less than 40 years old. Among the organization disciplines, we are the youngest.

Technology for data processing was not new with computers. Punched cards for use in data processing were introduced in the 1890s. This technology was limited by the 80-character capacity of a punched card and the simple capabilities of punched-card sorting, calculating, and printing devices. Because of these limits and simple range of uses, punched-card processing did not generate academic research interest or academic coursework.

Computers removed punched-card data processing constraints and improved upon existing data processing methods. Very quickly, innovative organizations used computers to improve data analysis and increase the quality and value of information for managing organizations. With rapid advances in technology, not only the reporting and management support systems but most of the work systems in organizations began to be redesigned. These activities required specialized skills, new methods and new analysis. A new organization function emerged to manage the technology and perform the analysis, design and implementation of new computer-based systems. Almost every work system in an organization proved to be amenable to improved performance and new capabilities through the affordances of information and communications technology. The activities excited academic interest both because of the need to teach students about them and because of the opportunity to understand the affordances and the processes of design, implementation and use.

As an academic field, we started by focusing on the emerging uses of computers for data processing and improving management information. Early research emphasized the support for analysis and decision making. We soon began also to study the organization function that plans, develops, implements and manages the information system resources (hardware, software, databases, personnel, etc.). We studied processes and methods for obtaining requirements, developing applications and implementing systems. We researched the strategic impact organizational impact and economic value of information systems.

These academic teaching and research activities were conducted in a context of an incredible rate of change in computer and communications technology. If it seems as if we are always studying new applications of IT in organizations, it is because it is true. New or improved technologies provide new affordances that lead to new or redesigned work systems and to new research issues.

The field of information systems has been fortunate to attract a large number of intellectual entrepreneurs. A variety of ideas, concepts, paradigms and philosophies have flourished. New technologies, new affordances and new applications are quickly studied for insights into productivity, necessary revisions to organization forms, and evidence of the impact of the new technology-enabled work systems on workers at all levels, from senior executives to clerks. Traditional assumptions are routinely questioned. For example, some researchers assume that increased productivity is beneficial; other researchers challenge that view and find unsatisfactory consequences, both intended and unintended. The teaching and research boundaries of the field have been fluid. To an outsider, there may be a perception that we are 'application chasers' with no boundaries on what we include in the field. While some in the field may share this view, others view the shifting, expanding boundaries as a good sign of intellectual vigor. Related to discussion of issues of applications and their effects is an ongoing debate about research methods.

This ferment of ideas about the field produced much discussion. I have followed the 'debate' not only because I know and value the participants as scholars and friends but also because I believe we need to understand ourselves and how we fit into a dynamic, interesting field. One of the central issues in the discussion began to be the boundary (what is part of the field and what is not) and if there is a core of the field that defines it as a separate academic discipline. Ron Weber initiated much of the discussion about the core, but it took some time for 'the core' to become a major topic of discussion. Two articles in this book sparked increased academic discourse about definition and boundary:

- 'Desperately Seeking the "IT" in IT Research: A Call to Theorizing the IT Artifact,' by Wanda J. Orlikowski and C. Suzanne Iacono, was published in 2001. The article created much discussion because it proposed that the essential condition for information systems research was that the object of study included an IT artifact. Their argument was often simplified to focus only on the computer and information technology (IT), but this seems to be too narrow. In my terms, they are saying that information systems as an academic, research community has a central focus of IT-enabled systems in organizations. Any system is an artifact, but only systems that depend on IT can be characterized as IT artifacts. In other words, if a manager designs a system that does not employ IT, it is not part of the field; if IT enables the system, it is part of the IS field. This is an important distinction. IT-enabled systems tend to be complex because they involve the intersection of individual preferences, organization issues, work system design and technology. The work of designing and building such systems (artifacts) requires a broad range of expertise involving technology, individual human behaviors and social behaviors.
- 'The Identity Crisis within the IS Discipline: Defining and Communicating the Discipline's Core Properties' by Izak Benbasat and Robert W. Zmud was published in 2003. This article can be viewed as a broader view of the field than just the IT artifact. They present a nomological net for the information system discipline as a

useful way to define the field. It includes the IS function and IS management as well as IT artifacts. The article provides a basis for discourse about the field, and it did generate discussion. It was followed by a number of articles and commentaries, some that supported their ideas and some that did not.

The collection of articles in this book includes some of the articles that sparked new interest in the issues related to the identity of the field. There are also new articles written especially for the book. The authors of the original articles explain their ideas further and respond to comments. The articles selected for this book do not merely talk about the original articles; they also point to new ways of thinking about the issue of identity and boundary. For example, the article by Gerardine DeSanctis suggests the lens of community of practice as a useful, different way of looking at the development of the IS field. Her untimely death prevented her from amplifying her ideas.

There has been vigorous debate in the field about research methods. My own development as a scholar was influenced by the debate, because my view from my training was positivist. The debate in the field began with discussion of positivist versus post-positivist interpretive research. That debate has largely been resolved with substantial acceptance of either method if the method is most appropriate and done well. The exploration of appropriate research has continued. One very important emerging issue is the place of research that designs, builds and tests system ideas, often termed design science. This type of research is common in computer science and engineering, but there has been some lack of clarity as to how it fits research concepts for systems in organizations. A classic article by Sal March and Gerald Smith, written while they were at Minnesota, changed my thinking about design science. A more recent article on the subject and a new essay are included in the book. To be able to justify design science research in a community of scholars is vital, and the two articles in the book are important to all IS scholars.

The discussion of the core of the field (those concepts, properties and processes that are unique or for which the field provides unique understanding) is very useful. While not yet resolved in a nice, tidy way, the articles will help the process of articulating the important elements of the field. Why does an organization need information system specialists? The same question can be applied to all organization functions. Why do organizations have accounting or marketing or finance functions? Every person in the organization needs to know something about these functions but, for example, it would be chaos to have end-user accounting and no accounting function. Likewise, the information systems function has unique roles and unique capabilities that are necessary for organizations. Some of these may be defined as core properties of the field, some are associated with the activities of the function, and some are associated with the applications of information and communications technology in work systems. Framed in this way, the boundaries of the field will always be fluid because IT-enabled systems are changing and expanding in scope. Each new application system presents a shared research space. The function employing the system is interested in the value and use of the application, but information systems is also interested because the design properties, operational properties, value obtained and impact on jobs and people are important to the design knowledge of the IS function and important to the operations and maintenance knowledge needed to support the systems. This view may be extended. As Galliers points out in his trans-disciplinary view of the field, the central role of technology-enabled systems offers an opportunity for IS to incorporate a broad, societal perspective in the design of systems and not be bounded by narrow, technology perspectives.

The discussion about the IS field has a full range of expectations from optimistic to pessimistic. The selection of articles contains the full range. I tend to be an optimist. I believe we are part of an incredibly important field that is at the center of some of the most significant past changes in organizations and that similar changes will continue into the future. In their Introduction, King and Lyytinen pose a question about the future in a somewhat awkward way. They ask 'will the IS field not be okay?' and give their answer as 'perhaps'; in other words, they express a cautionary view that perhaps the IS field will not be okay. My own view is more positive and optimistic; I believe that most probably the IS field will be okay.

In summary, this book of reprinted articles and original pieces is a significant contribution to the field. It brings together material to focus the discussions of the field on essential issues. There is much to be done to improve our understanding and sharpen our explanations, and all this is likely to be challenging and interesting. Clarity will not come in a moment; it takes time and effort. This set of papers helped me, and I believe it will help others.

Gordon B. Davis
Honeywell Professor of Management
Information Systems (Emeritus)
University of Minnesota

Series Preface

The information systems community has grown considerably in the twenty years that we have been publishing the Wiley Series in Information Systems. We are pleased to be a part of the growth of the field, and believe that this series has played, and continues to play, an important role in the intellectual development of the discipline. The primary objective of the series is to publish intellectually insightful works which reflect the best of the research in the information systems community. Books in the Series should help advanced students—particularly those at the graduate level—understand the myriad issues surrounding the broad area of management of IS. Additionally, these works should help guide the IS practitioner community regarding what strategies it ought to adopt to be successful in the future.

To this end, the current volume—*Information Systems: The State of the Field*, edited by John King and Kalle Lyytinen—is an especially welcome addition. This volume brings together a number of the most well-known researchers in the field expressing their views about the nature and future of the IS discipline. The book is based on a collection of seminal articles discussing the underlying assumptions of the IS discipline. The collection provides a fascinating view of the diversity present among the most senior scholars in the field. What makes the book especially interesting is that the editors asked the authors of these articles to write new papers based on what they learned after their earlier articles were published. In effect, the book offers a unique opportunity to see how these authors' thinking about the IS field changed over time. These commentary pieces present a diverse set of opinions and beliefs which should help the field grow and evolve in the future. It is refreshingly well-argued and insightful. There is no question that this book, with its impressive collection of readings, should be on the bookshelves of every serious student of the field. We are delighted to have it as part of our Wiley Series in Information Systems.

Rudy Hirschheim

Introduction

John Leslie King and Kalle Lyytinen

This book is a harvest of perspectives on the growth of the information systems field over the past quarter-century. At first glance, that seems like a straightforward description of how the book was created and what it contains, but appearances can be deceiving: the story is more complicated than that. This effort is not the first to describe the state of the information systems field, but it is the first to do so through the diverse views of authors who disagree with each other as often as they agree. The reader seeking a coherent and consistent description of the state of the IS field will be baffled: that is not to be found in this book. This collection of perspectives reveals the plurality of the field at present. It might have been more honest to subtitle the book, 'The States of the Field', but that seemed like over-reaching, even for the editors.

The plurality of the IS field is a central theme in much of the commentary in this collection. Some authors feel there is a trade-off between plurality and intellectual focus, and that a willingness to incorporate too many different interests in the center of the field dilutes the field's focus and effect. Others feel that the plurality of the field is what makes it exciting and strong, and that the field is, if anything, insufficiently diverse in intellectual perspectives, methods and intentions. Yet, most of those whose opinions align with these caricatures would object that their views are not *exactly* as stated, and that they, in fact, understand and respect the views of those on the other side. The discussion is appropriately heated, but the effort is to create more light than heat.

The general design of the book is a set of original papers, presented in chronological order of appearance, followed by a set of commentaries by most of the authors of those original papers updating their views for the purposes of this collection. The decision to present the papers in chronological order of appearance was primarily a matter of convenience, but it was also a consequence of the fact that we were unable to devise a suitable alternative order. This does not imply that there is no order to the discussion: on the contrary, the authors make clear in all these papers that they see an intellectual tradition of discussion about these topics dating from the earliest days of the field. The problem in coming up with a sensible order other than chronological is that any such order would impose on the papers a precedence entirely of the editors' choosing, and one that would almost certainly receive no greater agreement among the authors than the perspectives expressed. Moreover, the chronological order of the original papers does demonstrate that the discussion has been evolving in the literature, even if not in a completely coordinated manner. Many of these papers were being written contemporaneously, and the latency inherent in review and publication disrupted the ability of the authors to discuss the issues with each other in the manner of a normal conversation. The original readings presented here are an approximate trace of the key issues, over time, as seen from the personal perspectives of authors who read and think about each other's work when they get a chance to see it.

The order of the commentaries could not be chronological—they all came to the editors at about the same time. It would have been easy to assemble the commentaries in order of the appearance of the original papers, but the content of the commentaries suggested an ordering that could be used to package the material. This order is that of the editors, of course, but it is built less from the views of the authors than from the nature of the conversation among the authors during the commentary phase. The editors synthesize the papers and commentaries into a brief conclusion at the end of the book, which is the closest the book comes to describing the state of the field.

We greatly appreciate the help of all the authors who participated in this endeavor. This book has been a community effort, in which the editors were merely the coordinators of assembly and production. (That said, the admonition that the editors are responsible for errors and omissions still applies.) In addition, a debt of gratitude is due to many people in the IS field and in related fields whose thoughts and insights have guided the authors whose work appears in this volume. None of the authors represented here claims to have an exhaustive understanding of this complicated topic, and there is a great deal more that might have been included in this volume with good effect. The choice of what to include in no way marginalizes other important contributions, and the editors stand ready to nod sympathetically at claims that other works should have been included. It should also be said that some of the brightest lights in the IS field spend all their time making direct research contributions, and none discussing the work of the field itself. In any case, as this set of readings makes clear, the discussion is far from finished. Even if all the authors represented here retire from the discussion, recent history suggests that a similar book of entirely new papers cannot be long in coming.

We also thank the editors of this book series, Dick Boland and Rudi Hirscheim, for being assertive and brave; Anneli Anderson, Sarah Booth, Sarah Corney, Matt Duncan, and Rachel Goodyear from John Wiley & Sons for their support and guidance; Gordon Davis for his leadership in our field and his willingness to write a preface for this book; Nikhil Srinivasan for helping to pull the pieces together and managing the nightmare of normalizing n+1 different formats of source text; Kathleen King for her editorial assistance and indexing; and finally, but with most affection, our families for patience as we dealt with yet another of our seemingly interminable projects.

At this point, we shift to the personal voice. This book is dedicated to our dear colleague Gerardine DeSanctis, who died on 16 August 2005, as this book was being finished. To those who knew Gerry, the simple language of the dedication page contains all there is to say. But many who see this book will not have had the privilege of knowing her, so we take this opportunity to address the legacy she left us. Gerry was a prolific and influential scholar and teacher. As part of her legacy, she wrote one of the papers that appears in this volume. As with the other authors of papers that appear in this volume, Gerry was asked to write a commentary. However, unlike our practice with the other original paper authors, we sent Gerry all of the commentaries we had received, and asked her to write a master commentary that integrated the key concepts contained in the commentaries, and by extension, the original papers on which those commentaries were based. We did this because of our deep respect for her insight and judgment. Gerry agreed to do this, and we eagerly awaited her insights. After a short time, she notified us that she could not complete the assignment due to her health problems. Her notification was exactly one week before she passed away. What can we say in response to this?

As a modest beginning, we say that Gerry was willing, quite literally on her deathbed, to contribute to our field. She knew the importance of place, and she was willing to take her place in the vanguard of the field's thinking, irrespective of her physical condition. She lost that bet, but it was a bet worth making. This is not a tale of naïve heroics. Gerry battled the disease that eventually took her for many years, and she knew well its crooked course. She was an idealist, but above all, she was a pragmatic idealist. In her effort to provide a meta-commentary for this book, she hoped to help us make sense out of a dilemma that is central to our sense of ourselves. She did not have the time to do that, but we do. We cannot offer in this book what

Gerry would have said in her commentary, but we can provide through her example a commitment to the challenge she was willing to engage. The larger story to come from Gerry's role in this book, and her role in our field from beginning to end, is the observation that we are all engaged in an endeavor that we shall not live to see the end of. As St James said, our lives are but a vapor that appears for a little while (James 4:14). The glory of our mission, if we see it right, must transcend us. It is not about us. It is about the idea of what we might be.

Original Papers

1
Scoping the Discipline of Information Systems[1]

David Avison and Steve Elliot

INTRODUCTION

In reflecting on the academic discipline of information systems (IS) we might first look at what we mean by 'discipline'. Here we mean 'a branch of instruction or learning' though we do not wish to imply the desirability of, nor actual, agreement on a limited field of study nor total 'control', 'obedience' nor too much 'order' about what we research. This would give grounds for concern, for information systems is a pluralistic field, founded on knowledge from other, more established, source disciplines and frequently borrowing from these disciplines. On the other hand, a lack of 'discipline'—for example, not having an agreed general area for teaching, research and practice—is also a concern, as it leads to a perceived lack of coherence in the discipline and a low status as a consequence. It is this balancing act, between too much control about limiting the issues relevant to the discipline on the one side and the danger of incoherence on the other, which is a central theme of this chapter. This balancing act might be considered to be only of academic interest except for the importance of information systems to industry and to society.

Since the 1990s, applications of information and communication technology (ICT) have been fundamentally changing the way organizations conduct business. These changes create opportunities for

An earlier version of this chapter appears in Avison, D. E. and Pries-Heje, J. (eds) (2005), *Research in Information Systems: A Handbook for Research Supervisors and Their Students*. Copyright 2005, reproduced with permission from Elsevier.

researchers to make significant contributions to knowledge while they assist organizations to manage this change better. The Organization for Economic Cooperation and Development (OECD) acknowledges the structural impact of these technology-enabled innovations:

> The Internet and related advances in information and communication technology (ICT) are transforming economic activity, much as the steam engine, railways and electricity did in the past (OECD, 2001).

But we have reservations about the above as a basis for understanding the discipline of information systems in its concentration on economic activity with technology, rather than the broader activity between people and organizations and technology, and also in its comparison between ICT and the more static technologies mentioned. Major developments in ICT seem to occur every day and there are so many different strands and applications. Further, there can be no doubt that it is transforming society, at least in the developed world and some regions in the developing world.

IS is a relatively new discipline. We consider the start of the discipline to be the widespread use of computers to process data in the 1950s. Of course they existed well before the advent of computers. There can today be IS without computers. The grapevine is a powerful information system. Further, if technology is used, it does not have to be sophisticated. But in practice, information systems are now almost invariably computerized, and can be very sophisticated in their use of technology. The rejoinder is that the organizational context is key, that people will be involved as much as computers, and that not all parts of the information system will be automated.

IS as a field of study developed in response to the increasing necessity of organizations to improve their capabilities to process and to manage data. Reflecting this origin, an information system was initially seen to be an application of computers to help organizations process their data so they could improve their management of information. Indeed, information systems used to be referred to as data processing systems.

While the types of computer technologies developed and potential areas of their application increased, so too did the role of an information system and the scope of the discipline. Information and communication technologies are now ubiquitous in industrialized nations and widespread in much of the rest of the world. Their impact extends from business, across a broad range of application areas, including health and government, to the community at large and into many private homes.

By looking at some potential definitions for the discipline, we will set the scene for our discussion on its scope. Our starting point for a definition of information systems is that of Avison and Fitzgerald (2003, p. xi): 'The effective design, delivery, use and impact of information [and communication] technologies in organizations and society.' This definition captures an important part of IS, that is the development of IT applications, and it recognizes that successful applications of ICT require broader attention than just that on the technology. The IS discipline has steadily developed from its initial 'techno-centric' focus to a more integrated technology, management, organizational and social focus.

But this definition does not capture the excitement of the discipline. We are now in a period of great transformation, as organizations change to address their challenges or achieve their goals. It is also a period of structural transformation of the global economy. ICT supports and enables most of these changes, and IS is the only discipline with a primary focus to study the applications of technology by organizations and society. It is therefore particularly relevant during this period of great change.

The following definition suggested by the UK Academy for Information Systems is somewhat broader than the definition looked at previously:

> The study of information systems and their development is a multi-disciplinary subject and addresses the range of strategic, managerial and operational activities involved in the gathering, processing, storing, distributing and use of information, and its associated technologies, in society and organizations.

The above definition is, however, somewhat passive about IS as it does not give a sense of the creativity and innovative effort that is part of the potential contribution of IS. The definition might also include some scholars from other disciplines, such as the computing disciplines or some management and social science ones, such as sociology or psychology. In his definition, Allen Lee tries to distinguish information systems from other disciplines without presenting too narrow a view. He argues that the IS discipline is distinct in that it:

> examines more than just the technological system, or just the social system, or even the two side by side; in addition it investigates the phenomena that emerge when the two interact. (Lee, 2001, p. iii)

As Lee points out: 'This embodies both a research perspective and a subject matter that differentiate the academic field of information systems from other disciplines' (Lee, 2001, p. iii). However, although it provides a focus, it lacks a sense of the richness of the discipline and its possible contribution.

The above discussion has set the scene on our perspective on the scope of the discipline and, having suggested a fairly broad scope, we turn to differentiating between IS and other related disciplines, both on the technology side and the social side, using Lee's definition above.

DIFFERENTIATING IS FROM RELATED DISCIPLINES

On the technology side of information systems, it is differentiated from computer and IT disciplines by its focus. In a controversial article in the *Harvard Business Review* of May 2003, Nicholas Carr argues that IT doesn't matter. He compares IT to the electricity or telephone infrastructure: the early mover advantage has gone, everyone has it and organizations cannot gain competitive advantage because of it (Carr, 2003). In some respects this is similar to the OECD perspective given at the beginning of the chapter.

But IS is different from IT. As illustrated graphically in Figure 1.1, compared with two other IT-related disciplines, computer science and computer systems engineering, IS emphasizes the applications of technology rather than a focus on fundamental technologies and theories. It focuses more on interactions between people and organizations

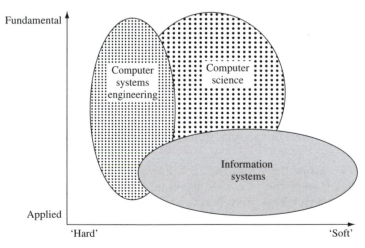

Figure 1.1   *Differentiating IS from other IT-related disciplines (adapted from ACS, 1992)*

(the 'soft' issues) and technology rather than on the technologies (the 'hard' issues) themselves. (It should be noted that Figures 1.1 and 1.2 represent the focus of the different disciplines, not the quantum of work conducted in or contributed by any of the disciplines.)

Figure 1.3 is a comic-strip representation of the different viewpoints of the computer scientist and the IS researcher vis-à-vis the computer. Whereas the computer scientist and systems engineer will be looking at the technology, interested in technology itself, the

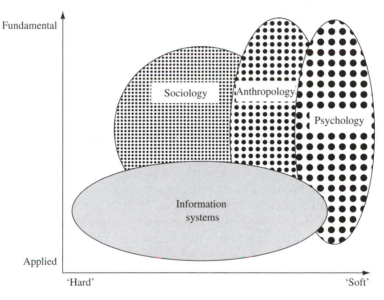

Figure 1.2 *Differentiating IS from other social science disciplines*

Figure 1.3 *The computer scientist and the IS researcher (or the software developer and the systems analyst)*

information systems researcher is looking away from the computer to its impacts on people and organizations. In the same way, in practice, the software developer is focused on the technology, whereas the systems analyst is focused on the business.

This emphasis on soft, or human and organizational, issues may suggest that IS should be seen more as a social science discipline rather than science or engineering. But as shown in Figure 1.2, sociology, psychology, anthropology and other social sciences do not share our emphasis on the applications of technology to organizations and society.

Like computer science, these other disciplines can be seen as both related disciplines and foundation disciplines of IS. But, while there may be considerable overlap of the disciplines at the boundaries, the disciplines are still differentiated by the focus, purpose and orientation of their activities.

FOUNDATIONS OF IS

We now turn to some of the foundations that support the discipline, beginning with the theoretical foundations. We have seen that the IS discipline is in essence an applied social science pertaining to the use and impact of technology. As researchers were drawn to the discipline, they began by applying the theories, methods and research practices from their original disciplines, primarily computer science on the one side and social sciences and management on the other. A diversity of theory from reference disciplines, including economics, mathematics, linguistics, semiotics, ethics, political science, psychology, sociology and statistics, along with computer science, was applied.

For example, we can see how economic theories might be used to cost-justify an information system to the organization's management; how psychology might be used to assess the impact of the system on individual users; how sociology might be used to assess the impact of the system on organizations and society; and semiotics to study the meaning of signs, how people and computers can communicate, as well as computer science to study the efficiency of software.

One potential problem is that, within these disciplines, different theories exist and these may be mutually inconsistent. As Orlikowski and Baroudi (1991) argue, the social sciences are 'marked by a plethora of "schools of thought," each with its own metatheoretic assumptions, research methodologies, and adherents'.

The theories include systems theory, information theory, design theory, the theory of science and scientific method. It is true that many disciplines (including medicine, management and geography) also do not have a simple and single disciplinary status and can further be described as a collection of social practices. However, as we have already suggested, such a discipline can be seen by other academics as confused and lacking in coherence and academic rigor: in short, the discipline of information systems could lack credibility because it does not have theoretical clarity.

The interdisciplinary nature of the subject is no excuse for a lack of rigor. One of the problems with the use of concepts from another discipline is that they may be used uncritically. Avison and Myers (1995) give an example of the uncritical use of a concept within information systems with the use of the term 'culture'. Researchers in information systems may be unaware of their historical development within the source discipline, and may gloss over the fact that there may be a range of perspectives that operate concurrently.

The way that IS seems to take on board major theoretical underpinnings of other disciplines has been lax at times. In attacking the once-prevalent view that systems theory can be used to underpin IS, Checkland (1999) argues that this should be dispelled as 'naïve optimism…there is no simple link between systems theory and information systems'. Similarly, information theory (Shannon and Weaver, 1949) is a very technical, indeed mathematical, way to perceive communication between humans and organizations that is the essence of IS. It is not mathematical complexity that underpins IS. Stamper (1997) argues the case for the related theory of semiotics (and also linguistics) to be fundamental to IS. The unifying work of Simon (1981) continues to be influential in branches of economics, sociology, psychology, computer science and elsewhere, as well as in IS. The theory of communicative action (Habermas, 1979), structuration theory (Giddens, 1987), and actor-network theory (Latour, 1987) have also become popular in some IS academic circles. As an emerging discipline, IS has also been influenced by writers giving a sociological perspective from within and outside the discipline (for example, the socio-technical theory expressed in Mumford, 1995, and also by Kling, 1996).

Even well-established concepts in IS research such as 'users' have been found simplistic and unrepresentative of the multitude of roles undertaken by users in their interactions with a diversity of applications and people within varying social contexts (Lamb and Kling, 2003). The authors consider earlier research approaches based on the concept of an individualistic user to be limited, leading to an inadequate understanding of information selection, manipulation, communication and exchange in a variety of social contexts.

New insights into the strategic role of IT have also been sought, for example by Sambamurthy, Bharadwaj and Grover (2003), by drawing on recent thinking in strategy, entrepreneurship and IT management. Stressing the critical impact on organizational performance related to its capabilities (agility, digital options and entrepreneurial alertness) and strategic processes (capability-building, entrepreneurial action and co-evolutionary adaptation) these authors consider their antecedents to be research into IT investments and capabilities.

Thus IS has been reliant on the theories espoused in other disciplines. Interestingly, the view that IS serves as a reference for emerging disciplines in a discourse with other reference disciplines has also been promoted recently. Baskerville and Myers (2002) note the development of new fields of study that refer to IS theory for explanations; for example, biotechnology. They also note the increasing influence of IS on disciplines, including accounting, banking and marketing, experiencing structural transformation resulting from application of ICT. As illustrated in Figure 1.4, they present an argument that no single discipline is able to completely address today's multi-faceted research issues so well as IS. A more viable reference model is a network of disciplines in continuous dialogue and exchange, with IS at the center of the network.

These diverse perspectives on the focus of IS theory development, with compelling arguments on all sides, should be recognized as being complementary. The discussion is beneficial to the discipline. The dynamic IS domain requires both excitement and enthusiasm in its research as well as reflective consideration on how dynamically developing research may contribute to, and be consistent with, the

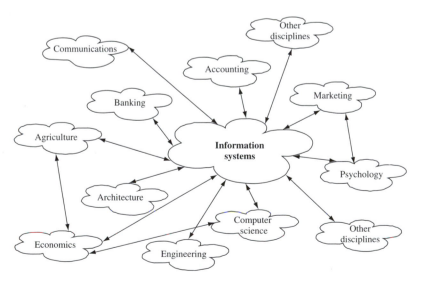

Figure 1.4   *IS as a reference discipline in discourse with other reference disciplines (adapted from Baskerville and Myers, 2002)*

discipline's overall development. The diversity of perspectives means that IS is vibrant both as a discipline and as an area of research.

But the discipline does not rest on its theoretical foundations alone, there need to be practical foundations as well. Major landmarks in the development of the IS discipline were the publication of the first research-oriented IS journal, *Management Information Systems Quarterly (MISQ)*, published in 1977 and the first *International Conference of Information Systems (ICIS)* held in 1980. It is interesting that, at that first conference, Dickson et al. (1980) suggest that IS has an image problem due to an identity crisis, definitional uncertainty, moving target, communication and integration, practitioners vs. academics, research quality and fragmentation, and being the new kid on the block. As we have seen, some of these are still concerns, although much has been achieved since that time.

More recently, the *Association for Information Systems (AIS)* was formed in 1994 as the international organization for IS academics, to add to the many national organizations already existing. Reference to the AIS website at http://isworld.org/ is time well spent and it reveals a very exciting but diverse discipline. To give only two examples, at the time of writing (in 2005) 60 conferences were listed that have taken place or would take place in the first six months of the year, with over 200 journals listed as relevant to the IS researcher.

UNITY AND DIVERSITY

Since the range of ICT is rapidly developing, applications of ICT are also developing rapidly. In consequence, IS research, teaching and practice are characterized by diversity, flexibility and dynamic development. As we have seen, these characteristics may be seen to provide the discipline with both strengths and weaknesses.

The IS discipline's strength lies in its ability to support research into applications of ICT that are structurally transforming traditional business practice and the global economy. The weakness is that the discipline may focus on such a diversity of phenomena that it may appear to lack a central core.

This potential weakness is examined in Benbasat and Zmud's (2003) paper where the authors express concern that the IS research community is contributing to an identity crisis by under-investigating what they call core issues in IS and over-investigating non-core issues. They scope the IS field narrowly and, while acknowledging its multi-disciplinary principles, seek to limit multi-disciplinary practice in IS research. The authors also challenge the current approach discussed above of borrowing and adapting theories from other disciplines to explain IS phenomena better and suggest that focus would be applied more beneficially to original contributions to the IS field. On the other hand, this view has been challenged widely by the IS community.

The narrowness of their proposed scope for IS appears to be too restrictive. It excludes the 'information' aspects of information systems and the rich tradition of diversity in IS. Instead it promotes a narrow focus in research approaches (there is a strongly positivist flavor in their research examples). It omits the major role played by IS in the transformation of organizations, industries and the community which have occurred particularly recently as a result of e-business applications; and much of the excitement and the energy that is associated with assisting to address major issues confronting organizations and the community.

Ironically, in the same *MISQ* issue that Benbasat and Zmud propose limiting the application of reference disciplines to IS theory, two essential concepts of IS theory (both mentioned previously), 'users' and the 'role of IT in firm performance' have been reviewed and substantially revised through exactly this process (Lamb and Kling, 2003; Sambamurthy, Bharadwaj and Grover, 2003).

While Benbasat and Zmud (2003) raises many contentious issues, it does serve as a timely reminder to IS researchers that while a plethora of research opportunities constantly confront us, we need to ensure our focus remains distinctly IS in order to develop our discipline. We turn now, therefore, to suggesting categories of IS research and key concepts in IS from an academic and practice perspective.

Major Categories in IS Research

In June 1988, *MISQ* published a classification scheme of IS keywords 'to provide a description of the discipline, introduce a common language, and enable research of the field's development'. This scheme was updated in 1993 with an additional 175 keywords bringing the total to nearly 1300 'to incorporate the new research topics and methods, hence reflecting better the evolution of the IS discipline' (Barki, Rivard and Talbot, 1993). Table 1.1 shows the scheme with nine major categories.

In a dynamically developing technology and business environment, individual keywords may become out of date and emerging research areas may not receive specific mention. The categories do, however, help to identify the focus of research within the IS discipline. Even where a new phenomenon is not identified explicitly as a keyword, analysis of the categories can provide a framework for its research.

Table 1.1 *Major categories in IS research (Barki, Rivard and Talbot, 1993)*

A   Reference disciplines, including behavioral science, computer science, decision theory, information theory, organizational theory, social science, management science, economic theory, ergonomics, political science and psychology

B   External environment: economic, legal, political and social

C   IT, computer systems and software

D   Organizational environment, including characteristics, functions and tasks

E   IS management, including hardware, software, personnel, projects, planning, evaluation, security and other management issues

F   IS development and operations, life cycles, IS development, implementation and operations

G   IS usage, by organizations and users, and their support, access and processing

H   IS types, application areas, components and characteristics

I   IS education and research

For example, although e-business is not included as a keyword in the classification scheme, e-business research could be located within several different categories depending on the particular topic. These categories include: B, for external drivers and inhibitors of Internet purchasing; C, for specific e-business technologies; D, for organizational aspects of e-business adoption; E, for planning, evaluation and security of e-business applications; F, for development of e-business applications; G, for usage of e-business by organizations; H, for characteristics of e-business systems; and I, for research into the levels of education and research activity in the e-business area.

Indeed, we could complete all the categories if we consider the reference disciplines influencing e-business, thereby adding A. If the research was, for example, concerned with website design characteristics to facilitate online consumer purchasing, then theory from other disciplines including decision theory, ergonomics and psychology may also be considered applicable. The research could be located in category A which is the category relating to reference disciplines (for example, AC sub-discipline decision theory; and AP sub-discipline psychology) and, potentially, categories F (for example, FC development methods and tools) and H (for example, HD IS characteristics).

The research would be classified as IS research not because it could be allocated totally to an IS category, but because the primary focus of the research was within the IS classification categories. If the primary focus of the research was, for example, within a reference discipline such as psychology or ergonomics, rather than in its application to the IS discipline, then the research may be more properly classified and conducted within the other discipline. Indeed, with IS research now impacting on other disciplines, this may well be the case. This categorization of website design also shows how essential it is that IS research issues are sustainable. The particular phenomenon being examined may change, but the underlying IS research issues remain.

Key concepts in IS—educational perspective

As this chapter is attempting to acknowledge the broad scope of IS, it may be useful to examine the perspective of IS educators and of business. Forty of the world's most influential IS educators jointly specified the key concepts in IS for business students (Ives *et al.*, 2002). Among the authors are those who, in another forum, sought to limit the scope of the IS discipline (Benbasat and Zmud, 2003)! It is suggested that this list (Table 1.2) comprises the essence of the discipline in its business and organizational contexts. The breadth of scope and the balanced focus on technology, organizational, management and social issues are noteworthy.

This suggests that IS must retain a broad focus on issues at the intersection of technology and business, and the conclusion of these eminent authors is that: 'We believe that information technology is now the prime driver and enabler of business strategy for many, if not most, organizations' (Ives *et al.*, 2002).

Key IS issues—industry perspective

Given that the focus of IS is on applications of technology in organizations and by individuals, then analysis of the key IS management issues confronting business can assist in defining the core focus of IS. Table 1.3 compares the top ten issues from the international study (CSC, 2004) and a study of 301 Society of Management and the Conference Board members in the USA across more than ten industries (Luftman and McLean, 2004). Although the terminology

Table 1.2   Key IS concepts—educational perspective

1 What are information systems?
2 How do information systems influence organizational competitiveness?
3 Why have databases become so important to modern organizations?
4 Why are technology infrastructures so important to modern organizations?
5 What is the role of the Internet and networking technology in modern organizations and how is e-business transforming organizations and markets?
6 What are the unique economics of information and information systems?
7 How do information systems enable organizational processes?
8 How do organizations develop, acquire and implement information systems?
9 What is the nature of IS management?
10 What ethical, criminal and security issues do organizations face when using information systems?

Table 1.3   *Comparison of key IS/IT issues for executives 2003*

CSC international study 2003 (CSC, 2004)	SIM/TCB USA study 2003 (Luftman and McLean, 2004)
1 Maximizing the return on IT for the business	IT and business alignment
2 Enterprise architectures for business agility	IT strategic planning
3 Safeguarding information assets	Security and privacy
4 Driving competitive advantage through innovation	Attracting / retaining IT professionals
5 Selecting and managing sourcing options	Measuring value of IT
6 Structuring for global organizations	Measuring performance of IT
7 Managing business change	Creating information architecture
8 Managing business relationships	Reducing complexity
9 Connecting with CEO and peers	Speed and agility
10 Adopting new roles and responsibilities	IT governance

differs across the two studies, there is a high level of consistency between the studies about the major IS/IT challenges confronting industry. This high degree of consistency across numerous studies (see also Elliot and Avison, 2005) helps in defining the core focus of the academic discipline of IS.

ALIGNMENT

Concern has been expressed that the IS discipline suffers from a lack of focus due to excessive diversity in its research. Table 1.4 shows a cross analysis of seven sources that contribute to determining IS research focus and theory using the research categories proposed by Barki et al. (1993). The table demonstrates remarkable uniformity in breadth and depth of focus by industry and education over the past 20 years. Despite specific emphasis by one or more sources, taken as a whole, there is a high degree of alignment on core issues.

The outlying categories, reference disciplines and research, could not be expected to be included as issues of concern to industry, but research and education on a specific discipline may reasonably be considered part of that discipline. The IS discipline should continue to engage in a discourse with other reference disciplines as they all seek to cater for technology-enabled transformation of industries and organizations. This appears to be one of the weaknesses of the argument that IS educators and researchers should deliberately exclude potentially relevant theory from other disciplines.

Table 1.4   *Cross-analysis of sources determining core focus of IS research*

Research categories (Barki, Rivard and Talbot, 1993)	Reference	External environment	IT systems	Organizational environment	IS management	IS development and operations	IS usage	IS types	IS education and research
ACS submission, 1992	√	√	√	√	√	√	√	√	√
Benbasat and Zmud, 2003	—	—	√	*	√	√	√	√	*
Baskerville and Myers, 2002	√	√	√	√	√	√	√	√	√
Ives *et al.*, 2002	—	√	√	√	√	√	√	√	√
Key IS management issues, CSC, 2001	—	—	√	√	√	√	√	√	—
Key IS management issues, CSC, 1988	—	√	√	√	√	√	√	√	—
Key technology issues, CSC, 2000	—	√	√	√	√	√	√	√	—
Barki, Rivard and Talbot, 1993	√	√	√	√	√	√	√	√	√

Key: √ core focus; — not mentioned or excluded; * limited applicability

This overview of the IS discipline acknowledges the rapidly developing nature of the IS discipline as it responds to the essential dual roles of IS in enabling organizations to realize potential strategic and operational benefits while facilitating the fundamental transformation of traditional business and government practice and, in a wider context society, through the processes of global transformation.

The IS discipline is located to assist these organizations and industries through both research and education. The energy that powers organizational innovation fuels the energy and excitement that enthuses IS researchers to contribute to the development and revision of IS theory.

Although this chapter acknowledges different views and orientations of researchers in this comparatively new and exciting discipline, core concepts and issues identified by researchers, educators and industry over the period from 1988 to 2003 display fundamental alignment and agreement in their focus. We have demonstrated that there is much more coherence in the discipline than is frequently observed, and this has not meant narrow boundaries in its focus of study.

IS has reached a level of maturity where it has gone beyond merely incorporating seminal works in other disciplines: it now acts as a reference discipline in its own right. Its status has changed from an emerging to an accepted academic discipline, impacting on teaching, research and practice. Its work is both important and permanent.

NOTE

1 Editors' Note: This paper was produced as an original contribution to this volume, but appears first in the chronological order of the papers because it is an update of a paper first published by Avison and Fitzgerald in 1991, and developed further in Elliot and Avison in 2005, and provides a good general introduction to the topics.

REFERENCES

ACS (1992) *Submission to Review of Computing Disciplines*, Australian Computer Society, Canberra.

Avison, D. and Fitzgerald, G. (1991) 'Information systems practice, education and research', *Journal of Information Systems*, 1(1), pp. 5–17.

Avison, D. E. and Fitzgerald, G. (2003) *Information Systems Development: Methodologies, Techniques and Tools*, 3rd edn, McGraw-Hill, London.

Avison, D. E. and Myers, M. D. (1995) 'Information systems and anthropology: An anthropological perspective on IT and organizational culture', *Information Technology and People*, 8(3), pp. 43–56.

Barki, H., Rivard, S. and Talbot, J. (1993) 'A Keyword classification scheme for IS research literature: An update', *MIS Quarterly*, 17(2), pp. 209–26.

Baskerville, R. and Myers, M. (2002) 'Information systems as a reference discipline', *MIS Quarterly*, 26(1), pp. 1–14.

Carr, N. (2003) 'IT doesn't matter', *Harvard Business Review* (May), pp. 1–10.

Checkland, P. B. (1999) 'Systems thinking', in W. L. Currie and R. G. Galliers (eds), *Rethinking Management Information Systems*, OUP, Oxford.

CSC (2004) *16th Annual Survey of IS Management Issues*, Computer Sciences Corporation, El Segundo, California.

Dickson, G. W., Benbasat, I. and King, W. R. (1980) 'The management information systems area: Problems, challenges and opportunities', in *Proceedings of the First International Conference in Information Systems*, McLean, E. R. (ed.), pp. 1–8.

Elliot, S. and Avison, D. (2005) 'Discipline of information systems', in D. Avison and J. Pries-Heje (eds), *Research in Information Systems: A Handbook for Research Supervisors and Their Students* (Butterworth Heinemann), pp. 185–206.

Giddens, A. (1987) *Social Theory and Modern Sociology*, Polity Press, Cambridge.

Habermas, J. (1979) *Communication and the Evolution of Society*, Beacon Press.

Ives, B., Valacich, J. S., Watson, R. T. and Zmud, R. W. (2002) 'What every business student needs to know about information systems', *Communications of the Association for Information Systems*, 9, pp. 467–77.

Kling, R. E. (1996) *Computerization and Controversy*, Academic Press, San Diego.

Lamb, R. and Kling, R. (2003) 'Reconceptualizing users as social actors in information systems research', *MIS Quarterly*, 27(2), pp. 197–235.

Latour, B. (1987) *Science in Action: How to Follow Scientists and Engineers through Society*, Harvard Universilty Press, Cambridge, Mass.

Lee, A. S. (2001) Editorial, *MIS Quarterly*, 25(1), pp. iii–vii.

Luftman, J. and McLean, E. R. (2004) 'Key issues for IT executives', *MISQ Executive*, 3(2), pp. 89–104.

Mumford, E. (1995) *Effective Requirements Analysis and Systems Design: The ETHICS Method*, Macmillan, Basingstoke.

OECD (2001) *The Internet and Business Performance*, OECD, Paris.

Orlikowski, W. J. and Baroudi, J. J. (1991) 'Studying information technology in organizations: Research approaches and assumptions', *Information Systems Research*, 2(1), pp. 1–28.

Sambamurthy, V., Bharadwaj, A. S. and Grover, V. (2003) 'Shaping agility through digital options: Reconceptualizing the role of information technology in contemporary firms', *MIS Quarterly*, 27(2), pp. 237–63.

Shannon, C. E. and Weaver, W. (1949) *The Mathematical Theory of Communication*, University of Illinois Press, Chicago.

Simon, H. A. (1981) *The Sciences of the Artificial*, MIT Press, Cambridge, Mass.

Stamper, R. (1997) 'Organisational semiotics', in J. Mingers and F. Stowell (eds), *Information Systems: An Emerging Discipline*, McGraw Hill, Maidenhead.

2

Desperately Seeking the 'IT' in IT Research: A Call to Theorizing the IT Artifact

Wanda J. Orlikowski and C. Suzanne Iacono

INTRODUCTION

We begin this commentary with what we believe is a telling observation: that the field of Information Systems (IS), which is premised on the centrality of information technology in everyday life, has not deeply engaged its core subject matter—the Information Technology (IT) artifact. While there have been a number of attempts over the years to conceptualize IT artifacts in various ways (as we will describe below), we find that, by and large, IT artifacts—those bundles of material and cultural properties packaged in some socially-recognizable form such as hardware and/or software—continue to be under-theorized. Indeed, IS researchers tend to focus their theoretical attention else-where, for example, on the context within which some usually unspec-ified technology is seen to operate, on the discrete processing capabilities of artifacts (as separate from how they operate in context), or on the dependent variable—that which the technology presumably affects or changes as it is developed, implemented, and used. The outcome is that much IS research draws on commonplace and received notions of technology, resulting in conceptualizations of IT artifacts as relatively stable, discrete, independent, and fixed. As a consequence,

Reprinted by permission, Orlikowski, W. J., S. Iacono, 2001, 'Desperately seeking the IT in IT research: a call to theorizing the IT artifact', *Information Systems Research* 12(2), pp. 121–34. Copyright 2001, the Institute for Operations Research and the Management Sciences, 7240 Parkway Drive, Suite 310, Hanover, MD 21076, USA.

IT artifacts in IS research tend to be taken-for-granted or are assumed to be unproblematic.

The status of technological artifacts as taken-for-granted is not restricted to the IS field, but has permeated most studies of technology, including those in sociology (Bijker, 1995) and organizational studies (Orlikowski and Barley, 2001). For example, Pinch and Bijker (1987, p. 21) argue that '…in the economic analysis of technological innovation everything is included that might be expected to influence innovation, except any discussion of the technology itself.' Articulations of the nature and role of technology, and theories of its interdependence with social contexts are also missing from classic social theory, where technology is either 'black-boxed' and treated as a monolith (Latour, 1987), or it 'vanishes' from view in the preoccupation with social constructions (Button, 1993). Processes such as innovation and change are conceptualized largely in socio-economic terms, while 'things' are not considered or are treated as self-evident (Pinch and Bijker, 1987). Technology, as the quintessential 'thing,' dissipates into the atmosphere around us, or it becomes emblematic of our 'age.' We throw it up as a banner of our times, but then instantly let it recede from view by stereotyping or ignoring it.

In this paper, we present evidence for our assertion that IS research has not seriously engaged its core subject matter—the IT artifact. Our evidence is based on a review of the full set of articles (N=188) published in the *Information Systems Research* journal since its inception ten years ago. For each article, we examined whether and how IS researchers conceptualized and dealt with information technology, and then analyzed the results. After presenting the findings, we discuss their implications, and then offer some directions for research that are premised on the critical importance of developing and using theories of information technology in IS research.

CONCEPTUALIZATIONS OF THE IT ARTIFACT

During the 1980s, several IS researchers attempted to overcome shortcomings in what they perceived to be overly narrow views of technology in the IS field. They offered alternative conceptualizations of what technology is, how it has effects, and how and why it is implicated in social change. Kling and Scacchi (1982), for example, developed the concept of 'web models' of computing in contrast to what they saw as the dominant 'discrete-entity' model of computing. From their perspective, information technology is more than just the tools deployed on the desktop or the factory floor. It is the ensemble or 'web' of equipment, techniques, applications and people that define a social context, including the history of commitments in making up that web, the infrastructure that supports its development and use, and the social relations and processes which make up the terrain in which people use it. A few years later, Markus and Robey (1988) presented a number of different ways of understanding and studying the relationship between technology and organizational change. In their analysis, technology can be theorized as playing different roles—as an independent variable, a dependent variable, or as one of a number of players in an emergent process of change, where the outcomes are indeterminate because they are situationally and dynamically contingent.

Given Kling and Scacchi's and Markus and Robey's articulations of alternative conceptualizations of technology in the 1980s, we wondered what IS researchers had done with them since then. Had they used or built on these conceptualizations, elaborated or expanded them, or perhaps even created new ones? And how had such alternative conceptualizations influenced our collective understanding of the nature and role of technology in organizational and socio-economic practices? To answer these questions, we examined the evidence, reviewing every article that has been published in *Information Systems Research (ISR)* since the journal's commencement in 1990 through to the end of 1999—a decade's worth of data on research in the IS field. Categories of information technology conceptualizations were derived inductively from the data, using the grounded theory approach known as 'open coding' (Strauss, 1987). The interpretations and labels we gave to those conceptualizations were informed by the literature on technology, as reflected in the fields of IS, computer science, organization studies, and sociology.

Based on our coding of the 188 articles published in the past decade of *ISR*, we identified 14 specific conceptualizations of information technology. We then compared these 14 conceptualizations, looking for commonalities and differences, and found we could cluster them into five broad meta-categories each representing a common set of assumptions about and treatments of information technology in IS research. Our labels for these meta-categories signal the primary conceptualization of technology that distinguishes each category: the *tool* view, the *proxy* view, the *ensemble* view, the *computational* view, and the *nominal* view. Below, we first discuss these various views of information technology evident in the *ISR* literature, before turning to a discussion of their representation in the literature and the implications of such results for current and future IS research.

I. *Tool* View of Technology

The tool view represents the common, received wisdom about what technology is and means. Technology, from this view, is the engineered artifact, expected to do what its designers intend it to do. As such, what the technology is and how it works are seen to be largely technical matters—matters that are separate, definable, and unchanging, matters over which humans have control. Two scholars—Rob Kling and Bruno Latour—have conceptualized this view in the course of moving beyond it. Kling (1987, p. 311) describes the 'tool' view of information technology as: 'A computing resource [that] is best conceptualized as a particular piece of equipment, application or technique which provides specifiable information processing capabilities.' He argues that such a view conceives of information technology independently of the social or organizational arrangements within which it is developed and used. Latour (1987), in turn, argues that the tool view 'black boxes' technologies and assumes that they are stable, settled artifacts that can be passed from hand to hand and used as is, by anyone, anytime, and anywhere. George *et al.* (1990)—in a study that investigates the impacts of GDSS on group decision-making—provide an example of this view. They conceptualize the IT artifact as a set of group communication tools with specifiable features that are hypothesized to produce more effective group outcomes than would result from face-to-face communications without those tools.

We found that the 'tool' view was represented in the *ISR* literature in four different ways—as a tool for labor substitution, a tool for enhancing productivity, a tool for information processing, and a tool for changing social relations. These four conceptualizations share a view of information technology as a relatively unproblematic computing resource, and have in common the treatment of such technology as the primary independent variable in the studies undertaken. Little conceptual or theoretical attention is paid to the technology. Often it is just named—as in 'Lotus 1-2-3'—and its technical features are listed. What matters most in these studies is the dependent variable—that which is affected, altered, or transformed by the tool. What this view suggests is that tool-using humans and organizations can vary labor needs, increase performance, enhance information-processing capabilities, and shift social relations.

Technology as labor substitution tool

Since the days of mechanization and automation, it was assumed that new technologies would substitute for and replace labor. Organizations would be more productive because fewer people could do more work (and more reliable work). Early studies of technologies such as shop-floor numerical control machines ignited age-old fears that machines would replace workers (Castells 1996) and led to predictions of mass unemployment. Similar arguments were made for information technology (Attewell and Rule 1984). Applegate *et al.* (1988, p. 129), for example, argue that management information systems are organizational 'tool[s] for downsizing and restructuring' as they can replace scores of analysts and middle managers and enable organizations to work more cheaply and efficiently.

Technology as productivity tool

Subsequent notions of technology shifted from labor-substitution to labor-augmentation. Technologies here are seen to be 'productivity tools,' prosthetic devices that enable individuals and social institutions to extend their reach and achieve performance benefits in the course of their ongoing socio-economic activities. To describe the technical features of a new technology is to understand what that technology will do, as its performance capabilities are assumed to be designed *in* the technical features. For example, in the 1980s, the flexible features of PCs were thought to enable more productivity because workers could more easily shift from one task to another. In the 1990s, the collaborative features of groupware were thought to enable increased productivity as workers could more easily develop and maintain work collaborations. In this view, performance outcomes are assumed to be positive and to result from replacing older (read: slower, less efficient, less accurate, more cumbersome, and more time-consuming) ways of working with new technology-enabled ways of working.

Technology as information processing tool

In practice, simple substitution of new technologies for older ways of doing things did not always produce the expected labor reductions or performance enhancements. An alternative 'tool view' argued that what technology does best is to alter and enhance the ways that humans and organizations process information. For example, at the institutional level of analysis, Leavitt and Whistler (1958) hypothesized that computerization of the firm would allow for information collected at the bottom levels of the firm to flow to the top, thus, recentralizing decision-making authority. More recently, the Internet has been conceptualized in information processing terms, being seen as a large-scale repository of information that can be searched, manipulated, and used for socio-economic gain. IS researchers have also conceptualized individuals and small groups as information processing entities and have focused on the ways in which new technologies—for example, email, spreadsheets, electronic brainstorming applications, and executive support systems—can alter information flows and enhance feedback and learning or, more negatively, result in information overload.

Technology as social relations tool

The fourth 'tool' of conceptualization evident in the *ISR* literature recognizes that in addition to substituting for labor, enhancing performance, and processing information, technologies can and do alter social relations. Following the introduction of new technologies, social roles may change, hierarchies may become more or less salient, business processes may be modified, and communication may require choices among different media and tasks. Over the years, IS researchers have examined shifts in social networks, communication patterns, and work activities associated with the introduction of new technologies that offer different capabilities. For instance, new electronic media have been portrayed as providing different opportunities to convey social presence, social context, and information richness, and such differences have been hypothesized to alter communication behavior and effectiveness.

II. *Proxy* View of Technology

The conceptualizations of technology that we have clustered under the 'proxy' label have in common a focus on one or a few key elements that are understood to represent or stand for the essential aspect, property, or value of the information technology. In our set of *ISR* articles, we found three types of proxy logics. All share in common the assumption that the critical aspects of information technology can be captured through some set of surrogate (usually quantitative) measures—such as individual perceptions, diffusion rates, or dollars spent. For example, the study by Moore and Benbasat (1991) develops an instrument for assessing individual users' perceptions of the new technologies they might consider adopting.

The first proxy logic posits the importance of human understandings in technology use, and thus focuses on technology as viewed by individual users. Perceptual, cognitive, and attitudinal responses to computers become the critical variables in explaining technology and its effects in the world. The second proxy logic concentrates on the diffusion and penetration of technologies within firms, industries, and economies. Here, the critical aspect of technology is the rate with which particular IT artifacts (hardware, software, techniques) become spread across social systems and the extent to which they become integrated into operational activities. The final proxy logic is constituted by monetary measures of technology, the premise being that a useful indicator of the value of technology to a firm or economy is the amount of money spent on it. Thus, dollar amounts of technological investments and changes in them are tracked over time to understand the essential role of technology in organizations and economies.

Technology as perception

In this conceptualization, information technology is represented in terms of measures of users' perceptions of the technology. The variables of study typically include 'ease of use,' 'usefulness,' and 'intention to use the technology.' Researchers are interested in examining individuals' perceptions to better understand what motivates them to accept or use new technologies such as spreadsheets, electronic mail, word processing applications, etc. Many of the articles categorized here draw on theories such as the Technology Acceptance Model (TAM) and the Theory of Planned Behavior (TPB). These theories assume that how individuals perceive a new technology (and make choices about their intention to use it) is based on an internal cost-benefit analysis. Users assess a technology's usefulness and evaluate whether that usefulness exceeds the costs associated with gaining access to it or learning to use it. Over the years, more variables have been added to these theories resulting in more sophisticated approaches to understanding user perceptions and attitudes towards new information technologies.

Technology as diffusion

Technology is represented in this category by measures of diffusion and penetration of a particular type of IT artifact (e.g., electronic mail) within some socio-institutional context such as a firm, industry, or society. What researchers want to know is how many people, organizations, or nations are currently using the technology. The focus is on understanding the processes of diffusion (Rogers 1983) and/or penetration of the technology within and across these settings. If the technological innovation is not diffusing or being used as widely as expected, researchers want to understand the barriers to such processes. These barriers tend to be conceptualized in cultural, organizational, or economic terms, and typical questions include: Why are firms slow to implement the new technology? How can the new technology be integrated into an organization's workflow? What is the critical mass that is needed for widespread use of the new technology? What can a nation do to not be left behind technologically? Such questions have been used to help understand important societal problems such as why developing countries are slow to embrace the Internet or why there appears to be a digital divide in the United States today.

Technology as capital

In this category, technology is conceptualized and measured in terms of dollars—usually the costs associated with the tools themselves (e.g., dollars spent on hardware and/or software) or the information systems infrastructure (e.g., dollars of IS department budget)—and then treated as either an independent or a dependent variable. This view of technology is grounded in the economics discipline, and focuses specifically on the value of the information technology resource or investment to firms, industries, or economies. Typical questions addressed by this literature include: What is the spending on information technology in firms and/or industries? How has spending on information technology changed over time? What is the productivity impact of investing in information technology? These studies examine all manner of industries, firms, and technologies, an analytic move made possible by the abstraction of technology to a homogenized and fairly general (if not completely universal) representation of value—dollars. Such conceptual abstraction facilitates this literature's interest in seeking regularities that hold across organizations and types of information technologies. In particular, this stream of research has been helpful in articulating the so-called 'productivity paradox,' a phenomenon recognized in the late 1980s and early 1990s as organizations increasingly invested in information technologies with apparently little return on their investments.

III. *Ensemble* View of Technology

Over the years, a number of researchers have been dissatisfied with the tool and proxy views of technology. Kling and Dutton (1982) point back to a key insight of Ivan Illich (1973) who argued that while the technical artifact may be a central element in how we conceive of technology, it is only one element in a 'package,' which also includes the components required to apply that technical artifact to some socio-economic activity. Kling and Scacchi (1982) further developed this insight into what they called the 'web of computing,' which includes the commitments, additional resources such as training, skilled staff, and support services, and the development of organizational arrangements, policies, and incentives to enable the effective management and use of new technologies. Latour (1987), similarly dissatisfied with prevailing views, took a different tack. He argued that social scientists tended to make new technologies into 'black boxes' and argued for unpacking those boxes. He observed that if one takes a tool such as a pestle grinder, ties it to a wooden frame, which is then tied to sails that catch the wind, and, then, if the wind can be cajoled to cooperate, one has an 'assembly of forces' or what he refers to as a 'machine.' For Latour, these forces comprise 'systems of alliances' which tie together not only cogs, winds, and sails, but inventors, research and development organizations, commercial companies, and national governments, which can all be enrolled to develop and maintain a machine's existence. Latour examines various technologies—the diesel engine, Eastman's new Kodak camera, and the telephone—and asks, 'How did this machine get to be the way it is? What were the various alliances that had to be formed? What were the various interests that had to be negotiated, so that a black box could emerge?' He claims 'Understanding what...machines are is the same as understanding who the people are' (1987, p. 140). Thus, Latour theorizes about how new technologies come to *be*; Kling and Scacchi theorize about how new technologies come to be *used*.

We identified four variants of the 'ensemble' view in the *ISR* data, with all variants focusing on the dynamic interactions between people and technology—whether during construction, implementation, or use in organizations, or during the deployment of technology in society at large. For example, Robey and Sahay (1996) examined the processes and outcomes associated with the introduction of a geographical information system into two different user groups, and investigated how differential use of the system was influenced by a variety of cultural and social factors. Among the four variants of the ensemble view in the *ISR* data, we found—following the Kling/Latour theoretical split—two conceptualizations focused primarily on the ways in which technologies come to be developed (with secondary emphasis on use), and two conceptualizations focused primarily on how technologies come to be used in certain ways (with secondary emphasis on development).

Technology as development project

The conceptualization of technology represented by the articles in this category is that of an artifact in formation, a 'work in progress.' The focus is on the social processes of designing, developing, and implementing technical artifacts, usually in specific organizational contexts. These articles examine the roles of key stakeholders in IS development projects, how such roles engender conflict, power moves, and symbolic acts, and the influence of more or less inclusive methodologies on development processes. Many of the articles adopted a socio-technical perspective, and most of the articles were field studies, examining one or more particular information systems development projects. These studies have helped to deepen understanding of information systems development as a complex socio-political process, and the ways in which these processes are played out in actual organizations and over time.

Technology as production network

In this conceptualization—like that of the development project— the focus is on the supply-side of technology. But here, technology development is viewed at the levels of industry and nation-state, and much like Latour's view, the focus is on the building of 'systems of alliances,' which tie together inventors, research and development organizations, corporations, and governments who work together to develop new technologies and maintain their competitiveness. Unlike Latour, however, the questions in these articles were not focused on understanding how a particular 'machine' emerged into its current form. Rather, the questions included: 'How did this [part of the] computer industry evolve into its present global structure?' 'Why have some [particular] countries succeeded more than others?' To answer these questions, researchers examined national and international IT policies and the market forces operating within specific countries and regions.

Technology as embedded system

The conceptualization of technology represented by the articles in this category is that of an evolving system embedded in a complex and dynamic social context. Technology is neither an independent nor dependent variable, but, instead, is seen to be enmeshed with the conditions of its use—hence, our label 'embedded system.' This view is similar to the 'web model' articulated by Kling and Scacchi with a focus on better understanding of how technologies come to be used in particular ways. These articles examined the ways in which various social influences shaped how a technology is introduced into a situation, and how different user groups engaged with that technology. Most of the articles viewing technology as an embedded system drew heavily on socio-historical, cultural, and political perspectives, and tended to examine a specific technology as it was embedded in one or a few particular social contexts.

Technology as structure

The conceptualization of technology as structure is also focused on the ways in which technology is enmeshed in the conditions of its use. However, this conceptualization is grounded specifically in ideas drawn from the structuration theory of social theorist Anthony Giddens (1984). Technology here is seen to embody social structures (conceptualized in terms of Giddens' notion of structure as sets of rules and resources), which presumably have been built into the technology by designers during its development and which are then appropriated by users as they interact with the technology. Typical questions addressed by this literature include: How do users appropriate the social structures embodied in a given technology, and with what outcomes? What are the intended and unintended consequences of using a given technology? The articles categorized here were informed by either Orlikowski's (1992) structurational model of technology or DeSanctis and Poole's (1994) adaptive structuration theory. They tended to focus on technologies as concrete, particular technical artifacts such as a specific group decision support system, a type of electronic meeting software, or a customized groupware application.

IV. *Computational* View of Technology

Not all research in the field of IS, however, is interested in the interaction of people with technology in various social contexts. Some research concentrates expressly on the computational power of information technology. Articles embracing this view are interested primarily in the capabilities of the technology to represent, manipulate, store, retrieve, and transmit information, thereby supporting, processing, modeling, or simulating aspects of the world. For example, Trice and Davis (1993) describe a project that generated an algorithm for reconciling discrepant knowledge bases and then built a working program to implement and test it.

We found two types of computational views represented in the *ISR* literature. The first involves the actual development of algorithms and the production of running code by researchers to demonstrate the computational power of the technology as applied to particular domains (e.g., medical diagnosis). The second involves the development and use of computational capabilities by researchers to create models that represent or simulate specific social, economic, or informational phenomena of interest (e.g., decision making, information retrieval).

Technology as algorithm

Technology is represented here through algorithmic endeavors to build new or enhance existing computational systems that can support some human activity. All the articles in this category both named and described (in considerable technical detail) the computational system in question. In addition, most articles also reported on the prototyping and testing of the system, which was not simply modeled, but actually implemented and operating. Most of the studies specified the actual design and building of the computational system—typically through detailed articulation of innovative or improved algorithms—and then offered some validation through testing or provisional use. Articles in this category assumed (whether implicitly or explicitly) that once the algorithmic issues had been resolved, the technology would necessarily be effective and would usefully support the intended human endeavor.

Technology as model

Research in this category attempts to represent social, economic, and informational phenomena (e.g., processes, structures, events, knowledge, etc.) through the methodology of data modeling or simulation. The focus is on developing mathematically specified mechanisms, techniques, and approaches for what Agre (1997) has called the craft of 'research programming' or using computers as 'language machines.' Specifying, building, and programming models—often based on game theory, information theory, or systems dynamics—are distinctive ways of representing (and thus examining) a range of organizational phenomena. Some of the research we have categorized here might fit database research, while other articles might be labeled as decision science, information retrieval, or artificial intelligence research. We have put them together here because these streams of research have in common the intent to build new computational capabilities that facilitate the representational and modeling work of the researcher.

V. Nominal View of Technology: *Technology as Absent*

Our label for this category is intended to indicate that the articles in this group invoke technology 'in name only, but not in fact' (as 'nominal' is defined in Webster's dictionary). Typically, the terms 'information technology,' 'information system,' or 'computer' are used a few times in the articles, but these references to technology are either incidental—as in studies of CIO compensation or computer security—or used as background information—as in studies of IS personnel or outsourcing practices in the IS industry. The conceptual and analytical emphasis is elsewhere, typically focused on a range of topics of broad interest to the IS field. For example, Beath and Orlikowski (1994) describe a content analysis of a particular systems development methodology (Information Engineering), and highlight contradictions in the methodology's prescriptions for user involvement. Their study makes no reference to any specific technology that might support the use of the methodology, or any technology that might be developed using the methodology in question.

Thus, in the nominal view, IT artifacts are not described, conceptualized or theorized; technology is essentially absent from these articles. Constituting neither an independent nor a dependent variable, technology here is the *omitted variable*.

IMPLICATIONS OF THE CONCEPTUALIZATIONS OF THE IT ARTIFACT

ISR published 188 articles in the decade beginning in 1990 and ending in 1999. While analyzing these articles to see how IS researchers had conceptualized information technology in their studies, we encountered 11 articles that offered broad commentaries on the literature (e.g., Orlikowski and Baroudi 1991, Robey and Boudreau 1999). We excluded all such meta-research articles (distributed across the ten years of *ISR*) from consideration, leaving a total of 177 articles. Our analysis of the 177 articles yielded the 14 categories and the five meta-category clusters (tool, proxy, ensemble, computational, and nominal views of technology) described above. Table 2.1 shows the distribution of the 177 articles across these 14 categories and 5 clusters.

As evident in Table 2.1, those articles that engage with information technology minimally or not at all represent the largest cluster of *ISR* articles. This cluster, which we labeled the *nominal* view, accounted for 25 percent of all the articles published in a decade of *ISR* issues. As we noted, these articles essentially treat technology as absent, referring to it in passing as the context, motivation, or background against which to set examinations of phenomena such as IT governance mechanisms, IS professionalism, and IS strategy or planning approaches. In many of these articles, we noticed that we could have substituted another term for 'IS'—for example, 'HR' personnel, 'logistics' outsourcing, or 'marketing' strategy—and the articles would still have made sense. But, IS personnel, IS outsourcing, and IS

Table 2.1   *Classification of articles in ISR (1990–1999) by conceptualization of information technology*

Cluster	Conceptualization of technology	Freq.	%	Freq.	%
Nominal view	Absent			**44**	**24.8**
Computational view				**43**	**24.3**
	Algorithm	6	3.4		
	Model	37	20.9		
Tool view				**36**	**20.3**
	Labor substitution tool	1	0.5		
	Productivity tool	12	6.8		
	Information processing tool	15	8.5		
	Social relations tool	8	4.5		
Proxy view				**32**	**18.1**
	Perception	8	4.5		
	Diffusion	8	4.5		
	Capital	16	9.0		
Ensemble view				**22**	**12.5**
	Development project	7	4.0		
	Production network	2	1.1		
	Embedded system	7	4.0		
	Structure	6	3.4		
Total				**177**	**100%**

strategy are different from the personnel, outsourcing, and strategy issues of other disciplines and functional areas in that they must engage with a changing and evolving set of IT artifacts. Yet, this distinction was not always evident in the IS research articles, and an opportunity was missed for such studies to offer more grounded insights into IS phenomena by including and articulating the role of information technology—for example, in the lives of IS professionals, in the practices of IS outsourcing, and in the processes of IS planning.

Almost tied for first place, the second largest cluster of *ISR* articles is the group of articles that we have labeled as taking a *computational* view of the IT artifact, where the focus is on the underlying processing capabilities of the technology, expressed through the construction and running of algorithms (3.4 percent) or through the creation and processing of computational models and simulations (20.9 percent). This view reflects the traditional computer science approach to the IT artifact, representing a strong and lively research stream within the *ISR* research community. However, there is often an unproblematic reliance in these studies on assumptions that may be outdated or one-sided, and an opportunity exists for this paradigmatic view of information technology to include the insights from more recent social and economic theories that account for how people understand, adopt, use, and change their artifacts in complex and dynamic social contexts.

The third largest view of information technology in a decade of *ISR* literature is represented by the *tool* view at 20.3 percent of the articles. This cluster includes articles that treat information technology as a relatively straightforward, unchanging, and discrete technical entity with the focus being on the impacts/effects of this independent variable on such outcomes as information processing (8.5 percent), productivity (6.8 percent), social relations (4.5 percent), and labor substitution (0.5 percent). We were surprised to find the variety of ways that the tool view has been applied since Kling and Scacchi (1982) first articulated it in the early 1980s. While the tool view helps to explain how technologies alter various aspects of social and organizational life, many of the studies retain the kind of latent determinism that Markus and Robey (1988) cautioned us against. As they argued, there is much potential in seeing technologies and organizations as mutually dependent and dynamically emergent, and there is still much opportunity for the IS field to move beyond relatively simple black-boxed views of technology towards more powerful conceptualizations of the role of IT artifacts in organizations.

The fourth largest cluster of *ISR* articles is represented by a *proxy* view of information technology, where one or a few abstracted elements are focused on and assumed to represent the critical aspects of the technology. This cluster represented 18.1 percent of the articles published in a decade of *ISR*, and was comprised of three categories— articles that focus on users' perceptions of and intentions to accept the technology (4.5 percent), articles that focus on the rate of diffusion and penetration of technology within and across organizations (4.5 percent), and articles that focus on the monetary value of the technology as capital (9 percent). Studies conducted from this proxy view have pointed out interesting socio-psychological and socio-economic patterns, such as the lack of acceptance or diffusion of apparently useful new technologies, and the presence or absence of business value from investments in information technology. A risk of this view is that the proxy becomes confused with that which it is intended to represent or measure. Because such studies deal with technologies through surrogates, they tend not to conceive of historical or cultural variations in IT artifacts given that those variations may not be evident in the surrogate measures. Thus, proxy studies lack the means to account for temporal and contextual variations in the patterns discerned. To do so will require more careful theorizing about differences in IT artifacts, their role and use in different contexts and over time. Such theoretical elaboration would have to give up some conceptual parsimony to gain increased explanatory power.

Those articles that we have grouped under the ensemble view represent the fifth and smallest cluster. Accounting for 12.5 percent of the total set of articles, this cluster is characterized by treatments of technology as a socio-technical development project (4 percent), as a system embedded in a larger social context (4 percent), as a social structure (3.4 percent), and as enmeshed within a network of agents and alliances (1.1 percent). Given the high visibility of Kling and Scacchi's and Markus and Robey's work in articulating versions of the ensemble view during the 1980s, we were surprised to see the low number of articles adopting such a view during the 1990s. Given the kind of emergent IS phenomena we are witnessing today—open source software, electronic commerce, virtual teams, globally-distributed work, new challenges to privacy and intellectual property rights, etc.—there clearly is scope for more work to be done from an ensemble view.

Taken together we see that 88 percent of all papers published in *ISR* over the past ten years adopt a nominal, proxy, tool, or computational view of the IT artifact. Examined over time, this combination of four views dominates each of the past ten years, ranging from a low of 64 percent in 1991 to a high of 100 percent in 1993 and 1995. The number of published articles taking the remaining ensemble view was low throughout the ten years, including 0 percent (in 1993 and 1995), 1 percent (in 1994 and 1999), and 2 percent (in 1990 1992, and 1997). However, it reaches an important peak in 1996 when 7 articles representing the ensemble view were published (representing 28 percent of the articles for the year). Six of the seven articles were published in a single special issue calling specifically for this type of research, and edited by researchers specializing in the ensemble view.

In summary, a review of the articles published over the past ten years of the *ISR* journal reveals a broad array of conceptualizations of IT artifacts. Despite this array, however, it seems that even today—in the year 2000 and several decades into the development of our field—many people are still relying on received notions of technology and viewing technology primarily through their disciplinary lenses. Thus, management and social scientists tend to engage IT artifacts only minimally—as seen by our largest category, the nominal view—or to focus primarily on their effects (or those of their surrogates)—as seen by the tool and proxy views. And computer scientists publishing in the *ISR* journal tend to abstract IT artifacts from contexts and practices of use to focus principally on their computational capabilities. We believe that moving beyond received disciplinary notions towards broader and deeper interdisciplinary conceptualizations of IT artifacts is not only possible, but essential, if the IS field is to make important contributions to the understanding of a world become increasingly interdependent with ubiquitous, emergent, and dynamic technologies.

RESEARCH DIRECTIONS: RECONCEPTUALIZING THE IT ARTIFACT

Currently, in the one journal most focused on publishing IS research, we see that information technology is not a major player on its own playing field. In the majority of articles over the past decade, IT artifacts are either absent, black-boxed, abstracted from social life, or reduced to surrogate measures. We believe that this lack of attention to the core subject matter of our field represents both a unique opportunity and an important challenge for us to engage more seriously and more explicitly with the material and cultural presence of the information technology artifacts that constitute the 'IT' in our IT research. The opportunity arises because the diversity of IS researchers uniquely qualifies our field to pay special attention to the multiple social, psychological, economic, historical, and computational aspects of an evolving array of technologies and the ways in which they are developed, implemented, used, and changed. The challenge in realizing this opportunity lies—as Adam (1995) notes about the role of time in social analysis—'in making the implicit visible and turning our attention to the taken-for-granted.' We have tended to take information technology for granted in IS research, and we now need to turn our attention to specifically developing and using interdisciplinary theories of IT artifacts to inform our studies. Such theories would provide a distinctive foundation for the IS field and serve to guide ongoing research into all manner of IT phenomena.

In this final section, we propose a research agenda that can begin to take up this challenge. In particular, we see two general directions for such an agenda: developing conceptualizations and theories of IT artifacts; and incorporating such conceptualizations and theories of IT artifacts expressly into our studies. In proposing these research directions, we are not arguing for or against any particular perspective or methodology. On the contrary, we believe all perspectives and methodologies offer distinct and important analytic advantages. What we are arguing for is increased attention and explicit consideration of IT artifacts in all studies—whatever their epistemological perspective or methodological orientation. Thus, all studies of IT, quantitative or qualitative, large-scale or in-depth, experimental, survey-based, modeling, ethnographic, or case study, can advance our theoretical understandings of IT artifacts. But to do so, they will need to stop taking IT artifacts for granted, and begin to take them seriously enough to theorize about them. We believe all IT research will benefit from more careful engagement with the technological artifacts that are at the core of óur field.

Theorizing about IT artifacts might take many forms, but as a starting point we offer the following five premises (Orlikowski and Iacono 2000):

1. IT artifacts, by definition, are not 'natural,' neutral, universal, or given. As Grint and Woolgar (1995, p. 292, emphasis added) note, objects 'are never merely and automatically *just objects*; they are always and already implicated in action and effect.' Because IT artifacts are designed, constructed, and used by people, they are shaped by the interests, values, and assumptions of a wide variety of communities of developers, investors, users, etc.
2. IT artifacts are always embedded in some time, place, discourse, and community. As such, their materiality is bound up with the historical and cultural aspects of their ongoing development and use, and these conditions, both material and cultural, cannot be ignored, abstracted, or assumed away. For example, when studying the use or productivity impacts of electronic mail, it makes a difference to the findings whether the technology in question is IBM's *Profs* system or Qualcomm's *Eudora*, and whether the study is being conducted in large manufacturing companies in 1980, or small startups in 2000.
3. IT artifacts are usually made up of a multiplicity of often fragile and fragmentary components, whose interconnections are often partial and provisional, and which require bridging, integration, and articulation in order for them to work together. We have a tendency to talk of IT artifacts as if they were of a piece—whole, uniform, and unified. For example, we talk about 'the Technology,' 'the Internet,' 'the Digital Economy,' as if these are single, seamless, stable, and the same, every time and everywhere. While such simplifications make it easy to talk about technologies, they also make it difficult to see that such technologies are rarely fully integrated, flawless, and unfailing, and that they can and often do break down, wear down, and shut down.
4. IT artifacts are neither fixed nor independent, but they emerge from ongoing social and economic practices. As human inventions, artifacts undergo various transitions over time (from idea to development to use to modification), while co-existing and co-evolving with multiple generations of the same or new technologies at various points in time. For example, the World Wide Web (WWW) technology was first proposed in 1989 by Tim Berners-Lee of

CERN as a hypertexted, networked system for sharing information within the high-energy physics research community. Planned and designed as a particular information technology for a particular community, the WWW has been (and continues to be) taken up by other individuals, organizations, and communities (both here and around the world), used in different ways, and adapted, enhanced, and expanded to accommodate a diversity of evolving interests, values, assumptions, cultures, and other new technologies.

5. IT artifacts are not static or unchanging, but dynamic. Even after a technological artifact appears to be fixed and complete, its stability is conditional because new materials are invented, different features are developed, existing functions fail and are corrected, new standards are set, and users adapt the artifact for new and different uses. Understanding how and why IT artifacts come to be 'stabilized' in certain ways at certain times and places are critical aspects of understanding the range of social and economic consequences associated with particular technologies in various socio-historical contexts. Together, they comprise a critical baseline for understanding the consequences of IT artifacts in different conditions, and how such artifacts (and their uses and consequences) come to be changed over time.

Thus, our first premise requires a shift of attention from taking IT artifacts for granted towards explicit theorizing about specific technologies with distinctive cultural and computational capabilities, existing in various social, historical, and institutional contexts, understood in particular ways, and used for certain activities. Given the context-specificity of IT artifacts, there is no single, one-size-fits-all conceptualization of technology that will work for all studies. As a result, IS researchers need to develop the theoretical apparatus that is appropriate for their particular types of investigations, given their questions, focus, methodology, and units of analysis. We anticipate that multiple conceptions and theories of technology will emerge and be modified, generating a rich and growing repertoire of useful concepts and theories of IT artifacts. The point is not to develop *the* theory of IT artifacts (that is not possible in any case), but that we begin to develop *some* useful theories—both for ourselves and for researchers in other fields who will want to learn from our examinations and explanations of IT phenomena.

Second, to conceptualize IT artifacts as embedded in specific social and historical contexts requires that the detailed practices of their use be recognized and integrated into extant theories. Thus, how people engage with various technological artifacts in the course of working, learning, communicating, shopping, or entertaining themselves must become a central theoretical concern (Orlikowski 2000). At a recent *Academy of Management* meeting, one interesting session raised the question of whether virtual teams were different from co-located ones. To our surprise, a vote taken at the end of the session showed that almost half the audience believed that the teams were the same. In essence, they were saying that the ongoing use of technology by virtual team members did not matter. With such a starting premise, we can hardly expect these researchers to theorize how virtual team members engage with IT artifacts in the course of working, and to consider the consequences of such engagement for changes in work practices and modifications in the use and design of work technologies. If, as IS researchers, we believe that information technology can and does matter—in both intended and unintended ways—we need to develop the theories and do the studies that show our colleagues how and why this occurs.

Our third premise requires researchers to conceptualize and explain IT artifacts as multiple, fragmented, partial, and provisional. Letting go of a monolithic view of technology implies recognizing that technologies such as the Internet and other distributed applications do not provide the same material and cultural properties in each local time or context of use. Differences in system configurations, infrastructures, bandwidth, interfaces, accessibility, standards, training, business models, and citizens rights' and responsibilities guarantee that the experience of, say, 'being on the Internet' in China will be different from that in Saudi Arabia or in the United States, let alone in various micro-contexts of use. Research on the uses of distributed complexes of applications may require new theories and methods to understand how the various elements of interdependent systems (and their uneven development) interact to provide different types and levels of service. For example, more research on the kinds of workarounds (Gasser 1986) and forms of articulation work (Suchman 1996) that enable people to make dynamically complex systems work in practice may be critical.

Our fourth and fifth premises point to the emergence and evolution of IT artifacts as complex and changing techno-social processes existing in time and over time. We need to generate new theories to help us make sense of these processes, particularly if we are to understand the dynamic and unprecedented technologies and uses comprising contemporary initiatives in electronic business and virtual organizing, innovations in mobile computing and telecommuting, developments in wireless and wearable technologies, and the predicted convergence of nanotechnology, biotechnology, and information technology, to name a few. Even the ensemble views of technology, which do engage with the social and embedded aspects of technology development and use, tend not to take into account the multi-generational and emergent aspects of technological artifacts that arise as designers, developers, users, regulators, and other stake-holders engage with evolving artifacts over time and across a variety of contexts.

To better understand such evolving dynamics, ongoing and longitudinal studies of information technology are particularly useful—whether conducted by individuals or teams of researchers. By following specific artifacts over periods of time, it should become clear that changes occur not only in the social, behavioral, and economic circumstances within which the artifacts are embedded—resulting in the so-called 'societal' or 'organizational transformations' that we hear so much about—but also that changes are constantly occurring in the IT artifacts themselves—whether through invention, innovation, regulation, expansion, slippage, upgrades, patches, cookies, viruses, workarounds, wear and tear, error, and failure. The Internet that we are developing and using in new ways today is not the Internet that we developed and used in new ways in the 1980s or even the 1990s. That the Internet is not static or fixed should be obvious. But, where are the theories of how such large-scale and densely interconnected IT artifacts co-evolve with the various social institutions and communities (both local and global) that develop, regulate, use, and change them? For example, how, exactly, is the 1980's Internet different from the 1990's Internet, how do those differences shape contemporary uses of the Internet, and what do these differences bode for the future—for the Internetworked technologies of the 2000s and the ways in which they will mutually constitute organizations and society?

It seems that we have left much of our understanding of IT arti-facts to the technology vendors and the mass media journalists and pundits who cover them, while the associated social changes have been left to social scientists, economists, and media theorists (Iacono and Kling 2001). However, none of these groups attempts to understand the complex and fragmented emergence of IT arti-facts, how their computational capabilities and cultural meanings become woven in dense and fragile ways via a variety of different and dynamic practices, how they are shaped by (and shape) social relations, political interests, and local and global contexts, and how ongoing developments in, uses of, and improvisations with them generate significant material, symbolic, institutional, and historical consequences. Yet, this is precisely where the IS field—drawing as it does on multiple disciplines and different types of analyses—is uniquely qualified to offer essential insights and perspectives.

CONCLUSION

Our paper has been motivated by a belief that the tendency to take IT artifacts for granted in IS studies has limited our ability as researchers to understand many of their critical implications—both intended and unintended—for individuals, groups, organizations, and society. We believe that to understand these implications, we must theorize about the meanings, capabilities, and uses of IT artifacts, their multiple, emergent, and dynamic character, as well as the recursive transformations occurring in the various social worlds in which they are embedded. We believe that the lack of theories about IT artifacts, the ways in which they emerge and evolve over time, and how they become interdependent with socio-economic contexts and practices, are key unresolved issues for our field and ones that will become even more problematic in these dynamic and innovative times.

Our future is becoming increasingly dependent on a multiplicity of pervasive and invasive technological artifacts. As IS researchers we have the opportunity—and responsibility—to influence what future is enacted with those technological artifacts. To do so, however, we must engage deeply and seriously with the artifacts that constitute a central component of that future. Otherwise, we will remain passive observers of the techno-social transformations occurring around us, and we will risk fulfilling our own worst prophecies of technological determinism. A basic presumption of the IS field is that IT matters in everyday social and economic practice. We also need to make it matter in our research practice.

REFERENCES

Adam, Barbara. 1995. *Timewatch: The Social Analysis of Time*. New York, NY: Polity Press.

Agre, Philip E. 1997. *Computation and Human Experience*. Cambridge, UK: Cambridge University Press.

Applegate, Lynda M., James I. Cash Jr., and D. Quinn Mills. 1988. 'Information Technology and Tomorrow's Manager.' *Harvard Business Review* November-December: 128–136.

Attewell, Paul and James Rule. 1984. 'Computing and Organizations: What we know and what we don't know.' *Communications of the ACM* 27, 12: 1184–1191.

Beath, Cynthia M. and Wanda J. Orlikowski. 1994. 'The Contradictory Structure of Systems Development Methodologies: Deconstructing the IS-User Relationship in Information Engineering.' *Information Systems Research* 5, 4: 350–377.

Bijker, Wiebe E. 1995. *Of Bicycles, Bakelites, and Bulbs: Toward a Theory of Sociotechnical Change*. Cambridge, MA: MIT Press.

Button, Graham. 1993. 'The Curious Case of the Vanishing Technology.' Pp. 10–28 in *Technology in Working Order: Studies of Work, Interaction and Technology*. Graham Button (ed.). London: Routledge.

Castells, Manuel. 1996. *The Rise of the Network Society*. Malden, MA: Blackwell.

DeSanctis, Gerardine and Marshall Scott Poole. 1994. 'Capturing the Complexity in Advanced Technology Use: Adaptive Structuration Theory.' *Organization Science* 5, 2: 121–147.

Gasser, Les. 1986. 'The Integration of Computing and Routine Work.' *ACM Transactions on Office Information Systems* 4, 3: 205–225.

George, J. F., Easton, G. K., Nunamaker, J. & Northcraft, G. B. 1990. 'A Study of Collaborative Group Work With and Without Computer-Based Support.' *Information Systems Research* 1, 4: 394–415.

Giddens, Anthony. 1984. *The Constitution of Society: Outline of the Theory of Structure*. Berkeley, CA: University of California Press.

Grint, Keith and Steve Woolgar. 1995. 'On Some Failures of Nerve in Constructivist and Feminist Analyses of Technology.' *Science, Technology, &Human Values* 20, 3: 286–310.

Iacono, S. and Kling, R. 2001. 'Computerization Movements: The Rise of the Internet and Distant Forms of Work.' Pp. 93–135 in *IT and Organizational Transformation: History, Rhetoric, and Practice*. JoAnne Yates and John Van Maanen (eds.). Newbury Park, CA: Sage Publications.

Illich, Ivan. 1973. *Tools for Conviviality*. New York, NY: Harper and Row.

Kling, Rob. 1987. 'Defining the Boundaries of Computing across Complex Organizations.' Pp. 307–362 in *Critical Issues in Information Systems Research*. Richard J. Boland Jr. and Rudy Hirschheim (eds.). New York, NY: John Wiley & Sons.

Kling, Rob and Walt Scacchi. 1982. 'The Web of Computing: Computer Technology as Social Organization.' *Advances in Computers* 21: 1–90.

Kling, Rob and William H. Dutton. 1982. 'The Computer Package, Dynamic Complexity.' Pp. 22–50 in *Computers and Politics: High Technology in American Local Governments*. J. N. Danziger, W. H. Dutton, R. Kling, and K. L. Kraemer (eds.). New York, NY: Columbia University Press.

Latour, Bruno. 1987. *Science in Action*. Cambridge, MA: Harvard University Press.

Leavitt, H. J. and Whisler, T. L. 1958. 'Management in the 1980s.' *Harvard Business Review* 41–48.

Markus, M. Lynne and Daniel Robey. 1988. 'Information Technology and Organizational Change: Causal Structure in Theory and Research.' *Management Science* 34, 5: 583–598.

Moore, Gary C., and Benbasat, Izak 1991. 'Development of an Instrument to Measure the Perceptions of Adopting an Information Technology Innovation.' *Information Systems Research* 2, 3: 192–222.

Orlikowski, Wanda J. 1992. 'The Duality of Technology: Rethinking the Concept of Technology in Organizations.' *Organization Science* 3, 3: 398–427.

Orlikowski, Wanda J. 2000. 'Using Technology and Constituting Structures: A Practice Lens for Studying Technology in Organizations.' *Organization Science* 11, 4: 404–428.

Orlikowski, Wanda J. and Jack J. Baroudi. 1991. 'Studying Information Technology in Organizations: Research Approaches and Assumptions.' *Information Systems Research* 2, 1: 1–28.

Orlikowski, Wanda J. and Stephen R. Barley. 2001. 'Technology and Institution: What can Research on Information Technology and Research on Organization Studies Learn from Each Other.' *MIS Quarterly* June 25, 2: 145–165.

Orlikowski, Wanda J. and C. Suzanne Iacono. 2000. 'The Truth is Not Out There: An Enacted View of the Digital Economy.' Pp. 352–380 in *Understanding the Digital Economy: Data, Tools, and Research*. Erik Brynjolfsson and Brian Kahin (eds.). Cambridge, MA: MIT Press.

Pinch, Trevor J. and Wiebe E. Bijker. 1987. 'The Social Construction of Facts and Artifacts.' Pp. 17–50 in *The Social Construction of Technological Systems: New Directions in the Sociology and History of Technology*. W. E. Bijker, T. P. Hughes and T. J. Pinch (eds.). Cambridge, MA: MIT Press.

Robey, Daniel and Sahay, Sundeep. 1996. 'Transforming Work Through Information Technology: A Comparative Case Study of Geographic Information Systems in County Government.' *Information Systems Research* 7, 1: 93–110.

Robey, Daniel and Marie-Claude Boudreau. 1999. 'Accounting for the Contradictory Organizational Consequences of Information Technology: Theoretical Directions and Methodological Implications.' *Information Systems Research* 10, 2: 167–185.

Rogers, Everett. 1983. *The Diffusion of Innovation*. New York, NY: Free Press.

Strauss, Anselm L. 1987. *Qualitative Analysis for Social Scientists*. New York, NY: Cambridge University Press.

Suchman, Lucy A. 1996. 'Supporting Articulation Work.' Pp. 407–423 in *Computerization and Controversy* (2nd ed.). Rob Kling (ed.). San Diego, CA: Academic Press.

Trice, Andrew and Davis, Randall. 1993. 'Heuristics for Reconciling Independent Knowledge Bases.' *Information Systems Research* 4, 3: 262–288.

3

Still Desperately Seeking the IT Artifact

Ron Weber

Since the early 1970s, scholars within the information systems discipline have been concerned about the nature of and the future of the discipline. For instance, in 1972, John Dearden from the Harvard Business School wrote an article in the *Harvard Business Review* entitled, 'MIS Is a Mirage.'[1] Dearden argued (p. 90) that management information systems as a 'conceptual entity' were 'embedded in a mish mash of fuzzy thinking and incomprehensible jargon.' Dearden's comments sparked substantial controversy, and among some scholars they were roundly condemned as destructive and unhelpful to a nascent discipline. Nonetheless, they were a harbinger of concerns that have persisted to this day.

As a young scholar in the 1980s, I confronted my own personal and professional crisis with the information systems discipline. My secondary school education had been heavily oriented to physics, chemistry, and mathematics, and my initial tertiary education had been in economics. In the information systems discipline, I searched in vain for the powerful, general theories that underpinned research in disciplines like physics and economics. As I indicated in my March 2003 editorial, I first voiced my concerns publicly in a presentation I gave to attendees at the 1983 Doctoral Consortium of the International Conference on Information Systems.[2] I learned subsequently that other colleagues harbored similar concerns to mine about the discipline. For instance, Phillip Ein-Dor[3] and Ali Farhoomand[4] had written papers that articulated

First published in *MIS Quarterly* 27(2), pp. iii–xi. Copyright 2003 by the Regents of the University of Minnesota. Reprinted by permission.

various problems they perceived were undermining progress within the discipline.

In the ensuing years, concerns about the information systems discipline have waxed and waned. Recently, however, they have emerged again in various forms. In a research commentary published in the June 2001 issue of *Information Systems Research* entitled 'Desperately Seeking the "IT" in IT Research—A Call to Theorizing the IT Artifact,' Wanda Orlikowski and Suzanne Iacono expressed concerns about the lack of centrality of the information technology artifact in much of the information systems research that has been conducted to date. In 2002, the Association to Advance Collegiate Schools of Business (AACSB) for a time contemplated removing information systems as a core course in its undergraduate and graduate accreditation standards. Only intense lobbying by the Association for Information Systems averted this outcome. At the 2002 International Conference on Information Systems, the then-President of the Association for Information Systems, Phillip Ein-Dor, convened a meeting to discuss concerns about the state of the discipline. At the conference, two lively panel sessions were held that addressed various aspects of the state of the information systems discipline—one organized by Wanda Orlikowski and Suzanne Iacono in response to the interest gener-ated among colleagues by their research commentary, and another organized by Rick Watson and Elena Karahanna to canvass the need for developing a theory of information systems. Earlier this year, Phillip Ein-Dor, as President of the Association for Informa-tion Systems, also convened a committee on information systems disciplinary matters to advise and prepare a report for the Council of the Association for Information Systems on the state of the information systems discipline.

In this issue of the *MIS Quarterly*, we have a paper in the Issues and Opinions section by two senior colleagues within the inform-ation systems discipline, Izak Benbasat and Bob Zmud, which provides their perspective on the 'identity crisis' they believe faces our discipline. In their paper, Izak and Bob propose a 'core set of properties' for the information systems discipline that they believe provides a basis for establishing an identity for our discipline. From conversations I have had with colleagues who have already read earlier versions of Izak and Bob's paper, I am aware that some of the views expressed in the paper are controversial. I hope, therefore, that Izak and Bob's paper will provide a stimulus for further debate about the nature and meaningfulness of the research in which we engage within the information systems discipline. As I indicated in my March 2003 editorial statement in the *MIS Quarterly*, I believe we need to focus more on 'the problem of the problem' in the conduct of our research. In other words, we need to be more circumspect about our choice of research topics and their implications for the long-term future of our discipline.

IS THERE A CRISIS IN THE INFORMATION SYSTEMS DISCIPLINE?

I doubt we will ever achieve unanimity within the information systems discipline about whether we have a serious identity problem within the discipline. In 1989, for example, Claude Banville and Maurice Landry characterized the discipline as a 'fragmented adhoc-racy'—a discipline characterized by a low level of political independence among its members, a low level of conceptual coherence, and a low level of coherence in terms of standardization of research methods and interpretation of results.[5] Rudy Hirschheim, Heinz Klein, and Kalle Lyytinen have also argued that a 'call for a unifying paradigm is not desirable.'[6] Similarly, Dan Robey would prefer to embrace diversity within the discipline than attempt to unify it.[7] From the discourse that has occurred at a number of panel discussions and meetings that I have attended recently, it is clear that many colleagues, some of whom are very senior members of our discipline, believe the problems pertaining to identity that others have articulated are vacuous. Some colleagues are also quick to point out that the sorts of concerns we have about identity within the information systems discipline are typical concerns in other disciplines (not that this stance provides sufficient justification, in my view, for ignoring our concerns).

In any event, achieving unanimity about whether we have a problem of disciplinary identity is not important in my view. In this regard, I have a Darwinian perspective on the matter: let the different 'species' coexist for the moment, and over time only the fittest will survive. As scholars we need to argue our viewpoints in forthright, constructive, and respectful ways. In due course, we will either convince colleagues (especially younger colleagues) of our views, or they will be attracted to other views that they find more compelling. We need to accept that colleagues (and ourselves for that matter) may change their views and not denigrate them if they do so. While the debate over disciplinary identity is now longstanding and somewhat hackneyed, nonetheless I believe it remains a healthy aspect of our discipline. When we engage with it, we are reminded that we ought always to reflect carefully on what we do as scholars.

HOW MIGHT THE INFORMATION SYSTEMS DISCIPLINE ESTABLISH AN 'IDENTITY'?

Benbasat and Zmud argue that a collective, such as a discipline, establishes its identity via 'a set of important, essential core properties that distinguish the collective from others in its environment.' They define the core of a discipline as the 'central character, that connotes, in a distinctive manner, the essence' of the discipline. For Izak and Bob the key to establishing an identity for the information discipline is to articulate its core.

Of course, their basis for establishing the identity of a discipline provokes the question: How do we identify the core of a discipline? Benbasat and Zmud answer this question in two ways. First, they 'conceptualize the IT artifact' in terms of its application to a task embedded within a structure that in turn is embedded within a context. Second, they look at the phenomena studied by information systems scholars and, in a sense, induce the core properties of the information systems discipline based on the phenomena that have been and are being studied.

I am somewhat at odds with Izak and Bob in terms of how we identify the core of a discipline and the way that the discipline establishes its identity. By looking at what information systems scholars do as a basis for identifying the core, we simply perpetuate our current problems with disciplinary identity. I doubt an inductive approach to identifying the core of our discipline will work successfully.

Instead, I believe we need to follow a two-step process. First, I agree with Izak and Bob that we need to identify and to classify the types of phenomena that are the focus of researchers who call themselves members of the information systems discipline. In some sense, presumably these researchers must believe the phenomena they are studying are special in some way. In the search for the core of the information systems discipline I agree that these phenomena are a good place to start.

Identifying and classifying these phenomena, however, is only half the story in my opinion. The second step involves a crucial test. Specifically, we need to ask whether other disciplines have provided theories (or theories that might be adapted in a relatively straightforward way) to account satisfactorily for the phenomena we have identified. If such theories exist, in my view the information systems discipline will not be capable of establishing a separate identity by claiming these phenomena as a component of its core. If we include them in our core, we will forever be characterized as a reference-theory discipline—one that simply borrows theories from other disciplines to explain or predict phenomena that interest us. As a result, the problems that have occurred because we have failed to establish a disciplinary identity (described by Izak and Bob in their paper) will become even more endemic.

For instance, assume that the things that are our focus are 'information systems' and 'users of information systems.' Furthermore, assume the properties on which we focus are the various characteristics of human-computer interfaces that might be used with information systems and various characteristics of users that manifest their performance in their use of human-computer interfaces. At first glance, these phenomena might seem like reasonable phenomena for an information systems scholar to address, especially relationships among them. If we conclude that psychological theories can be used or readily adapted to account for user performance with different types of human-computer interfaces, however, we will have done little to contribute to the core of the information systems discipline. Instead, at a basic-research level, we will be contributing to the discipline of psychology rather than the discipline of information systems.

Clearly, we are off to a promising start when seeking to articulate the core of a discipline if we can identify things or properties of things that are not the focus of other disciplines. Nevertheless, I believe that such an outcome is neither a necessary nor sufficient condition for identifying the core of a discipline. If we find that we can use theories from other disciplines to account for the behavior of these new things or new properties of things, we have no basis for the core of the information systems discipline. For me, the key to identifying a core is finding phenomena where existing theories are non-existent or deficient. The key to creating the core is then building theory that is novel—theory that colleagues in other disciplines will acknowledge as belonging to the information systems discipline. Conceivably, it might be a completely new theory—one that has no genesis in other disciplines. I suspect that the more-likely outcome is that the theory is a marked adaptation of or extension of a theory that has its roots in another discipline. It will be sufficiently different from its ancestors, however, that ownership will be ascribed to the information systems discipline.

To establish a core for the information systems discipline, I believe we need two creative acts. First, we need to 'see' things or phenomena that are not the focus of other disciplines. Alternatively, we need to see things or phenomena that are the focus of other disciplines in new, rich, insightful ways (see the world through a dramatically different lens). Second, we need to build powerful, generic theories to account for these phenomena that are not applications of theories from other disciplines or straightforward extensions of these theories.

The 'value-add' associated with the theories we propose must be sufficient for other disciplines to ascribe ownership of these theories to the information systems discipline. In other words, we cannot establish our identity as a discipline by fiat. Instead, our identity will emerge only as the outcome of a social process—one in which members of other disciplines acknowledge that the theoretical contributions we have made are important to their own understanding and prediction of some phenomena.

In short, I believe the identity of a discipline is established through the contributions it makes to theory. The core phenomena of the discipline are circumscribed via the theories 'owned' by the discipline that account for these phenomena. Disciplinary identity and ownership of theories that other disciplines deem important are linked inextricably. Likewise, the theories owned by a discipline and its core phenomena are linked inextricably.

INFORMATION TECHNOLOGY-RELATED PHENOMENA: A MISPLACED FOCUS?

For those of us who seek the core of the information systems discipline, there is one line of enquiry that I believe will be unproductive and thus should be avoided. Specifically, I believe the core, if one exists, will not lie in theories that account for information technology-related phenomena. Rather, it will lie in theories that account for information systems-related phenomena. The two sets of phenomena are not the same. They are fundamentally different. Moreover, for the moment I believe our understanding the likely different implications of our researching the two sets of phenomena is important to our chances of success in creating theories that differentiate us from other disciplines and thus finding the core of our discipline.

If we believe a theory of the core lies in information technology-related phenomena, presumably we believe theories of the core also exist for other sorts of technology-related phenomena—for instance, a theory of the core of automobile-related phenomena, or space shuttle-related phenomena, or electric toothbrush-related phenomena. I have canvassed senior colleagues in the disciplines of sociology and anthropology about whether theories of the core have been developed for these sorts of technology-related phenomena. They were somewhat bemused by my questions, but nonetheless they indicated they knew of no such theories of the type I was describing. Clearly, much research has been undertaken on the impacts of various types of technologies on humans. Where this research is informed by theory apparently existing social science theories (or some adaptation thereof) have sufficed to explain or predict the phenomena of interest.

It is true that in some cases the emergence of new technologies has spawned new disciplines. For example, the discipline of computer science owes its existence to the invention of computers. Based on conversations I have had with colleagues in computer science, however, it seems the nature of the core of the computer science discipline remains elusive (although I believe good progress has been made). Ultimately, the knowledge created by computer scientists that has the most impact may be important applications of theory from other disciplines or engineering-based knowledge rather than theory-based knowledge. If this outcome occurs, a theory of the core of the computer science discipline might not emerge.

I hoped to be proved wrong about my belief that a theory of the core of the information systems discipline does not lie in information technology-related phenomena. If information technology-related phenomena formed part of the core of our discipline, we would have a richer, larger core and potentially a more interesting and exciting discipline. Perhaps one way forward is to try to identify a set of generic characteristics of information technology that cause existing theories about technology to fail. In this way, the basis for building new theory and the identity of the information systems discipline would be established. In some ways, the somewhat tentative status of computer science as a discipline with its own identity has been founded on generic characteristics of information technology that differentiate it from other technologies. For example, compiler theory has been developed because of special needs associated with computing machines as opposed to other sorts of machines.

Again, I am not hopeful of this path leading to productive outcomes for the information systems discipline. Our discipline is called the information systems discipline, not the information technology discipline. Surely our focus ought to be information systems, therefore, and not information technology. Information technology is simply the platform or resource on which we build information systems.

WHAT IS THE CORE OF THE INFORMATION SYSTEMS DISCIPLINE?

In the mid-1980s, Yair Wand and I wrestled at length with the question of what constitutes the core of the information systems discipline.[8] As an initial step, we followed the course of action proposed by Benbasat and Zmud: we classified the phenomena that information systems researchers had studied and were studying at the time. For the different classes of phenomena we then applied the second, critical test I described above. We asked whether theories from other disciplines were likely to account for the different classes of phenomena we had identified. After a long period of discernment, we found we could identify only one class of phenomena for which theories sourced from other disciplines seemed deficient—namely, phenomena associated with building conceptual models and designing databases. This was an 'unhappy' conclusion for us for several reasons. First, through our undergraduate and postgraduate studies, neither of us had built the knowledge base that allowed us to research these sorts of phenomena with confidence. Second, research on these phenomena had fallen somewhat into disrepute. Third, the discipline of computer science had already staked substantive claims on these phenomena via extensive work that had been carried out on the topics of semantic modeling and database normalization.

As we reflected on these phenomena further, however, we reached two additional conclusions. First, we became convinced that 'representation' was the essence of all information systems. The raison d'être for information systems was that they tracked states of and state changes in other systems. By observing the behavior of an information system, we obviate the need to observe the behavior of the system it represents. We thereby avoid having to incur the costs associated with observing the represented system. For example, with an order-entry information system, we track states of and state changes in customers, which means that we do not have to consult with each customer individually to determine the goods or services they wish to purchase. Moreover, in some cases an information system provides us with the only means we have available to observe the behavior of the represented system. For example, in a simulation, the represented system may not exist, except in our minds. The simulation is an information system that allows us to gain insights into the behavior of the represented system.

Second, even though a substantial amount of work had been done on building conceptual models and designing databases, some of it was a-theoretical. In particular, while research on data normalization was grounded in solid theory, research on conceptual modeling was virtually devoid of theory. This situation seemed curious, given we had concluded that representation was the essence of an information system. Moreover, as we searched in other disciplines for theories that might account for the sorts of representational phenomena that were relevant in an information systems context, we were unable to find any that were compelling. Ultimately, we concluded that theories of ontology potentially provided us with the best base for building theories about information systems representational phenomena. Nonetheless, it was also clear that these theories had to be adapted and extended substantially if they were to provide us with powerful accounts of information systems representational phenomena.

Like Wand, I continue to believe that we will establish a theory of the core of the information systems discipline (and potentially a separate identity for the information systems discipline) if we can articulate powerful, general theories to account for the characteristics of representations that enable 'faithful' tracking of other systems. Whereas natural information systems evolve to be faithful representations of the systems they track, artifactual information systems have to be designed to achieve this objective. Moreover, the sorts of representations built by, say, artists and engineers provide us with limited insights in terms of how we might accomplish this objective. For the most part, artists are not concerned with building representations that undertake one-to-one tracking of the 'worlds' they are representing. Similarly, engineers are concerned with building artifacts that accomplish some type of work, but the artifacts that are their focus are not intended to represent another system (unless, of course, the engineers are also building information systems). For these reasons, how we design good or faithful representations of other systems has remained the focus of Wand's and my work.

I fully accept that other types of information systems-related phenomena might exist for which theories borrowed from or adapted from other disciplines provide an inadequate account. If so, such phenomena potentially provide the basis for theories of the core of the information systems discipline. For the moment, however, I am unable to identify such phenomena. Nonetheless, for two reasons I hope such phenomena exist. First, having a core that includes more than representational phenomena would likely make for a richer, more-interesting discipline. Second, in due course I may have to resile from my belief that representational phenomena form part of the core of the information systems discipline (e.g., a colleague may convince me that I hold mistaken views). If this outcome occurs, my consolation would be that we have other foundations on which to build an identity for our discipline.

PUBLISHING WITH AND WITHOUT A THEORY OF THE CORE

If we subscribe to the notion that we need to develop a theory of the core of the information systems discipline if our discipline is ever to develop its own clear identity, then the type of research we undertake ought to reflect this belief. If called to account by our colleagues, we ought to be able to explain why we believe our research is contributing to a theory of the core of our discipline. In short, we ought to practice what we preach; otherwise, with some justification, we might be accused of hypocrisy.

Moreover, if we are faithful to our belief, some important implications arise. We ought not to seek publications for the sake of increasing the length of our vitae. We ought to be forthright with our Ph.D. students about our belief. We should also advise them about their choice of topic and the conduct of their research in ways that are consistent with our belief. We ought to be especially circumspect about continuing to pursue a line of research if we conclude it is not contributing to a theory of the core of our discipline. We ought to accept that citations to our work will fall, at least in the short run. If we are senior scholars within the discipline, as I argued in my March 2003 editorial, we have a special responsibility to bring about change. Relative to our more-junior colleagues, we are better placed to withstand the setbacks that often accompany fundamental changes in the direction of a discipline.

If we do not subscribe to the notion that we need a theory of the core of the information systems discipline if our discipline is ever to develop its own clear identity, then we face a 'boundaries' problem. We need criteria that we can use to judge what types of research fall within the boundaries of our discipline and what types of research fall outside the boundaries of our discipline. Subsequent to the publication of Orlikowski and Iacono's paper, I have noted that members of the *MIS Quarterly*'s Editorial Board and reviewers for the *MIS Quarterly* increasingly are asking how papers contribute to knowledge within the information systems discipline as opposed to other disciplines. They also now appear to be more unwilling to deal with papers that engage in only superficial ways with information technology and information systems.

In this regard, Benbasat and Zmud's paper in this issue of the *MIS Quarterly* provides putative criteria we might use to evaluate whether research should reasonably be deemed to be information systems research. First, they provide a 'nomological net' of constructs that they believe captures the major phenomena immediately associated with the information technology artifact. Second, they caution informa-tion systems researchers against 'errors of exclusion'—undertaking research that includes 'neither the IT artifact nor at least one of the elements associated with its immediate nomological net.' Third, they caution information systems researchers against 'errors of inclusion'—undertaking research that examines constructs 'best left to scholars in other disciplines' because of their 'significant causal distance' from the IT artifact. In the absence of a theory (or theories) of the core of the information systems discipline, I suspect we must resort to criteria like those Izak and Bob suggest to evaluate whether a piece of research constitutes information systems research. I anticipate, however, that Izak and Bob's criteria will be scrutinized and debated.

DISCIPLINARY IDENTITY, THE CORE, AND SOME EDITORIAL POINTERS TO PUBLISHING IN THE MIS QUARTERLY

My purpose in articulating my views in this editorial in a fairly forceful and forthright way is to provoke discussion and debate on enduring concerns that I have about our discipline. I accept fully that many colleagues believe strongly that the concerns I hold about the identity of and nature of the core of our discipline are spurious. In short, they see no problems that ought to concern us and believe instead that my concerns are badly misplaced. Moreover, some colleagues who share my concerns about our discipline disagree strongly with my diagnosis of the problems and my views on appropriate ways to try to address them. Whatever our views, I believe we will benefit from open, constructive, and respectful debate. In this regard, as I have indicated above, I hope to be proved wrong in some of my views. It would make my life as a scholar easier!

Let me also underscore that my personal views will not be the standard by which manuscripts are deemed suitable or unsuitable for the *MIS Quarterly*. I believe authors, reviewers, and members of the Editorial Board who have dealt with me will vouch that I am willing to work with and support a wide range of topics and approaches when I have editorial responsibilities to discharge. I fully understand, also, that we need work done outside the core of our discipline, however we might define the core. Information systems practitioners face a wide range of problems. The application of theories from other disciplines to better understand the nature of these problems clearly is an important contribution to our overall portfolio of knowledge about information systems- and information technology-related phenomena. Insofar as this work is the only sort of research done within our discipline, however, I believe it exacerbates rather than mitigates problems associated with our identity as a discipline. On the other hand, if it is seen as supportive of but ancillary to research on the core, I believe it will enhance rather than undermine our identity as a discipline.

At the *MIS Quarterly*, increasingly we seem to be facing the problem of receiving manuscripts that stretch the boundaries of our discipline to an extreme. At least prima facie, they contain little content that bears on information technology or information systems. Each Senior Editor has the prerogative to make a decision on whether a manuscript's topic is congruent with the mission of the *MIS Quarterly*. Nonetheless, I suspect that most, if not all, would find the sorts of criteria discussed in Izak and Bob's paper to be a reasonable basis for evaluating whether a paper falls within the boundaries of our discipline and thus potentially is a suitable publication in the *MIS Quarterly*. Of course, a Senior Editor will also use other criteria to evaluate whether a manuscript is congruent with the *MIS Quarterly*'s mission—for example, whether the overall contribution to knowledge made by the research reported in the paper is sufficient. Nevertheless, for authors who intend to submit their papers to the *MIS Quarterly*, I believe it will be helpful if they reflect on whether they have made 'errors of exclusion' or 'errors of inclusion.' If so, their papers might best be submitted elsewhere.

NOTES

1 J. Dearden, 'MIS Is a Mirage,' *Harvard Business Review* (50:1), 1972, pp. 90–99.
2 R. Weber, 'Toward a Theory of Artifacts: A Paradigmatic Basis for Information Systems Research,' *The Journal of Information Systems* (1:2), 1987, pp. 3–19.
3 P. Ein-Dor, 'An Epistemological Approach to the Theory of Information Systems,' Proceedings of the 18th Annual Meeting of the Decision Sciences Institute, Honolulu, Hawaii, November 1986, pp. 563–565.
4 A. Farhoomand, 'Scientific Progress in Management Information Systems,' *Data Base* (18:4), 1987, pp. 48–56.
5 C. Banville and M. Landry, 'Can the Field of MIS Be Disciplined?' *Communications of the ACM* (32:1), 1989, pp. 48–60.
6 R. Hirschheim, H. K. Klein, and K. Lyytinen, 'Exploring the Intellectual Structures of Information Systems Development: A Social Action Theoretic Perspective,' *Accounting, Management and Information Technologies* (6:1/2), 1996, pp. 1–64.
7 D. Robey, 'Research Commentary: Diversity in Information Systems Research: Threat, Opportunity, and Responsibility,' *Information Systems Research* (7:4), 1996, pp. 400–408.
8 See, for example, Y. Wand and R. Weber, 'On the Deep Structure of Information Systems,' *Information Systems Journal* (5:3), 1995, pp. 203–223.

4

The Identity Crisis within the IS Discipline: Defining and Communicating the Discipline's Core Properties[1]

Izak Benbasat and Robert W. Zmud

INTRODUCTION

The Information Systems (IS) scholarly community, like any new collective, has strived, since its inception in the 1970s, to develop a meaningful, resilient identity within the institutions that comprise its organizational field—namely, the organizational science and information science research communities, business and information science academic institutions, and the various organizations, industries, and professional groups that comprise the information technology (IT) industry. Such a community objective is admittedly ambitious, given the high failure rate associated with organizational foundings (Aldrich, 1999). Still, we maintain that, after 30 years, insufficient progress has been made in establishing this collective identity. Further, recent events—the collapse of the dot.coms, the 'e-ing' of both business and other scholarly disciplines, the recent tightening of the IT job market seems to have raised anew concerns across the discipline that the viability and unique contributions of the IS discipline are being questioned by influential stakeholders.

First published in *MIS Quarterly*, 27(2), pp. 183–194. Copyright 2003 by the Regents of the University of Minnesota. Reprinted by permission.

IS scholars research and teach a set of diverse topics associated with information technologies (IT), IT infrastructures and IT-enabled business solutions (i.e., information systems), and the *immediate* antecedents and consequences of these information systems (e.g., managing, planning, designing, building, modifying, implementing, supporting, and/or assessing *IT-based systems* that serve, directly or indirectly, practical purposes). The focus of this commentary is not about whether such a diversity of topics is beneficial for the IS field (Benbasat and Weber, 1996; Robey, 1996). Our concern is more fundamental: We are worried that the IS research community is making the discipline's central identity even more ambiguous by, all too frequently, under-investigating phenomena intimately associated with IT-based systems and over-investigating phenomena distantly associated with IT-based systems.

In this commentary, we begin by discussing why establishing an identity for the IS field is important. We then describe what such an identity may look like by proposing a core set of properties, i.e., concepts and phenomena, that define the IS field. Next, we discuss research by IS scholars that either fails to address this core set of properties or addresses concepts/phenomena falling outside this core set. We conclude by offering suggestions for redirecting IS scholarship toward the concepts and phenomena that we argue define the IS discipline.

THE NEED FOR ESTABLISHING AN ORGANIZATIONAL IDENTITY FOR IS

Albert and Whetten (1985) argue that an organizational identity must satisfy three necessary and sufficient criteria: claimed *central character*, claimed *distinctiveness*, and claimed *temporal continuity*. These criteria indicate that a collective's identity is based on a set of important, essential core properties that distinguish the collective from others in its environment. While these core properties will inevitably evolve in response to environmental exigencies, shifts in a collective's identity would exhibit strong path dependency.

Adopting a theoretical lens from institutional and ecological theory (Aldrich, 1999),[2] it is insightful to view IS scholars as a community of nascent entrepreneurs attempting to create a new population, i.e., the IS discipline, within an organizational field populated by other scholarly disciplines or populations. Aldrich argues:

> Together, founders and members of new organizations create communities of practice, molded by forces that heighten the salience

of organizational boundaries. Boundaries become more salient as the contrast between organizational activities and surrounding environments deepen...Only when bounded entities emerge can selection pressures change the organizational composition of populations. (p. 161)

We argue that the primary way in which a scholarly discipline signals its boundaries—and in doing so, its intellectual core—is through the topics that populate discipline-specific research activities.

Two related problems confront the members of a new population as they strive to succeed in their environment: they must discover or create effective routines and competencies with regard to this environment, and they must establish ties with elements of the environment that might not understand or acknowledge their existence. Aldrich (1999) categorizes the first as a *learning* issue and the second as a *legitimacy* issue. We believe that the IS discipline has made significant progress in resolving the learning issue, as reflected through its methodological and theoretical rigor, its methodological and theoretical diversity, and the respect afforded the discipline's major journals, *MIS Quarterly* and *Information Systems Research*.[3] Still, this learning issue will never be resolved fully until a dominant set of standards and designs—for a scholarly field, a coalescence regarding the phenomena about which knowledge is developing—is accepted by the population's members. Without a *dominant design*, population boundaries will be ambiguous and organizational knowledge fleeting (Aldrich, 1999). We argue that a dominant design for the IS discipline has yet to be realized.

This lack of consensus regarding a dominant design proves particularly troublesome as the IS discipline strives to resolve the second of Aldrich's problems, the legitimacy issue. Aldrich (1999) argues that two types of legitimacy exist: cognitive legitimacy and sociopolitical legitimacy. He defines each as follows (p. 230):

- '*Cognitive legitimacy* refers to the acceptance of a new kind of venture as a *taken for granted* feature of the environment.'
- '*Sociopolitical legitimacy* refers to the acceptance by key stakeholders, the general public, key opinion leaders, and government officials of a new venture as appropriate and right. It has two components: *moral acceptance*, referring to conformity with cultural norms and values, and *regulatory acceptance*, referring to conformity with government rules and regulations.'

We believe that the IS discipline has made significance progress regarding sociopolitical legitimacy, as seen via: the institutionalization of IT as an integral part of today's organizational and economic contexts; the acknowledgement of the importance of IS by academic accreditation bodies; the presence of IS academic departments and degree programs at most public and private universities; a professional society (Association for Information Systems) able to demonstrate influence within the organizational field; and the aforementioned respect afforded *MIS Quarterly* and *Information Systems Research*. What seems less affirmed, however, is the discipline's cognitive legitimacy. For too many key actors within the discipline's organizational field (e.g., governing bodies, executives from public and private organizations, university and college administrators and, most importantly, scholars from other disciplines), the core phenomena being explored through IS scholarship—and, hence, the nature of the discipline—remains amorphous.

Because of the interdisciplinary nature of IS research, IS scholars have emerged from varied academic backgrounds: organization science, computer science, information science, engineering, economics and management science/operations research. As a result, the theories embraced, the methods applied, and the topics addressed by IS scholars are themselves varied, producing the diversity exhibited across the discipline. Like Robey (1996), we accept this breadth in intellectual background. The complex and imposing challenges associated with IT management, development, and use demand interdisciplinary approaches to their resolution. However, topical diversity can, *and has*, become problematic *in the absence of a set of core properties*, or central character, that connotes, in a distinctive manner, the essence of the IS discipline. If influential stakeholders are unable to comprehend the nature, importance, and distinctiveness of the role being served by the IS discipline, these stakeholders are unlikely to acknowledge its legitimacy within the organizational field.

AN IDENTITY FOR THE IS DISCIPLINE

In fact, a natural ensemble of entities, structures, and processes does exist that serves to bind together the IS subdisciplines and to communicate the distinctive nature of the IS discipline to those in its organizational field—the IT artifact and its *immediate* nomological net.

We conceptualize the IT artifact (see Figure 4.1) as the application of IT to enable or support some task(s) embedded within a structure(s) that itself is embedded within a context(s). Here, the hardware/software design of the IT artifact encapsulates the structures, routines, norms, and values implicit in the rich *contexts* within which the artifact is embedded. Table 4.1 illustrates this view of the IT artifact through two examples, one in a business setting and one in a personal setting.

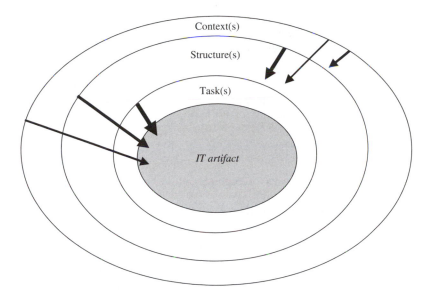

Figure 4.1   *The IT artifact*

The IS discipline involves much more, however, than the study of the IT artifact. Specifically, IS scholars and IS practitioners strive to increase their collective understandings of (1) how IT artifacts are conceived, constructed, and implemented, (2) how IT artifacts are used, supported, and evolved, and (3) how IT artifacts impact (and are impacted by) the contexts in which they are embedded. Hence, our view (Figure 4.2) of the phenomena studied by IS scholars—and, hence, the set of core properties of the IS discipline—includes:

- The managerial, methodological, and technological *capabilities* as well as the managerial, methodological, and operational *practices* involved in planning, designing, constructing, and implementing IT artifacts.
- The human behaviors reflected within, and induced through both the (1) planning, designing, constructing, and implementing, and (2) direct and indirect usage of these artifacts.
- The managerial, methodological, and operational practices for directing and facilitating IT artifact *usage* and evolution.
- As a consequence of use, the *impacts* (direct and indirect, intended and unintended) of these artifacts on the humans who directly (and indirectly) interact with them, structures and contexts within which they are embedded, and associated collectives (groups, work units, organizations).

Table 4.1   *Defining elements of the IT artifact*

	Budget Planning	Gardening Club Internet Presence
Information Technology	• Collaborative budget planning software • Central archive of historical and anticipated expenditures • PCs connected via LAN	• ISP hosting service • Email, bulletin board and message threading software • PCs, browser and Internet connections
Task	• Specification of corporate and divisional budgets • Analysis of budget alternatives that meet corporate and divisional needs	• Point to useful gardening information and product sources • Share gardening practices • Answer gardening problems • Review gardening products
Task Structure	• Formal enterprise budget planning process • Institutional budgeting policies, rules and practices • Corporate and divisional objectives	• Interaction etiquette and rules • Content management processes
Task Context	• Enterprise and divisional values and norms • Industry and firm business conditions • Personal agenda and relationships • External and internal jolts	• Membership rules • Members interests • Member expertise levels • Membership values and norms • Periodic face-to-face club meetings

Two aspects of the nomological net shown in Figure 4.2 are vital. First, the constructs involved are *intimately* related to the IT artifact. For example, IS development team practices involve behaviors lodged deeply within IT development activities rather than reflective of more generic interpersonal or group interactions. Second, as observed from Figure 4.2, the nomological net accounts for both forward and reverse causation.

All too often, however, elements from this nomological net are seemingly absent from much IS scholarship (Orlikowski and Iacono 2001). Such an observation is not unique, having also been raised, for example, by Massey, Wheeler, and Keen (2001):

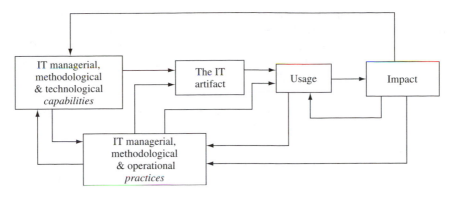

Figure 4.2   *IT artifact and its immediate nomological net*

Although IS researchers have rightly concluded that the meaning of technology is socially constructed...our discipline's unique contribution to the broader field of social science requires that we understand technology as well as the organizational and individual issues surrounding its use. If the IS community chooses a future that moves us away from a rigorous understanding of technology itself, then we are choosing wrong. (p. 27)

Our specific concern herein involves two troubling trends regarding the current conduct of IS research: *errors of exclusion* of constructs reflecting the core properties of the IS discipline, i.e., the IT artifact and its immediate nomological net; and, *errors of inclusion* of constructs that lie outside this scope.

Errors of Exclusion

Based on an examination of the research articles published in *MIS Quarterly* and *Information Systems Research* over the last two years (2001 and 2002), we believe that about one-third offer and/or examine research models that include neither the IT artifact nor at least one of the elements associated with its immediate nomological net (see Figure 4.2). A variety of topical themes span these articles, including on-line consumer behavior, trust-building, research methodology, on-line services delivery, collaboration, decision making, knowledge management, resource allocation, on-line communities, and supply chain management.

To illustrate what we mean by exclusion, we offer below (Figure 4.3) a simplified, hypothetical research model. Here, the study context involves software development groups, the outcome variable reflects client satisfaction, and the predictor variables are expected to influence the outcome variable as follows:

- The greater the mutual understanding among project team members, the greater the client satisfaction.
- The greater the interdependency of tasks assigned project team members, the greater their mutual understanding.
- The greater the task interdependency, under a low goal clarity condition, the greater the client satisfaction.
- The lower the task interdependency, under a high goal clarity condition, the greater the client satisfaction.

While we are not aware of such a study having been undertaken, it is situated within an IS context, could easily be situated within the IS literature, and is similar in spirit to other studies that have been published in the IS literature.

Note, however, that neither the IT artifact nor elements from its immediate nomological net are explicitly present in this research model. Further, the instrumentation (most of which would be borrowed from reference disciplines) likely to be applied in examining the research model would as well lack explicit linkage with either the IT artifact or elements from its immediate nomological net (except, perhaps, through extensive item rewording, which would then jeopardize the instrumentation's psychometric properties). Finally, a study undertaken to assess the above research model could have involved any project team context, IS-focused or otherwise. In other words, the research

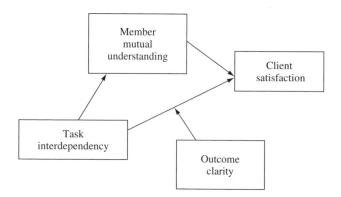

Figure 4.3   *An example of an error of exclusion*

model *at its core* is not about the influence of software development team member interaction on software success. Rather, it is about the influence of project team (or group) member interaction on client (or stakeholder) satisfaction. While such a study examines an important phenomena (whose research outcome might inform IS research), the study is based firmly in the organizational behavior and group behavior disciplines and not the IS discipline. Clearly, it is appropriate for an IS scholar to propose and study such a research model, especially as the project-based nature of IT activities has provided IS scholars with keen insights into project-based work. Our concern rises only when the products of such research are positioned (via submission to and publication in a top IS journal) as IS scholarship.

Why is it problematic to publish research excluding the IT artifact and/or elements from its immediate nomological net in IS journals? Because such research makes ambiguous the boundaries of IS scholarship, thus raising questions regarding its distinctiveness—and hence its legitimacy—with respect to related scholarly disciplines. If IS research is no different from that undertaken in more entrenched scholarly disciplines (e.g., marketing, operations management, organizational behavior), why should institutions in the organizational field continue to invest in this new intellectual capability?

We emphasize that our intention is neither to discourage IS scholars from pursuing research that excludes the constructs and phenomena depicted in Figure 4.2 nor to discourage non-IS scholars from publishing appropriately focused research in IS journals. IS scholars have much to contribute to scholarship, regardless of the core issues involved (e.g., service delivery, trust among members of a collaborative group, customer or supplier relationships, organizational learning). Such contributions can prove valuable in reinforcing the *individual reputations* of IS scholars and in enhancing the *collective reputation* of the IS discipline. However, such research should not be positioned as IS research. Instead, it should be submitted to scholarly journals whose readership includes the communities of scholars most readily associated with the (non-IS) phenomena being investigated. Moreover, when non-IS scholars publish research on IS phenomena in IS journals, they bring new theories, methodologies, and insights to enrich the study of these phenomena and serve to enhance the legitimacy of these IS journals and, hence, of the IS discipline.

Errors of Inclusion

We are also concerned with the issue of inclusion—namely, when IS research models involve the examination of constructs best left to scholars in other disciplines. Even when the IT artifact and/or other elements associated with its immediate nomological net are included in such research models, the significant causal distance that tends to separate the IS and non-IS constructs produces extensive theoretical ambiguity regarding if and how the IS constructs influence or are influenced by the non-IS constructs.

Because e-commerce is a current area of major interest to IS scholars, we will illustrate the error of inclusion using an example from this field of study. E-commerce has a multidisciplinary focus, with marketing being one of the major disciplines that IS academics have relied upon to study online purchasing behavior. Indeed, marketing researchers have done more than IS researchers to study online consumer behavior. This leads to an important question: What should be the nature of the contributions made by IS scholarship to e-commerce research? Or, to put it differently, what is the nature of the specific expertise held by IS scholars that distinguishes our e-commerce research from that undertaken by scholars from other disciplines?

As an example, consider the research model shown in Figure 4.4 that was used in an examination of how IT could provide a customer with a virtual product experience, i.e., an experience enabling the customer to better appreciate the product's qualities when the product is being purchased through an online channel and, hence, cannot be 'experienced' directly (Jiang and Benbasat 2004).

In Figure 4.4, the two types of control represent the IT treatments. Visual control, enabled by software such as QUICKTIME or FLASH, allows a customer to manipulate a product image via mouse and keyboard, e.g., move, rotate, and 'zoom' a product so as to view it from different angles and distances. Functional control, supported by software such as SHOCKWAVE, allows a customer to explore a product's functionality via mouse and keyboard. Perceived diagnosticity, the dependent variable, is defined as the extent to which the

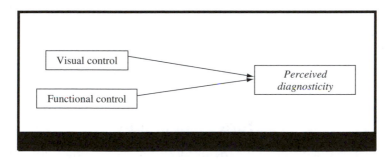

Figure 4.4   *An example to illustrate errors of inclusion*

consumer believes the shopping experience is helpful in evaluating the product (Kempf and Smith 1998).

When this study is presented in research workshops, two questions are often raised. The first is: Why isn't there a construct representing buying behavior in the model? After all, isn't IT being used here in order to improve the likelihood of a sale? An off-the-cuff answer is that the interest of the researchers lies primarily with how the IT manipulations have been able to (positively) influence customers' perceived understanding of the online product and that this objective, alone, is a worthwhile goal. (Note that this research model has *one degree of separation*[4] between the IT variables and the consequent variable.)

Usually, the questioner is not satisfied with the above response. Another answer is that there are a number of factors that might intervene between understanding a product and buying it, such as the consumer having a need for the product or having the monetary resources to buy the product. Understanding a product does not mean that one will necessarily buy it. Another, usually more accepted, argument is that because one's understanding of a product might lead to a positive, neutral, or negative reaction of the product, the evaluation and hence the purchase behavior is indeterminate. (Note that including mediating variables and a purchase behavior produces a research model with multiple degrees of separation between the IT variables and the consequent variable, i.e., purchase behavior.)

The second question that is often raised is: Why hasn't the study investigated *all* the factors that could potentially influence diagnosticity? Indeed, a number of other factors—in addition to *direct product experience* as simulated or effected by IT—are potentially salient, such as a customer's *a priori* familiarity with the product in question. While this second question is likely to be of great interest to marketing scholars, our view is that it is of far less interest to IS scholars. The research objective for the study represented by the research model in Figure 4.4 was to examine the contribution of IT to online product understanding, not to study the total set of factors that might have such an influence. There are, of course, other IS-related factors, such as a customer's expertise with or comfort in using the IT in question, that certainly could be added to this research model. The non-IS factors associated with a customer's product understanding have already been studied in the marketing literature, are in the domain of marketing, and are better left to scholars in marketing—scholars with more expertise in such matters.

Our view, therefore, is that we should not increase this research model's complexity by including more 'marketing' constructs in either measuring all potential influences on diagnosticity or measuring the influence of diagnosticity on other customer behaviors. Could we do so if we wanted? Probably, but at the cost of a more complex study and the burden of investing time in learning the theories and measures of another discipline, with little to be gained for the IS field by so doing.

There are adverse consequences to both increasing the degrees of separation in models being investigated or decreasing the ratio of IT-related constructs to total number of constructs in a research model. First, it takes focus away from our primary goal, which is to theorize about and study the enabling role of IT (and associated IT activities). Second, we spend a significant amount of energy in making marginal additions to the theories that we have borrowed, rather than thinking about original contributions to the IS field. Consider the direction that IT adoption studies have taken over the last decade. A large number of papers have been preoccupied with minor improvements to the theory of reasoned action and other technology adoption models. Instead, our focus should be on how to best design IT artifacts and IS systems to increase their compatibility, usefulness, and ease of use or on how to best manage and support IT or IT-enabled business initiatives. Interestingly, this is what we used to do in experimental studies in the 1970's and 1980's, e.g., the studies on Decision Support Systems. It is possible that the current emphasis with theories from other disciplines has distracted the IS research community from developing its own theories. Third, IS faculty allegiance develops in these other disciplines, rather than the IS discipline. Last, the less we focus on IS concepts and phenomena in our research, the less likely it is that we contribute to the principal consumer of our research—the IT practice community.

Two types of criticisms[5] may legitimately be raised to our 'errors of inclusion' arguments. First, who is responsible for integrating the findings and models from different fields to provide a larger picture? Here we have no objections to IS researchers integrating their models with those already developed in non-IS fields to inform the IS audience of the wider context enveloping a phenomenon.

Second, might there not be an under-specification problem that could lead to several concerns? We agree that under-specification can prove problematic:

- It is possible to overlook non-IT variables that have important interactive, or moderating, effects with the independent variables of the study. In the virtual product experience study mentioned above, it is likely that the nature of the product will have a moderating effect on the impact of the IT-related variables of visual and functional control. If the product is one that can be described mainly by quantitative attributes—such as weight, size, and durability—then we would expect that visual and functional control to have less impact on diagnosticity than if the product needs to be experienced to be evaluated, i.e., to enable the customer to acquire a richer feel for the product's appearance and/or functionality. As a consequence, omitting variables that characterize a product's essential nature will likely lead to research outcomes that fail to fully reveal the benefits of an IT-enabled, virtual product experience.

- When the outcome variable is IT-related, such as is the case in a study aiming to understand the organizational factors that promote successful strategic IT planning, it is certainly important to fully understand all the influences that result in successful strategic IT planning.
- When the research objective is to understand the relative importance of IS variables *vis-à-vis* non-IS variables, then the inclusion of non-IS variables is certainly necessary. An example of such a study, in the e-commerce context, would be one desiring to determine if trust in the merchant was a more influential determinant of purchase behavior than the attractiveness of the merchant's web site.

CONCLUDING COMMENTS

The central argument in this commentary is that the problems of 'exclusion' and 'inclusion' hamper efforts towards developing and reinforcing a central identity for the IS discipline. What are the reasons for this state of affairs? Is it a consequence of borrowing too much from reference disciplines, a strategy we adopted in the early 1980's to achieve legitimacy (Benbasat and Weber 1996)? It might be so, because heavy reliance on theories that neither have a basis in IT-related behaviors nor are founded on IT-related constructs would naturally distract us from reaching agreement regarding the core set of phenomena associated with IS scholarship. This would then cause us to gravitate towards investigating constructs, and associated phenomena, that lie in others' domains. We see no problems in adopting theories from reference disciplines, as long as we either apply them in investigating a phenomenon included within our offered delineation of the IS discipline (see Figure 4.2) or adapt them to reflect a unique IT or IS component. For example, the 'quality-effort tradeoff' model in behavioral decision theory could be adapted to include the cognitive cost reduction effected by IT (a DSS) on the effort side of the equation to predict the behaviors that would ensue in computer-supported decision-making (Todd and Benbasat 1999).

A few simple rules of thumb (or questions) that IS researchers and IS editors might pose to heighten the distinctiveness of our work and our journals are the following:

- Does a study investigate the relationships that fall within the IS *nomological net*—that is, investigate relationships involving one or more of the constructs included in Figure 4.2?
- How many *degrees of separation* are there between the IS constructs and the key consequent construct(s) in a study's research model— that is, how far *outside* the boundaries of the nomological net shown in Figure 4.2 are the primary constructs being investigated? (Here, by 'primary constructs' we refer to those constructs associated with a study's principal scholarly contribution.)
- What is the *nomological density* of the IS constructs in a study's research model—that is, do relationships involving only IS constructs represent a majority of the relationships in a research model? To measure nomological density, count the number of two-way relationships among the constructs in the research model that fall within the nomological net (i.e., those relationships that exist between constructs in Figure 4.2). Then, divide this total by the total number of two-way relationships in the research model.[6]

Further, IS researchers should avoid treating IT artifacts or IS systems either as a 'black box' or as being synonymous with a more generic entity (e.g., innovation, investment, or Internet). Instead, the IS aspects of the phenomena being examined should be brought to the forefront to make clear the unique, specific contributions of IS scholarship. Finally, in our research questions and research models, we should focus on delineating the contribution being made (or to be made) in enhancing our understanding of IS phenomena. We should neither focus our research on variables outside the nomological net nor exclusively on intermediate-level variables, such as ease of use, usefulness or behavioral intentions, without clarifying the IS nuances involved. Instead, we should identify the contribution being made either at a global level (such as a GSS or a virtual development team) or, preferably, at a finer level of analysis (e.g., mechanisms for labor replacement, for cognitive enhancement, for relationship enhancement, for ease of searching). We believe that the above suggestions, if followed, would enable substantial progress to be made in clarifying the nature of IS scholarship and, hence, the identity of the IS discipline.

NOTES

1 Ron Weber was the accepting senior editor for this paper.
2 While Aldrich's (1999) ideas are primarily couched in the context of for-profit collectives, his ideas are intended to apply to non-profit collectives as well: '...I will do the best I can to ground the book in the substance of organizations in all their diversity; rather than write as if the Fortune 500 were the only creatures in the organizational zoo. I focus primarily on businesses, but other kinds of organizations are also covered.' (p. 1)
3 Both journals are included in the list of administrative sciences journals used by the *Financial Post* and *Business Week* to rank business schools.
4 This term was used originally by psychologist Stanley Milgram.
5 We thank one of the anonymous referees for bringing up these issues.
6 As a simple example, consider an expansion of the model shown in Figure 4.4. Assume that the model represents the following relationships: Diagnosticity (extent to which consumers believe the shopping experience is helpful to evaluate a product) is influenced by visual and functional control (namely, the IT capability that allows a customer to understand the form and functionality of the online product better). In turn, diagnosticity together with the reputation of the online merchant influences the customer's willingness to shop online. In this example, the relationships between visual control/functional control and diagnosticity fall within the nomological net shown in Figure 4.2. The relationships between diagnosticity/reputation and willingness to shop online do not. Thus, two of the four, or 50 percent, of the relationships in this model fall within the nomological net.

REFERENCES

Albert, S. and Whetten, D. A. 'Organizational Identity,' *Research in Organizational Behavior* (7), 1985, pp. 263–295.

Aldrich, H., *Organizations Evolving*, Sage Publications: Thousand Oaks, CA, 1999.

Benbasat, I. and Weber, R. 'Rethinking diversity in information systems research' *Information Systems Research* (7:4), December 1996, pp. 389–399.

Jiang, Z. and Benbasat, I. 'Virtual Product Experience: Effects of Visual and Functional Control on Perceived Diagnosticity in Electronic Shopping' *Journal of MIS*, Winter 2004–2005, Vol. 21, No. 3, 111–147.

Kempf, D. S. and Smith R. E. 'Consumer Processing of Product Trial and the Influence of Prior Advertising: A Structural Modeling Approach,' *Journal of Marketing Research* (35:3), August 1998, pp. 325–337.

Massey, A., Wheeler, B. C., and Keen, P. 'Technology Matters' in *Information Technology and the Future Enterprise: New Models for Managers*, Dickson, G. W. and DeSanctis, G. (eds.), Prentice-Hall, Upper Saddle River, NJ, 2001, pp. 25–48.

Orlikowski, W. and Iacono, S. 'Desperately Seeking the "IT" in IT research—A call to Theorizing the IT Artifact,' *Information Systems Research* (12:2), June 2001, pp. 121–134.

Robey, D. 'Diversity in Information Systems Research: Threat, Promise, and Responsibility,' *Information Systems Research* (7:4), December 1996, pp. 400–408.

Todd, P. and Benbasat, I. 'Evaluating the Impact of DSS, Cognitive Effort, and Incentives on Strategy Selection,' *Information Systems Research* (10:4), December 1999, pp. 356–374.

5
Crisis in the IS Field?
A Critical Reflection on
the State of the Discipline

Rudy A. Hirschheim and Heinz K. Klein

1 INTRODUCTION

The need to step back and consider the central issues of IS as an academic discipline[1] and practical profession has never been more apparent. Consider the view of Lynne Markus (1999) who in a provocative article poses the question: 'what happens if the IS field as we know it goes away?' For her, the field is in a state of crisis and at a crossroads. On the one hand, it could grow to become one of the most important areas for business since no organization can ignore the inexorable development and application of new information technology and expect to survive. On the other hand, there is a move to emasculate and devolve the field, moving IS tasks and skills into other business functions and/or overseas.[2]

Lucas (1999) supports Markus' concern noting that the migration of IS skills to other business disciplines is occurring, and that many US business school deans have adopted this 'disturbing belief'. Indeed, our informal discussions with colleagues at peer institutions suggest that many universities no longer support a vigorous and expanding IS group. Deans justify this decision citing declining IS student numbers. Many schools have seen drops of almost 50% in the number of IS majors. Markus and Lucas seem to attribute this drop to the migration of IS skills into other disciplines. However, there is a need to consider another reason: the dramatic increase in the 'offshoring' of IS jobs to places like India and China. Even the popular press (*Business Week* 2003; *USA Today* 2003) has reported on this issue, noting that as much as 50% of IT jobs will be 'offshored' to India and other off- and near-shore destinations in the next 10 years. Such change—the pundits argue—is nothing more than the natural progression of first moving blue-collar work (manufacturing, textile production, etc.) overseas followed by white-collar work (Morstead and Blount 2003). IT jobs are the most visible to us in the IS field, but the same is happening (or will happen) in accounting, HR, and other business functions/processes (this is the so-called BPO or business process outsourcing phenomenon). Companies typically start with small offshore projects as a proof of concept. If successful, larger and more complex projects follow. Companies are scurrying to find offshore 'partners' because of the significant cost savings such arrangements bring. With labor costs in India about 1/5 of what they are in the US and Europe, and the technical skills equal or better, the argument for offshoring is compelling indeed.

No wonder deans are sometimes reluctant to support IS. They see a bleak future for the field.

We thus believe the time is right to consider whether Markus' contention is correct, i.e., that the field is at a crossroads. Is there a legitimate concern that the field as we know it will disappear? What can we in the field do to prevent such dispersal, assuming of course that we believe the field should not disappear? If one assumes the field is indeed in a state of crisis, then using a medical analogy, four options would appear possible: (1) *let it die* or whither away. Such an opinion might well be held by many of our colleagues in the other business disciplines who feel separate IS departments have exceeded their usefulness and that whatever we have learned can now be integrated within other domains (e.g., accounting, marketing, etc.). (2) *keep it on life-support* in the sense of upholding the status quo in spite of reduced demand. Such a view might be held by some deans who have little interest in killing IS because of the political battles that would likely ensue and believe the lean years will eventually come to an end. A similar position (outcome) could emerge from those within the field who feel there is no crisis, i.e., denial. In this case, the field keeps ticking on without taking any significant corrective action. This means that IS as a field might never realize that it could be perilously close to the precipice and its continued strength or mere survival would become a matter of external chance factors beyond its vision or control. (3) *take corrective action*. This requires making significant change to set the field on a more stable course, leading to a long-term existence. Some in our field have sought such change, particularly in relation to professionalization and accreditation. (4) *re-birth/transformation*. Nolan and Croson (1995) have termed this 'creative destruction' with reference to Schumpeter calling for a total transformation leading to a new Phoenix arising from the ashes. This would be a dramatic and radical change, perhaps causing much pain in the IS community. 'Warriors for change' typically prescribe such treatment to overcome the malaise and stagnation that can occur in many fields over longer periods. The need for radical change is, thus, not confined to IS.

On the other hand, some may feel that such talk of crisis is alarmist and misguided. Assuredly, there have been declines in IS student numbers during the years 2000–2003, but this is ephemeral. Such declines are part of the normal cyclical nature that can be observed in many fields (not just IS) from time to time. Whilst the decline in student numbers is dramatic for IS, this can partly be explained by the dot.com effect. The dot.com period was a bubble resulting in artificial growth numbers. When the bubble burst, the numbers returned to a normal state. Moreover, the depressed student numbers also reflect the current state of the economy. Once the economy picks up, so too will student numbers. It happened before in the early 1990s, so why not assume the same will happen when the economy returns to its buoyant self.

In either case, we feel that some underlying structural patterns in IS are in definite need of attention because they could portend trouble in the longer run (possibly even in the short run). Rather than proposing a radical transformation of the field, we believe that taking 'corrective action' could be sufficient to 'right the ship,' so to speak. We feel such corrective action is necessary regardless of whether the field is actually in a state of crisis at this very moment. In this paper, we offer our diagnosis of why we believe this is so, analyze the causes that have led to the current situation and give some indication of possible corrective actions. For those skeptical that the field is in a crisis, we contend that even a situation of relative calm is a good opportunity to engage in a reflective analysis, because it contributes to the field's continued health and stability. If such an analysis reveals reasons for concern, then our proposal for taking corrective action holds, irrespective of whether the field is in a crisis right now. If the field is not in crisis, then our paper should be interpreted as advocating 'proactive change' as a way of avoiding a crisis. In either event, our analysis should have merit.[3]

Engaging in such a critical reflection is of course neither an easy undertaking, nor one to be taken lightly. We approach this challenge by interpreting what has occurred in the field over the past thirty odd years, capturing as many IS specialties as is humanly possible. Fortunately, we can draw upon some of our earlier work for inspiration and guidance. Our prior work has on the one hand been more concrete yet on the other, more narrowly focused. The internal issues of the field that we will raise have, to some extent, been foreshadowed in Hirschheim (1986a), Klein and Hirschheim (1991) and Klein (1999). This second article introduced the dualism between purposive and communicative rationality in the context of IS development methods and tools. This distinction plays a critical and much broader role in this paper. The external issues of the field were touched on in Hirschheim and Klein (2000) where we first started to worry about the field's disconnects with its external stakeholders. Some of these concerns were also foreshadowed in an earlier paper which looked at societal change and its potential impact on the field (Klein and Hirschheim 1987).

In this paper, we will make a case for the members of the IS field to devote more attention than in the past to the potential role of IS in supporting sincere, reflective, agreement-oriented, yet critical conversations and debates. IS can support the achievement of agreement through the force of rational argumentation in two ways: as a convenient communication medium that reduces the transaction costs of communications; and as potential content provider that gives access to relevant information for evidence giving in critical debates that otherwise would not be available to the participants. This conversational-critical potential of IS was described in Klein and Lyytinen (1992) and then again in Hirschheim *et al.* (1995, pp. 165–169).

With this in mind, we chose to structure the paper as follows. In section 2, we first offer a preview of the line of argument that the paper takes. This may seem somewhat unusual, but because of the nature and complexity of our argument, some up front summary/ preview will help the reader follow our train of thought. After the preview, we attempt to assess the status of the IS field,[4] i.e., from where we have come. We offer a brief reflective history noting that the field is fragmented, and our historical treatment helps to better understand why it is fragmented. In sections 3 and 4, we explore the current state of the field. We note that because of the disparate stakeholders the field tries to satisfy, a number of communication gaps are apparent. We term these 'disconnects'. These disconnects are discussed in terms of two communities: the external community and the internal community. The external disconnects are associated with (1) IS researcher-executive, (2) IS practitioner-IS researcher, and (3) executive-IS practitioner communication gaps. The internal disconnects relate to communication gaps between (4) IS researcher-IS researcher, and (5) IS researcher—other disciplinary researcher that significantly influence the well being of IS in the academy. In section 5, we offer a proposal for the direction that corrective action could follow. This is our suggestion for 'where might we go from here?' We discuss the different types of knowledge that may be useful in IS and following on from there, the potential value of creating a shared structure which creates a core Body of Knowledge (BoK) out of parts that are now mostly disjoint. In section 6, we derive some implications and then recommendations from our ideas, particularly as they relate to the setting of research agendas, changes in the institutional publication practices, and the development and use of knowledge creation and transformation networks. Last, we speculate on a new frontier for IS revolving around a new cyber democracy.

2 FROM WHERE HAVE WE COME

2.1 Synopsis of Our Argument[5]

Having been in the field for a combined 60+ years, we have seen considerable growth in and maturation of the field. This includes many fads, but also substantial structural and institutional changes, as well as numerous calls for the need to change research methods, publication practices, tenure and promotion criteria, editorial policy, and so on. However, even with the normal 'give and take' and the cycles that are common to any field, we feel particularly uncomfortable with the current state of the IS field because we see certain underlying structural patterns that give us serious cause for concern. In this paper, we attempt to analyze what these structural patterns are and why they have come about. We also articulate what is deeply disturbing about these patterns. Additionally, we offer a knowledge structuring and social communication perspective on assembling and sharing IS knowledge; *viz.* the concept of an IS Body of Knowledge.[6] This paper will proceed from a historical background sketch, to a diagnosis of structural deficiencies in IS as a field, to suggesting some directions for corrective action.

We need to start first by identifying the underlying structural patterns from which our concerns arise by presenting a brief historical reconstruction of the evolution of IS as an academic field. We believe that the field needs to understand where it has come from in order to better discern where it might go.[7] This will also shed light on the fundamental assumptions that lie behind our concerns for the viability of IS as a discipline. The goal of this paper then is to reflect upon what has occurred in our discipline over the past thirty plus years and to consider the possible course of events that would favor or jeopardize the long-term survival of the field. This goal suggests two purposes for this paper: a *diagnostic* one, which is the key focus of the paper, and a *therapeutic* one where we offer our recommendations on how the field needs to change its strategic research priorities and institutional arrangements.

2.1.1 Diagnostic purpose

First, from a diagnostic perspective, we find that the IS discipline suffers from two problematic structural patterns: (1) a state of fragmentation, and (2) a number of significant communication gaps, which we term 'disconnects.' These lead to at least the following major threats: intellectual rigidity and the subsequent lack of fruitful discipline-wide communication; and a lack of relevance leading to possible emasculation through dispersal into other disciplines or business functions or through 'offshoring.' If so, the institutionalized IS discipline, as we know it, may cease to exist, at least in most of the Western World. Unless the academic leaders of the field begin to address these structural threats, they will eventually undermine the viability of the field. IS as a discipline could fail internally from a lack of integration, splitting into separate specialties that can then easily be allocated to other management disciplines or be offshored.[8] Practitioners are facing a similar threat directly and, if they are absorbed or dispersed, academicians will soon follow, for without a thriving practitioner community, there is little need for an academic one. If so, IS would have failed externally for the lack of service it provided to its principal external clients: IS practitioners, business unit users including senior management—CEOs, CFOs, COOs, etc. In this paper, we seek to address these structural deficiencies that are not connected to any economic cycle or 'market crash.' To meet this goal, we present a problem diagnosis that arises from a historically informed reflection on the current state of our discipline.

2.1.2 Therapeutic purpose

Second, from a therapeutic perspective, we contend that IS as a discipline has both *communicative* and *purposive-rational* functions,[9] and that IS research and practice straddle the methodological divide between these functions. Both functions are equally important for IS as a whole, but not necessarily for each of its sub-specialties. Because of the important role that the purposive-rational and communicative functions play, we offer a brief discussion of them.

Purposive rationality is exclusively concerned with achieving given ends with the minimum expenditure of means. The purposive-rational function of IS takes the calculative optimization of the means-ends relationship as the guiding principle of human action, as is presumed in mainstream economic theory and the engineering sciences. For example, a database programmer seeking to minimize response times while keeping duplication and storage needs to a minimum acts in a purposive-rational manner. In distinction to the means-ends orientation of purposive-rational action, the communicative function of IS research and practice attempts to contribute to the achievement of mutual understandings or at least compromises between different agents through negotiated arrangements. The analyst trying to nego-tiate the definition of requirements with different user groups is oriented toward reaching mutual understanding and agreement (unless he chooses to act strategically using deception, *cf.* Keen's 1981 description of implementation and counter-implementation games). Therefore, the communicative function of IS needs to examine how mutual understanding and agreements can be achieved in different situations. For this purpose, it is concerned with forming shared interpretations of norms, meanings and values and with maintaining social relationships. The further explanation of the communicative function draws on a general theory of the nature of human communi-cation in everyday life. It analyses how through sincere conversations and discourses on any topic of interest, people can reach mutual understanding through having a minimum of common background assumptions about the world. This also applies to academic discourse in research communities (*cf.* Heath 2001, p. 17; McCarthy 1982, Ch. 4; Habermas 1984, p. 75). We have elaborated on this in earlier research (e.g., Klein and Hirschheim 1991; Hirschheim, *et al.* 1996) based on the general framework of Habermas 'Theory of Communicative Action' (Habermas 1984, 1987).

It is important to realize that the type of knowledge and its role is very different in the purposive-rational and communicative functions of IS research and practice. The principal role of knowledge in the pursuit of rational-purposive action is to acquire powers of prediction and outcome control. The type of knowledge that is most useful for this is nomological, of which the laws of nature are the most typical example. If purposive-rational strategies are directed against human agents, they involve a claim to social power and treat people either as passive, inanimate objects or as opponents capable of intelligent counter-strategies (for an example of this in IS see Keen, 1981). In contrast, communicative action is based on knowledge of social norms, conventions, habits and historically accepted viewpoints as are typi-cally expressed in ordinary language. Other agents are not treated as inanimate objects or opponents, but as fellow human beings and part-ners. The kind of knowledge that is most useful in agreement oriented interactions comes from the humanities, especially history, study of foreign languages and cultures, comparative literature and social anthropology Therefore, the communicative function brings IS close to the methods of history, social anthropology, social psychology, sociology and—at the philosophical level—hermeneutics.[10]

While important strides have been made in both the communicative and purposive-rational functions of IS research and practice, their full extent and the interconnections between them have never been widely recognized nor become integral to our culture as an applied discipline—as pointed out in the literature analysis in Hirschheim *et al.* (1996). The communicative function for IS professionals and researchers first should include a shared understanding of our short history—the major intellectual waves that shaped our perspectives. Most of these intellectual waves originated in Europe, in particular the U.K. and Scandinavia, and the U.S. We believe the first time prominent representatives of the differing research world views of the U.S. and Europe engaged in an intense, face-to-face dialogue, was during the so-called 'Manchester conference' (Mumford *et al.* 1985). Since then, the US/ Europe divide has gradually been broken down. For example, the original Conference on Information Systems (CIS) has become ICIS (the International Conference on Information Systems); AIS—our institutional IS academic body—has a membership consisting of a significant and growing number of international affiliates. Yet, only a few old-timers, who directly participated in the beginnings of the globalization of IS research, know the intellectual foundations that drove these institutional changes and which now legitimize them. Therefore, a historical reflection, biased and incomplete as it necessarily must be here, can provide an essential foundation for a broader dialogue—internally. The second important focus of the communicative function looks outward to our clients. It suggests that all IS researchers need a better understanding of their clients' 'lifeworld' and existential concerns (*cf.* Habermas 1984). The past examples for conveying such understandings were important, but too limited. They consisted of yearly surveys of 'Key Issues Facing CIOs,' SIM APC grants, and a few select conferences. Some of the most successful ones were the IS research centers at various universities. However, their reach was rather limited as they served only a handful of elite universities that enjoyed the location and resources to afford them.

2.1.3 A proposed solution—a consensual body of knowledge

To achieve the diagnostic and therapeutic purposes for this paper, we note the need for a shared language. Without such a language, it is difficult to arrive at a consensual core body of knowledge or even to begin framing the issue of coding such a shared BoK for the discipline as a whole. Categorization schemes that make up the subject areas of IS (*cf.* Barki *et al.* 1988; Bacon and Fitzgerald 2001) are a useful start for developing a shared language for the field, but have not led to a discussion on how IS knowledge as a whole should be structured.

Moreover, most of the current research efforts have been devoted to knowledge that can serve a technical interest in prediction and control: ISD methods, tools, and other process knowledge such as database design, technology adoption, and so on. This type of knowledge is often widely dispersed (appearing in different disciplinary journals, e.g., management science, computer science, parts of applied psychology, etc.) and therefore not easily accessible. Furthermore, its relevance is often not seen because IS was unable to establish the kind of boundary spanning, social networks—what Klein and Lyytinen (2003) term 'knowledge creation and transformation networks (KCTNs)'—that are possessed by other applied fields like medicine, law, and engineering. These disciplines have had a long history where members of their transformational network convert abstract research insights into understandable and action-oriented, practically relevant knowledge. The relevance of research results is not so much an attribute of their research papers' wordings, but the product of the interaction occurring within a network of different agents and their motivation to transform knowledge similar to components in a food chain. Both the providers and the receivers must expend effort to communicate on the one hand and understand (interpret) on the other. To improve the relevance of its products, IS as a field must invest in establishing the appropriate knowledge creation and transformation networks. We shall return to this idea later in the paper.

In this paper, we shall propose a high-level classification scheme that includes practical, action oriented 'applicative knowledge.' We trust that our proposal will not endanger the currently very fertile pluralism that exists in the field. Our proposal for such a body of knowledge needs to be seen as merely a 'trial balloon' and not a concrete object. It is a 'first cut' to illustrate what we mean. It will hopefully lead to serious follow up research.

2.2 The Information Systems Field: A Reflective History

The field of Management Information Systems (or simply Information Systems, as is now more commonly used) has been around since the 1960s and has been evolving ever since. It formed from the nexus of computer science, management and organization theory, operations research, and accounting (Davis and Olson 1985, pp. 13–14). Each of these areas or disciplines brought a unique perspective to the application of computers to organizations, but each was also far broader in orientation. None focused specifically on the application of computers in organizations.

2.2.1 The emergence of theory

As computers began to be successfully applied to business problems in the late 1950s and early 1960s, interest grew in the development of 'theory' to support continued success. Blumenthal (1969) proposed what might have been the first comprehensive attempt at the development of a MIS (Management Information Systems) theory in his landmark book *Management Information Systems: A Framework for Planning and Development*. The author claimed his book 'is the long awaited intelligent, scientific approach to determining an organization's information needs and developing the kind of system that is responsive to sound decision making.'

Along the same timeframe as Blumenthal, Börje Langefors in Sweden was developing his own thoughts about IS. This culminated in Langefors' (1973) seminal work *Theoretical Analysis of Information Systems*, which provided 'a formal theory [of information systems].' Langefors drew on systems theory noting: '...we try to support statements by drawing analogies from other systems theories, for which precise solutions to the specific problems or techniques for solutions, have already been devised (p. 17).' Dickson (1968) proclaimed a dawn of a new era. He wrote: 'A new academic discipline, "management information-decision systems" is emerging to integrate these techniques and to provide the analytical frames of reference and the methodologies necessary to meet the new management requisites (p. 17).' Other authors rallied around the growth of MIS 'theory' and saw the development of total information systems solutions for organizations (*cf.* Young 1968; Zani 1970; Gorry and Scott-Morton 1971). But not all were enamored by the emergence of total information systems solutions (*cf.* Ackoff 1967; Dearden 1966, 1972). A debate ensued in the early years of the field about the efficacy of MIS (*cf.* Rapport 1968; Emery and Sprague 1972). Nevertheless, the field grew and flourished as discussed in Dickson's (1981) thoughtful history of the field. There he noted that the 'genesis' of the IS concept could be linked to decision making and 'viewing the management process as a cybernetic control system within the organization, relying heavily upon the computer as the control mechanism (p. 6).'

Keen's (1987) articulation of the field's mission reaches beyond Dickson's focus on decision making and cybernetic control within organizations:

The mission of Information Systems research is to study the effective design, delivery, use and impact of information technologies in organizations and society. The term 'effective' seems key. Surely the IS community is explicitly concerned with improving the craft of design and the practice of management in the widest sense of both those terms. Similarly, it looks at information technologies in their context of real people in real organizations in a real society. (pg. 3)

Because of its roots in multiple disciplines, such as computer science, management, and systems theory, it is hardly surprising that the field of IS cast a wide net when defining its boundaries, sweeping in many themes and areas. Nor is it surprising that there is considerable disagreement about what the field actually includes and does not include, and what its core features are. Mason and Mitroff (1973), for example, in their classic framework of IS, characterize the core components to be: psychological type (of the user), class of problems to be solved, organizational context, method of evidence generation and guarantor of evidence, and mode of presentation of the output. Ives *et al.* (1980) define IS in terms of five environments (external, organization, user, IS development and IS operations), three processes (user, IS development and IS operations), and an information subsystem. Lyytinen (1987) divides the field into nine components: the information system itself, IS operations environment, IS development environment, user environment, organizational environment, external environment, use process, development process, and operations process.

Swanson and Ramiller (1993) discuss the field in terms of the broad areas on which people write papers: computer-supported cooperative work, information and interface, decision support and knowledge-based systems, systems projects, evaluation and control, users, economics and strategy, impact, and IS research. Others have used co-citation analyses to identify intellectual subfields upon which IS draws (*cf.* Culnan 1986, 1987; Culnan and Swanson 1986; Cheon *et al.* 1992). Culnan (1986) for instance, noted the existence of three categories of 'referents' upon which IS draws: fundamental theory (e.g., systems science); related applied disciplines (e.g., accounting, computer science, finance, management, and operations research); and underlying disciplines (anthropology, political science, psychology, sociology). Keen (1987) categorized the field in terms of the problem areas each historical era chose to focus on. For example, in the early 1970s the focus was on 'managing systems development, design methodologies, economics and computers.' In the mid 1970s the focus changed to 'decision support, managing organizational change, and implementation.' In the early 1980s the focus was on 'productivity tools, data base management, personal computing, organizational impacts of technology, and office technology.' And in the mid 1980s, it changed to 'telecommunications, competitive implications of information technology, expert systems, impact of IT on the nature of work (pg.1).'

2.2.2 The beginnings of institutional infrastructures and diversity

The growth of the IS field over the past three decades has manifested itself in three ways. First, as the field has grown, *new specialties and research communities* have emerged, and the level of research has increased dramatically. Second, n*ew journals, new conferences, new departments, and new IS programs* are indicative of the dramatic growth of the field. We have witnessed the generation of a wealth of literature in information systems. Third, as the field moved into the nineties, this literature could be characterized as diverse and pluralistic. This is manifested in *diversity of problems addressed, diversity of theoretical foundations and 'referents',* and *diversity of research methodologies* (Benbasat and Weber 1996).[11] Regardless of whether diversity is considered a blessing (e.g., Robey 1996) or a curse (e.g., Benbasat and Weber 1996), it is widely accepted as a defining characteristic of the field (Cooper 1988; Banville and Landry 1989; Alavi *et al.* 1989; Keen 1991; Orlikowski and Baroudi 1991; Swanson and Ramiller 1993; Markus 1997; Mingers and Stowell 1997; Mathiassen 1998; Benbasat and Zmud 2003; King and Lyytinen 2003).

In view of the rich diversity, it is not surprising that no unifying perspective on the nature of IS and IS research has gained widespread acceptance. The abundance of different schools of thought in the field is suggestive of its rich and diversified nature. The proliferation of different schools of thought in IS research, however, has its disadvantages as researchers in the different schools appear to work on disjoint or non-pertinent topics (Bjorn-Andersen 1984; Huber 1983) without much cross-communication. This has raised the concern that IS research does not contribute to a cumulative research tradition (Keen 1980), thereby throwing into question the value of IS research. To answer this challenge, several attempts have been made to find a common conceptual platform (paradigm) on which to ground, build and organize IS research (Mason and Mitroff 1973; Ives *et al.* 1980; Weber 1987; Farhoomand 1987; Ein-Dor and Segev 1981; Wand and Weber 1990; Hirschheim *et al.* 1996).

2.2.3 From diversity to the beginnings of fragmentation

However, Banville and Landry (1989) shed doubt on the possibility of achieving such a common conceptual platform. Through a sociological analysis of dependencies among researchers in IS, they concluded that the field is more a 'fragmented adhocracy' than a unified discipline. Why a fragmented adhocracy? Because in order to work in IS one does not need a strong consensus of one's colleagues on the significance and importance of the problem to be addressed in research as long as there exists some outside community for support. Nor are there widely accepted, legitimized results or procedures on which one must build 'in order to construct knowledge claims which are regarded as competent and useful contributions (Banville and Landry 1989, p. 54).' In addition, there exists high task uncertainty in IS research, because problem formulations are unstable, research priorities vary among different research communities, and there is little control over research goals by a professional leadership establishment (such as bars or licensing boards for physicians and engineers). For example, IS research groups may choose to define projects that do not follow the familiar patterns of engineering or empirical social science. There exists considerable local autonomy to formulate research problems and standards for conducting research and evaluate research results. In fact, this has been a matter of lively debate for many years (Ives *et al*. 1980; Keen 1980; Mumford *et al*. 1985; Culnan 1986, 1987; Farhoomand 1987; Cash and Lawrence 1989; Benbasat 1989; Kraemer 1991; Nissen *et al*. 1991; Backhouse *et al*. 1991; Landry and Banville 1992; Galliers 1992; Hirschheim *et al*. 1995; Lee *et al*. 1997; Mingers and Stowell 1997; Checkland and Howell 1998; Currie and Galliers 1999; Klein and Myers 1999).

2.3 The State of IS Today

Today, we believe that fragmentation is a root cause of the field's potential crisis. Whereas Banville and Landry (1989) described the field as a fragmented adhocracy, they did not explain why this condition arose nor whether this was a problem. Indeed, they believed it to be a strength.

In contrast, we believe the fragmentation is evidence of a structural problem for the field that portends a crisis. To be clear, we do not equate fragmentation with pluralism. Pluralism—for us—relates to diversity of ideas, perspectives, research approaches, paradigms, etc. But there is at least some underlying core set of knowledge or beliefs that all in the field share. There is a sense of shared belonging and empathy to others in the field. This is different from fragmentation, where there is insufficient (insignificant) communication between the different communities such that no core knowledge set exists. Individuals work in their own sub-communities without reference to other sub-communities. For us, this is a serious concern and in this paper, we shall explain why we feel this way. To do so requires us to reflect on the state of the field as it currently is. We start by considering the role of IT.

Critical to the evolution of the field was the development of technology—IT to be precise. The advancements in IT spawned new areas of IS research. This is a point cogently made by Orlikowski and Iacono (2001) and Benbasat and Zmud (2003).

From a historical perspective, the discipline that at first used to be called data processing (DP), then MIS and later IS, has been undergoing another subtle name change to IT, particularly in industry. Each of these name changes reflects the discarding of an identity in search of another. The identity changes are not so much related to generations of hardware capabilities as to usage patterns associated with new technologies. According to Dahlbom (1996), there have been at least four such information technology usage eras. The first, DP, was epitomized by the automation of transaction processing. The second, MIS, was characterized by using computers as instruments of control and rationalizing administrative systems. The notion of an integrated IS perhaps best characterizes this second stage of MIS. To the third era belongs 'personal computing,' which boosted personal productivity and end-user computing to create a measure of independence of individuals from the centralized power centers of 'administrative computing.' With the arrival of wide-spread networking from LANs to the Internet we have entered a fourth era, where computers begin to look more like information appliances: mere access points to a vast array of services available to all with minimal computing literacy. The commercial exploitation through e-commerce and e-entertainment has just begun and we don't know yet whether this will lead to another qualitative identity change into a fifth era of the global e-village.

As IT evolved, it has clearly influenced the IS profession. To be sure, IT is neither the root cause nor the technological fix for the structural patterns which lie at the base of the 'crisis.' The offshoring, the disconnects, and the internal communication gaps that we identify in the next sections as the basis of the crisis are not caused by IT. But there is one exception: as the IS field embraces technical specializations, the widely recognized rapid change and proliferation of technology encourages ever finer divisions of labor and with this comes more and more rapid social differentiation contributing to the communication gaps: the 'techies' versus the 'softies' research cultures for example. Otherwise, IT has an enabling or mediating role in the underlying patterns. The following three points illustrate the role of IT from our perspective. It is the attention to the mediating role of IT that differentiates IS from other business disciplines.

2.3.1 IT as enabler of sourcing and offshoring

The phenomena of outsourcing and offshoring would be impossible without the high speed and reliable global networks on which industry has come to rely since the mid to late nineties. In this case, IT is clearly an enabler that has opened up new strategic options for structuring IT and business operations. However, the causal driver of exploring and implementing these options is clearly economics: improving profits through cost savings. In addition to the availability of the new high bandwidth technologies, it was important to prove the concept (e.g., that outsourcing IT to a third party provider could be done), and to develop the detailed know-how and skills that would lead organizations to trust in the viability of such options. It took several years to do this. Hence those pundits believing in a current crisis point out that most of the U.S. industry is now poised to take full advantage of options such as offshoring with the long-term view that few IT jobs will be left in the US and Europe. Moreover, a new business cycle upswing will not bring back the jobs lost domestically even though the offshoring target countries may benefit, especially India and China.

2.3.2 IT as enabler and catalyst for commoditization

The new buzzwords of 'IT-enabled services' (Kern *et al.* 2002) and 'utility computing' (Westerman and Ross 2003) point to another important side effect of technology that has been one of the key characteristics of 'modernization' since the beginning of the first industrial revolution—the expropriation of individual skills into explicit methods and techniques that are then coded in specific turn-key technology 'solutions.' From a systems perspective, the same phenomenon has been labeled as 'black-boxing.' The operators of the turn-key solutions need no longer be able to master the level of detailed craftsmanship that is necessary to perform the work that the turn-key solution automates, because the original complexity has been hidden behind the levers and buttons of an interface. As a result, the operator of a programmable lathe needs fewer skills than the old blacksmith, or the factory-trained laborer in a semi-automated shoe factory has a fraction of the skills of the old shoemaker workshop. Modern IT has allowed extending this market logic of commoditization to white collar work—clerical work initially (e.g., payroll computations) and now all the way to business processes (business process outsourcing—BPO). Hence, IT has served both as a medium and catalyst of turning subjective skills and know-how into a market commodity that can be contracted out to the lowest bidder.

If the crisis pundits are correct, this process has now come full circle by ironically hitting the IT profession itself: they will suffer what they have done unto others. The key point here is that whilst commoditization is not wholly dependent on IT, the causes of commoditization are deeply rooted in the progress ideal of the enlightenment and liberalist ethics of market economics. IT simply extends its reach and speed with which it spreads throughout the economic system.

2.3.3 IT—a part of the solution?

In section 2.1, we alluded to the important role of social knowledge creation and transformation networks (KCTNs). We see them as a possible vehicle for overcoming the communication gaps that manifest themselves in multiple disconnects that we will explore in the next two sections. Clearly IT cannot provide the initial motivation, commitments and social bonds required to make these networks a reality and keep them functioning. However, once established, IT can provide an important support function to make them more effective and reduce the costs of communications. Once the motivation for establishing such networks leads to widespread commitment, it is a matter of socio-technical research to determine which type of interfaces (video conferencing vs. telephony vs. email), information repositories and symbol transformation capabilities could support and to some extent replace expensive face-to-face communication. From the perspective of Actor-Network-Theory (A-N-T), IT components could serve as complex 'actants' in KCTNs enabling them to behave differently than they would without these techno-actants.[12] We shall return to the idea of KCTNs at the end of the paper.

2.4 Summary and Preview

With this reflective history in mind, we turn our attention to an assessment of the field. In the next section we assess where we are now from two alternative perspectives: an external perspective where we focus on the view of the field from the eyes of management; and an internal perspective where we look at the state of the discipline from the eyes of the academic community.

3 WHERE ARE WE NOW: THE EXTERNAL VIEW FROM THE MANAGEMENT WORLD

It has been and continues to be commonplace to bemoan the lack of relevancy of IS research for professional practice (*cf.* Keen 1987, 1991; CAIS 2001). In the current state of discussion, it is now widely agreed that we need to ask who the stakeholders for our research are and what relevancy means for them. In exploring the meaning of relevancy 'one rather critical distinction is between relevance to and serves the interests of or is of value to' (Cresswell 2001, p. 2). With this distinction, Cresswell points out that some research could be rather critical of practice and could undermine a stakeholder's interests, yet this would not make the research irrelevant. In fact, Creswell's point needs to be taken one step further. It would be ideologically biased and therefore ethically questionable to require that publicly funded researchers like University faculty should place the interests of one external stakeholder group, i.e., industry shareholders or their agents (management), above those of other stakeholders. Other stakeholders who should benefit from academic IS research are the employees of firms and organizations, their agents (e.g., unions), community and other levels of government and the general public. In addition to multiple external constituents for IS research relevancy, IS researchers have important stakeholders within academia, for example funding agencies, colleagues in other disciplines, university administrators, and last, but not least, students (*cf.* Bhattacherjee 2001). Insofar as different stakeholder groups tend to possess conflicting interests arising from differing value systems, IS relevancy depends on value judgments that should be made explicit while not engendering opportunities to learn from the interaction with any stakeholders that are willing to open themselves to IS researchers.[13]

In this paper, we can deal with the IS research relevancy issue only selectively. Therefore, under the heading of 'external' relevance, we shall focus only on the 'serves the interest of' relationship of IS research for the most commonly espoused *external* stakeholder groups, i.e., industry management.[14] In section 4, we shall consider how the relevancy issue presents itself from the internal perspective of the IS research community, i.e., we shall examine whose interests IS research is required to serve to achieve academic success.

For analyzing the external relevance issue, we must not consider industry management as one homogenous stakeholder group. At a minimum, we need to consider two groups of actors in addition to the IS researchers themselves. These are senior management and the practitioners in IS departments. By focusing on the interdependences among these two groups and IS researchers, we conclude that the current situation is characterized by three 'disconnects'. *First*, there is a disconnect between expectations as formulated by senior management and the practice of IS departments in the way they interpret their mission. *Second*, there is a disconnect between current IS research and senior management expectations. *Third*, there is a disconnect between IS researchers and the practitioners in IS departments because IS research is insufficiently relevant to the concerns of professional IS practice. For the sake of completeness there are two additional disconnects with which we shall deal under the 'internal view.' Disconnect *four* exists within the IS research community itself due to numerous IS research sub-communities that insufficiently communicate with each other. It involves the internal fragmentation of IS research. A *fifth* disconnect exists between the IS academic research community and academics in other disciplines. We shall explore these latter two disconnects in section 4, *the internal view of the state of the research community*.

3.1 Disconnects between the Worlds of Business and Academia

The disconnect of both IS researchers *and* practitioners from senior management expectations is a matter of outsider perceptions and expectations of IS academics and practitioners alike and therefore concerns *the external view of the state of the community*. Our interpretation of the external view is based on formal and informal interviews of hundreds of IS managers on three continents over a fifteen year period. These culminated in a variety of publications (Hirschheim *et al.* 1988; Hirschheim and Miller 1993; Lacity and Hirschheim 1993a, b, 1995a, b; Bhattacherjee and Hirschheim 1997; Hirschheim and Lacity 2000; Sabherwal *et al.* 2001; Hirschheim and Sabherwal 2001; Hirschheim *et al.* 2003). Our interpretation also reflects the results of other IS researchers who have studied the actual practices of IS (*cf.* Ward and Peppard 1996; Earl 1996; Willcocks *et al.* 1997; Henderson and Venkatraman 1999; Currie and Galliers 1999; Brown and Sambamurthy 1999; Pepper and Ward 1999; Zmud 2000). They point to five expectations that senior management and peers in other business functions have for IS managers.[15] These five expectations stand in contrast to the regularly published 'top issues facing the CIO' published in places like *MISQ*, because they have more persistence about them. As our data have been accumulated for well over a decade, we reached the conclusion that they have continually shaped the quality of the relationships of IS practitioners with the organizational environment in two ways: horizontally with the other business functions and vertically with senior corporate management. These expectations are: (1) lower costs of the IS function; (2) increased speed of delivery of IS products and services; (3) comprehensive, cross-functional data availability; (4) demonstrable value add; and (5) leadership in shaping corporate strategic direction.

Even a cursory examination makes it apparent that the IS community as a whole (consisting of practitioners and IS researchers) has not been able to meet these 'external' expectations in the past nor is it likely to do so in the foreseeable future. This is not to imply that we believe all of the following expectations are legitimate or even reasonable. They may in part be based on misconceptions and part of the future challenge for IS academics is to discern legitimate expectations from misconceptions.

(1.) Lower costs of the IS function. While it is true that hardware functionality in terms of processor speed, bandwidth and storage capacity has been increasing as prices decrease (and this trend seems likely to continue), this simply misses the point. Lower IT costs typically do not translate into lower overall costs for IS functionality,[16] but the IS practitioner community has historically had difficulty arguing why this is so. Simply put, IT costs only make up a fraction of overall IS costs. As the IS function delivers more and more products and services to the business units, its overall costs go up inevitably (Lacity and Hirschheim 1995a). Consider the analogy with the car industry: consumers expect greater functionality from cars, yet do not necessarily expect them to go down in price, even given a decrease in price of some car components. So does it make sense for senior business executives to expect lower costs from their IS units?

(2.) Increasing speed of delivery of IS products and services. One of the persistent challenges confronting IS departments is the speed with which it can deliver products and services. As the number of products and services demanded from it increase, the function struggles to meet expectations. Just as senior management uses the decline in hardware costs to buttress its belief that IS costs should go down, it also believes that new technology should aid IS in delivering products and services more expeditiously. And it does, to some extent. But this point of view is misguided. The IS function is increasingly attempting to balance a greater and greater number of system demands. Whether it is implementing an ERP across the organization, maintaining legacy applications, putting in a new telecommunications infrastructure, and/or preparing the organization for electronic commerce, these demands simply place an enormous burden on IS. And the burden grows daily as more and more business units request new and ever more complex services.

(3.) Comprehensive, cross-functional data availability. Although organizations for some time have wished for and—to some extent— have been promised information systems that could deliver data that was comprehensive and spanned the entire organization (and even spanned across organizations), such a desire was more pipe-dream than reality. Nor did IS organizations help themselves with the overselling of data base technology, decision support systems and executive information systems, promising senior executives exciting integrative possibilities now that data were accessible from across the entire organization. In fact, these systems, while potentially beneficial to management, were not the panacea they were often sold to be. While they did provide richer data that was easier to access and understand, they were neither comprehensive nor truly cross-functional. Senior management needs this kind of information, but perhaps until recently—with the advent of client/server based ERP applications and data warehouses—such wishes could not be met. Again, in many ways this mismatch of expectations is in part IS's fault. Delivering cross-functional data and applications is not only a technological problem but a political one as well. Getting disparate organizational units to share 'their' data is typically a political minefield. The IS function has simply not done a good job in making this situation visible to all.

(4.) Demonstrable value-add. Perhaps the most intractable problem that IS faces is the issue of how to get management to see the value-add of the IS function. This issue is connected to the evaluation of IS, i.e., the evaluation of IS products and services. While IS evaluation has received a fair amount of attention in research,[17] the results have been disappointing in that no reliable method has been found to measure the value of an IS before it has been built (and even after it is built, *cf*. Smithson and Hirschheim 1998). *A fortiori* it follows that the evaluation of the IS function as a whole is even more intractable. According to Lacity and Hirschheim (1993a), the IS function is often perceived as an overhead; that is, a cost of doing business but one to be minimized. In such an environment, it is hard for IS to demonstrate its strategic contribution to the organization when it has had to focus its attention on justifying why it charges what it does to the business units (*cf*. Ross *et al*.'s 1999 discussion on the need for IS to chargeback the costs of its services). Simply put, IS continues to be seen as an overhead rather than a valuable investment. With all the negative connotations this brings with it, it will be increasingly difficult for the IS executive to focus on IS's strategic role, and more specifically, to convince senior management to focus on IS's strategic potential. It does not help matters when an IS function's successes (e.g., new applications successfully implemented on time and on budget) are perceived as 'business unit successes' yet IS failures (e.g., new applications where budgets are overrun) are labeled 'IS failures.' According to Hirschheim *et al.* (2003), one of the major failures of IS has been its inability to provide credible success stories that become part of company folklore.

(5.) Leadership in shaping corporate strategic direction. Somewhat paradoxical to the last point where IS is typically perceived as overhead, organizations often wish IS to take an active role in shaping a corporation's strategic direction. The belief seems to be that the IS function is uniquely suited for this role for two reasons. First, because IS develops systems for all the business units in the organization, it is believed that it has to understand how the different systems fit together. Therefore IS leaders are well suited to having a good over-view of all the functions and systems of the organization. Second, IS is perhaps the most knowledgeable group of individuals in the organization on new technologies. Given these new technologies may provide opportunities for the organization to get into new businesses, new markets, etc., such technology expertise could prove invaluable for setting strategic direction (Wheeler 2002). Hence IS is uniquely placed to provide leadership both in an integrative role and in shaping a company's strategic direction (Luftman 1996; Ross *et al.* 1996). Yet, here too we note a serious inconsistency. On the one hand, IS has been perceived as being an overhead, as too expensive, as failing to provide comprehensive data across the organization and insufficient value for money; while on the other hand, it is supposed to provide leadership in strategic direction. The first set of problems with IS has led the function to being ignored as a source for corporate senior management positions. How often does one find a former IS director in the capacity of chief officer of a corporation? Answer: not very often. To us, it is totally inconsistent to expect IS to take a lead role in shaping strategic vision and direction without giving IS the necessary access to senior management positions and the knowledge and motivation that comes with it.

3.2 Reflection on the Disconnects between the Worlds of Business and Academia

So where does this leave us? Clearly there is a problem with the non-IS practitioners' view of IS. They have an unrealistic image of IS and concomitantly, unrealistic expectations about what IS can and cannot accomplish. But there is also a significant disconnect between IS practitioners and IS academics that is well known. IS practitioners feel academics live in ivory towers engaging in research that is devoid of any practical relevance. IS academics, on the other hand, feel that practitioners do not understand the need for theory and are only interested in vocational training. (This is a theme we will take up again in the Conclusions.)

In placing these unmet expectations into a historical perspective, we have reached the conclusion that the image of information systems to which the IS research community has subscribed over some time has been incongruous with that held by the external consumers of IS research. As a result, they do not look for enlightenment through IS research, because they have given up on our research a long time ago. If we truly believe that at least some IS theories are, indeed, relevant for practitioners, we must have done a very poor job of communicating it in a convincing way. (We do not want to imply that every bit of theoretical exploration has to be immediately relevant for practitioners.)

There are two sides to this incongruence issue. First, the view of IS that is held by IS practitioners is at best only partially supported by some of the theories that guide IS research (e.g., structuration theory, agency theory, and actor network theory). In part this is a result of the pressure in MBA education to keep all courses focused on purposefully rational concepts and relevant skills. Second, the view held by non-IS practitioners, i.e., senior management or business unit managers, is even more at odds with the academic notions of information systems and also quite different from the IS practitioners' beliefs about the nature of IS. Many of these managers have degrees outside of management. Their views are then shaped by the assumptions underlying these degrees (provided they have degrees at all) moderated with crash courses in 'executive education,' which often are even more narrowly focused than MBA curricula. This contributes to a credibility crisis for IS as a whole that engulfs both academia and practice.

As researchers, we must ask ourselves: is there anything that we can do to illuminate the issues at stake from a longer-term perspective? For a start, we believe that research should be undertaken in at least two areas:

(1.) There is a need for increasing the amount of research directed at *understanding IS practitioners* and engaging them in a discourse about a realistic set of expectations for what the IS academic research community can and cannot deliver. As an applied discipline, we need to better understand what each community expects from the other.

(2.) There is a need for increasing the amount of research directed at *understanding non-IS practitioners, especially senior management*, and engaging them in a discourse about a realistic set of expectations for what the IS function can and cannot deliver. We also need to provide well-articulated arguments to the IS practitioners by which they can state their case to senior management that a thriving IS department is needed along with the other functional units.

One pointer on how the above might be accomplished can be found in Lynne Markus' address to the 1997 IFIP8.2 conference in Philadelphia. She argued that one of the directions the field should now take is 'the appreciation of practicality in IS research (Markus 1997, p. 18).' The intent of what she terms practical research is not to replace or over-shadow research that builds or tests academic theory, but rather to complement theoretical research with 'rigorous research that describes and evaluates what is going on in practice (Markus 1997, p. 18).' This is underscored by the conference theme of ICIS 1997 with its emphasis on the issue of relevance and relationship of IS research to practice (Kumar 1997, p. xvii). Later, *MISQ* announced a renewed thrust aimed 'at better imbuing rigorous research with the element of relevance to managers, consultants, and other practitioners (Lee 1999a, p. viii).' The discussions presented in Benbasat and Zmud (1999), Applegate and King (1999), Lyytinen (1999), and Lee (1999b) support this thrust. (We shall return to the external relevancy issue in section 6 of the paper—Recommendations.)

3.3 Summary and Preview

If, in its current state, IS research appears to be ill equipped to address these issues, it will be necessary to face several intellectual issues and social dynamics that are driving IS research from within the academic community. These issues neither resonate with the five expectations of senior management nor align themselves with IS practitioner interests. The first of these issues to consider, is the frag-mentation that characterizes the internal state of the IS research community.

4 WHERE ARE WE NOW: THE INTERNAL VIEW OF CRISIS SYMPTOMS IN ACADEMIA

We now turn to the internal view of the state of the research community and the disconnects that exist within the IS research community arising from the lack of communication among the numerous research sub-communities. This leads to an internal fragmentation of the field. Within the 'internal view' we also address the disconnect that exists between the IS academic research community and academics in other disciplines.

4.1 Internal Disconnects

We postulate that there are four expectations that come from our internal constituencies that again do not resonate with the current state of the field: (1) we are supposed to accept or be tolerant of different research sub-communities, implying tolerance of alternative paradigms; (2) we are supposed to have general theories; (3) we are supposed to be rigorous; and (4) we are supposed to be relevant, but for whom?

(1.) Pluralism, yet a need for common ground. It is our belief that the discussion of preferred reference disciplines and paradigms have shaped the current ways of thinking and agendas in the IS research community more than anything else.[18] The effects of conflicting paradigms and commitment to incompatible visions of the nature of IS have fragmented the IS research community along several dimensions to the point that it has reached the so-called 'fragmented adhocracy.'[19] Hence the greatest issue that the IS community faces internally is its fragmentation into numerous specializations (or what we might call 'sects'). They need an intellectual synthesis that could emerge from a fruitful discourse. However, we lack a set of shared assumptions and language, and as a result the various sub-specializations lack the motivation and capability to communicate with each other. Our large conferences like ICIS, AIS or HICSS are reincarnations of the Tower of Babel. Fruitful, cross-sectional debate almost never occurs. And it has been like this for decades (*cf.* Hirschheim 1986b).

Traditionally, the relationship between alternative paradigms was conceived as being one of the following: dominance, synthesis, incommensurability, eclecticism or pluralism (Morgan 1983). For example, positivism, through the centuries, has enjoyed great success. Its position was one of dominance. More recently, however, critics have surfaced calling into question positivism's dominance. A call has gone out for pluralism rather than dominance in research (*cf.* Lincoln and Gupa 1985). From an historical perspective, one can distinctly see the uneasy tension that has existed in the application of positivism in the social sciences. This has given rise to what Tashakkori and Teddlie (1998) have termed 'the paradigm wars:' battles fought by the adherents of positivism against those from other paradigms.

For Landry and Banville (1992), the paradigm wars can be recast into three types of researchers each with its own outlook on paradigm appropriateness. They have characterized these types or groups as 'mainstream navigators,' 'unity advocates,' and 'knights of change.' The first group, mainstream navigators, is composed of supporters of the dominant orthodoxy. Their epistemological roots are in logical positivism, which cements them in the functionalist paradigm. The second group, unity advocates, is more concerned with the acceptance of information systems as a scientific discipline than with a specific paradigm. In the unity advocates' view of the world, an immature or pre-science discipline is characterized by the existence of several competing paradigms. A more desirable state—that of a full-fledged scientific discipline—is characterized by the reign of a single dominant paradigm. They would be agreeable to using any paradigm as long as it granted them scientific respectability. Since the current state of information systems research is dominated by positivism, unity advocates tend to cluster towards this end of the paradigm dimension. The third group, knights of change, is of the opinion that reality is multifaceted, and forged from the interpretations and interactions of individual actors. They also give credence to the belief that no single research approach can fully capture the richness and complexity of what we experience as reality. Thus they champion a collection of assorted research approaches arising from multiple paradigms.

Yet, even the knights of change, with their clarion call for methodo-logical pluralism, argue for change *within* Burrell and Morgan's (1979) four paradigms. Others argue that Burrell and Morgan's framework, by virtue of its widespread acceptance and impact, has normalized and rationalized emerging streams of research, constraining alternative perspectives.

> In time, influential frameworks can become as restraining and restrictive as those they originally challenged...we are sometimes presented through responses to a conceptual framework...with a new, rich set of alternative perspectives through which we can continue our study and talk about our subject matter. (Frost 1996; p. 190)

In addition to the three types of paradigm warriors identified by Landry and Banville, a new group is emerging that is calling for an end to the paradigm wars—the pacifists. These theorists and researchers argue that there are strengths and weaknesses in both the positivist and non-positivist positions, and point out that the conflicting paradigms have, in spite of the best efforts of their most ardent supporters, achieved a state of coexistence (Tashakkori and Teddlie 1998). Datta (1994) has presented five compelling arguments in support of this assertion. (1) Both paradigms have been in use for a number of years. (2) There are a considerable (and growing) number of scholars arguing for the use of multiple paradigms and methods. (3) Funding agencies support research in both paradigms. (4) Both paradigms have had an influence on various policies and (5) much has been learned via each paradigm.

In the IS research arena, the existence of such paradigm pluralism can be found, but it is not as wide spread as Datta (1994) and Tashakkori and Teddlie (1998) suggest. Worse, the supposed interplay between researchers of different paradigms does not occur—as was noted above—because of the communication gap that exists among the alternative paradigms.

(2.) Generality: the unresolved challenge. IS as a field has had difficulties with generalization from its beginnings. It started with story telling of experiences that were generalized into insights that should apply to many situations (e.g., the five lessons from Ackoff 1967 or the 'myths' of Dearden 1966). Such reasoning was later debunked as 'unscientific' and replaced with 'rigorous' hypothesis testing. It now appears as if IS research has come full circle by returning to new forms of story telling (the politically correct term is, of course, 'narratives'). Whereas the new story telling movement can point to much better and more explicit philosophical grounding than 'the great wise men' had for their story telling, this does not necessarily make it 'more general.' In fact some forms of narrative research lag in generality behind the insights offered by the earliest authors. Moreover, it shares this weakness with the failure of positivist research to offer a few broad theories that contribute to general orientation and bring some measure of order to the perpetual confusion in our field. So far the application of interpretivist theories has not resulted in more general theory formulations than the positivists. Should it turn out that the interpretivist approach is equally unable to deliver results of general interest, i.e., that reduce the complexity of coping with reality by applying to a large number of instances, it may fall into disrepute quicker than the attraction of positivism is waning. (*cf.* Klein and Myers 1999 for a proposal to strengthen the generalization potential of interpretivist research). So how does one deal with this dilemma?

It appears that the generalization deficit is a concern that affects interpretivists and positivists alike, yet is largely ignored by both. However, there may be hope here. We propose that this deficit could be addressed by a change in paper reviewing practices in the direction of giving generalization the same weight as methodological rigor.

Often authors are discouraged from generalization, because they cannot support it with the same degree of plausible evidence as narrowly conceived hypotheses. This practice discourages prospective authors from connecting specific hypotheses or ethnographic findings to broader theoretical lines of reasoning that might qualify as some form of general theory, at least within a specific sub-community. If papers are rejected for lack of rigor, then the same should apply for lack of generalization. The degree of rigor required should be tempered in relation to the degree of generalization attempted. The more generalization, the less rigor would be expected. Lee and Baskerville (2003) make a welcome attempt to place the topic of generalization on the agenda of serious discussion. They diagnose certain limits of statistical generalizability and propose a framework of different types of generalizability. Hopefully their proposal will spark further debate on this important topic.

We believe that a new genre of papers should be encouraged, which takes a major block of specific studies and molds them into a larger theoretical framework. There are examples of this kind of work (e.g., Zmud 1979; Ives *et al.* 1980), but they are far too few. Of course, engaging in such work not only requires considerable effort, but also typically leads to papers that are longer and conceptual rather than empirical in nature. Most journals have page limitations that specifically militate against such efforts. Thus in encouraging these new papers, journal editors would have to revise their editorial policies in the following ways. (1) Engage sympathetic Associate Editors and reviewers to broaden their view about what types of papers are acceptable to their journals; (2) set different and realistic new page limitations for such papers; and (3) revise the scope and aims of their journals to reflect the broader focus. (See section 6.4 for additional suggested changes to the field's institutional publication practices.) For the sake of completeness, we do need to mention that a number of books exist such as Checkland (1981), Checkland and Scholes (1990) and Walsham (1993), which offer good generalizations drawn from action research and detailed field studies respectively.

(3.) Rigor: what does it mean? A dictionary definition of rigor typically uses terms such as 'severity, sternness, strictness, stringency, harshness' to describe its nature.[20] In academic research, the term rigor has become the touchstone for quality and scholarship. 'If it isn't rigorous, it isn't scholarly. If it isn't rigorous, it shouldn't be published.' Rigor seems to have taken on a life of its own in academic research. Rigor is usually manifested in research through Greek symbols, mathematical formulas, number of experimental controls and conforming to the standards of the best research the community of scholars interprets it has done so far. Typically, this means applying the hypothetico-deductive method—the accepted method of science. Such a view of rigor however, excludes other forms of scholarly research that do not subscribe to such positivist standards.[21]

We contend that there are many scholarly vehicles for knowledge creation and they need to be recognized as rigorous as long as they employ sound forms of reasoning and evidence giving. Indeed, we believe that any knowledge claim emanating from research should be scrutinized using a sound reasoning process. This might embrace Habermas' (1984) notion of the 'force of the better argument' where competing knowledge claims are evaluated, and the knowledge claim based on the better reasoning, arguments, and evidence is judged as 'accepted.' Such a process can be used to evaluate interpretive as well as positivist research even though interpretive research is considered inherently more difficult to be 'evaluated objectively,' because the community consensus about its standards have not yet solidified. Nevertheless, it can be done. An objective evaluation would typically involve considering three aspects of the research: intelligibility, novelty and believability. Intelligibility relates to how well the research approach and results are comprehensible, i.e., how closely others can follow them with similar qualifications and how much effort they have to expend to absorb them in the sense of making the new knowledge a part of their mind set. Novelty can be judged in at least three ways: (1) by the amount of new insight added; (2) by the significance of the research reported in terms of the implications it has for seeing important matters in a new light and/or provide a new way of thinking about the phenomenon under study; and (3) by the completeness and coherence of the research report(s). Can the author provide an overall picture so that its components link up to each other without major holes in the picture that is being painted? Believability, on the other hand, relates to how well the research arguments make sense in light of our total knowledge. The key question for believability is how well the research in method and results fits with other ideas and arguments that are taken for granted within the current state of knowledge. A first measure of this is the number of references with which it is consistent (or which it challenges). This is based on Quine's idea that the current state of research forms a web of beliefs that is only sparsely connected to 'hard' evidence (Quine 1970). New research inevitably challenges a part of the web of beliefs introducing inconsistencies suggesting that some parts of the knowledge web need to be reformulated if not discarded. References provide the links to those parts of the belief web with which the new research is consistent. In this way, the references connect the new research to other parts of the belief web that so far had not been considered as pertinent. In this way knowledge is updated and restructured by a bump and shift process. Another useful image of the state of knowledge is the fact net and its proliferation in the sense of Churchman (1971). The more references are challenged, the less believable, but potentially the more significant is the research. For believability, each author must demonstrate how his research 'fixes' the net of our knowledge. If the research 'takes out' certain parts of the knowledge net, the author must reconnect the loose parts. Often this requires relating to some forgotten or remote parts of the web of belief (which may be the domain of some other research community). By bringing in more references from other areas, authors can often successfully challenge major parts of a local (within one discipline) web of belief.

For sociological reasons, intelligibility and believability are inextricably linked and together are often inversely related to the degree of novelty in the following way. The more radical a new idea is the more difficult it is to explain and comprehend and the more evidence is required to make it believable. Alas the newer an idea is, the less 'hard' evidence is usually available to support it. Moreover, anything that is difficult to explain tends to be less believable than what is 'clear and simple.' In addition, there often exists an attitude in management circles that truth is recognized by its clear and simple formulation, which contrasts with attitudes in physics and engineering (e.g., Einstein's theory of relativity or particle theory is neither clear nor simple for most people, yet believed to be useful by most). Ultimately they are a measure of what the research community terms 'the validity of the research.' Although all research projects must produce results that are intelligible, novel and believable for the community of scholars to label them a contribution to the state of knowledge, the criteria are perhaps more subjective in interpretive research projects. To this end, Klein and Myers (1999) offer assistance. They present a set of criteria on how to judge knowledge claims generated from interpretivist research. We feel this is critically important for the IS discipline because interpretivist research can often offer better insights for practice than its counterpart. Interpretive research is typically descriptive and explanatory, hence practitioners can usually better relate to it as the research is closer to practice, involves actual case studies, involves real people in real situations, and is undertaken in real world settings. They talk about the results offering new insights, and the results are more translatable into the ways people actually work in organizations. However, interpretive research is not prescriptive. It is typically weak in providing clear normative advice on what to do or how to improve matters in practice. Therefore, it is doubtful that interpretive research as practiced today is any more relevant for management and practitioners than its counterpart, especially if one considers its normative value. So why then has it gained in popularity in the IS research community? This leads us to the issue of internal relevancy.

(4.) Relevancy but for whom? From the internal perspective of the IS research community, stakeholders from within academia are equally or even more important than external stakeholders, because they control the advancement of IS researchers and the field as a whole more than anything else. The fact is, much IS research is done with an eye to other academics—academics from other departments in the business school and other faculties on campus. These communities, often at odds with each other, may have entirely different sets of goals and expectations for IS. Even if they share the applied focus of IS (like the other management disciplines), that does not mean that marketing, finance, management, operations management have consistent expectations for their IS colleagues. Hence there is continuing pull on IS academics to make their research and teaching useful for others, i.e., to serve the interests of too many masters. These pressures can be especially strong for junior IS faculty if they know that their tenure committees are dominated by non-IS faculty. They need to strike alliances lest they do not perish even if they publish.

Beyond this, many of the disciplines on campus are not applied, and see applied research as 'unacademic' and hence not valued. And if such work is not valued, this poses a problem for the IS academic whose rewards (tenure and promotion) and punishments (failed tenure and promotion cases, rejected research proposals) heavily depend on other academic groupings. IS academics can ill afford to ignore what these groups consider to be relevant. Many IS researchers have succumbed to this pressure by undertaking highly theoretical work, which is relevant not only for the broader university community but for IS academics themselves. Whilst such a strategy has helped make IS an arguably accepted discipline,[22] it has done so at the expense of practitioner relevancy.

In fact, the strategy has led to the rather dubious condition of what might be termed 'the vicious cycle' of academic research. Many academics with an applied perspective feel caught in this particularly unflattering condition. In the traditional or 'virtuous' model of research, the purpose of research is to generate knowledge. The model starts out with a problem, which leads to research, which in turn leads to knowledge, which in turn informs practice, which in turn encounters new problems, which starts the whole cycle over again. In the vicious version of this cycle model, the purpose gets distorted to one where a research problem leads to research, which leads to new research problems, which leads to research, which leads to more research problems and on without end. The feedback control loop to practice has been lost entirely; research remains entirely in the ivory tower.[23]

4.2 Summary of Communication Deficits

To summarize, there are many different recipients of IS research, each with their own particular interests and views of what relevance means. Our diagnosis of the current state of the IS discipline leads us to recognize a double communication deficit. Internally, this deficit manifests itself in structural fragmentation with a lack of discipline-wide discourse, or even worse, the undermining of the motivation to engage in such discourse. This diagnosis should not be confused with the argument for a single paradigm or disciplinary unification. Such singularity of focus is dangerous, because it tends to lead to rigidity and dogmatism. Rather, we argue that pluralism needs to be accompanied by interaction to translate the most important insights from different research approaches and interests into a language that most IS researchers can understand so that each specialty can contribute its key results to a living core body of knowledge.

The second communication deficit affects the field's relationships with its external stakeholders. It surfaces as doubts about the relevance of IS research and the superficial diagnosis that currently, IS research *de facto* has pursued relevance more in the context of relevance for academic communities. This is superficial, because the real causes for the perceived lack of relevance—at least as we see them—are the disconnects between IS research and the external stakeholders: practitioners, executives, and ultimately political leaders and their constituencies supplying the financial support for university research and teaching. We note that a better understanding of the relationship between IS and the senior management of profit and non-profit organizations may take on a larger role than in the past, thereby leading to refocusing research and curricula on methods and contents that cannot easily be outsourced. The solution cannot be more Java programming and ERP software skills, but a focus on managerial problems and expectations. The consideration of these matters needs to become a two-way street that is mediated through discourses in boundary spanning that involve social knowledge creation and transformation networks. If we fail to establish such interaction networks, the field could slip ever deeper into a crisis, if it has not already started to do so. We in the discipline need to broaden our notion of relevancy to include other groups who use or could use the knowledge generated by IS research.

4.3 From Diagnosis to Therapy

To better understand the forces that affect the ever changing IS research directions and priorities, we need research on how all the various stakeholder groups come to understand IS and how they form their perceptions about the proper role of IS as an academic discipline. This certainly includes, but it is not limited to the need for understanding the interaction patterns among business unit management among themselves and with senior executives in industry (and not-for-profit organizations). And if there is a mismatch between what business unit managers and senior executives see as the role of IS, then hopefully IS research can contribute persuasive arguments so that all parties reconsider their positions with a view to communicatively address the mismatch. Fundamentally, we must extend our notion of relevancy to include stakeholders other than just IS practitioners and management, and from this it follows that IS research will have to deal with a much broader set of values than the proverbial bottom line. To some extent, this has happened earlier under the banner of the participation and quality of work life debate in ISD. However, these classical debates about the values that should drive ISD and IS use still adhere to a view of values, which is too limited.

Future research on relevancy will have to consider the general relationships between values and the meaning of human action in all walks of life, given that computers have penetrated even the private sphere as never before. If we follow the pointers of recent philosophical debates, perhaps interpretive research (*ceteris paribus*) is the preferred methodology for improving the communicative rationality of our work. Interpretivism is closer to the reference disciplines that deal with human sense-making and understanding: language theories (in particular speech act theory), social anthropology, philosophy and history. While these have recently gained increasing influence on the IS research community, most interpretive research has had a rather narrow focus. Typically, it has dealt with specific cases and thereby improved our appreciation of practice. It needs to broaden its focus to look at discipline-wide communication gaps of strategic importance. This could significantly strengthen the communicative functions of the IS discipline just as the empirical-analytical methods of engineering contributed to advancing the effectiveness and efficiency of IT applications to support the instrumental and strategic imperatives of purposive rationality. With these considerations, we have already moved from diagnosis to the issue of possible corrective action, the topic of the next section.

5 WHERE DO WE GO FROM HERE: ADDRESSING THE COMMUNICATION DEFICIT THROUGH THE DEVELOPMENT OF A BODY OF KNOWLEDGE IN INFORMATION SYSTEMS

We have outlined a number of internal and external problems that by themselves may go unnoticed in the short run. However, in the context of global outsourcing and the commoditization trends of market economies, they take on the nature of a serious threat that appears beyond the control of IS—a small cogwheel in the large scale evolutionary pattern of Western societies. Is there something that IS can do to influence the course of these evolutionary patterns that will improve chances for its continued viability and legitimacy?

While there can be no guarantees, we feel our prior analysis points to one major piece of advice: the need to strengthen the communicative functions of our research and teaching programs. By strengthening these functions internally, many different voices will contribute to a few major themes (paradigms). By strengthening them externally, IS contributions will be better perceived and understood. We suggest that two avenues need to be concurrently pursued. First, we need to build motivated and committed institutional arrangements to better integrate IS to its societal support base. The support base includes all of those whose daily work can and should benefit from IS research, including: consultants, teachers at vocational schools, text book writers, industry trainers and many others, ultimately including the highest levels of decision makers in industry and government. As this is taken up elsewhere (Klein and Lyytinen 2003), we shall focus in this paper on the second avenue—the intellectual side of improving the communicative function of IS as a field, i.e., the sense-making, meaning creations, and negotiations among ourselves. One side of this issue is *linguistic*. The IS specialization has come to such a point that we can no longer understand each other—the Tower of Babel syndrome. Others have pinpointed this too (*cf.* Benbasat and Zmud 1999). The other side relates to *content*. But before we spend any effort on developing an appropriate set of core concepts that can help to overcome the Tower of Babel syndrome, we need the *content* that all feel is worth expressing to stimulate more discourse across the adhocracy.

To address this issue we need a rallying point across all IS subspecialties, something that all feel is important to strive for. We do not advocate a drastic restructuring or reformulation of all research programs. Rather adding something that lends a communicative dimension to what all in the field are doing, including those members of the discipline whose primary research interests relate to the goal of improving technical, purposive rationality. We propose that a discipline wide focus on a properly structured, core body of knowledge (BoK) could provide this rallying point. Moreover, a broad-based discussion on what to include and how to structure and code such a BoK would create the key terms of a shared, continuously extended language as well. Clearly, if everyone is committed to contributing *something* that our external stakeholders find useful, then we should be able to say which subset of our specialty knowledge is intended for that purpose. This will then be proposed for the core BoK. Such a professionally oriented core BoK would then also be an important vehicle around which KCTNs can coalesce and would help external stakeholders to better perceive the identity and value add of our field.

Therefore, in this section, we wish to expand on the concept and need for such a core BoK. In order to keep this section within reasonable bounds, we shall focus on a possible framework for structuring the knowledge needed by members of the IS community. We do this in the spirit of providing a first cut into what will hopefully become a discipline-wide debate.

5.1 The Importance and Possibility for a Professional BoK for IS as a Whole

The specification of a discipline wide BoK is a challenge that to the best of our knowledge has proved largely elusive.[24] Even established classical disciplines like mathematics, physics, accounting, and medicine struggle with this continuously. In order to tie attempts at generalizations to the nuts and bolts of specialized research results, it is necessary to capture the interplay between specific knowledge fragments and alternative frameworks that are more speculative but able to relate the fragments in a meaningful way across sub-disciplines. We have reached the conclusion that defining a theoretically appealing, yet practically relevant, action—oriented body of knowledge could provide a type of 'Rosetta Stone' for IS as an applied discipline. It also closely relates to better understanding the core competencies of IS specialists and to advancing the identity of IS as a discipline among its fragmented membership. Institutions like AIS and ICIS need a shared worldview that is flexible and built from the ground up. They need to draw on a community that shares meaningful visions and stands for more than a coalition of loosely aligned interest groups, yet engages in vigorous debate rather than submits to fallacious consensus through 'group-think.' In this paper we offer some thoughts on how such a BoK might proceed. (This is based on the ideas presented in Iivari *et al.* 2004).

In order to define the body of knowledge for the IS discipline as a whole, we need to proceed from several specific bases, i.e., we should begin with specifying the BoK of one of the more mature IS sub-specializations.[25] Only after we better understand the BoK of several core specializations can we hope to join these to a central BoK. To the best of our knowledge, no IS sub-specialization has defined its BoK to date. Thus, we looked to the oldest sub-specialization that once defined the core of the IS discipline during its emergence in the late sixties and early seventies, i.e., information systems development. We felt encouraged to do this because of significant prior work in ISD, which has aimed at synthesizing the vast extant literature on the subject (*cf.* Hirschheim and Klein 1989; Hirschheim, *et al.* 1995, 1996; Iivari *et al.* 1998, 2000; and Klein and Hirschheim 1992, 2001). We believe that the literature on ISD could provide an exemplary test case for defining the BoK in other sub-specialization such as DSS, CSCW, Knowledge Management, Information Systems Planning, etc. Proceeding to a shared understanding of the BoK of IS as a whole is, of course, even more complex than focusing on the BoK of IS sub-specializations.

A possible starting point for identifying the distinguishing characteristics of the BoK in ISD is the discussion about defining the BoK of professional software engineers. Such a discussion can be found in SWEBOK (2000), a joint project of the ACM and IEEE Computer Society on a software engineering BoK. An analysis of the ten knowledge areas listed in SWEBOK (2000)[26] shows that they do not include any knowledge about applications (see also Denning *et al.* 1989). The software engineering process, on the other hand, is extensively addressed. According to Iivari *et al.* (2004) there are five specific knowledge areas in ISD: *technical knowledge, application domain* (i.e., business function) *knowledge, organizational knowledge, application knowledge,*[27] and *ISD process knowledge.*[28] Further, ISD process knowledge is broken down into four distinctive competencies that IS experts are suggested to possess: *(1) aligning IT artifacts* (IS applications and other software products) with the organizational and social context in which the artifacts are to be used, and with the needs of people who are to use the system as identified through the process of *(2) user requirements construction*, including engineering, analysis, elicitation and specification.[29] The third area of process knowledge *is (3) organizational implementation* from which *(4) the evaluation/assessment* of these artifacts and related changes is factored out. (We make a distinction between the first two because organizational alignment and user requirements construction may be quite distinct activities, for example in an ISD project involving business process redesign or reengineering.) These competences are virtually ignored or at best weakly taken into account in the ten knowledge areas of SWEBOK.

Further details of our proposal for a possible description of the applied BoK in ISD are beyond the scope of this paper but see Iivari *et al.* (2004). Nevertheless, the prospects are encouraging in that it appears possible to present a specific proposal for defining the body of knowledge of a particular sub-specialization (like ISD) in the space of a single journal paper (albeit a long paper). Hence, it would be possible to construct one set of proposals for identifying the body of knowledge for several sub-specializations in a number of journal papers. Clearly, one needs two or three such proposals for each sub-specialization, as defining the relevant BoK is very likely to be controversial even within a specific sub-specialization. However, without any documentation of the body of knowledge, no matter how tentative and controversial, we cannot even begin a discussion on what constitutes relevant knowledge, let alone work toward some consensus. The reason for this is that the relevant BoK is very widely dispersed over many books, journals, etc. and hence difficult to find and even more difficult to retrieve. We therefore have reached the conclusion that access to systematically conceived, but concise descriptions of the BoK for at least a few major areas of specialization could lift the discourse on the state of knowledge in the IS research community to a new level for both the internal and external constituencies. To initiate this discussion, it does not matter if the first specifications of the BoK are very controversial. As the critical discussion of these initial specifications proceeds, it will be possible to work toward ever broader (and updateable) practice-oriented BoK specifications that at any given time will embrace much (though never all) of what is accepted wisdom in IS, similar to the clinical literature in medicine or law.

Building and reflecting on this work, we now wish to speculate on what might be appropriate high level umbrella categories that could organize the more detailed core knowledge of IS specialties other than ISD. Clearly these cannot be derived from looking at the ISD literature, but need a more general conceptual base. Perhaps the philosophical theory of knowledge, which is broader than the philosophy of science, is the preferred place to look for inspiration on the most general knowledge typologies.

5.2 Four knowledge types

In this paper, it is of course impossible to do justice to the issue of 'knowledge' given the voluminous literature on the subject. Instead, our discussion of knowledge is based, in large part, on our understanding of the philosophy of knowledge, and in particular, the writings of classic philosophers/social scientists such as Aristotle, Kant, Gadamer and Habermas who had much to say about the theory of knowledge.

From the perspective of the philosophy of knowledge, it is logical to structure knowledge into four types: *technical knowledge, normative (ethical) knowledge, theoretical knowledge of an explanatory-descriptive-predictive nature*, and *applicative knowledge that is practical and action oriented*.

Technical knowledge deals with specific 'rules of skill' or technique which is ostensibly the knowledge needed to carry out specified operations to achieve a more or less well-defined end product. It typically improves purposive-rational action. *Technical knowledge* appears to be a good label for this, because it retains the root of Aristotle's use of the term 'techne' and points to our earlier claim that such knowledge is often packaged as a commodity as part and parcel of technical turn-key solutions. *Ethical knowledge* involves the moral value choices to be made between competing alternatives. It includes both ethical theories and cases in which a choice has to be made by applying sometimes conflicting principles of ethical theories. We do not expect that these two knowledge types will cause much controversy, but they are insufficient. Two more knowledge components are highly relevant for research, teaching and practice. The first of these is also widely accepted, but much more difficult to capture because it is very abstract. It is *theoretical knowledge*. This type of knowledge focuses on articulated understanding, including the understanding of the consequences of one's research for action (as exemplified in the classic Oppenheimer nuclear energy case), the potential of predictions and hypothesis formation through various modes of inference, and last, but not least, conceptual frameworks that help to organize large bodies of knowledge. It covers everything from testable hypotheses and models (such as the TAM—Davis, 1989, or Lucas' 1975 classical IS failure framework) via very general social theories and frameworks to paradigms, as have more recently have been introduced in IS research. Examples of *theoretical knowledge* are Gidden's (1984) Structuration Theory and Latour's (1987, 1999) Actor Network Theory, or the paradigm knowledge elaborated in Chua (1986), Hirschheim and Klein (1989), and Iivari *et al.* (1998).[30] In spite of its diffuse and abstract nature, we expect that it can be imported from the current IS literature with some modifications.

The fourth important knowledge component is the kind of knowledge that is required in dealing with everyday problem solving, which includes getting along with people at work (e.g., management and office politics) and in one's personal life. No commonly understood word exists for this kind of knowledge in our everyday language except that it is often referred to as 'wisdom' or simply 'seasoned experience.' Kant (1964, p. 27) referred to important parts of it as 'imperatives of prudence' or 'counsels of prudence' (contrasting them with imperatives of skill and command of morality). In the contemporary philosophical literature, this type of knowledge has been labeled applicative knowledge or simply practical knowledge, because it captures an important aspect of what we mean by saying that someone possesses good practical common sense.

Application or practical knowledge does not mean to neglect theory. Rather it is concerned with a special type of knowledge beyond theoretical knowledge that is required to apply theoretical knowledge to specific circumstances, similar to the way a judge has to interpret the law to solve a court case in litigation. It may be thought of as common sense. To connote the full meaning of practical knowledge with its Aristotelian connection, we prefer to call it *applicative knowledge* with reference to Gadamer (1975, p. 275) and Habermas (1988, p. 163).[31] Some further discussion of this category is needed to better understand its meaning.

5.3 The Special Characteristics of Applicative Knowledge

Freely interpreting Gadamer (1975) and Habermas (1988), we can identify three characteristics in which applicative knowledge differs from the other three types. First, it has a close relationship to a person's identity. It typically takes hard work and painful mistakes to acquire it and therefore becomes part of an individual's personality. It is mostly learned through various forms of apprenticeships, mentoring and the 'school of hard knocks.' This suggests that applicative knowledge can at least be partially shared among frequently interacting groups, but much of it remains tacit knowledge. As such, it is closely related to personal insight and wisdom. The preferred research approach to make such knowledge visible to outsiders would be hermeneutic field studies (in the form of ethnographies using participatory observations and intensive interviewing, *cf.* Klein and Myers 1999).

Second, because of the above characteristics, applicative knowledge closely connects to personal emotions and interests. It depends on the whole complex of presuppositions, fundamental beliefs (prejudices) and attitudes that are part and parcel of a person's character. In contrast, technical knowledge is relatively neutral and external to a person's inner core. Insofar as applicative knowledge is acquired from the environment, the process is more one of socialization than cognitive learning even though cognitive, intellectual abilities are important to filter and digest what is acquired through social interaction. This naturally leads to the third characteristic, the holistic nature of applicative knowledge. It cannot be easily split into goals and means, but rather is rooted in the lived experience consisting of work, play, and travel, various forms of symbolic communication and, last but not least, the tradition into which someone is born or into which a person has chosen to integrate when leaving his/her native community.

It is particularly the last characteristic that makes applicative knowledge so critical for achieving mutual understanding and consensus. By relating other cultures to one's own experiences, applicative knowledge allows for cross-cultural dialogue, and by understanding one's place in the tradition in which one lives, it helps to overcome vertical communication barriers, e.g., between government and citizens, between old and young, and in organizations, and between rank and file. Therefore it is not surprising that applicative knowledge is one of the areas of expertise in which successful politicians and managers excel compared to technical experts or the common person. In summary then, applicative knowledge is a fourth category of knowledge, because it is not simply acquired as a byproduct of learning the other three. Without it, a person would have difficulty benefiting from the theoretical knowledge that he may have learned. Of course, in practice, all four types of knowledge will also inform every action that a person takes, but to differing degrees.

If one accepts the above knowledge classification—at least as a working hypothesis—there is yet another reason why the IS field faces an external communication deficit (in addition to the missing institutional use of KCTNs). We believe that one reason for the so-called relevancy deficit is not so much that our theoretical knowledge is too conceptual or unnecessarily complicated (even though this may also contribute to the deficit) as has been argued by the relevancy vs. rigor debaters, but rather because research into applicative knowledge has been very weak. And even if it were already available, we seem unable to communicate it very well because we lack the social infrastructure of KCTNs.

The problem that this poses for strengthening the external communication function of IS as a field becomes more apparent if we relate the knowledge types to a particular IS specialization. In Table 5.1, we attempt such a classification, relating the various knowledge types to information systems development. The four knowledge types are mapped with the four ISD process core competencies (organizational alignment of IT; user requirements construction, organizational implementation, and evaluation/assessment of IT artifacts) possessed by IS specialists and that distinguish them from Software Engineers (this is further discussed in section 5.4). We believe that ISD is a good exemplary specialization to choose, because during its

Table 5.1   *Components of an IS BoK applied to the ISD area of specialization*

ISD process core competency	Types of knowledge with examples			
	Technical knowledge	Ethical knowledge (insight and wisdom)	Applicative knowledge	Theoretical knowledge
(1) organizational alignment of IT	technical IT knowledge	understanding the diversity of demands from different departments	ability to negotiate acceptable alignment criteria	Strategy theories, organization theories
(2) user requirements construction	technical specification	understanding the competing needs of users	ability to develop acceptable ISD requirements criteria	cognitive psychology, sociology, engineering
(3) organizational implementation	technical implemen- tation	understanding values of individuals using IS	ability to develop acceptable implementa- tion criteria	organizational conflict theories
(4) evaluation/ assessment of IT artifacts	technical evaluation	understanding competing values/ perceptions associated with IS	ability to develop acceptable assessment criteria	cost benefit analysis, managerial accounting

early days, ISD was the principal core area around which IS as an academic discipline coalesced. Even today, ISD is an integral part in most sub-specializations from DSS and groupware, to enterprise systems, to e-commerce and other Internet applications. Using the extensive literature on ISD and relating it to the left side of Figure 1, which was already discussed above, we propose that, in principle, it should be possible to create a BoK for the IS discipline.

However, to create a BoK for the IS discipline in general, two questions immediately surface. (1) What would be the principal procedure for applying the highest level categories of the four knowledge types to other IS specialties? (2) What are the principal gaps in the contents of the four knowledge types?

(1) Presumably, each discipline would ultimately map its contributions to the four knowledge types on the column headings. The table rows would be discipline specific. The collection of all of these matrices would comprise the total IS BoK at least for the consensual core body. This suggests that the IS field (a) define its boundaries, (b) identify all of the processes or tasks that take place within the boundaries, (c) form the matrices and thereby document and perhaps generate the knowledge.

(2) From Table 5.1, it is clear that technical and theoretical knowledge exists in abundance for all four areas of ISD process competencies. Yet the same cannot be said about ethical knowledge and applicative knowledge. These types of knowledge are difficult to develop and not abundant. Indeed, we would argue there is a gap in both these knowledge areas as the literature on them is rather sparse (but see Klein and Hirschheim 2001 for one example which addresses ethical knowledge). Thus, the biggest gap in the BoK currently is applicative knowledge.

An essential part of this classification is that all four knowledge types are of equal importance and hence deserve equal respect. Even though they do not submit to the same quality criteria, ultimately all have equally exactingly high quality standards. We emphasize this, because today, pure theoretical knowledge has been devalued to some extent, especially in the practitioner literature. It is, therefore, important to reintroduce the value of pure theorizing, but give applicative knowledge an equal status. Paradoxically, many academic communities devalue applied research oriented toward applicative knowledge. One of our key messages is that these negative attitudes in industry and academia toward certain types of knowledge can and should change. The four types of knowledge may have somewhat differing quality criteria, but ultimately are equal in the level and difficulty of their standards. (Knowledge quality standards are an important special issue, but beyond consideration here.)

5.4 Implications for Ethical and Applicative Knowledge

If the above knowledge types are accepted as a valid characterization of the knowledge that should be developed in IS, then a serious gap appears to exist between the types of knowledge that IS researchers attempt to develop and the types of knowledge the field needs. The field has focused almost the entirety of its resources on theoretical and technical knowledge, ignoring ethical and applicative knowledge (although there are some notable exceptions, *cf.* Szajna 1994). The reasons for this are varied, but one obvious remedy is to reallocate some of the field's research resources toward ethical and applicative knowledge. This, of course, raises the question of how could the two under-researched knowledge types (i.e., ethical and applicative) be strengthened in IS. In the case of ethical knowledge, this should be relatively easy because there exists a substantial body of well-conceived textbook and research monographs on ethical theory (e.g., Brandt's 1959 *Ethical Theories*; Rawl's 1971 *Theory of Justice*, and so on). Moreover, there have been some attempts (two of which we were involved in— Hirschheim and Klein, 1994; Klein and Hirschheim 2001) to apply some of the logic of ethical reasoning to core areas of IS (*cf.* Mason 1986). Of course, this kind of theoretical knowledge in ethics will have to be supported with appropriate knowledge transfer vehicles. Cases seem to be the most appropriate mechanisms for this[32] and Table 5.2 provides a classification of the common types of cases available. Given the existing case writing expertise in IS, it should be possible to create a good case base for dealing with ethical knowledge.

However, the matter is much more difficult for applicative knowledge (AK) for reasons that are somewhat different for the two subtypes of AK. The first subtype is the kind of knowledge required to move from recognized theory (assuming good theories do exist) to practice. This kind of applicative knowledge is similar to the insight a judge needs when using a body of law to decide a court case; the engineer when using a mathematically formulated theory to solve a practical design problem; or the physician when diagnosing a patient by applying the state of the art of theoretical medical training. For this kind of applicative knowledge IS could follow the institutionalized models of professional apprenticeships well established in legal articling or medical clinics. The difficulty here is not conceptual, but lies in the lack of an educational tradition that legitimizes the substantial resources needed to transfer these models to IS. Ethnographic field studies and ethnomethodology appear to provide recognized research approaches to track the evolving nature of this type of knowledge.

It is often suggested that cases provide a good vehicle for teaching applicative knowledge. However, while cases are somewhat useful, our analysis of typical textbook case material suggests that they are much more limited than is commonly believed. As is evident from Table 5.2, cases are written mostly for researchers or beginners and not for seasoned practitioners. Therefore, we lack a good vehicle to document the AK that should go along with good theories. The conceptual and methodological difficulties arising from the lack of a good elicitation and representation mechanism are even more severe for the second type of AK.

Table 5.2   *Tentative classification of common types of case reports*

- **Research Cases** (positivist, interpretive, critical): report something new, make the claim that what is reported should be considered new knowledge, emphasizing method: *oriented towards researchers*
- **Teaching cases**: call for a solution applying knowledge learnt before: *oriented toward students, not seasoned practitioners*
- **Illustrative cases** (usually 'vignettes'): demonstrate an abstract concept or idea in a concrete setting. *They have some relevancy for practitioners, but tend to be narrow in scope and simplistic.*

Main Point: *Cases are useful for some forms of knowledge transfer, but as a vehicle for capturing and communicating new applicative knowledge for seasoned practitioners, they appear to be somewhat inadequate.*

The second type of AK consists of 'pure craftsmanship,' i.e., mostly tacit knowledge for which either no adequate theory exists or which for other, poorly understood reasons, cannot be articulated. A classical example of this type of knowledge is the sculptor or painter who practices his calling (i.e., makes sculptures or paintings) without having studied the medical theory base of anatomy (in sculpting human postures as the Greek statues) or the chemistry of minerals yet can become master of his craft. Similarly, our ancestors built good ships without the benefit of aerodynamic or hydrodynamic models. Of course, the limits of this kind of knowledge are often less clear than that of theoretical knowledge leading to disaster. For example, the shipbuilders of the VASA overextended their knowledge base under pressure from Sweden's King and the VASA sank within view of the King's palace on its maiden voyage.

There are good reasons to believe that an essential part of the practice of IS depends on this kind of 'atheoretical' knowledge that tends to be acquired by socialization into a community of practice. (*cf.* Matthiassen 1998). (Maybe software engineers should take the lesson of the VASA case to heart and resist the pressures for constantly overextending the experiential knowledge base of ISD; this might then contribute to getting software development failures under control.) As far as we know, the only known vehicle to acquire applicative knowledge appears to be the master—(talented) student apprenticeship, which typically takes 2 to 4 or more years depending on the craft to be learned.[33] To better understand how such knowledge evolves and how it is *really* passed on in various types of craftsmanship would take new types of research projects. Whereas such projects could build on the currently known stock of research methods, especially interpretive ones, they would likely have to invent substantial adaptations of these methods. Based on the analogy of handicrafts, we are also led to hypothesize that this kind of research would take much longer than most current IS research to come to publication stage. For example, we guess it would take at least 3 years to understand how an apprentice acquires a tradesman level of skill and how tradesmen become recognized masters in their area of expertise. Hence, we reach the conclusion that an essential part of AK will require substantial new research resources and research skills, and a significant reallocation of existing research capacities.

6 RECOMMENDATIONS

The main body of this paper has been built around the idea that there exist significant communication gaps in the field—both internally and externally—and that these gaps are a serious concern for the future of the field. More pointedly, if we do not address these gaps—and address them soon—we may not have any field to worry about in the future. So the question is: what can we do now?

It seems to us, that we must first look at ourselves, i.e., the IS academic community. In order for our field to become more relevant to its external stakeholders, IS research must become more relevant for ourselves and to become more relevant for ourselves we must strengthen the communicative function of IS research. The internal communication deficit that has been building since the mid 80s weakens our ability to meet evolving legitimate needs of our immediate stakeholders and, we may add at this point, also our societal stakeholders. Except for researchers with a specific interest in social issues or social impacts of computers (*cf.* Kling 1980), the societal stakeholders have so far not played a major role either in mainstream IS research or in this paper. (But we will return to this issue in section 7.)

In order to overcome the internal communication deficit, both the amount and quality of communication between different IS research schools and subspecialties would have to increase dramatically. This means that we must devote more effort into discipline wide discourse to achieve a better understanding of the differences between us and based on this, work towards more synthesis of ideas and integration of results by building on each others' work. Yet, what is being preached is that IS as a field will become more relevant if it better caters to the interests of our immediate stakeholders, i.e., if it better serves the purposive rational interests of a managerial elite and their masters, the shareholders. IS are primarily seen as instruments of effectiveness and efficiency. The focus on cost cutting, to which offshoring is simply the newest strategy, is an example of what we mean. Thus, substantial external pressures exist to become more externally relevant by putting most of our resources into research that serves externally given, purposive rational ends while neglecting research on the 'communicative aspects' of human action and the potential role of IS and IS research to support the communicative side of organizations (and society).

In this section, we shall first outline which resources are primarily under our control that could help to overcome the internal communication deficit. Having clarified this, we shall then ask whether strengthening the internal communication function might help us to meet future challenges that will assign a larger role to IS within the societal information infrastructure.

Information technology has been metaphorically described as the 'information highway' implying that the traffic for the highway will come from elsewhere. This is the equivalent of saying that newspapers are just printing machines and distribution channels that deliver contents submitted to them from independent outsiders. Clearly, this is not so. Just as the press combines contents with distribution, so IT will soon come to play a similar role of mixing content and distribution as the press in the societal process of policy debate and social will formation. To some extent, the mixing of content and technology is already happening on the Internet: Browser technologies provide content portals. If so, IT will and should respond to the same policies that, in theory at least, should govern the operation of a democratic press: freedom of inquiry, universal access and an equal chance for the widest possible diversity of opinions to be heard. These are values of communicative rationality which have not been given the attention in mainstream IS research that they deserve because IS research has ignored the importance of discourse in creating and conveying information and knowledge in social settings. Practicing better discourse internally could very well be a good starting point to more external relevance if our prediction is on the mark that IS as part of IT plays an important role in overcoming the communication deficit in modern mass societies (Dahlberg 2000, 2001). For many reasons the press has fallen behind in filling this important societal role which has led to a deterioration of the public sphere (Habermas 1971, 1989, 1993).

So what can we do to address our internal communication deficit? We see five action items the resources of which are primarily under the control of the field. Each of these items addresses an important aspect of the internal communication deficit. Taken together, they could significantly improve the cohesion and cooperation of the different sub-communities that currently make up the fragmented adhocracy from which the field suffers.

- Change our research priorities: Work from paradigms towards broader, more general theories.
- Focus on the viability of a discipline wide core BoK that is not legislated but emerges from consensual negotiation which would contribute to the communicative role of IS research in two ways. First, the process of identifying and formulating the elements of a discipline wide core BoK, would intensify interactions across specialties; and second, the result would serve as a guide post for a shared orientation.
- Study our stakeholders' 'forms of life' to better understand their 'being,' i.e., their time frames, lifeworlds and expectations. This should include helping them understand the 'IS Research World' so as to allow them to form realistic expectations and overcome misconceptions, which underlie some of the current external disconnects as noted in section 3.1.
- Reconsider our institutional communication and publication practices from the perspective of how they can support different research priorities, stakeholders, and the negotiation of a core BoK.
- Build Knowledge Creation and Transformation Networks (KCTNs) as a new way to disseminate the results of our research, thereby helping to address the field's communication deficit.

Each of these five action items is now discussed in greater detail.

6.1 From Paradigms to Generalizations

Our review of the paradigm debate in section 4 illustrated that the discourse on research methodology has risen to a new level of sophistication. Whilst this is generally positive, it does have the undesirable side-effect of adding to an already existing significant communication barrier. The difficulties arise from both new terminology and different epistemological orientations. Both point to new barriers to fostering more and better communication among IS researchers. Just as the statistical-mathematical jargon of positivism is difficult to understand, so too are the new philosophical concepts of interpretivism and critical research (e.g., axial coding, discursive formation, communicative competence, lifeworld colonization, etc.). The way one research specialty expresses its findings and approaches is not in terms understandable and useful to other research specialties. Benbasat and Zmud (1999) called for a translation of specific jargons into more widely understood terms. We agree, but this is only part of the problem. Based on the notion of 'dualism in the social sciences,' positivism and its counterparts foster very different attitudes of what constitute worthwhile research questions and good methods to explore them. Add this to the complicated jargon and you have a highly charged atmosphere not conducive for 'rational discourse.' So how can we overcome this?

Certainly, not by dropping the precision of technical vocabularies that are needed in the 'trenches' of day-to-day research, but rather by broadening how we think about generalizations. In order to establish the broader meanings of specialized research results, it should be possible, perhaps, to generalize very specific findings from time to time across more than one specialized research contribution, even if the generalization is based on 'insufficient' evidence. Yet the current academic culture of rigor tends to inhibit this—a point that could be addressed by introducing a new category of research papers (see section 6.4 below). In addition, generalization is inherently very difficult: it requires a creative, intellectual leap to see the general behind the specific. Because of these reasons, IS as a whole lacks internal transparency and suffers from the following generalization deficit, which neither positivists nor interpretivists have seriously addressed.

In most papers, generalization is only concerned with abstraction from data to middle-range hypotheses or conjectures. It rarely advances to the building of broad theories that span multiple systems of hypotheses or conjectures as building blocks. Even though the generalization deficit is a concern that affects all paradigms, positivist, interpretivist and critical alike, it is also largely ignored by all. Without a concerted effort from opinion leaders in some of the major research subcommunities, fragmentation is likely to get worse as subspecialties spawn new sub-communities at a greater rate than older sub-communities die out. To mitigate this trend, more attention needs to be paid to the theoretical side of publications. The current theoretical part of most papers consists of minor theory building blocks (hypotheses usually diagrammed as boxes and arrows) for broader theories of human action and interaction that at best are implied (*cf.* Habermas 1988 for an outline of classical action theories) and at worst do not even exist. The result is a multitude of hypotheses with associated statistical significance tests (or ethnographic insights with associated thick descriptions), which as a whole go nowhere. They go nowhere, because their interconnections do not exist or are at best transparent only to the insiders who have to spend an extraordinary amount of time with the literature of a specific sub-community. (An example cogently illustrating this situation is Fjermestad and Hiltz's 1998 cross-tabulation of variables, methods and results of approximately 200 controlled experiments in group support research. Similar indexing work could be done for interpretive research). Add to this the different preferences of what constitutes 'good research' and it is easy to see why the findings of one research community are typically not known and valued by another, let alone by researchers from other disciplines or practitioners. We are stuck too much into one corner of the literature and lose sight of the greater, overarching issues. In fact, there is currently little broad-based debate on identifying overarching issues let alone on exploring them. In the following three sections on setting new research priorities and changes in institutional publication practices, we explore how this problem might be addressed.

6.2 The Communicative Role and Viability of a Core Body of Knowledge for the Field

It is difficult to see how generalizations and discipline-wide debate can come about by self-organization only without some landmarks to which all can relate. In Computer Science, the *Communications of the ACM* has played such a role for many years and to some extent has continued to do so after the 1993 change in editorial policy. But other, more 'action oriented' guideposts are needed for research that will contribute to better communication among IS specializations. One such guidepost could be the project of identifying and reformulating the elements of a core body of knowledge, to which all specializations would contribute their most important findings. This does sound a bit like reinventing the Tower of Babel, but the idea is not for all to agree on such a BoK as an instrument of defining what good knowledge is. On the contrary, it would be the debate and disagreements about what is and is not good core knowledge that would produce the most important and almost immediate benefits to overcoming the internal communication deficits. As partial agreement emerges, the growing partial BoK would also become a convenient vehicle for addressing the external communication deficit.

While it became apparent in section 5 that defining the relevant BoK for IS would be a very controversial project, we surmise that most would agree that it is important for the field because without *any* agreed body of knowledge, we cannot identify the externally relevant knowledge for IS. Engaging the conceptual, epistemic and practical issues of specifying a recognized body of knowledge in IS provides us with an immense challenge that we all can welcome and that by its nature *must be shared*. According to Banville and Landry (1989, p. 54), it is the high strategic task uncertainty that gives us the status of a fragmented adhocracy.[34] The BoK could reveal the underlying reasons why strategic task uncertainty exists. Hence, we believe the time is right to consider possible approaches to building a theoretically appealing, and practically relevant, action oriented body of knowledge for the field. Such a BoK should reflect the fact that the field is an applied discipline like law, medicine and engineering and identify the core competencies of IS specialists. It should also help in advancing the identity of IS as a discipline among its fragmented membership. Our IS institutions such as AIS, ICIS and ECIS, need such a shared worldview. Moreover, they need to draw on a community that shares meaningful visions and stands for more than a coalition of loosely aligned interest groups.

However, the project of a core BoK needs to be undertaken with some enlightened policies. On the one hand, a grass-roots debate on the contents and structure of a core BoK is likely to further stimulate the intellectual rigor and flexibility of IS as an academic discipline rather than robbing it of its pluralism. Discussing the contents and format of a practically relevant BoK would surface many fundamental issues about methodology and substance. On the other hand, with the creation of a shared BoK comes the worry that the community's efforts might shift from research to institutionalization. Once a certain BoK becomes officially 'approved' by the professional institution, the usual bureaucratic dysfunctions are likely to emerge. Powerful interests gain a stake in the status quo and hence criticism and revision of the accepted BoK could begin to suffer from myopic politicization. This would endanger the pluralistic debate about the nature of knowledge and preferred research methods, which has recently stimulated many interesting contributions to the IS literature. The thriving methodological diversity is one of the distinguishing features of IS as a field from Software Engineering which has a more narrow research perspective. The true mark of intellectual penetration and vigorous research is the ability to function with dualistic, contradictory conceptualizations and fragmentary understandings. In contrast, professional bodies view fundamental criticism and dialectical debate as confusing the public and hence as threatening their status and recognition. They are, therefore, often inclined to decide epistemic issues by political fiat, which forces premature closure to what is better left to free and open debates. We hope that most researchers in the field will treat any such moves towards the institutionalization of professionalization with healthy skepticism.[35] Whilst in principle it may be possible to define and structure a professional body of knowledge for IS as a whole, we are practically nowhere near achieving it.

So where should we as IS researchers direct our limited resources? We suggest that IS researchers ought to focus their efforts on alternative structures and coding schemes[36] for a discipline wide BoK. On the other hand, some community resources should be devoted to exploring the issues of professionalization on a broad scale so that IS as a field will be prepared to contribute and respond to professionalization initiatives in related disciplines. Next, as the core BoK should

explicitly identify externally relevant knowledge (but not be limited
to such knowledge), we must gain a better understanding of what
kind of knowledge might be useful for external stakeholders. It
would be a rather myopic view that this will be primarily instrumental knowledge to fix given problems. Applying DiMaggio's
(1995) view of theories to knowledge, we see knowledge not only
helping to predict and control, but also enlightening. It tells us a story
(with a lesson or moral to be learned) and describes the complex
world in which we live thereby helping us to find our way just as
maps help us to plan a trip. This would permit fairly broad frameworks into the relevant BoK because they serve to organize large
bodies of detailed concepts and facts.

6.3 Understanding Our Organizational Stakeholders: A New Research Priority?

In contrast to the broad view of knowledge as advocated in this
paper, which includes reflection and critique, practitioners often
insist that IS researchers should be in constant touch with industry to
address the problems truly relevant to them. This attitude can be
framed in the following question: 'Should practice lead research or
research lead practice?' This question tends to put IS researchers on
the defensive but this doesn't have to be the case.

First we cannot make our research more relevant for external interests, unless we understand their ways of thinking and doing. It is
essentially an ethnographic-hermeneutic issue of interpreting meanings across the dividing lines in modern societies. It is surprising how
little emphasis this line of inquiry has received probably because of
the fallacious assumptions that our business or economic degrees are
sufficient to 'read' the needs of our managerial stakeholders (in the case
of IS in 3rd and 4th world cultures, this question did receive more
attention). By trying to understand how our external stake-holders
work and live, we do not unduly cater to them or become dependent
on them, but, of course, we cannot understand them unless 'they' let
us into their forms of life.

There is the possibility that undue influence from industry could
result from vested interests or myopic fads shaping short-term industry
practices. Thus, in order to make research agendas responsive to
practice without becoming controlled by undue influence, we need to
distinguish between two types of research questions. *Type one* are
timely issues, which are topic-of-the-day research issues. *Type two* are
timeless issues which are recurring questions and dilemmas that have
emerged over time and continue to be problematic. Undoubtedly,
practice is often in a better position to lead research when it comes to

type one. It is here, where research on the 'appreciation of practice' as earlier discussed is indispensable. Often timeliness is of utmost importance for such research because the half-life of the issues tends to be relatively short. Having papers under review and successive author revisions for 1 to 4 years is simply inappropriate for type one problems. This kind of research also contributes to better understanding the needs of the ultimate 'customers' for our research. The premier academic journals primarily deal only with the internal audience of IS researchers. They largely ignore other customers such as different classes of practitioners (including the ideal of the 'reflective' practitioner), applied researchers like consultants, researchers in other disciplines, administrators, and students including undergraduates, MBAs, Executive MBAs and PhDs. Reproducing and reflecting the management buzzwords or technological silver bullet of the day do not satisfy the needs of many of these customers. Considering *all* our different customers will require type two IS research.

While *type two research* also depends on studying practices, the time scale is much longer, measured in years rather than months. In fact, these issues have a timeless quality to them. An example might be what has been learnt from different approaches to IS planning or how the role and forms of user participation have changed over time with regard to changes in methods and tools of ISD, and increased user understanding of IT. Another example of a type two research problem is how to measure IS success as IT capabilities increase. There is a danger that earlier lessons are forgotten and the wheel is reinvented continuously as each of these questions keeps reappearing in slightly different forms. For type two research questions, academia is often in a better position to lead practice. However, an unresolved issue in this context is how we can better stimulate and validate such research. Peer reviewing is extremely difficult here because one cannot judge the quality of this type of applied research easily for several reasons. First, the practicality of research would ultimately have to be established by industry use of the results and these may take years to become visible. Second, this kind of research requires funding over extended periods including dissemination of results over industry-friendly channels and tracking the effects on professional practices. It is likely to be difficult to attract funding for this type of research given that it does not count as new knowledge in the traditional sense, yet would be perceived as being very risky, with uncertain payoffs. Nevertheless, it is one important category contributing to 'applicative knowledge' and exists in other disciplines like medicine and civil engineering. If it were to take hold, the resulting interactions would also address the external communication gaps.

It would be unrealistic to believe that the above research priorities have any chance to be considered on a broad scale unless we make some changes to the practices by which research output is filtered for publication and distributed. We take up these two points in sections 6.4 and 6.5.

6.4 Required Changes in Institutional Publication Practices

With the previous points in mind we reached the conclusion that IS research needs to advance on two fronts. First it needs to target research on better understanding its external constituencies—who they are, what they want and what they need (which may not be the same). This in turn might then also lead to advancement on the second front, *viz.* providing the motivation and direction required for overcoming its internal deficits of relevance and generalization. To this end some of the academic 'conventions of truth construction' would have to change in that the current publication game places insufficient emphasis on providing generalizations and conclusions of broad interest and how they might contribute to the core of a shared BoK reaching beyond specific IS specializations. Only if these issues are addressed effectively will the vigor of IS research yield the benefits that are commensurate with the efforts expended.

To achieve all of this, the field needs to reform certain institutional practices. First there are content changes some of which can be addressed through special journal issues. We pointed to the need for increasing the amount of research directed at understanding non-IS practitioners and engaging them in a discourse about a realistic set of expectations for what the IS function can and cannot deliver. We also suggested a role of IS research in providing well-articulated arguments to the IS practitioners by which they can state their case to senior management that a thriving IS department is indispensable to organizations along with the other business functions. Perhaps the Texaco case (Hirschheim *et al.* 2003) could serve as an example how—through historical case analysis—senior management could be let to reconsider if their expectations for IS departments are realistic or tainted by false assumptions. Second the filtering mechanisms of quality control need to be reconsidered. Our institutional publication practice needs to redefine the concept of 'rigor' in research. It should be augmented to include a wide range of scholarly inference and evidence giving genres on the one hand and tightened on the other to include the linking of detailed models or hypotheses to more general theory or at least conjectures. This serves the purpose of arriving at expanded categories of knowledge that can communicate across the narrow boundaries of our preferred academic sub-communities. For that purpose all publication venues, in particular the large conferences like AMCIS, ICIS, HICSS, and ECIS and all first tier journals need to provide some visible vehicles (e.g., special sessions, special subsections or issues) for broad syntheses that are interesting and comprehensible to all members of the IS community. Panel discussions have already contributed to this need and tend to be well attended if broadly conceived. What we are suggesting here is the publication of high quality surveys and/or tutorials which everyone in the field can read and understand. In computer science, the journal *ACM Computing Surveys* serves such a purpose. There is, unfortunately, no equivalent in our field although the new section of *MISQ* called *MISQ Review* and *Communications of the AIS* are presently vehicles for this. IS needs more high quality outlets. Additionally, we need more participation in outlets like our online community *ISWorld* to facilitate internal communication amongst ourselves. Vehicles like *ISWorld* could be expanded to include participation of external stakeholders—such as IS practitioners—as well. We also need more historical analyses of the various areas which make up the IS domains. (Actually, the field needs more in-depth historical analyses period.) Moreover, we need to shape the perception of the IS community to truly value such contributions.

In the current situation we seem to have an overabundance of specialty papers for in-group members with the result that the IS community as a whole suffers from serious communication gaps. The current publication culture favoring narrowly focused, highly specialized papers is one of the major impediments to making our research more relevant to practitioners (albeit not the only one, as was pointed out earlier). Specialized research is important because it supplies the building blocks for correcting misconceptions, updating our knowledge and eventually progressing on a broader front, but it has its limitations. To overcome these, we simply must also attempt the difficult and risky, but nevertheless invaluable syntheses that pull together special research results from the various sub-communities into broader analyses of potential interest to practitioner communities. To this end, we have suggested the need for building a broader and practically relevant knowledge base in IS based on defining an action oriented, professional body of knowledge (BoK). Given all of the above, we also need to build new social networks: *Knowledge Creation and Transformation Networks*. They play a special role for disseminating and absorbing the results of the new research community spirit.

6.5 Knowledge Creation and Transformation Networks (KCTNs) as a Means of Helping to Overcome the Field's Communication Deficit

We already briefly introduced the notion of KCTNs in section 2 of the paper. Here we return to this notion and suggest why such networks could be critical for overcoming the IS field's internal and external communication deficit. We start by elaborating what KCTNs are.

Klein and Lyytinen (2003) developed the concept of KCTNs by generalizing Baskerville and Myers' (2002) definition of 'knowledge creation networks' and adding the notion of transformation. Because the latter paper focuses on the impact of reference disciplines within the IS field they limited their definition to the interactions of scholars between different disciplines:

> Rather than conceptualizing the process of knowledge creation as unidirectional (being part of a food chain with IS at one end), we can conceptualize this process as multidirectional. IS scholars along with scholars in other fields can be seen as part of many knowledge creation networks throughout the world. The focus then shifts to the linkages between the networks. (Baskerville and Myers 2002, p. 7)

Baskerville and Myers see knowledge creation networks as operating among reference disciplines. As such, they are primarily of importance for achieving relevance in academic communities, what we have termed 'internal relevance.' This is certainly valuable, but too limited for overcoming the external communication deficit. KCTNs, on the other hand, are broader and span many different communities including IS stakeholders outside of academia. For example, they would include consultants, part time faculty, textbook writers, industry researchers and management. In general, they include all who give feedback to the research process in various ways, thus becoming part of the knowledge 'food chain,' manufacturing the broader knowledge ecology of IS. Practitioners play a major role in this food chain. Examples of transformations in such networks include: repackaging knowledge when teaching courses for students, writing textbooks, drafting questionnaires, and learning from the feedback of different academic and practitioner audiences. Additionally, those participating in field studies or in industry seminars conducted by researchers can significantly affect knowledge transformation. Luftman and Brier (1999), for example, identified alignment enablers and inhibitors from seminar participants. A key aspect of KCTNs is that knowledge produced by some researcher can become relevant to a researcher in another community even though this was unintended by the original researcher. In such a case, the knowledge affects another community and is regarded as a relevant knowledge contribution. This is an aspect of the 'communities of practice' notion and reflects how knowledge is created and legitimized within such communities (Latour 1987; Seely-Brown and Duguid 2000; Carlisle 2002).

If such a view of knowledge creation and exchange is adopted, then we need to abandon how the field currently conceives of research knowledge transmission as a linear, direct link between academia and practitioners. Complex interdependence, circularity, feedback, emergence and other knowledge transformation mechanisms abound when we start examining how IS research knowledge is circulated through different constituencies. We need to investigate empirically how the knowledge translation among these various sub-communities really works along with the resulting 'genealogy' of research contributions. For example, even though we often observe that many IS innovations were first conceived in practice, their refinement, generalization and transfer is often a complex social interaction process between multiple communities, in which the IS research community plays a critical role. This type of view assigns a different but equally useful role for IS academics, which we could term 'scientific hermeneutics': IS scholars act like Hermes—the go-between of the Gods—in understanding, representing and translating some specific forms of knowledge and skills in specific organizational contexts to other constituencies. Academics are often good at abstracting and generalizing ideas that are first put into practice in a limited way but which need further refinement (early database development is a good example). Academic debate is often able to transform a new idea or tools originally conceived in practice into a package of abstract principles and logic, which expands its potential. The academic interpretation then feeds back to the practitioner community, often via consulting firms screening the academic discussion, for the next round of collective learning. Interpreted in this sense, IS research could be proud of what it has done even though its role may have so far been too subtle and needs better showcasing, which in turn could strengthen it further. (A case example for a well-functioning KCTN in a specific region that greatly benefited from it, is described by Oinas-Kukkonen *et al.* 2003.) KCTNs could include recurring IS academic-practitioner conferences that are designed to increase the significance of communications between the two groups. There are enough persons of good will in each community to ensure the success of such an endeavor. This is the sort of bridging that professional societies, in their most enlightened actions, could and should sponsor.

In the future, we need to better understand the factors that nurture relevancy and the ways in which IS research knowledge is circulated within KCTNs. We need to understand what incentives and efforts are needed to produce research that is relevant as well as what incentives can be used to improve IS scholars participation in effective knowledge transformation networks. We must also re-examine what time periods are used to assess the impacts of knowledge transfer processes and changes in recipients' behaviors. We suspect that there is an unrealistic expectation of how quickly knowledge is adopted. Lastly, we should distinguish between intended and unintended transfers, e.g., leaks, serendipity, etc.

6.6 Summary and Preview

Table 5.3 summarizes our five action items and recommendations to help implement them.

Table 5.3   *Summary of action items and the recommendations to support them*

IS Action Items	Recommendations
Change research priorities	1. translate specific jargons into more widely understood terms 2. broaden how we conceive of generalizations 3. move from middle-range hypotheses or conjectures to the building of broad theories that span multiple systems of hypotheses or conjectures as building blocks
Develop a discipline wide core BoK	1. engage the conceptual, epistemic and practical issues of specifying a core body of knowledge that is widely shared 2. maintain discussion on controversial knowledge
Understand our Organizational Stakeholders	1. distinguish between two types of research questions: *Type one* are timely, topic-of-the-day research issues, and *type two* are timeless, recurring questions and dilemmas that have emerged over years and continue to be problematic 2. let industry lead research in the former, and let research lead industry in the latter
Change Institutional Publication Practices	reform institutional practices so as to (1.) redefine rigor; (2.) encourage papers that offer histories and provide syntheses; (3.) support the development of scholarly tutorials
Develop Knowledge Creation and Transformation Networks	1. build KCTNs that connect IS with reference disciplines, industry and the public sphere of society 2. recognize that both the producers and recipients of research results must expand efforts to communicate new research, the first to make it comprehensible and the latter to interpret and absorb the new knowledge 3. allow for long term evaluation of the potential usefulness of research results

Before concluding this paper, we would be remiss if we did not take advantage of this opportunity to offer some thoughts on the possible direction the field could take. Whilst we have primarily focused on the communication deficit within the internal community, and secondarily, looked at the deficit associated with the external community; we have bounded our analysis at the organizational level. Yet, this leaves out the wider domain of society. In our concluding thoughts, we wish to address this missed external stakeholder group, and speculate on a possible new frontier for the field: Where IS is the information media of the future.

7 A POSSIBLE NEW FRONTIER: IS—THE FUTURE INFORMATION MEDIA?

With the emergence of the Internet, IS entered the arena of a public information media. Eventually it might be on par with—if not superior to—print, radio, and TV. Consider the introduction to Dahlberg, (2001):

> The Internet's two-way, decentralized communications are seen by many commentators as providing the means by which to extend informal political deliberations. Indeed, a cursory examination of the thousands of diverse conversations taking place everyday online and open to anyone with Internet access seems to indicate the expansion on a global scale of the loose webs of rational-critical discourse that constitute what is known as the public sphere.[37] However, some commentators argue that online discourse is not presently fulfilling its deliberative potential.

The symptoms why IT in its current form cannot fulfill its 'deliberative potential' are not difficult to discern. Most websites are developed to support purposive rational actions: to facilitate the buying and selling of products. It inundates the casual browser with advertising that is often manipulative, offensive and intrusive, while at the same time collecting personal information which is subsequently used for spamming. Few resources appear to be devoted to building cyber forum prototypes that have the potential for becoming institutions supporting 'rational-critical discourse' and informative debates among large numbers of participants as had been the case in the 18th and 19th century when democracies and free enterprise became established in most parts of the Western hemisphere. An informed public opinion that cannot be ignored or easily manipulated by the leaders of government and big business is an essential prerequisite for the continued strength of Western democracies. Such an informed public depends on the social institutions of a 'public sphere' which in recent times has substantially deteriorated.

Today, the public sphere in the political realm consists of the institutional interactions of the public press, political parties, and parliament with its ancillary participants like lobbyists. Within the public sphere, opinions emerge and form a tension-charged social environment in which official government authority and publicity confront each other (adapted from Habermas, 1989, p. 73). Important prerequisites of a public sphere are that citizens address each other as an audience, that forums exist where audiences can meet, and that social practices have been created entitling all citizens to an informed opinion on matters of general concern and granting them the right of expressing their opinions freely. The public sphere concerns itself not only with politics but all matters of general interest which are the principal domains of publicity. These include the economy, the arts, scholarship, the sciences, education, and matters of law and morality.

But herein lies the rub: One of the key tenets of social theorists is that modernization has led to 'cultural impoverishment' which is equivalent to 'loss of meaning, which is one of the principal obstacles for 'the emergence of critical consciousness and action' (White 1988, p. 121; Habermas 1987, pp. 140 and pp. 383). In order to see how this has deteriorated the public sphere, we must compare its current state and functioning to its earlier, much more powerful state and decisive influence.

Originally, it was through the emergence of the institutions of a public sphere at the beginning of the 18th century, that democratic 'opinion' in the Western world toppled the power of authoritarian monarchs and the intellectually stifling dogmatism of the churches (*cf.* the detailed analysis in Habermas 1989). Contrary to today, the public sphere had much influence on the life of a nation. Via the interactions between scholars, artists, aristocrats and leading citizens in the salons and coffeehouses of the 18th century,[38] public opinion eventually brought about the general recognition of the human rights of free inquiry, free speech and free peaceful assembly—the prerequisites for an independent press, which became the most important institution of the public sphere. This happened first in Great Britain where censorship was eliminated in 1695 and the *Times* was founded in 1785. Eventually it spread to France and Germany. Everywhere, subordinate subjects turned into autonomous subjects emancipated from the tutelage of state and church through the enlightenment of their reason in public discourse. Such informed subjects could no longer be treated simply as receivers of regulations from above, but had to be respected as critics and potential opponents.

Unfortunately, in the modern world, through the 'scientization of politics' (*cf.* Habermas 1974, 1989), big government and big industry turned enlightened subjects into manipulated citizens. This became possible through fundamental changes in the public sphere that robbed science of its liberating force for the public and turned the press along with the other mass media into instruments of 'distorted communication' (*cf.* the detailed historical analysis in Habermas 1989). This came about through the increasing isolation of science, law and the arts from the public so that they became almost exclusively the domain of full time professionals. Many members of the public sphere including journalists and politicians, no longer have the time and necessary education to absorb the key insights from the principal domains of publicity and to examine their potential social and political impacts.[39]

The question then is: does the Internet have the potential to counteract if not reverse these dangerous trends. The many experimental cyber communities that do engage in serious debates and the many individualized discourses of email list servers clearly demonstrate that the potential for deliberative, communicative functions of IT does, indeed, exist. Heng and Moor (2003) review a number of examples of such communities. We suggest that the deeper reasons why such serious communicative functions of the Internet have not yet materialized on a larger scale stem from the fact that one-sided values have driven most IT development. This has led to the emphasizing of purposive rational effectiveness and efficiency over supporting rational communication.

This observation is somewhat surprising given that the communicative functions of IT have been highly touted since the inception of the computer (e.g., Hedberg 1975; Sackman 1967) and it is part and parcel of the American credo that public information distribution should be governed by policies that serve the better good of all. Historically, the values that were supposed to be advanced in public policies governing information technology from print to radio and TV, were those associated with the notion of a free press, i.e., freedom of inquiry, expression of the greatest diversity of opinion, and universal access. From the press they were transferred to other media that played a similar role as communication technology advanced: radio, TV and to some extent the telephone. *A fortiori* they should have also been extended to the new IT. Yet, as was previously noted that has not happened so far. IT mostly serves specific interest groups, for example the management of corporations and owners of the communications industry. In order to keep the discussion within reasonable bounds, in this paper we refrained from raising the thorny issue of how our society uses information technology and what values should govern such use. At the level of individuals and organizations, the traditional values of a free press link to what we called the communicative function of IS.[40] Once extended to the new information media, they will raise fundamental challenges to the role of IT in modern democracies. To meet these challenges, the communicative function of IS will have to assume a higher moral priority than its purposive rational function, at least in principle if not in practice as has been the case with the older information and communication technologies.

If we look upon IS (as systems) as the newest and maybe in the near future most powerful 'kid on the block' of the public information and communication arena, then we as IS researchers need to ask, how well IS (as a field) is prepared for this role (keeping in mind that IS makes up only a part of the IT industry)? In this paper we made the point that IS as a field might be in crisis and a field in crisis is going to find it very difficult to deal with new challenges such as these. We concluded that IS as a field needs to address its internal problems first so that it can better perform its external social roles whatever they maybe. They will continue to include its current immediate external stakeholder's interests who appear mostly concerned with efficiency and effectiveness. But a new communicative function for IS as societal systems is in the wings. We believe that for the IS discipline to prosper, will require it to meet the challenge of broadening its purposive rational value base to include that which is needed for taking on the larger societal issues. In so doing, the field will also become better equipped to handle the current pressures of immediate relevancy for all its stakeholders. Indeed, it is interesting to consider that the future of the field may well lie in the forgotten discussions of the late 60s and early 70s where scholars theorized about how the new information technology would impact society. So our future may well lie—at least in part—in rejuvenating the past.

ACKNOWLEDGEMENTS

We would like to thank Juhani Iivari for his helpful input on the formulation of our ideas about an IS Body of Knowledge; Kalle Lyytinen for his thoughts on knowledge creation and transformation networks; and Tim Goles for his assistance on paradigms wars. We gratefully acknowledge the comments of Izak Benbasat, Margaret Hendrickx and Andy Schwarz who read various versions of the paper. Additionally, we would like to thank the Editor for this paper—Detmar Straub—and the three anonymous reviewers for their valuable comments and suggestions.

NOTES

1 In this paper, we use the terms 'discipline' and 'field' synonymously.
2 An interesting twist to the Markus argument—if one believes the field is in crisis—is that even if the function is of critical importance to an organization, it could still be outsourced and/or sent offshore. That is precisely what many companies are doing. So while the function could be important, this does not necessarily mean the jobs and associated skills will stay internally or even in the same country or continent.
3 Both of us agree that there will be a crisis if a significant number of the jobs for our graduates permanently disappear, i.e. if offshoring or other factors cause the current volume of IS students to continue to decline even if the economy picks up. But that is not our main focus here. Rather than analyzing the basis behind a crisis claim, our purpose in this paper is to reflect on the state of the discipline, crisis or no crisis. We would also contend that a critical reflection on the state of the field is an important prerequisite for any future strategizing.
4 When we use the term 'IS field' in this paper, we are primarily focusing on the IS academic community (in general) and in particular, the research performed by the IS academic community.
5 It has been pointed out to us that many of the claims we make such as fragmentation, the need for a strong communicative function, etc. are not unique to IS. Indeed, perhaps our paper can be used as a template for academics in other disciplines to reflect upon the state of their own fields.
6 Such a structure should not be seen as an attempt to 'unify the field'. Like King and Lyytinen (2003), we question the wisdom of any calls for unification, be it paradigmatic, institutional, or otherwise. On the other hand, some vehicle for structuring a common body of IS knowledge does seem to have merit to us.
7 It is somewhat surprising to us that the discipline of IS has few published reflective pieces tracing the historical roots of the field. We are not sure whether the field considers itself too young to need such a reflection or whether there simply are not enough 'old timers' around who could provide such a view. Whatever the case, we believe this to be a serious shortcoming of the IS discipline.
8 Examples of such disjoint specialties might be web programming, logical database design, database maintenance, ERP customization, e-comm applications, IS security, GUI design, legacy application maintenance, and so forth (whatever the latest phase of IT innovation suggests).
9 This is a distinction that is fundamental to the treatment of human action in different branches of the social and cultural sciences (*cf.* Polkinghorne 1983; Heath 2001, p. 35).
10 Traditionally social anthropology was concerned with understanding the evolution of the human species as a whole, tracing different cultures to their ultimate remote origins in time and space. History has focused on the tradition of specific cultures and its ethnic and spiritual integrity across different time periods. In both cases the assumption is that understanding the past helps to grasp the depth and breadth of contemporary meanings. (An example of this is found in this paper where the meaning of the cultural sphere is traced back to its origins in the 17th and 18th century.) The study of literature goes together with the study of the languages in which the literature was written, be it historical or contemporary literature including the evolution of different literature genres. It thus focuses on a specific product of history—its texts. By studying the texts of different cultures

we can better understand our own and overcome the barriers of communication to others. For example, by studying the Koran, Christians can better understand what Muslims mean and do and vice versa for Muslims and the New Testament. Finally, hermeneutics is concerned with conditions that make understanding possible including its limits. 'It seeks to throw light on the fundamental conditions that underlie the phenomenon of understanding in all its modes, scientific and nonscientific alike, and that constitute understanding as an event over which the interpreting subject does not ultimately preside.' Linge (1977, p. XI)

11 Consider, for example, the phenomenon of IS implementation. It has been examined from such diverse perspectives as technical implementation (DeMarco 1978; Gane and Sarson 1979), planned change models of Lewin and Schein (Keen and Scott-Morton 1978; Alter and Ginzberg 1978), political theories (Bardach 1977; Wilensky 1967; Keen 1981; Newman and Rosenberg 1985), action learning (Argyris and Schon 1978; Kolb 1984; Heiskanen 1994), Marxist economic theory (Sandberg 1985; Nygaard 1975) and institutional economics (Williamson 1975; Alchian and Demsetz 1972; Kemerer 1992; Heikkila 1995). To make matters worse, there are probably as many conflicting messages about what constitutes 'good IS implementation' as there are perspectives.

12 A-N-T uses the term 'actant' to refer to both human and non-human actors or agents in complex socio-technical networks (*cf.* Walsham 1997).

13 Ormerod (1996) for example, called for 'the synergistic combination of consulting and academic research in IS'. Davenport and Markus (1999), in like fashion, note the value of consulting and academic research learning from each other. Similarly, Avison *et al.* (1999) advocate a greater use of action research to make IS academic research more relevant to practitioners.

14 Klein and Hirschheim (2001) analyze the fundamental value choices that would have to be considered to make IS research relevant for multiple stakeholders.

15 In part these expectations and where they come from, how they are formed and what they lead to are taken up in Hirschheim *et al* (2003).

16 Of course there have been times, such as in the early 1990s when many IS departments did lower their budgets typically through downsizing, but this often led to a concomitant rise in hidden IT spending in the business units that did not show up in the corporate IS spending figure. Hence, the perception that IS costs had actually gone down during this period is somewhat illusory. And where it was not illusory, organizations typically suffered degradations in IS service quality due to too few IS employees trying to handle increasing service demands.

17 See for example the latest rage based on the so-called 'balanced scorecard' (Martinsons *et al.* 1999).

18 We do not overlook the importance of reference discipline focus as a source of differentiation, i.e., training in preferred references disciplines and professional experience as an engineer, accountant, economist, etc. This source of influence was of particular importance during the early era of IS when there were no internally trained IS faculty. This influence works through the personality of influential researchers. It affects their vision of an IS and their paradigmatic assumptions. Hence it is indirectly acknowledged. A more detailed treatment of this source is beyond the scope of this paper.

19 By applying Whitley's (1984a, 1984b) model of cognitive and social institutionalization of scientific fields (or academic disciplines), Banville and Landry (1989) conclude that the field of IS is a 'fragmented adhocracy'. This is so because in order to work in IS one does not need a strong consensus with one's colleagues on the significance and importance of the research problem as long as

there exists some outside community for support. Nor are there widely accepted, legitimized results or procedures on which one must build 'in order to construct knowledge claims which are regarded as competent and useful contributions' (Whitley, 1984a, pp. 88–123 as quoted by Banville and Landry, 1989, p. 54). In addition, research involves high task uncertainty, because problem formulations are unstable, priorities vary among different research communities, and there is little control over the goals by a professional leadership establishment (such as bars or licensing boards for physicians and engineers). For example, some IS research groups may choose to define and cherish projects that do not follow the familiar patterns of engineering or empirical social science, although such groups are generally in the minority. There appears—to some extent at least—local autonomy to formulate research problems, and standards for conducting and evaluating research results (*cf.* Goles and Hirschheim 2000).

20 For some interpretivist researchers, such notions of rigor seem totally understandable as that is the way their research often seems to be treated by reviewers, i.e., harshly!

21 The fact that IS is struggling with the issue of rigor should come as no surprise. It is an issue that has been debated in most disciplines, often without any consensus being reached. In sociology, for example, rigor is thought to embrace six elements: (1) properly theorized questions; (2) clearly defined concepts; (3) method appropriate to the question and to the context; (4) good technique involving careful execution; (5) subjected to attempts to 'disconfirmation'; and (6) open to checking (not replication) (Castleman, 2000).

22 We are, of course, aware that not everyone would agree with this view, but we will have to leave that discussion for another time.

23 This description is not to imply that each research publication must immediately inform practice. Hence it is compatible with the first and fruitful version of this cycle that IS research stimulates other research, as long as some of it is eventually translated into ever more applicable results via different research specializations including consultants and textbook writers. We refer to this as the 'social network view of knowledge creation, transformation and diffusion'.

24 There have been a number of undergraduate and post-graduate IS curriculum proposals (*cf.* ACM 1968, 1979; Couger 1973; Nunamaker *et al.* 1982, Buckingham *et al.* 1987; Gorgone *et al.* 1994; Couger *et al*, 1997) which have offered, often implicitly, a description of the general types of knowledge that IS professionals supposedly need. But such knowledge has traditionally been translated into subject areas (e.g., telecommunications, IS management) that an IS student should know and certain skills (e.g., data base design, Java programming) that the student should have mastery of. Nor was there much consideration of an IS professional body of knowledge. We believe the knowledge areas in IS are broader than the ones articulated in the many undergraduate and graduate curriculum proposals.

25 Of course a potentially thorny question is what are the IS sub-specializations and where would such a listing of them come from? Special Interest Groups (SIGs) might be one way to distinguish various sub-specializations. The Swanson and Ramiller's (1993) categorization of research topics in IS may be another.

26 The SWEBOK knowledge areas are: Software configuration management, software construction, software design, software engineering infrastructure, software engineering management, software engineering process, software evaluation and maintenance, software quality analysis, software requirements analysis and software testing.

27 Application knowledge as used in Iivari *et al* (2004) refers to the knowledge of typical applications which is knowledge about software applications in a given application domain. It involves the knowledge about typical applications, their structure, their functionality, behavior and use with a view to identify the possibilities to support user tasks with IT. This is different from applicative knowledge which emerges from applying theories and abstract principles to solve practical problems in a creative way, as defined earlier.

28 These knowledge areas correspond closely to the knowledge areas identified by Vitalari (1985): application domain knowledge is compatible with his 'functional domain knowledge,' application knowledge to his 'application domain knowledge,' organizational knowledge to his 'organizational specific knowledge,' and ISD process knowledge to his 'knowledge of methods and techniques'.

29 The term 'requirements construction' was coined by Flynn and Jazi (1998). This term like 'requirements engineering' implies that requirements are not out there to be gathered and analyzed, but that they are socially constructed. We prefer 'requirements construction' because it does not imply a specific engineering paradigm.

30 In principle, *theoretical knowledge* could also be defined to include reasoning with ethical theories, but because values and ethical issues in modernity have often been banned from the cognitive realm, it is appropriate to recognize the special status of *ethical knowledge* by listing it separately to emphasize its equal significance and role along with other types of knowledge.

31 Aristotle called applicative knowledge *phronesis* to refer to political-ethical knowledge and distinguish it from *episteme* (theoretical knowledge) and *techne*. We referred to *techne* (the etymological root of technique) as rules of skill and technical knowledge. Modern science tends to include some application knowledge with its teaching of theory (and with this introduces a technical attitude towards theories), whereas Aristotle meant by *episteme* primarily the kind of theoretical contemplation that is not necessarily action oriented, but 'pure' thinking or reflection.

32 Whilst cases may well be the most appropriate vehicle, they are not the only one. Role-playing, focus groups, and other team-oriented exercises may also prove valuable knowledge transfer mechanisms.

33 The European tradition for PhDs is built on this master-student apprenticeship.

34 With reference to Whitley (1984a, p. 205–206), Banville and Landry (1989, p. 54) write 'strategic task uncertainty is low when members of the field agree on a hierarchy of research problems, when there is a tight control over research goals and minimal local autonomy in the formulation of research problems and significance standards. Conversely, a high strategic task uncertainty is associated with the presence of loosely coupled schools of thought.'

35 We note that the AIS appears to have already begun exploring professionalization through its formal participation in professional standards committee meeting in related associations such as ACM and IEEE where there are discussions on-going about an IS specialization. As long as this serves the purpose of knowledge and experience transfer, this is no doubt fruitful. Sooner or later professionalization is likely to transform itself from its rather inconspicuous existence of today to become one of the key concerns of the field in the future.

36 As suggested earlier, how to code the available knowledge in an action oriented format is far from clear. For example, it still is not clear what the role of cases is versus abstract knowledge in packing knowledge for practice.

37 Proponents of the idea that cyberspace may, under the right social conditions, offer a renewed public sphere include Aikens (1997), Fernback (1997), Hauben and

Hauben (1997), Kellner (1999), Moore (1999), Noveck (1999), Rheingold (1993), and Slevin (2000).

38 The Marquise de Rembouillet (1588–1665) held the first salon on the site of the current Louvre in Paris. Salons mostly took place in large private homes, which provided a forum where artists, intellectuals and aristocrats could meet for intellectual pursuits in the arts and literature. Salons then spread to England and to Germany in the form of table societies (Tischgesellschaften) and literary clubs. Particularly in England the salons and coffee houses soon took up matters formerly reserved almost exclusively for government, i.e. economics and politics, to the point that the political parties of the Whigs and Tories found it necessary to get involved in the English salons (*cf.* Habermas 1989). The modern usage of 'salon' might be related to the fact that from the very origins of the salons, women played a much more significant role in them than in official politics.

39 With the term 'scientization of politics' ('Verwissenschaftlichung der Politk'), Habermas (1974, p. 120–140) refers to a change in the relationship between professional and scientific specialists and politicians. Originally, scientific experts were to provide political decision makers with the principal alternatives from which politically legitimized authority would make informed choices. With the advance of the so-called decision making technologies (models and other complex information processing methods), the choices themselves became mostly predetermined. The values and biases entering the scientific processes of decision support methods are removed from critical articulation and reflection to the point that they may not even be perceived by the scientists themselves. At that point, the instrumental values of applied science and its bias to ignore what is not measurable, function as an ideology to sell the politics of the elites as the inevitable outcome of the application of the scientific method to the current problems of society. The voices of those without access to the industrial-scientific decision making apparatus are dismissed as irrelevant and have little chance to be taken seriously. This is the core of the so-called 'technocratic decision model.' The alternative is a pluralistic decision model of deliberative democracy that depends on the interactions of an informed public sphere with the officialdom of elected governments and their scientific staff cadres.

40 To make this link explicit, requires the introduction of several constructs from discourse theory. These include the notions of why, in each communicative act oriented towards mutual understanding, all parties involved have to assume that they mean what they say or write (sincerity), that they express themselves in ways comprehensible to their audience (intelligibility), and that the claims they make can be supported by good reasons. It also would require distinguishing different types of discourses (theoretical, moral, aesthetic) and their different truth claims (such as truth of propositions, technical efficacy, legitimacy of norms of action, adequacy of standards for good taste). Finally, the character of the arguments that are effective to redeem the different truth claims associated with different types of discourses would have to be sketched. An introduction to these issues can be found in Howe (2000, pp. 18–62) and White (1988, pp. 90–127, chapter 5, 'Modernity, rationalization and contemporary capitalism' and White (1995) pp. 3–16. For a fuller treatment of the link between discourse theory and democracy see Chambers (1995, pp. 233–259), and Moon (1995, p. 143–164); and for a critical treatment of Habermas' two models of deliberative democracy, see Scheuerman (1999, p. 153–177) and Poster (1999).

REFERENCES

Ackoff, R. (1967), 'Management misinformation systems,' *Management Science*, December, pp. B147–156.

ACM Curriculum Committee on Computer Science (1968), 'Curriculum 68: Recommendations for the Undergraduate Program in Computer Science,' *Communications of the ACM*, 11(3), March, pp. 151–197.

ACM Curriculum Committee on Computer Science (1979), 'Curriculum 78: Recommendations for the Undergraduate Program in Computer Science,' *Communications of the ACM*, 22(3), March, pp. 147–166.

Aikens, S. (1997), 'American Democracy and Computer-Mediated Communication: A Case Study in Minnesota,' Doctoral Dissertation in Social and Political Sciences, Cambridge University.

Alavi, M., Carlson, P., and Brooke, G. (1989), 'The ecology of MIS research: A twenty year review,' in J. I. DeGross, J. C. Henderson, and B. R. Konsynski (eds.), *Proceedings of the Tenth International Conference on Information Systems*, pp. 363–375.

Alchian, A. and Demsetz, H. (1972), 'Production, Information Costs and Economic Organizations,' *American Economic Review*, 62(5), pp. 777–795.

Alter, S., and Ginzberg, M. J., (1978), 'Managing Uncertainty in MIS Implementation,' *Sloan Management Review*, Vol. 19, pp. 23–31.

Applegate, L. and King, J. (1999), 'Rigor and Relevance: Careers on the Line' *MIS Quarterly*, 23(1), pp. 17–18.

Argyris, C. and Schon, D. (1978), *Organizational Learning: A Theory of Action Perspective*, Addison-Wesley, Reading.

Avison, D., Lau, F., Myers, M., and Nielsen, P. A. (1999), 'Action Research,' *Communications of the ACM*, 42(1), pp. 94–97.

Backhouse, J., Liebenau, J. and Land, F. (1991), 'On the Discipline of Information Systems,' *Journal of Information Systems*, 1(1), January, pp. 19–27.

Bacon, J. and Fitzgerald, B. (2001), 'A Systemic Framework for the Field of Information Systems,' *Database*, 32(2), Spring, pp. 46–67.

Banville, C. and Landry, M. (1989), 'Can the Field of MIS be Disciplined?' *Communications of the ACM*, 32(1), pp. 48–60.

Bardach, E., (1977), *The Implementation Game*, MIT Press, Cambridge.

Barki, H., Rivard, S. and Talbot, J. (1988), 'An Information Systems Keyword Classification Scheme,' *MISQ*, June, pp. 299–322.

Baskerville, R. and Myers, M. (2002), 'Information Systems as a Reference Discipline,' *MISQ*, 26(1), pp. 1–14.

Benbasat, I. (ed.) (1989), *The Information Systems Research Challenge: Experimental Research Methods*—Vol. 2. Boston: Harvard University Press.

Benbasat, I. and Weber, R. (1996), 'Rethinking Diversity in Information Systems Research,' *Information Systems Research*, 7(4), December, pp. 389–399.

Benbasat, I. and Zmud, R. (1999), 'Empirical Research in Information Systems: The Practice of Relevance,' *MIS Quarterly*, 23(1), pp. 3–16.

Benbasat, I. and Zmud, R. (2003), 'The Identity Crisis within the IS Discipline: Defining and Communicating the discipline's Core Properties', *MIS Quarterly*, 27(2), June, pp. 183–194.

Bhattacherjee, A. (2001), 'Understanding and evaluating relevance in research,' Volume 6, Article 6, *Communications of the Association for Information Systems*, March.

Bhattacherjee, A. and Hirschheim, R. (1997), 'IT and Organizational Change: Lessons from Client/Server Technology Implementation,' *Journal of General Management*, 23(2), Winter, pp. 1–16.

Bjorn-Andersen, N. (1984), 'Challenge to Certainty,' in Bemelmans, T. (ed.), *Beyond Productivity: Information Systems Development for Organizational Effectiveness*. North-Holland, Amsterdam, pp. 1–8.

Blumenthal, S. C. (1969), *Management Information Systems: A Framework for Planning and Development*, Prentice-Hall, Englewood Cliffs.

Brandt, R. B. (1959), *Ethical Theory*, Prentice Hall, Englewood Cliffs.

Brown, C. V. and Sambamurthy, V. (1999), *Repositioning the IT Organization to Enable Business Transformation*, Pinnaflex Educational Resources, Cincinnati, OH.

Buckingham, R., Hirschheim, R., Land, F. and Tully, C. (1987), 'Information Systems Curriculum: A Basis for Course Design,' in *Information Systems Education: Recommendations and Implementation*, R. Buckingham, R. Hirschheim, F. Land and C. Tully, (eds.), Cambridge University Press, Cambridge, pp. 14–133.

Burrell, G. and Morgan, G. (1979), *Sociological Paradigms and Organizational Analysis*, Heinemann Books, London.

Business Week (2003), 'Outsourcing Jobs: Is it Bad?,' August 25, 2003, pp. 36–38.

CAIS (2001), *Communications of the Association for Information Systems*, Special Issue on Relevancy, Volume 6, March.

Carlisle, P. (2002), 'A Pragmatic View of Knowledge and Boundaries: Boundary Objects in New Product Development,' *Organization Science*, 13, 4, pp. 442–455.

Castleman, T. (2000), Rigor vs. relevance in sociological research, paper presented at the panel session 'Rigor vs. relevance in IS research', 8th *European Conference on Information Systems*, Vienna, Austria.

Cash, J. and Lawrence, P. (eds.) (1989), *The Information Systems Research Challenge: Qualitative Research Methods—Vol. 1*. Boston: Harvard University Press.

Chambers, S., (1995), 'Discourse and democratic practices,' in White, S. (ed.), *The Cambridge Companion to Habermas*, Cambridge: Cambridge University Press, pp. 233–259.

Checkland, P. (1981), *Systems Thinking, Systems Practice*, John Wiley & Sons, Chichester.

Checkland, P. and Scholes, J. (1990), *Soft Systems Methodology in Action*. John Wiley & Sons, Chichester.

Checkland, P. and Holwell, S. (1998), *Information, Systems and Information Systems: Making Sense of the Field*, Wiley, Chichester.

Cheon, M., Lee, C. and Grover, V. (1992), 'Research in MIS—Points of Work and Reference: A Replication and Extension of the Culnan and Swanson Study,' *Data Base*, 23(2), Spring, pp. 21– 29.

Chua, W. (1986), 'Radical Developments in Accounting Thought,' *The Accounting Review*, 61(4), pp. 601–632.

Churchman, C. W. (1971), *The Design of Inquiring Systems*, Basic Books, New York.

Cooper, R. (1988), 'Review of Management Information Systems Research: A Management Support Perspective,' *Information Processing & Management*. 24(1), pp. 73–102.

Couger, J. D. (1973), 'Curriculum Recommendations for Undergraduate Programs in Information Systems,' *Communications of the ACM*, 16(12), December, pp. 727–749.

Couger, J. D., Davis, G., Feinstein, D.L., Gorgone, J.T., Longenecker, H.E. (1997), 'IS'97, Model Curriculum and Guidelines for Undergraduate Degree Programs in Information Systems,' *Data Base*, 26(1), Winter, pp. 1–94.

Cresswell, A. (2001), 'Thoughts on relevance of is research,' *Communications of the Association for Information Systems*, Volume 6, Article 9, March.

Culnan, M. (1986), 'The Intellectual Development of Management Information Systems, 1972–1982: A Co-Citation Analysis,' *Management Science*, 32(2), February, pp. 156–172.

Culnan, M. (1987), 'Mapping the Intellectual Structure of MIS, 1980–1985: A Co-Citation Analysis,' *MIS Quarterly*, 11(3), September, pp. 341–353.

Culnan, M. and Swanson, E. B. (1986), 'Research in Management Information Systems, 1980–1984: Points of Work and Relevance,' *MIS Quarterly*, 10(3), September, pp. 286–301.

Currie, W. and Galliers, R. (eds) (1999), *Rethinking MIS*, Oxford University Press, Oxford.

Dahlberg, L. (2000), 'The Internet and the Public Sphere: A Critical Analysis of the Possibility of Online Discourse Enhancing Deliberative Democracy,' Doctoral Dissertation in Sociology, Massey University.

Dahlberg, L. (2001), 'Extending the Public Sphere through Cyberspace: The Case Minnesota e-Democracy,' *First Monday*, 6(3), March, *http://www.firstmonday.dk/issues/issue6_3/dahlberg/index.html#author*

Dahlbom, B. (1996), 'The New Informatics,' *Scandinavian Journal of Information Systems*, 8(2), pp. 29–48.

Datta, L. (1994), 'Paradigm Wars: A Basis for Peaceful Coexistence and Beyond,' in Reichardt, C. and Rallis, S. (eds.), *The Qualitative-Quantitative Debate: New Perspectives*, Jossey-Bass, San Francisco, pp. 53–70.

Davenport, T. and Markus, M. L. (1999), 'Rigor vs. Relevance Revisited: Response to Benbasat and Zmud,' *MIS Quarterly*, 23(1), pp. 19–23.

Davis, F. D. (1989), 'Perceived usefulness, perceived ease of use, and user acceptance of information technology', *MIS Quarterly*, 13(3), pp. 319–340.

Davis, G. and Olson, M. (1985), *Management Information Systems: Conceptual Foundations, Structure, and Development*, McGraw-Hill, NY.

Dearden, J. (1966), 'Myth of real-time management information,' *Harvard Business Review*, May–June, pp. 123–132.

Dearden, J. (1972), 'MIS is a mirage,' *Harvard Business Review*, January–February, pp. 90–99.

DeMarco, T. (1978), *Structured Analysis and Systems Specification*. New York: Yourdon Press.

Denning, P., Comer, D., Gries, D., Mulder, M., Tucker, A. Turner, A. J., and Young, P. (1989), 'Computing as a discipline,' Final report of the task force on the core of computer science, *Communications of the ACM*, 32(1), January, pp. 9–23.

Dickson, G. (1968), 'Management information-decision systems,' *Business Horizons*, Vol. 11, December, pp. 17–26.

Dickson, G. (1981), 'Management Information Systems: Evolution and Status,' in *Advances in Computers*, M. Yovits (ed.), Academic Press, NY.

DiMaggio, P. (1995), 'Comments on What Theory is Not,' *ASQ*, 40, pp. 392–397.

Earl, M. (1996) (ed.), *Information Management: The Organizational Dimension*, Oxford University Press, Oxford.

Ein-Dor, P. and Segev, E. (1981), *A Paradigm for Management Information Systems*, New York: Praeger.

Emery, J. and Sprague, C. (1972), 'MIS: A mirage or misconception?,' *Harvard Business Review*, 50(3), May–June, pp. 22–23.

Farhoomand, A. (1987), 'Scientific Progress of Management Information Systems,' *Data Base*, Summer, pp. 48–56.

Fernback, J. (1997), 'The Individual within the Collective: Virtual Ideology and the Realization of Collective Principles,' In: S. G. Jones (editor). *Virtual Culture: Identity and Communication in Cybersociety*. London: Sage, pp. 36–54.

Fjermestad, J. and Hiltz, S. R. (1998), 'An analysis of the effects of mode of communication on group decision making,' *Proceedings of the Thirtieth Annual Hawaii International Conference on System Sciences*, pp. 17–26.

Flynn, D. J. and Jazi, M. D. (1998), 'Constructing user requirements: a social process for a social context,' *Information Systems Journal*, 8(1), 1998, pp. 53–82.

Frost, P. (1996), 'Crossroads,' *Organization Science*, 7(2), March–April, p. 190.

Gadamer, H-G. (1975), *Truth and Method*, The Continuing Publishing Corporation, New York.

Galliers, R. (ed.) (1992), *Information Systems Research: Issues, Methods, and Practical Guidelines*, Blackwell Scientific, Oxford.

Gane, C. and Sarson, T. (1979), *Structured Systems Analysis: Tools and Techniques*, Prentice Hall, Englewood Cliffs.

Giddens, A. (1984), *The Constitution of Society: Outline for a Theory of Structuration*, Cambridge: Polity Press.

Goles, T. and Hirschheim, R. (2000), 'The Paradigm is Dead, the Paradigm is Dead . . . Long Live the Paradigm: The Legacy of Burrell and Morgan,' *OMEGA*, 28(3), May–June, pp. 249–268.

Gorgone, J., Couger, J. D., Davis, G., Feinstein, D., Kasper, G., and Longnecker, H. (1994), 'Information Systems 95,' *Data Base*, 25(4), November, pp. 5–8.

Gorry, G. and Scott-Morton, M. (1971), 'A framework for management information systems,' *Sloan Management Review*, Fall, pp. 55–70.

Habermas, J. (1971), *Der Strukturwandel der Öffentlichkeit. Untersuchungen zu einer bürgerlichen Kategorie der Gesellschaft*, 5th reprinting of the 2nd German edition 1965, Berlin, Luchterhand.

Habermas, J. (1974), *Science and Technology as Ideology*, References are to the German original, 'Technik and Wissenschaft als 'Ideologie', Suhrkamp Frankfurt, 7th ed.

Habermas, J. (1984), *The Theory of Communicative Action: Reason and the Rationalization of Society*, Vol. I, Beacon Press, Boston.

Habermas, J., (1987), *The Theory of Communicative Action: The Critique of Functionalist Reason*, Vol. II. Boston, MA: Beacon Press (references are to the paperback edition, 1989).

Habermas, J. (1988), *On the Logic of the Social Sciences*, MIT Press, Cambridge.

Habermas, J. (1989), *The Structural Transformation of the Public Sphere: An Inquiry into a Category of Bourgeois Society*. Cambridge, Mass.: MIT Press.

Habermas, J. (1993), 'Further Reflections on the Public Sphere,' in *Habermas and the Public Sphere*, Craig Calhoun (ed.), Cambridge, Mass.: MIT Press.

Hauben, M. and Hauben, R. (1997), *Netizens: On the History and Impact of Usenet and the Internet*, Los Alamitos, CA, IEEE Computer Society.

Heath, J. (2001), *Communicative Action and Rational Choice*, Cambridge, Mass.: MIT Press.

Hedberg, B. (1975), 'Computer Systems to Support Industrial Democracy,' in Mumford, E. and Sackman, H. (eds.), *Human Choice and Computers*, North-Holland, Amsterdam.

Heikkila, J. (1995), The Diffusion of a Learning Intensive Technology into Organizations: The case of PC technology, PhD Dissertation, Department of Computer Science, University of Tampere.

Heiskanen, A. (1994), Issues and Factors Affecting the Success and Failure of a Student Record System Development Process- A Longitudinal Investigation Based on Reflection-in-Action, PhD Dissertation, Helsinki School of Economics and Business Administration, Helsinki.

Henderson, J. C. and Venkatraman, N. (eds.) (1999), *Research in Strategic Management and Information Technology*, Volume 2, JAI Press, Stamford, CT.

Heng, M., de Moor, A. (2003), 'From Habermas's Communicative Theory to Practice on the Internet,' *Information Systems Journal*, 13(4), pp. 331–352.

Hirschheim, R., (1986a), 'The Effect of *A Priori* Views of the Social Implications of Computing: The Case of Office Automation,' *ACM Computing Surveys*, 18(2), June, pp. 165–195.

Hirschheim, R. (1986b), 'Office Systems: Themes and Reflections,' in *Office Systems*, A. Verrijn-Stuart and R. Hirschheim, (eds.), North-Holland, Amsterdam, pp. 193–199.

Hirschheim, R., Earl, M., Feeny, D. and Lockett, M. (1988), 'An Exploration into the Management of the Information Systems Function: Key Issues and An Evolutionary Model,' *Proceedings of the Joint International Symposium on Information Systems*, R. Jeffery (ed.), Sydney, Australia, March 1988, pp. 63–86.

Hirschheim, R. and Klein, H. K. (1989), 'Four Paradigms of Information Systems Development,' *Communications of the ACM*, 32(10), pp. 1199–1216.

Hirschheim, R. and Klein, H. K. (1994), 'Realizing Emancipatory Principles in Information Systems Development: The Case for ETHICS,' *MIS Quarterly*, 18(1), March, pp. 83–109.

Hirschheim, R., and Klein, H. K. (2000), 'Information Systems Research at the Crossroads: External vs. Internal Views,' in *Organizational and Social Perspectives on Information Technology*, R. Baskerville, J. Stage and J. DeGross (eds.), Kluwer Academic Publishers, Boston, pp. 233–254.

Hirschheim, R., Klein H. K. and Lyytinen, K. (1995), *Information Systems Development and Data Modeling: Conceptual and Philosophical Foundations*. Cambridge University Press, Cambridge, UK.

Hirschheim, R., Klein, H. K., and Lyytinen, K. (1996), 'Exploring the Intellectual Structures of Information Systems Development: A Social Action Theoretic Analysis,' *Accounting, Management and Information Technologies*, 6(1/2), pp. 1–64.

Hirschheim, R. and Lacity, M. (2000), 'Information Technology Insourcing: Myths and Realities,' *Communications of the ACM*, 43(2), February, pp. 99–107.

Hirschheim, R. and Miller, J. (1993), 'Implementing Empowerment Through Teams: The Case of Texaco's Information Technology Division,' *Proceedings of the 1993 ACM SIGCPR Conference Managing Information Technology: Organizational and Individual Perspectives*, M. Tanniru (ed.), pp. 255–264, St. Louis, April 1–3, 1993.

Hirschheim, R., Poora, J., and Parks, M. (2003), 'Forty Years of Information Technology Change at Texaco Inc.—A History and Change Analysis,' *Database*, forthcoming.

Hirschheim, R. and Sabherwal, R. (2001), 'Detours in the path toward Strategic Information Systems Alignment: Excessive Transformations, Paradoxical Decisions, and Uncertain Turnarounds,' *California Management Review*, 44(1), Fall, pp. 87–108.

Howe, L. (2000), *On Habermas*, Wadsworth/Thomson, Belmont, CA.

Huber, G. P. (1983), 'Cognitive Style as a Basis for MIS and DSS Designs: Much Ado About Nothing?,' *Management Science*, 29(5), pp. 567–577.

Iivari, J., Hirschheim, R. and Klein, H. K. (1998), 'A Paradigmatic Analysis Contrasting Information Systems Development Approaches and Methodologies,' *Information Systems Research*, 9(2), June, pp. 164–193.

Iivari, J., Hirschheim, R. and Klein, H. K. (2000), 'A Dynamic Framework for Classifying Information Systems Development Methodologies and Approaches,' *Journal of Management Information Systems*, 17(3), Winter, pp. 177–216.

Iivari, J., Hirschheim, R. and Klein, H. K. (2003), 'Towards a Distinctive Body of Knowledge for Information Systems Developers: A Knowledge Work Perspective,' submitted for publication.

Ives, B., Hamilton, S. and Davis, G. (1980), 'A Framework for Research in Computer-based Management Information Systems,' *Management Science*, 26(9), pp. 910–934.

Kant, I., (1964), *Groundwork of the Metaphysics of Morals*, (translated and analyzed by H. J. Paton), Harper Torch Books, New York, reprinting of the 3rd ed. 1956 by arrangement with Hutchinson & Co., London.

Keen, P. (1980), 'MIS Research: Reference Disciplines and Cumulative Tradition,' in *Proceedings of the First International Conference on Information Systems*, (ed.) McLean, E., pp. 17–31, Philadelphia.

Keen, P. (1981), 'Information Systems and Organizational Change,' *Communications of the ACM*, 24(1), pp. 24–33.

Keen, P. (1987), 'MIS Research: Current Status, Trends and Needs,' In Buckingham, R., Hirschheim, R., Land, F. and Tully, C. (eds.) *Information Systems Education: Recommendations and Implementation*, Cambridge University Press, Cambridge, pp. 1–13.

Keen, P., (1991), 'Relevance and Rigor in Information Systems Research: Improving Quality, Confidence, Cohesion, and Impact,' in H. E. Nissen, H. K. Klein, and R. Hirschheim (Eds.), *Information Systems Research: Contemporary Approaches and Emergent Traditions*, North-Holland, Amsterdam, pp. 27–49.

Keen, P. and Scott-Morton, M. (1978), *Decision Support Systems: An Organizational Perspective*, Addison-Wesley, Reading, Mass.

Kellner, D. (1999), 'Globalization from Below? Toward a radical democratic technopolitics,' *Angelaki: Journal of the Theoretical Humanities*, 4(2), pp. 101–113.

Kemerer, C. (1992), 'How the Learning Curve Affects CASE Tool Adoption,' *IEEE Software*, 9(5) May, pp. 23–28.

Kern, T., Lacity, M. and Willcocks, L. (2002), *NetSourcing: Renting Business Applications and Services Over a Network*, Financial Times Prentice Hall, Upper Saddle River, NJ.

King, J. L. and Lyytinen, K. (2003), 'When Grasp Exceeds Reach: Will Fortifying our Theoretical Core Save the Information Systems Field?,' working paper.

Klein, H. K. (1999), 'Knowledge and Methods in IS Research: From Beginnings to the Future,' in *New Information Technologies in Organizational Processes, Field Studies and Theoretical Reflections on the Future of Work*, Ngwenyama, O., Introna, L, Myers, M. and DeGross, J. (eds.), Kluwer Academic Publishers, Amsterdam, pp. 13–25.

Klein, H. K. and Hirschheim, R. (1987), 'Social change and the future of information systems development,' in *Critical Issues in Information Systems Research*, R. Boland and R. Hirschheim (eds.), J. Wiley, Chichester, pp. 275–305.

Klein, H. and Hirschheim, R. (1991), 'Rationality Concepts in Information Systems Development Methodologies,' *Accounting, Management and Information Technologies*, 1(2), pp. 157–187.

Klein, H. K. and Hirschheim, R. (1992), 'Paradigmatic Influences on Information Systems Development Methodologies: Evolution and Conceptual Advances,' *Advances in Computers*, Vol. 34, M. Yovits (ed.), Academic Press, New York, pp. 293–392.

Klein, H. K. and Hirschheim, R. (2001), 'Choosing Between Competing Design Ideals in Information Systems Development,' *Information Systems Frontiers*, 3(1), pp. 75–90.

Klein, H. K., and Lyytinen, K. (1992), 'Towards a new understanding of data modeling,' *Software Development and Reality Construction*, Floyd, C., Zuellighoven, H., Budde, R., Keil-Slawik, R. (eds.), Springer Verlag, Berlin, pp. 203–219.

Klein, H. K. and Lyytinen, K. (2003), 'Knowledge Creation and Transformation in Networks: The Case of Relevancy of Information Systems Research', submitted for publication.

Klein, H. K., and Myers, M. (1999), 'A Set of Principles for Conducting and Evaluating Interpretive Field Studies in Information Systems,' *MIS Quarterly*, 23(1), March, pp. 67–94.

Kling, R. (1980), 'Social Analyses of Computing: Theoretical Perspectives in Recent Empirical Research,' *ACM Computing Surveys*, 12(1), March, pp. 61–110.

Kolb, D., (1984), *Experiential Learning, Experience as the Source of Learning and Development*, Prentice Hall, Englewood Cliffs.

Kraemer, K. (ed.) (1991), *The Information Systems Research Challenge: Survey Research Methods—Vol. 3*. Boston: Harvard University Press.

Kumar, K. (1997), 'Program Chair's Statement,' *Proceedings of the Eighteenth International Conference on Information Systems*, K. Kumar and J. DeGross (eds), Atlanta, GA. December 15–17, 1997, pp. xvii–xix.

Lacity, M. and Hirschheim, R. (1993a), *Information Systems Outsourcing: Myths, Metaphors and Realities*, John Wiley & Sons, Chichester.

Lacity, M. and Hirschheim, R. (1993b), 'The Information Systems Outsourcing Bandwagon,' *Sloan Management Review*, 35(1), Fall, pp. 73–86.

Lacity, M. and Hirschheim, R. (1995a), *Beyond the Information Systems Outsourcing Bandwagon: The Insourcing Response*, John Wiley & Sons, Chichester.

Lacity, M. and Hirschheim, R. (1995b), 'Benchmarking as a Strategy for Managing Conflicting Stakeholder Perceptions of Information Systems,' *Journal of Strategic Information Systems*, 4(2), pp. 165–185.

Landry, M. and Banville, C. (1992), 'A Disciplined Methodological Pluralism for MIS Research,' *Accounting, Management, and Information Technology*, 2(2), pp. 77–97.

Langefors, B. (1973), *Theoretical Analysis of Information Systems*, Auerbach, Philadelphia.

Latour, B. (1987), *Science in Action- How to follow engineers and scientists through the society*, Harvard University Press.

Latour, B. (1999). 'On Recalling ANT,' in Law, J. and Hassard, J. (eds.). *Actor Network Theory and After*, Blackwell Publishers, Oxford, pp. 15–25.

Lee, A. (1999a), 'The MIS Field, the Publication Process, and the Future Course of MIS Quarterly,' *MIS Quarterly*, 23(1), pp. v–xi.

Lee, A. (1999b), 'Rigor and Relevance in MIS Research: Beyond the Approach of Positivism Alone,' *MIS Quarterly*, 23(1), pp. 29–33.

Lee, A. and Baskerville, R. (2003), 'Generalizing Generalizability in Information Systems Research,' *Information Systems Research*, 14(3), pp. 221–243.

Lee, A., Liebenau, J. and DeGross, J. (eds.) (1997), *Information Systems and Qualitative Research*, Chapman & Hall, London.

Lincoln, Y. and Guba, E. (1985), *Naturalistic Inquiry*, Sage, Beverly Hills, CA.

Linge, D. (1977), Editor's introduction, in H-G. Gadamer, *Philosophical Hermeneutics*, University of California Press, Berkeley, paperback edition.

Lucas, H. (1975), *Why Information Systems Fail*, Columbia University Press, New York.

Lucas, H. (1999), 'The state of the Information Systems Field,' *Communications of the AIS*, 5(1), January.

Luftman, J. (1996), *Competing in the Information Age: Practical Applications of the Strategic Alignment Model*, New York, NY: Oxford University Press.

Luftman, J. and Brier, T., (1999), 'Achieving and Sustaining Business-IT Alignment,' *California Management Review*, 42(1), Fall, pp. 109–116.

Lyytinen, K. (1987), 'A Taxonomic Perspective of Information Systems Development: Theoretical Constructs and Recommendations,' in Boland, R. and Hirschheim, R. (Eds.), *Critical Issues in Information Systems Research*, Wiley, Chichester, pp. 3–41.

Lyytinen, K. (1999), 'Empirical Research in Information Systems: On the Relevance of Practice in Thinking of IS Research,' *MIS Quarterly*, 23(1), pp. 25–27.

Markus, M. L. (1997), 'The Qualitative Difference in Information Systems Research and Practice,' in Lee, A., Liebenau, J. and DeGross, J. (eds.), *Information Systems and Qualitative Research*, Chapman & Hall, London, pp. 11–27.

Markus, M. L. (1999), 'Thinking the Unthinkable: What happens if the IS field as we know it goes away?,' in *Rethinking MIS*, Currie, W. and Galliers, R. (eds.), Oxford University Press, Oxford, pp. 175–203.

Martinsons, M., Davison, R., Tse, D. (1999), 'The balanced scorecard: a foundation for the strategic management of information systems,' *Decision Support Systems*, 25(1), pp. 71–88.

Mason, R. O. (1986), 'Four ethical issues of the information age.' *MIS Quarterly*, (10:1), pp. 5–12.

Mason, R. and Mitroff, I. (1973), 'A Program for Research on Management Information Systems,' *Management Science*, 19(5), pp. 475–487.

Mathiassen, L. (1998), 'Reflective Systems Development,' *Scandinavian Journal of Information Systems*, 10(1&2), pp. 67–117.

McCarthy, T. (1982): *The Critical Theory of Jurgen Habermas*. Cambridge: Cambridge University Press, 2nd printing of 1981 paperback ed.

Mingers, J. and Stowell, F. (eds.) (1997), *Information Systems: An Emerging Discipline?*, McGraw-Hill, New York.

Moon, D. (1995), 'Practical discourse and communicative ethics,' in White, S. (ed.), *The Cambridge Companion to Habermas*, Cambridge: Cambridge University Press, pp. 143–164.

Moore, R. (1999), 'Democracy and Cyberspace,' in: B. N. Hague and B. D. Loader (editors). *Digital Democracy: Discourse and Decision Making in the Information Age*. London: Routledge.

Morgan, G. (ed.) (1983), *Beyond Method: Strategies for Social Research*, Sage Publications, Beverly Hills.

Morstead, S. and Blount, G. (2003), *Offshore Ready: Strategies to Plan & Profit from Offshore IT-Enabled Services*, ISANI Press, USA.

Mumford, E., Hirschheim, R., Fitzgerald, G., and Wood-Harper, T. (eds.) (1985), *Research Methods in Information Systems*, North-Holland, Amsterdam.

Newman, M. and Rosenberg, D. (1985), 'Systems Analysts and the Politics of Organizational Control,' *Omega*, 13(3), pp. 393–406.

Nissen, H-K., Klein, H., and Hirschheim, R. (eds.) (1991), *Information Systems Research: Contemporary Approaches and Emergent Themes*, North-Holland, Amsterdam.

Nolan, R. and Croson, D. (1995), *Creative Destruction: A Six-Stage Process for Transforming the Organization*, Harvard Business School Press, Cambridge, Mass.

Noveck, B. (1999), 'Transparent Space: Law, Technology and Deliberative Democracy in the Information Society,' *http://webserver.law.yale.edu/infosociety/papers/democracy.html*

Nunamaker, J., Couger, J. D., Davis, G. (1982), 'Information Systems Curriculum: Recommendations for the 80s,' *Communications of the ACM*, 25(11), November, pp. 781–805.

Nygaard, K. (1975), 'The Trade Unions New Users of Research,' *Personnel Review*, Vol. 4, No. 2 as referenced on page 94 in K. Nygaard, 'The Iron and Metal Project:

Trade Union Participation,' in Sandberg, A., (ed.), *Computers Dividing Man and Work*, Arbetslivcentrum, Stockholm.

Oinas-Kukkonen, Henry, J. Similä, P. Kerola, P. Pulli, S. Saukkonen, (2003), 'Role of Systems/Software Methodologies Development in Growth Base of "Oulu Phenomenon",' in Bubenko, *et al.* (eds), 2003, *HiNC 1, The First Conference on the History of Nordic Computing,[http://hinc.dnd.no/] and Pre-proceedings*, IFIP WG 9.7 in cooperation with TC3, Trondheim, Norway, June 15–17, 2003, pp. 337–350.

Orlikowski, W. and Baroudi, J. (1991), 'Studying Information Technology in Organizations: Research Approaches and Assumptions,' *Information Systems Research*, 2(1), pp. 1–28.

Orlikowski, W. and Iacono, S. (2001), 'Desperately Seeking the IT in IT Research,' *Information Systems Research*, 7(4), pp. 400–408.

Ormerod, R. J. (1996), 'Combining Management Consultancy and Research,' *Omega*, 24(1), pp. 1–12.

Peppard, J. and Ward, J. (1999), '"Mind the Gap"- Diagnosing the relationship between the IT organization and the rest of the business,' *Journal of Strategic Information Systems*, 8(1), pp. 29–60.

Polkinghorne, D. (1983), *Methodology for the Human Sciences: Systems of Inquiry*, State University of New York Press, Albany.

Poster, M. (1999), 'The Net as a Public Sphere,' in *Communication in History: Technology, Culture, Society*, Third edition, London: Longman.

Quine, Willard Van Orman (1970), *The Web of Belief*, Random House, NY.

Rappaport, A. (1968), 'Management information systems—another perspective,' *Management Science*, 15(4), December, pp. B133–136.

Rawls, J. (1971), *A Theory of Justice*, Harvard University Press, Cambridge, Mass.

Rheingold, H. (1993), *The Virtual Community, Homesteading on the Electronic Frontier*. Reading, Mass.: Addison-Wesley.

Robey, D. (1996), 'Diversity in Information Systems Research: Threat, Promise, and Responsibility,' *Information Systems Research*, 7(4), December, pp. 400–408.

Ross, J., Beath, C. and Goodhue, D. (1996), 'Develop Long-Term Competitiveness Through IT Assets,' *Sloan Management Review*, Fall, pp. 31–42.

Ross, J., Vitale, M. and Beath, C. (1999), 'The Untapped Potential of IT Chargeback,' *MIS Quarterly*, 23(2), June, pp. 215–237.

Sabherwal, R., Hirschheim, R. and Goles, T. (2001), 'The Dynamics of Alignment: A Punctuated Equilibrium Model,' *Organization Science*, 12(2), pp. 179–197.

Sackman, H. (1967), *Computers, System Science and Evolving Society*, Wiley Interscience, NY.

Sandberg, A. (1985), 'Socio-technical Design, Trade Union Strategies and Action Research,' in Mumford, E., Hirschheim, R., Fitzgerald, G., and Wood-Harper, A. T., (eds.), *Research Methods in Information Systems*, North-Holland, Amsterdam, pp. 79–92.

Scheuerman, W. (1999), 'Between radicalism and resignation: democratic theory in Habermas's *Between Facts and Norms*,' in Dews, P, (ed.), *Habermas: A Critical Reader*, Blackwell, Oxford, pp. 153–177.

Seely-Brown, J. and Duguid, P. (2000), *The Social Life of Information*, HBS Press, Boston, Mass.

Slevin, J. (2000), *The Internet and Society*. Cambridge: Polity Press.

Smithson, S. and Hirschheim, R. (1998), 'Analyzing Information Systems Evaluation: Another Look at an Old Problem,' *European Journal of Information Systems*, 7(3), September, pp. 158–174.

Swanson, E. and Ramiller, N. (1993), 'Information Systems Research Thematics: Submissions to a new journal, 1987–1992,' *Information Systems Research*, 4(4), December, pp. 299–330.

SWEBOK (2000), *Guide to the Software Engineering Body of Knowledge, A Stone Man Version* (Version 0.6), February (www.swebok.org).

Szajna, B. (1994), 'How Much is Information Systems Research Addressing Key Practitioner Concerns?' *Data Base*, May, pp. 49–59.

Tashakkori, A. and Teddlie, C. (1998), *Mixed Methodology: Combining Qualitative and Quantitative Approaches*, Sage Publishers, London.

USA Today (2003), 'USA's new money-saving export: White-collar jobs,' August 5, 2003.

Vitalari, N. P. (1985), 'Knowledge as a basis for expertise in systems analysis: An empirical study,' *MIS Quarterly*, 9(3), pp. 221–241.

Walsham, G. (1993), *Interpreting Information Systems in Organizations*, John Wiley & Sons, Chichester.

Walsham, G. (1997), 'Actor-network theory and IS research: Current status and future prospects,' in Lee, A., Liebenau, J. and DeGross, J. (eds.), *Information Systems and Qualitative Research*, Chapman & Hall, London, pp. 465–480.

Wand, Y. and Weber, R. (1990), 'Toward a Theory of the Deep Structure of Information Systems,' in DeGross, J., Alavi, M. and Oppelland, H. (eds.) *Proceedings of the Eleventh International Conference on Information Systems*, Copenhagen, pp. 61–71, December 16–18.

Ward, J. and Peppard, J. (1996), 'Reconciling the IT/Business Relationship: A troubled marriage in need of guidance,' *Journal of Strategic Information Systems*, 5(1), pp. 37–65.

Weber, R. (1987), 'Toward a Theory of Artifacts: A Paradigmatic Basis for Information Systems Research,' *Journal of Information Systems*, Vol. 2, Spring, pp. 3–19.

Westerman, G. and Ross, J. (2003), 'Utility Computing and the Future of IT Outsourcing,' *IBM Systems Journal*, forthcoming.

Wheeler, B. (2002), 'The Net-Enabled Business Innovation Cycle: A Dynamic Capabilities Theory for Assessing Net-enablement,' *Information Systems Research*, 13(2), June, pp. 125–146.

White, S. (1988), *The Recent Work of Jürgen Habermas: Reason, Justice and Modernity*. Cambridge: Cambridge University Press, Cambridge, U.K.

White, S. (1995), 'Reason, modernity, and democracy,' in White, S. (ed.), *The Cambridge Companion to Habermas*, Cambridge: Cambridge University Press, pp. 3–16.

Whitley, R. (1984a), *The Intellectual and Social Organization of the Sciences*. Oxford: Clarendon Press.

Whitley, R. (1984b), 'The Development of Management Studies as a Fragmented Adhocracy,' *Social Science Information*, 23(4/5), pp. 775–818.

Wilensky, H. (1967), *Organizational Intelligence: Knowledge and Policy in Government and Industry*, Basic Books, New York.

Willcocks, L., Feeny, D. and Islei, G. (1997) (eds.), *Managing IT as a Strategic Resource*, McGraw-Hill, NY.

Williamson, O. (1975), *Markets and Hierarchies: Analysis and Antitrust Implications*. New York: Free Press.

Young, S. (1968), 'Organization as a total system,' *California Management Review*, Vol. X, No. 3, Spring, pp. 21–32.

Zani, W. (1970), 'Blueprint for MIS,' *Harvard Business Review*, November–December, pp. 95–100.

Zmud, R. (1979), 'Individual Difference and MIS Success: A Review of the Empirical Literature,' *Management Science*, 25(10), pp. 966–979.

Zmud, R. (2000), *Framing the Domains of IT Management: Projecting the Future ... Through the Past*, Pinnaflex Educational Resources, Cincinnati, OH.

6
Change as Crisis or Growth? Toward a Trans-disciplinary View of Information Systems as a Field of Study:[1] A Response to Benbasat and Zmud's Call for Returning to the IT Artifact

Robert D. Galliers

Tempora mutantur, et nos mutamur in illis.[2]

INTRODUCTION

This paper is in response to Benbasat's and Zmud's recent *MIS Quarterly* article in which they express '...concern that the [Information Systems] research community is making the discipline's central identity ambiguous by, all too frequently, under-investigating phenomena intimately associated with IT-based systems and overestimating phenomena distantly associated with IT-based systems' (Benbasat & Zmud, 2003; 183; cited hereafter as Benbasat and Zmud).

The case made by Benbasat and Zmud is that we need to become more disciplinary to survive. I seriously contend this point of view, and deny that we are at a crossroads in the field. Information Systems (IS) has been an interdisciplinary field in the past, and my sense is that the field should become less disciplinary, and more trans-disciplinary as we continue our development into the future.

I build my argument by focusing on—and then questioning— several basic underpinnings in their argument:

- The implied definition of information systems as being solely IT-based ('IS scholars research and teach...topics associated with information technologies, IT infrastructures and IT-enabled business solutions (i.e., information systems)...' (ibid; 184).
- The implied locus of Information Systems [IS] study as being organization-based ('If influential stakeholders are unable to comprehend the...role being served by the IS discipline, these stakeholders are unlikely to acknowledge its legitimacy within the organizational field' (ibid; 185).
- The unquestioned assumption that IS as a field of study is indeed— or is most helpfully treated as—a discipline ('The Identity Crisis Within the IS Discipline' (ibid; 183).
- The lack of consideration given to the inter- and trans-national nature of IS as a field of study ('...the discipline's major journals, *MIS Quarterly* and *Information Systems Research*[3]' (ibid; 185).

I first consider the manner in which fields of study develop over time. Such developments can be seen as entirely natural and consistent with an evolving understanding of our field of study and the changing nature of the phenomena we investigate, or they can be seen as a cause of crisis. I then discuss the meaning of IS as a term, and alternative 'cores' to Benbasat's and Zmud's 'IT artifact.' Following this, I consider an appropriate locus of study for IS as having a less constricting boundary than that of the organization, including societal and cross-cultural considerations, before moving on to questioning the very notion of discipline as applied to IS.

BACKGROUND: CHANGE AS CRISIS OR GROWTH?

One can view change in a field of study as a crisis, as Benbasat and Zmud do, or as an opportunity for growth. The latter point of view is more in keeping with the rapid changes that we see in information and the technology that delivers it. Viewing change as a crisis, I feel, could result in the field being left behind.

Benbasat and Zmud advocate that IS should be a discipline with a 'core,' one that is well defined and constant. But given significant shifts in the underlying technologies studied by academics in the field, a fixation on an old-fashioned core could lead to stasis. Trans-disciplinary approaches, on the other hand, are more likely to allow the core to change and knowledge of the field to grow naturally.

Consider how fields of study develop. I draw your attention to a seminal quotation that appeared in the first issue of the journal *Organization* back in 1994:

> The events which took place in 1989, two centuries after the French Revolution, did more than merely terminate the bipolar balance of terror which had kept the peace for nearly half a century; they also brought to an end the older ideological equilibrium and the habit-encrusted formulation of issues which went with it. The concepts we use to describe the world now urgently need to be reformulated ... We are facing a new situation in which the old polarities of thought can no longer apply, or at the very least require scrutiny' (Gellner, 1993; 3) ... The Editors of *Organization* concur, yet would go further. Gellner's characterization of the contemporary intellectual and institutional context of social theory applies equally to the socio-historical situation confronting organization theory and analysis. Today older ideological equilibriums and ingrained intellectual habits are being destroyed by fundamental social, economic, political and cultural change. The old polarities of thought between 'agency' and 'structure,' 'informal' and 'formal,' 'power' and 'authority,' and so on, no longer seem to apply or, at the very least, are in need of critical scrutiny. (Burrell, *et al.*, 1994; 5)

The point is made eloquently in relation to both social theory and organization theory. As the phenomena we study change, so must the very foundations of our theoretical constructs. We can either embrace this change as a natural development in (our treatment of) our subject matter,[4] or we can view it as representing some kind of crisis that, presumably, must be resisted if our field—our 'discipline'—is to remain intact and unsullied.

There is a hidden 'early' Kuhnian aspect to Benbasat's and Zmud's argument, which I believe, needs to be surfaced. Central to Kuhn's early consideration of scientific communities—in *The Structure of Scientific Revolution* (Kuhn, 1961) for example—was the concept of paradigm. For Kuhn, scientific communities could be identified by what many (e.g., Banville & Landry, 1989) viewed as a monistic vision of science, requiring revolution for there to be any movement away from the 'core.' Those who believe in such a core:

> ...seem to use the term paradigm as meaning that members of a scientific discipline...always know precisely the relevant research topics...the appropriate research methods and the proper interpretation of results. Therefore, a paradigm should dually indicate problems and methods not belonging to a discipline (ibid; 49).

Thus we see Benbasat and Zmud identifying errors (their term) of exclusion and errors of inclusion. Their model of the IT artifact and its nomological net (Benbasat & Zmud, 2003; 187) defines for them 'the set of core properties of the IS discipline' (ibid.; 186). Thus, they are able to argue that 'the problems of exclusion and inclusion hamper efforts toward developing and reinforcing a central identity for the IS discipline' (ibid.; 192).

The underlying arguments of this critique are: (1) the apparent logical inconsistency in identifying IS as an inter-disciplinary field of study and a discipline in the same breath, and (2) the point that any field of study is bound to have to embrace change—even in its fundamental concepts and subject matter—if it is to survive and prosper. Indeed, we see Kuhn coming round to this way of thinking (i.e., from revolution to evolution) in his later work (e.g., Kuhn, 1977). To be grounded in unchanging 'core properties' is to unnecessarily bound the subject to a particular age and context—a form of Zeitgeist if you will.

Surely, few would argue that the field of IS has undergone considerable change over the past four decades or so. Even were we to agree with Benbasat's and Zmud's focus on information technology, the very nature of these artifacts has changed so considerably over such a relatively short space of time as to make them unrecognizable to the early developers of business information systems (e.g., Caminer, *et al.*, 1998). The consequence of this has been that the nature and focus of our subject matter has also changed – with consequent changes to the manner in which we view, and approach, our field. Is there much point to identifying a core if we continually need to change it? And what if our field embraces a wide diversity of interests, with the core becoming a battlefield rather than a field of dreams?

ON INFORMATION, SYSTEMS AND INFORMATION SYSTEMS[5]

It may be useful to consider definitions of the terms 'information' and 'information systems' so that we can understand the nature of information systems and the associated field of study. Even as far back as 1973, Ronald Stamper argued that:

> The explosive growth of information technology has not been accompanied by a commensurate improvement in the understanding of information. It is undoubtedly easier to manufacture and distribute electronic hardware than to refine our concepts of information... The application of information technology to organizations demands a wider knowledge than many of its specialists now display. It calls for an understanding of both machine and human information systems (Stamper, 1973; 1).

Building on this line of argument, Land and Kennedy-McGregor (1981) unpack the notion of information systems to include:

- The informal human system comprising the system of discourse and interaction between individuals and groups...characterised by cultural and political attitudes...
- The formal, human system comprising the system of rules and regulations, of departmental boundaries and defined roles...
- The formal computer system comprising those activities which are removed from [what was] originally [a] human system because they lend themselves to formalization and programming...
- The informal computer system epitomised by personal computing and the possibility of using the formal system and computer networks as means of holding unstructured information and passing informal messages...
- The external system, formal and informal. No organization exists in isolation and links between it and the external world must exist (ibid., in Galliers, 1987; 86).

Most importantly, they make the point that we as human beings rely on informal as well as formal sources of information. 'The effective use of information technology as a source of internal information has been handicapped by a number of problems. Two of the most important [are]...The lack of flexibility of computer based systems [in]...adapting to changing requirements [and]...The related problem of having to build systems which leave little scope for interaction with the host of less formal systems which are pervasive in...organizations' (ibid.; 82–83). In other words 'information systems are essentially social systems of which information technology is but one aspect' (Land, 1992; 6).

This line of reasoning is picked up by Checkland and associates (Checkland & Scholes, 1990; Checkland & Holwell, 1998) and Galliers (1987; 1993). The last defines information as:

> ...that collection of data, which, when presented in a particular manner and at an appropriate time, improves the knowledge of the person receiving it in such a way that he/she is better able to undertake a [required] activity or make a [required] decision. (Galliers, 1987; 4)

Thus, information is 'both enabling and contextual, while data are context-free and simply the raw material from which information (meaning) may be attributed' (Galliers, 1993; 203; see also Galliers & Newell, 2003).

> From these considerations...two consequences flow. Firstly, the boundary of an [information system]...will always have to include the attribution of meaning...[and] will consist of both data manipulation, which machines do, and the transformation of data into information, [which humans do]...Secondly, designing an [information system] will require explicit attention to the purposeful action which [it] serves...(Checkland & Scholes, 1990; 55)

Insisting on the IT artifact as IS's core seems also to neglect what many in the field would see as an alternative set of cores:

> The roots of Information [Systems] are to be found in a number of different fields. One is Information Theory (see e.g. Shannon and Weaver, 1949; and Langefors, 1966). Another root is Systems Theory (see e.g. Langefors, 1966; Churchman, 1968; and Checkland, 1981). A third root comes from parts of Change Theory...(see e.g. Lewin, 1947; Langefors, 1966; Lundeberg et al, 1981; and Schein, 1985). (Lundeberg, *et al.*, 1995; 196)

Thus, were the preceding arguments to be accepted, there is a clear danger in focusing attention solely on IT-based systems at the expense of a consideration of the essentially human activity of data interpretation and communication, and knowledge sharing and creation. This is not to say that researchers in IS should be silent on the idiosyncrasies of various information technologies (cf., Orlikowski & Iacono, 2001). Indeed, were we to do so, we might fall into the trap of black-boxing IT. But this is not to say that we should assume that IS are anything other than social systems, albeit with an increasingly technological component. We leave consideration of how distant is 'distant' to Benbasat and Zmud, but will consider the important issue of boundary selection in the section that follows.

AN APPROPRIATE LOCUS OF STUDY FOR INFORMATION SYSTEMS

Neither the boundaries nor the locus of study of a field should be confined to a preestablished set. I argue that boundaries, distance from an emergent core, and the locus of this emergent core come forward in a natural and non-predetermined way as a field evolves. Much of this line of reasoning emerges from a consideration of Benbasat's and Zmud's focus on core.

Implied in Benbasat's and Zmud's (2003; 186) set of core properties of the IS discipline is a focus on IT's impacts on 'humans...and contexts within which they are embedded, and associated collectives (groups, work units, organizations).' We could first find a point of contention with the notion of IT and its impacts, given that IT arti-facts are themselves—or at least can be construed as – social constructions (Bijker, *et al.*, 1987).[6] Leaving this aside, however, I believe there are dangers in drawing our boundary too closely to organizational entities and making this the locus of all of our study. It goes without saying that, with the advent of EDI systems and the emergence of the Internet, inter-organizational systems have been an important aspect of the IS research agenda for many years (e.g., Cash, 1985). But there are clearly wider and deeply ethical issues that demand our attention. For example, in relation to societal issues associated with IT, there is a considerable research agenda confronting us with respect to the so-called 'digital divide' (NTIA, 1999; DTI, 2000). Indeed, more broadly speaking, there is an emerging agenda associated with IT and globalization (e.g., Castells, 2001; Walsham, 2001) and IT in the developing world (e.g., Avgerou, 2002) and the associated issues of culture and diversity (Beardon & Whitehouse, 1993).

Thus, I believe it is reasonable to argue that an appropriate locus of IS study is more broadly based than organizations or individuals. Societal, policy and ethical issues might reasonably be included within the ambit of the IS field. Indeed, returning to notions of system, the whole question of boundary drawing is a complex one and itself a social construction. The definition given by Checkland (1981, 1999; 312) demonstrates the latter point: '...a boundary is a distinction made by an observer which marks the difference between an entity he takes to be a system and its environment'. To know where to draw one's boundary in any problem context is an art form in and of itself. During the thirty years of developing and applying soft systems methodology in action projects, Checkland (1999) notes that the environment of any chosen system of activity can usefully be seen as the 'elements outside the system which it takes as given' (Checkland & Scholes, 1990; 35).

In other words, these are constraints on the system that has been chosen, and defined, for further analysis. Experience has shown that in dealing with complex real-world organizational problems, the choice of boundary is often key, and that a conservative choice may well not lead to insightful conclusions.[7] Indeed, in order to understand what actually are constraints on the system under consideration, those aspects over which there is little or no control, or those aspects that we choose to hold constant, an iterative process of boundary re-positioning is often useful. If we do not push the boundaries, then we may well be overly constraining ourselves and we will certainly not know whether a relevant choice has been made. Indeed there may be a number of different boundaries to consider:

> The problem situation...is itself located in a number of environments, some of which are concrete, and some others of which are abstract; all are important in the analysis as a source of influences, possibilities, and constraints. The first point to note is that an environment is somehow 'outside' the problem situation; that is to say, it is outside both the problem-content and problem-solving systems...If we can define a system's boundaries (and there may be a number of different kinds), then we have said something important about the system's environments. (Checkland, 1985; 159)

To relate this line of reasoning to the definition of one's field of study we, as an academy, can choose to draw and redraw our boundaries as we see fit. Indeed, given the breadth of subject matter and interest, our academy may choose to embrace a number of different boundaries simultaneously. 'Variety's the very spice of life.'[8] While Benbasat and Zmud (2003; 184) are not concerned 'whether such diversity of topics is beneficial,' they nonetheless wish to draw us back to '...investigating phenomena intimately associated with IT-based systems.' Thus, 'errors of inclusion' (ibid.; 190–192) might presumably have been committed by the editors of the *Journal of Strategic Information Systems* in commissioning special issues of the journal on 'Knowledge Management' and 'Trust in the Digital Economy,'[9] but this editor, for one, would wish to disagree.

SHOULD IS BE DISCIPLINED?

In this section, I wish to question the notion that IS is, or should be treated as, a discipline[10]—a question posed by Claude Banville and Maurice Landry some 14 years ago (Banville & Landry, 1989). Benbasat and Zmud clearly think so, and they clearly think that the fields of marketing, operations management and organization behavior are disciplines also—and are 'more entrenched scholarly disciplines' (Benbasat & Zmud, 2003; 189) to boot.

I want first to determine whether colleagues in these fields of study see this to be the case, and then will return to the question of boundary, and more specifically, boundary spanning.

If one reads the introduction of any textbook on the subject of marketing, operations management or organizational behavior, one might easily challenge the notion of the scholarly discipline label being easily applied to these fields of study. For example: '...marketing is the philosophy of management that recognises that the success of the enterprise is only sustainable if it can organise to meet the current and prospective needs of customers more effectively than the competition.' (Doyle, 1994; xiii) 'Operations management is about the way organizations produce goods and services... [it] is, above all else, a practical subject... (Slack, *et al.*, 1995; 4–5). Alternatively, 'operations management may be defined as the management of the direct resources that are required to produce and deliver an organization's goods and services.' (Davis, *et al.*, 2003; 4). It can be defined narrowly, or broadly, to exclude the activities of any of the other functional areas of management, or to 'include all activities which [have] any connection with the production of goods and services – in practice every activity with the exception of core marketing/selling and accounting/finance activities.' (Slack, *et al.*, 1995; 9) And when it comes to the field of organization behavior, '...the related theory and scientific study are extremely broad-based. It is an eclectic theory...comprised of...parts of sociology, psychology, anthropology, economics, political science, philosophy, and mathematics' (Kast & Rosenzweig, 1974; 9).

One could go further and point to new directions and critical reflections in such fields as accounting (e.g., Hopwood & Miller, 1994; Johnson & Kaplan, 1987), and economics and finance (e.g., Kahneman, 1994), where we see the influence of historical analyses, social psychology, and critical theory each playing an important role. If it is true that anything making 'ambiguous the boundaries of IS scholarship, thus rais[es] questions regarding its distinctiveness—and hence its legitimacy—with respect to related scholarly disciplines'

(Benbasat & Zmud, 2003; 189), then it is clear that IS in not alone in this regard.

Indeed, one could argue to the contrary: any field that is able critically to reflect on itself and range widely over related subject matter actually enhances its legitimacy. Such boundary spanning (Tushman & Scanlan, 1981) activity can lead to new thinking and innovation. If members of the IS academy not only publish in other disciplines' (sic.) leading journals such as *Organization* (e.g., Galliers, *et al.*, 1997), *British Journal of Management* (e.g., Newell, *et al.*, 2001) and *Decision Sciences* (e.g., Tukana & Weber, 1996), but are also members of their editorial boards,[11] it would seem reasonable to argue that IS academics are (rightly) held in high regard by their colleagues from other fields. And does it really matter where we—or they—publish the results of our research efforts?

THE TRANS-DISCIPLINARY NATURE OF INFORMATION SYSTEMS

Having demonstrated that IS is not alone with its 'ambiguous boundaries' and claiming the benefits of boundary spanning, I'd like to consider the benefits of a trans-disciplinary approach to the study of IS. First, I want to take note of the warnings about the more mechanist approaches to multi-disciplinary research in management fields, where there is little in the way of knowledge sharing and communication (Knights & Wilmott, 1997). There is a cogent argument (Gibbons, *et al.*, 1995) for investigating the spaces between traditional disciplines since this is where emerging issues and new learning are likely to occur. This is also more likely to lead to innovative solutions (Von Krogh, *et al.*, 2000).

As IS researchers, we have often accepted unquestioningly the assertion that IS has its 'reference disciplines,' often quoting Keen (1980) to make the point. Others (e.g., Davis & Olson, 1984; Culnan & Swanson, 1986) propose that the field of IS emerges from, or is at the intersection of, inter alia, computer science, behavioral science, decision science, organization theory, management, operations research, and accounting.

But are these reference disciplines actually disciplines themselves?[12] As I pointed out in the previous section, this assumption can very well be called into question.[13] Like IS, they may just as easily be viewed as applied fields of study. And, after all, a crucial point made by Keen is that an important goal of IS research is 'to improve practice through research' (Keen, 1987; 3). Thus, he emphasizes the need to improve the effectiveness of IS applications. Further, and while calling for a cumulative tradition in IS research, Keen makes the point that the field, by its very nature, is evolving. He also sets out not to define a single view of IS research: 'Our backgrounds, training and interests are very different. We must make that as a strength not a cause of argument.' (ibid.)

I agree with Keen. There is strength in diversity; new lessons and approaches and innovative solutions are more likely to emerge from taking a variety of perspectives on the phenomena we study. Being aware of these alternative perspectives, and applying a 'logic of opposition' (Robey & Boudreau, 1999), in an holistic, inclusive manner are more likely to lead to effectiveness than narrowly focused approaches. Information systems are complex phenomena that pervade a great deal of human existence in many (unseen) ways. Taking a lesson from Ashby's Law of Requisite Variety (Ashby, 1956), we must surely treat such complexity with all the requisite tools necessary, otherwise we will form only partial views. Narrowly focused, reductionist (cf., Descartes, 1968) thinking that assumes that the whole is no greater than the sum of the parts, that individual components of a complex entity will interact one with another in exactly the same way when certain of those components are taken out of the equation, that systems do not exhibit emergent properties – such thinking is unlikely to lead to the kind of insights that would emerge from a more systemic approach. This is the key to my argument. By attempting to define the core of IS, Benbasat & Zmud may be giving certain properties the value of zero – the one value that it is likely they do not have. By attempting to define this core, they confine our field of study to but one view of its current state, thereby denying its future development, and alternative perspectives. By attempting to predetermine the core, they run the risk of denying the emergent agendas that will arise as the field develops and the phenomena under investigation—and our understanding of them—develop. By focusing on the IT artifact, they deny the existence and relevance of other forms of information system. By seeking to define the boundaries of a pure IS discipline an unintended 'contradictory consequence' (cf. Robey & Boudreau, 1999) may be to relegate the field to a perceived state of irrelevance and isolation from the very disciplines from which it draws strength.

The trans-disciplinary nature of the phenomena we study dictates the need for trans-disciplinary scholars and approaches—boundary spanners (Tushman & Scanlan, 1981)—who are not wedded to a single perspective or line of reasoning. There is strength in diversity and pluralism, not weakness. The field of Information Systems will only be in crisis if we do not allow ourselves to develop and explore shared phenomena of interest with our colleagues from other (sometimes cognate) applied fields of study.

SOME IMPLICATIONS FOR THE IS ACADEMY

It is for the IS academy itself to weigh the arguments posed by our colleagues Benbasat and Zmud against those introduced in this paper. Let me, however, close by offering a brief outline of the main arguments for a trans-disciplinary, rather than a disciplinary, approach to our field, and suggest some implications, for us as an academy, of this line of argument. My argument is, of course, a social construction (cf., Berger & Luckman, 1966: Benson, 1977; Bijker, *et al.*, 1987). Table 6.1 attempts to summarize the polar opposites about our subject highlighted by the Benbasat and Zmud contribution and the current paper. By characterizing these two schools of thought in this way, I bring the different perspectives into stark relief. It is for the academy to choose in which direction it wishes to move.

I conclude with a call for acceptance and pluralism. My argument is similar to that of Benson (1977) in his treatment of organizations. If we were to replace 'organization' with 'the field of IS' we could paraphrase his argument as follows: 'Established perspectives fail to deal with the production of [IS knowledge] or to analyze the entanglement of theories in [that field]. ... [The field of IS] is seen as a concrete, multileveled phenomenon beset by contradictions, which continuously undermine its existing features' (ibid; 1). If we are to accept this as a starting point for our journey, it follows that we should both welcome and cherish new approaches to the study of our field, its emergent characteristics, and the disparate perspectives on its very locus of concern. IS as a field is, indeed, multi-leveled and multi-faceted. Overly constraining the IS academy to a narrow field of interest is self-defeating. Closed systems exhibit entropy; open systems do not.

Table 6.1 Characterizing disciplinary and trans-disciplinary perspectives on the field of IS

	Disciplinarity	Trans-disciplinarity
Boundary	Organization	Society
Central Artifact	IT	People/Information
Focus	Inward	Outward
Scope	Narrow	Broad
Reference disciplines	OB, Computer Science, etc	IS
Properties	Defined	Emergent
Inter-disciplinary	A threat	An opportunity

ACKNOWLEDGEMENTS

The author is grateful for the insightful comments of Sirkka Jarvenpaa, Detmar Straub, and the anonymous reviewers on earlier versions of this paper. Their contributions have added much to the central argument of this paper. Alas, however, it is I alone who should take full responsibility for the content.

NOTES

1 Detmar Straub was the accepting senior editor for this paper.
2 'Times change, and we change with them.' [Quoted in Harrison (1577), *Description of Britain*, Pt. III, Ch. iii.]
3 The selection of these two journals is based on the fact that they 'are included in the list of administrative sciences journals used by the *Financial Times* and *Business Week* to rank [NorthAmerican] business schools' (Benbasat & Zmud, 2003; 185).
4 See Somogyi & Galliers (1987) and Hirschheim (1985) for historical accounts of developments in business IT, and IS epistemology respectively.
5 The heading of this section is taken from Checkland & Holwell (1998).
6 See also, Bloomfield, *et al.*, 1997 and Scarbrough & Corbett, 1992.
7 A conservative choice may be to define the system such that its boundary is entirely consistent with the organization's existing (legal) boundary. A more insightful choice may be to draw the boundary to include external stakeholders or, conversely, focus attention on a particular aspect of the organization that requires attention. See, for example, Checkland & Scholes (1990; 31–36).
8 The quote is from William Cowper's (1731–1800) *The Task*, Book II; 606.
9 *Journal of Strategic Information Systems* volume 9 (2–3), September 2000 and volume 11 (3–4), December 2002 respectively.
10 dis·ci·pline (http://www.yourdictionary.com)
(dĭs'ə-plĭn) *n.* 1. Training expected to produce a specific character or pattern of behavior, especially training that produces moral or mental improvement. 2. Controlled behavior resulting from disciplinary training; self-control. 3. Control obtained by enforcing compliance or order. 4. A systematic method to obtain obedience: a military discipline. 5. A state of order based on submission to rules and authority: a teacher who demanded discipline in the classroom. 6. Punishment intended to correct or train. 7. A set of rules or methods, as those regulating the practice of a church or monastic order. 8. A branch of knowledge or teaching.
11 For example, Wanda Orlikowski (*Organization Science*), Izak Benbasat (*The Accounting Review*), Bob Zmud (*Academy of Management Review*) and Claudio Ciborra (*Human Relations*) to name just four.
12 Indeed, there are those in the Organizational Behavior (OB) field who are now calling for OB to be viewed as a 'neo-discipline' (Burrell, *et al.*, 2003).
13 Nambisan (2003) and Baskerville and Myers (2002) argue, in fact, that IS has become a reference discipline for other fields, so if one believes in the concept of a reference discipline, an argument can be made that boundary spanning is now taking place and even originating from other so-called 'disciplines.' In short, most disciplines lean toward a trans-disciplinary view of the world, and their topics of study and citation profile convincingly demonstrates this.

REFERENCES

Ashby, W R (1956) *An Introduction to Cybernetics*, London: Chapman & Hall.

Avgerou, C (2002) *Information Systems and Global Diversity*, Oxford: Oxford University Press.

Banville, C & Landry, M (1989) Can the field of MIS be disciplined? *Communications of the ACM*, 32(1), January, 48–60. Reproduced in Galliers (ed.) (1992), 61–88, op cit.

Baskerville, Richard and Michael Myers (2002) 'Information Systems as a Reference Discipline, *MIS Quarterly*, 26(1), March , 1–14.

Beardon, C & Whitehouse, D (eds.) (1993) *Computers and Society*, Oxford: Intellect Books.

Benbasat, I & Zmud, R W (2003) The identity crisis within the IS discipline: defining and communicating the discipline's core properties, *MIS Quarterly*, 27(2), June, 183–194.

Benson, J K (1977) Organizations – a dialectical view, *Administrative Science Quarterly*, 22(1), March, 1–21.

Berger, P & Luckman, T (1966) *The Social Construction of Reality: A treatise in the sociology of knowledge*, New York: Anchor Books.

Bijker, W, Hughes, T & Pinch, T (1987) *The Social Construction of Technological Systems*, Cambridge, MA: MIT Press.

Bloomfield, B P, Coombs, R, Knights, D & Littler, D (eds.) (1997) *Information Technology and Organizations: Strategies, Networks, and Integration*, Oxford: Oxford University Press.

Burrell, G, Reed, M, Alvesson, M, Calás, M & Smircich, L (1994) Why Organization? Why now? *Organization*, 1(1), July, 5–17.

Burrell, G, Calás, M, Reed, M, & Smircich, L (2003) Why neo-disciplinary? Why now? *Organization*, 10(3), August, 403–420.

Caminer, D, Aris, J, Hermon, P & Land, F (1998) *LEO: The Incredible Story of the World's First Business Computer*, New York: McGraw-Hill.

Cash, Jr., J I (1985) Interorganizational systems: an information society opportunity or threat? *The Information Society*, 3(3). Reproduced in E K Somogyi & R D Galliers (eds.) (1987), *Towards Strategic Information Systems*, Tunbridge Wells: Abacus Press, 200–220.

Castells, M (2001) *The Internet Galaxy: Reflections on the Internet, Business, and Society*, Oxford: Oxford University Press.

Checkland, P (1981,1999) *Systems Thinking, Systems Practice*, Chichester: Wiley.

Checkland, P B (1985) Formulating Problems for Systems Analysis. In H J Miser & E S Quade (eds.) *Handbook of Systems Analysis: Overview of Uses, Procedures, Applications, and Practice*, Chichester: Wiley, 151–170.

Checkland, P & Holwell, S (1998) *Information, Systems and Information Systems: Making Sense of the Field*, Chichester: Wiley.

Checkland, P & Scholes, J (1990) *Soft Systems Methodology in Action*, Chichester: Wiley.

Churchman, C W (1968) *The Systems Approach*, New York: Dell.

Culnan, M J & Swanson, E B (1986) Research in management information systems, 1980–1984: points of work and reference, *MIS Quarterly*, 10(3), September, 288–302.

Davis, G B & Olson, M H (1984) *Management Information Systems: Conceptual Foundations, Structure, and Development*, 2nd edition, New York: McGraw-Hill.

Davis, M M, Aquilano, N J & Chase, R B (2003) *Fundamentals of Operations Management*, 4th edition, Boston: McGraw-Hill Irwin.

Descartes, R (1968) *Discourse on Method; Meditations* (translated by F E Sutcliffe), London: Penguin Classics.

Doyle, P (1994) *Marketing Management and Strategy*, New York: Prentice Hall.

DTI (2000) *Closing the Digital Divide: Information and Communication Technologies in Deprived Areas*, London: HMSO.

Galliers, R D (ed.) (1987) *Information Analysis: Selected Readings*, Sydney: Addison-Wesley.

Galliers, R D (ed.) (1992) *Information Systems Research: Issues, Methods and Practical Guidelines*, Oxford: Blackwell Scientific.

Galliers, R D (1993) Towards a flexible information architecture: integrating business strategies, information strategies and business process redesign, *Journal of Information Systems* (now, *Information Systems Journal*), 3(3), July, 199–213.

Galliers, R D, Jackson, M C & Mingers, J (1997) Organization Theory and Systems Thinking: The benefits of partnership, *Organization*, 4(2), May, 269–278.

Galliers, R D & Leidner, D E (eds.) (2003) *Strategic Information Management: Challenges and Strategies in Managing Information Systems*, Oxford: Butterworth-Heinemann.

Galliers, R D & Newell, S (2003) Back to the future: from knowledge management to the management of information and data, *Information Systems and e-Business Management*, 1(1), January, 5–13.

Gellner, E (1993) What do we need now? Social Anthropology and its new global context, *The Times Literary Supplement*, 16, July, 3–4.

Gibbons, M, Limoges, C, Nowotny, H, Schwartzman, S, Scott, P & Trow, M (1995) *The New Production of Knowledge: The Dynamics of Science and Research in Contemporary Societies*, London: Sage.

Hirschheim, R A (1985) Information Systems epistemology: an historical perspective. In E Mumford, *et al.* (eds.) (1985), 13–36, *op cit*. Reproduced in R D Galliers (ed.) (1992), 28–60, *op cit*.

Hopwood, A G & Miller, P (eds.) (1994) *Accounting as Social and Institutional Practice*, Cambridge: Cambridge University Press.

Johnson, H T & Kaplan, R S (1987) *Relevance Lost: The Rise and Fall of Management Accounting*, Boston: Harvard Business School Press.

Kahneman, D (1994) New challenges to the rationality assumption, *Journal of Institutional and Theoretical Economics*, 150(1), 18–36.

Kast, F E & Rosenzweig, J E (1974) *Organization and Management: A Systems Approach*, 2nd international student edition, Tokyo: McGraw-Hill Kogakusha Ltd.

Keen, P G W (1980) MIS research: reference disciplines and a cumulative tradition, Proceedings: 1st International Conference on Information Systems, Philadelphia, 918.

Keen, P G W (1987) MIS Research: current status, trends and needs. In R A Buckingham, R A Hirschheim, F F Land & C J Tully (eds.), *Information Systems Education: Recommendations and Implementation*, British Computer Society Monographs in Informatics, Cambridge: Cambridge University Press, 1–13.

Knights, D & Wilmott, H (1997) The hype and hope of interdisciplinary management studies, *British Journal of Management*, 8, 9–22.

Kuhn, T S (1961) *The Structure of Scientific Revolution*, Chicago: University of Chicago Press.

Kuhn, T S (1977) *The Essential Tension*, Chicago: University of Chicago Press.

Land, F (1992) The Information Systems Domain. In R D Galliers (ed.) (1992), op cit., 613.

Land, F F & Kennedy-McGregor, M (1981) Information and Information Systems: Concepts and Perspectives. In R D Galliers (ed.), (1987), op cit., 63–91.

Langefors, B (1966) Theoretical Analysis of Information Systems, Lund, Sweden: Studentlitteratur.

Lewin, K (1947) Group decision and social change, in T N Newcomb and E L Hartley (eds.), *Readings in Social Psychology*, Troy, Missouri: Holt, Rinehart & Winston.

Lundeberg, M, Goldkuhl, G & Nilsson, A (1981) *Information Systems Development: A Systems Approach*, Englewood Cliffs, NJ: Prentice-Hall.

Lundeberg, M, Mårtensson, Sannes, R & Sundgren, B (1995) Information Management as a field, in B Dahlbom (ed.), *The Infological Equation: Essays in Honor of Börje Langefors*, Gothenburg Studies in Information Systems, Report 6, March, Department of Informatics, Göteborg University, Sweden, 195–209.

Nambisan, S (2003) 'Information Systems as Reference Discipline for New Product Development,' *MIS Quarterly*, 27(1), March, 1–18.

Newell, S, Swan, J & Scarbrough, H. (2001) From global knowledge management to internal electronic fences: Contradictory outcomes of intranet development, *British Journal of Management*, 12(2), 97–112.

NTIA (199) Falling Through the Net. Defining the Digital Divide: A Report on the Telecommunications and Information Technology Gap in America, Washington, DC: US Department of Commerce.

Orlikowski, W & Iacono, S (2001) Desperately seeking the 'IT' in IT research – a call to theorizing the IT artifact, *Information Systems Research*, 12(2), June, 121–134.

Robey, D & Boudreau, M C (1999) Accounting for the contradictory organizational consequences of information technology: theoretical directions and methodological implications, *Information Systems Research*, 10(2), June, 167–185.

Scarbrough, H & Corbett, J M (1992) *Technology and Organization: Power, Meaning and Design*, London: Routledge.

Schein, E H (1985) *Organizational Culture and Leadership*, San Francisco: Jossey-Bass.

Slack, N, Chambers, S, Harland, C, Harrison, A & Johnston, R (1995) *Operations Management*, London: Pitman.

Somogyi, E K & Galliers, R D (1987) Applied Information Technology: from data processing to strategic information systems, Journal of Information Technology, 2(1), March, 30–41. Reproduced with a Postscript by R D Galliers & B S H Baker in R D Galliers & D E Leidner (eds.) (2003), op cit., 3–26.

Shannon, C E & Weaver, W (1949) *The Mathematical Theory of Communication*, Chicago: University of Chicago Press.

Stamper, R (1973) *Information in Business and Administrative Systems*, London: Batsford.

Tukana, S & Weber, R (1996) An empirical test of the strategic-grid model of information systems planning, *Decision Sciences*, 27(4), 735–764.

Tushman, M & Scanlan, T (1981) Boundary spanning individuals: their role in information transfer and their antecedents, *Academy of Management Journal*, 24(2), 289–305.

Von Krogh, G, Ichijo, K & Nonaka, I (2000) *Enabling Knowledge Creation. How to Unlock the Mystery of Tacit Knowledge and Release the Power of Innovation*, Oxford: Oxford University Press.

Walsham, G (2001) *Making a World of Difference: IT in a Global Context*, Chichester: Wiley.

7

The Social Life of Information Systems Research[1]: A Response to Benbasat and Zmud's Call for Returning to the IT Artifact

Gerardine DeSanctis

Since its inception in the 1970s, the field of Information Systems (IS) has devoted significant effort to defining its domain, establishing its legitimacy, reflecting and critiquing its contributions, and tracking its progress as an academic discipline. Benbasat and Zmud's (2003) recent reflection and call for greater focus on the information technology (IT) artifact is within this genre. They laud the progress of the IS field in developing sociopolitical legitimacy through its journals, degree programs, and academic departments; but they lament the dilution of attention to the IT artifact itself and point to the corresponding poor progress in establishing the cognitive legitimacy of the field—especially in the minds of outsiders (i.e., non members).

No doubt the IS field lacks the legitimacy of disciplines more routinely found in business schools (such as marketing, accounting, and finance), engineering (e.g., electrical engineering) or the liberal arts and sciences (e.g., math and computer science). But such a situation is far from unique. Fields such as operations, decision science, strategy, and management science have murky identities as well, with wide-ranging topics of study, variant types of members, and mixed representation within universities.

Regardless, the issue at hand is legitimacy, and the question is how to sustain the IS discipline in the face of threats to such legitimacy. As a contribution to the debate, I offer three observations in this essay. First, that the legitimacy of the IS field is impressively high if it is viewed as a community of practice rather than as a formal organization; second, that shifting boundaries in the field may be associated with its maturing and the inclusion of a new generation of members and leaders; and third, that two related trends are jointly drawing the field away from the study of IT as artifact. These are technological transformation within industry and institutional changes within universities. Rather than resist the drift away from IT as artifact, I suggest that we move to embrace it.

Research is an enacted process within a community of practice, so leaders and pundits have limited influence. Research practices matter much more than dictates or directives. Nonetheless, this essay concludes with recommendations for improving the sustainability of the discipline, some of which are consistent with Benbasat and Zmud's recommendations and some of which are opposing.

THE IS COMMUNITY OF PRACTICE

Viewed as action more than as domain, research is the process of systematic inquiry, and coherence among researchers emerges as they interact with one another in the ongoing process of inquiry (Aldrich, 1999, p. 142). To understand the state or progress of a discipline, therefore, is to understand the social dynamics of the research community (Price, 1986). The measure of a discipline lies less in its outputs or artifacts than in the interactions of scholars. Scientific papers or other outputs (such as technology designs) are interesting insofar as they are reflective of these interactions (Sandstrom, 2001). The research process is inherently social—the joint processes by which scientists undertake their work. The active and changing nature of the scientific community, its membership and activities, represent its life. Communication is in the form of the discourse that takes place in journals and at conferences, and is reflective of the progress of the discipline, but it is not the whole story. An understanding of the discipline comes from a broad examination of its social life—of the characteristics of the scholarly community and of the communications among scholars over time.

Several approaches to understanding the social life of IS research are possible. For example, social network analysis could be used to map communication relationships among scholars, (e.g., Chin, Myers, & Hoyt, 2002); or citation analysis might be used to study the development of collaborations within the discipline (e.g., Price, 1986). For the purposes of this essay, I take another approach, which is to apply a community of practice perspective. I identify the major attributes of a community of practice and then comment on whether these exist within the field of IS. The community of practice perspective is consistent with recent advances in the knowledge-processing view of the firm; it emphasizes social interaction as the process through which knowledge is exchanged and created in an enterprise (Spender, 1996; Leonard, 1995; Nonaka & Takeuchi, 1995). Further, it allows us to examine the organizational attributes of the IS community and to consider how these have changed in the 30 years since the field's founding.

A community of practice view regards 'the discipline' to be more akin to a voluntary association (Knoke & Prensky, 1984) than a formal organization. As such, traditional organization theory tends to be less applicable in the evaluation of the field's progress than concepts drawn from the theories of community. Unlike more formal organizations, voluntary associations typically do not have economic interests per se; instead they promote the concerns of their members. Their boundaries are often fuzzy and porous and include 'episodic supporters and passively interested constituents' (Aldrich, 1971, pp. 3–4). The primary resources of a voluntary association are its members and the knowledge (especially the procedural knowledge) that they share (Argote, 1999; Kogut & Zander, 1996). The development of a community of practice occurs through the mutual engagement of members, the negotiation of a joint enterprise, and the creation of a shared repertoire (Wenger, 1998), resulting in an emergent, patterned form of social interaction among the participants (Wittgenstein, 1958).

Communities of practice are extremely difficult to develop and maintain precisely because they do not control formal authority, institutional boundaries, and other mechanisms of influence. Most important, they do not manage worker incentives and rewards; their influence is indirect, if at all. Within academe, where skilled researchers have the opportunity to join in and migrate to multiple communities, developing a new community from scratch is no easy feat. The fact that academic researchers have moved to establish a thriving community of practice around IS-related questions is impressive. Success in building this or other communities of practice lies more in efforts to build social identity among participants than in developing the cognitive legitimacy afforded by outsiders (see Wenger, 1998). It follows that—and here is where my argument differs with Benbasat and Zmud—maintaining the success of the community will require greater focus on internal matters than on external legitimacy. This is because, for a community of practice, formal organizational structure is more likely to result from participants' actions than be dictated by it. These arguments are further developed in the following sections.

EVIDENCE OF LEGITIMACY

Evidence of legitimacy of the IS field lies not so much in the establishment of organizations such as the Association for Information Systems (AIS), schools of information science, and university departments; instead, the evidence of legitimacy lies in the actions of people within and between these organizations as they pursue their scholarly work. Benbasat and Zmud (2003) acknowledge this point when they say that formal organizations can aid in sociopolitical legitimacy but not other forms of legitimacy. But whereas Benbasat and Zmud point to the need for cognitive legitimacy in the IS field, here I take a look at behavioral legitimacy and find the picture to be not so bleak. Whereas cognitive legitimacy is rooted in the mindset of outsiders, behavioral legitimacy is rooted in the actions of insiders (and those who choose to move from outside to inside).

Behavioral legitimacy refers to the following kinds of social interactions. These (and other) properties have been articulated by Wittgenstein (1958), Brown and Duguid (1991), Wenger (1998) and others (Brown & Duguid, 2001; Lave & Wenger, 1991; Scott, 1995) who have combined concepts of community with concepts of learning and knowledge exchange to describe the evolution of communities of practice.

- Frequent interaction among members. Frequent interaction increases opportunities for knowledge exchange and development of shared mental models. Interaction helps the community to build coherence and common practices.
- Routines of interaction. Communities of practice develop patterns, or rhythms of knowledge exchange, that facilitate effective participation in the community by the participants (Pentland, 1992). Routines also facilitate successful entry into the community by newcomers as they engage in meaningful interaction with others by joining in ongoing routines.
- Evolution of a core group. Communities of practice tend to be inclusive and their members active. This is not to say that there is

no turnover, but turnover is secondary to community growth. Over time, a core group emerges—i.e., the critical mass of active members who sustain the network (Wasko & Faraj, 2003).

- Ability to absorb newcomers. Communities of practice are not insular. They selectively absorb some (though not all) newcomers. In this way the community is able to import external information and practices (Lave & Wenger, 1991). Newcomers may operate in concert with existing routines; but they also retain some uniqueness in their interactions such that they are able to influence others. So, despite established routines of interaction, the community tolerates a range of interaction patterns and avoids becoming unitary.
- Boundary formation. Over time, communities of practice form boundaries that distinguish them from other communities and their surrounding context (Aldrich, 1999). These boundaries are porous such that the community of practice is separate from other communities yet operates with connection to them. Boundary formation is evident in networking behavior; there are higher levels of interaction within the community group than between insiders and outsiders. At the same time 'visits' (interactions) between the community and outsiders assures that external information is imported into the community and helps to prevent insularity.

If we cast these criteria against the behavior of IS scholars, evidence of the field's legitimacy is plentiful. Frequent interaction is evidenced in participation in conferences, list-serves, special interest groups (SIGs), and forums by researchers who identify with the IS field. In addition, small collections of scholars create informal gatherings for sharing of research findings.[2] It is notable that AIS recently has increased the number of conferences for participants through the creation of the worldwide CIS series of meetings (AMCIS, PACIS, ECIS, etc.). These forums provide extensive opportunity for newcomers to join the IS social network and influence its development. Most important, the forums provide opportunity for many types of members to become involved in the IS community and shape its evolution.

Newcomer absorption and retention within IS are likewise impressively high. Consider the fact that in 1980 there were only 35 researchers contributing to the program of the International Conference on Information Systems (ICIS), presenting a total of 25 papers. In 2002 the ICIS program included 205 researchers presenting a total of 93 papers.[3] This represents a 486% increase in conference participation. Further, ICIS attendance has been steady or growing over the past decade, making the gathering a going concern, so to speak, within the discipline. There are also much newer CIS conference venues. Other indicators of successful newcomer entrance into IS abound. For example, the IS World Faculty Directory lists a total of 6,736 researchers, reflecting a growth of more than 60% from 3–4 years earlier.[4] Overall, the field has grown at a rate far above the more typical doubling-per-decade rate of growth observed by Price (1986) for many scientific disciplines.

Newcomers are not only participating in the field, they are active in shaping its future. There is evidence that the core group of the community is expanding to accommodate its growing size. A review of the mastheads of leading journals such as *MIS Quarterly* and *Information Systems Research* shows that the new Ph.D.s and budding researchers of a decade ago are now serving as editorial board members, associate editors, and the like. More importantly, the breadth of schools and disciplinary backgrounds of people on the boards of the major journals has grown over time. Consider the following. At the time of its founding (1977), the *MIS Quarterly* review board consisted of 10 people. By 1990 both *MIS Quarterly* and *Information Systems Research* had 24 people on their review boards. In 2002 the numbers had more than doubled again; *MIS Quarterly* listed 41 review board members and *Information Systems Research* listed 58.[5] With very little exception, board members are from widely divergent schools. They are globally located, from universities of various levels of size and academic prestige, and positioned in various departments in their host institutions. (Most are located in information systems departments, but some are in computer science and others in communications, strategy, organiza-tion studies, and a variety of other disciplinary areas.) In sum, the IS community has demonstrated great success in attracting newcomers, retaining their participation, and providing opportunity for them to join core groups of influence. The discipline is impressively comprehensive and inclusive in its membership participation patterns. Dominant board participation by scholars within the discipline suggests boundary formation, but inclusion of scholars from other, related fields suggests porous boundaries associated with a viable community of practice.

Routines of interaction are subtler and so are more difficult to observe. They are found, for example, in repeat visits to conferences, ongoing conversations among members, and development of joint, repeated research projects among members with otherwise variant organizational ties. All of these kinds of behaviors are found within the IS research community and, one could argue, have grown over time as the field has matured. ICIS and the CIS-series of meetings, for example, attract a regular set of attendees. Further, these have spawned other venues for interaction, such as the Diffusion Interest Group in Information Technology (DIGIT), the Information Systems and Economics group (WISE), the Information Technology and Systems group (WITS), and the Cross-cultural Research Meeting in Information

Systems (CCRIS).[6] Members converse with one another in formal and informal venues and, over time, many of these gatherings become institutionalized while still others blossom as a result of new interactions.[7] The extent of repeated collaboration among scholars in the field likely matches that found in other disciplines.[8]

To the extent that new entrants continue to enter and be active in their participation, and the community successfully absorbs newcomers within its core group(s), the field should continue to thrive. Over time, some routines of interaction will persist, but new entrants will also bring new routines, and the practices of the field will inevitably change. Boundary shift is inevitable within this dynamic. To return to the issue that Benbasat and Zmud raise, we can ask the following question. If there is a shift away from the field's roots in the IT artifact, should influential leaders then act to set the boundaries of the field more firmly, and call on scholars to return their attention to the IT artifact? Benbasat and Zmud define the IT artifact as 'the application of IT to enable or support some task(s) embedded within a structure(s) that itself is embedded within a context(s)' (p. 186). IT is at the core of the discipline, and as one moves to the study of task, structure, and context, the movement is away from IT and toward the periphery of the field's nomological net. Too many studies, they lament, study the periphery without the core. So, for example, studies of software development teams that examine task, understanding, and satisfaction, but exclude the IT artifact, do not belong within the domain of the field (and so should not be published in IS journals). From the perspective of the community of practice as described above, a call to include IT in all IS studies is unlikely to bring the desired result. Indeed, it may be that the shift away from the IT artifact as the focus of study is adaptive and important for the maintenance and growth of the community. Let us consider the forces that may be moving the field away from the IT artifact.

DIFFERENTIATION AND SHIFTING BOUNDARIES—MATURITY EFFECTS?

The shifting boundaries of scholarly attention away from the IT artifact may be reflective of the field's maturing and the inclusion of a new generation of members and leaders whose interests center on topics that differ somewhat from those of the original founders. New generations bring new research practices; this is inevitable in the evolution of a community and a signal of its vibrancy. Many young scholars are deeply interested in interdisciplinary research, and so they may act to push the boundaries of the IS field (or other fields for that matter) away from its core roots. Further, absorption into the community of scholars with interests tangential to IS increases the likelihood that attention will shift to matters other than the IT artifact. Such a trend is not necessarily disturbing. There is value in the shifting of boundaries as the field opens up and seeks new grounds with a new generation of members and leaders. And there is value in a diverse set of participants in the field who bring variability of interests and practice. These trends make the community vibrant and lead it into new directions (Aldrich, 1999, p. 162).

Benbasat and Zmud undoubtedly appreciate these member and leadership shifts. They could reasonably counter argue that, despite benefits, the issue remains that the shift away from IT might lead the discipline toward submergence into another research community, where it might be absorbed forever, thus losing its IS identity. Clearly 'technology' is at the core of the IS field (just as 'behavior' is at the core of the organizational behavior field). But it does not follow that distance from the core is necessarily a worrisome state of affairs. As just one example, consider the fact that studies of emotion and cognition are currently very popular among OB scholars—more so than observable behavior it seems. But the field OB is not threatened with extinction. A scholarly field of study will ebb and flow toward and away from its core over time as part of the natural evolution of scholars' interests. The IS field is by definition broad and encompassing; Benbasat and Zmud's definition (2003, p. 186) reflects this inclusive view. I would argue that so long as scholars continue to participate in IS conferences, contribute to IS journals, and engage in other forms of ongoing interaction with one another, the field will retain its legitimacy—regardless of what scholars actually study. The field will sustain itself through the ongoing interaction of its participants. In this way, the social life of the community keeps the field alive and assures its future.

Indeed, a strong case for tolerance in the stretching of the field's boundaries can be made based on the view that growth through absorption and retention of newcomers—whatever they study—is the key to the field's survival. But before moving to this recommendation, it is useful to further consider the possible forces that are driving the shift in research focus among current, active participants in the IS field.

IT TRANSFORMATIONS AND INSTITUTIONAL CHANGES

A reasonable argument can be made that technological transformation within industry, along with institutional changes within universities, are jointly drawing the field away from primary attention to the IT artifact.

Technology transformations. In the 1970s and 1980s, when the IS field was blossoming, business organizations were struggling with immense and fundamental technology issues. IT design, development, and adoption issues pervaded the organizational landscape; there was a race to informate the organization, and IT was central to firms' ability to compete in the new information age (Zuboff, 1988). The IS function was formed to address and manage specialized, technology-centric challenges that could not be addressed by other areas of the firm because they lacked necessary expertise. Today the situation is quite different. Corporations have downsized and outsourced their IT staffs. IT artifacts are largely the concern of hardware and software vendors, system developers, and other industry specialists. Cadres of backroom specialists have been replaced by standardized hardware and packaged software. The transformation is that IT knowledge and creative use are pervasive—no longer the sole domain of specialists.

Within this context, the IS functional role has shifted primarily to one of leadership and support, not development. Markets care more about ability to manage IT than the technology itself (Chatterjee, Richardson, & Zmud, 2001). Some research even reports that the IT knowledge of business executives is not a significant factor in a firm's ability to successfully adopt and use the technology (Armstrong & Sambamurthy, 1999). More important than the IT artifact are matters such as the capability to transfer information to particular constituencies inside and outside the firm (Broadbent & Weill, 1999), IT governance, and the complexities of managing software implementation (Sambamurthy & Zmud, 1999; Ravichandran & Rai, 2000).

Mainstream managers increasingly view technology as a commodity whose value lies less in the specifics of design than in the ingenuity of its use. In a recent review of technology in our information age, *The Economist* put it this way:

> The engineers of Silicon Valley may still cling to the hope of finding, at long last, the Next Big Thing—a technology so whizzy it makes all those share options valuable again. But what if tech's next big thing turns out not to be a technology at all, but a better way to make it work? (*The Economist*, June 21, 2003, p. 56).

Within the current context, is it not surprising that the IT artifact has moved off center stage in IS research?

Institutional changes. The transformation of IT from a back-office development role to a strategic business partner requires new roles and competencies for IT leaders and professionals, and the challenges are largely human and organizational rather than technical (Roepke, 2000). For educational institutions, especially business schools, this can result in renewed interest in basic business training, driving more hard-technology pursuits back to their roots in engineering and computer science, or into new, specialized schools for information studies.

Although IS has made significant inroads into business schools and formalized its presence in the form of faculties, journals, and the like, it has been a niche area of study for many years and is likely to remain so. Indeed, the institutional paradox for IS is that the domain has become of interest to many faculty groups yet the sole purview of none. With the artifact no longer in the foreground, and IT knowledge and interests pervasive, many disciplines have taken on the study of IT-related phenomena. At the same time, an IS specialty function may not be viewed as needed, since most business students do not require the kinds of technical knowledge offered by the IT groups of the past. The implication is that IS is likely to remain a niche area of study—a luxury that is formally institutionalized (as a designated department or group) in a relatively small number of business schools. The more core disciplines of marketing, finance, and management constitute the pillars of the modern business enterprise and are likely to dominate business education and research for the foreseeable future.

But this is not to say that the IS community of practice cannot continue to thrive. On the contrary. As the concerns of the field broaden to consider matters of more general managerial interest, there is the opportunity to expand the discipline and entice the participation of those with more distant core pursuits. In an age of interdisciplinary research, the boundaries of many disciplines are blurring. For example, the fields of management and economics are extremely broad and overlapping. But the scholarship in both disciplines is vibrant none-theless, because community participants pursue interesting questions and sustain identity through ongoing social interaction and growth.[9] There is no reason why the IS field cannot follow a similar path.

RECOMMENDATIONS

Assuming that the IS field is a vibrant community of practice adrift from its roots in the IT artifact, how shall we proceed? We are no doubt witness to boundary shift and expansion within the field. Rather than resist this movement, we should anticipate it, embrace it, and let the field move in new directions. Maintenance of a research community of practice relies more on the interactions of participants than on core topics of study. As such, the emphasis should be on attracting and retaining newcomers and enhancing the interactions of all participants. Legitimacy will result from the community's ability to do these things well and, hence, sustain itself over time.

To date, the IS community has exhibited growth, institutionalization, and resilience despite forces that have shifted attention away from the IT artifact. To add further vibrancy to the field, recommendations such as the following might be considered:

(1) Focus on the questions not the domain. A vast number of questions can take on an IT perspective, and science revolves around important questions, not technology per se. Rather than focus on the IT artifact, or any other set topic for that matter, scholars would do well to identify the important, fascinating questions of the day and pursue those. IS has a history of doing this well. For example, the field in the past has generated excitement and impact in studies of decision support, user satisfaction, computer-mediated communication, and e-commerce. Streams of research in these areas have been spurred by the actions of researchers who articulated questions and rallied scholars to engage in their pursuit. Research questions serve to shape the discourse of the community and engage research energies.

We will do well to let the field migrate to the interesting questions with high potential impact in the eyes of interested researchers, whatever their discipline. If our journals publish the best research available, regardless of its 'core properties,' the effect will be to attract readers and spawn high quality work. These will help to sustain researcher interest in the community so that new members join, newcomers stay, and those at the core are energized to continue the field's development. Of course, journal editors and reviewers control the possibility for opening up and closing the gates of what readers see. But such gatekeeping should not be done on strict, nonchanging boundaries of the discipline. Otherwise, the community members will migrate elsewhere and the vibrancy of the discipline will be threatened. If the best research is on the periphery of the nomological net (and it is of interest to reviewers, etc.) then let the field (or segments of it) migrate there. We should take a chance on moving in varied directions and breaking new, exciting ground.

As an example, consider the argument that the nature of work that surrounds IT is center stage for much of organizational life today— not the IT itself. Some IT scholars (e.g., Brown & Duguid, 2000) have argued that designers and researchers of technology have paid far too little attention to the role played by social systems in technology and cannot afford to leave such research solely in the hands of those in other disciplines. Following this reasoning, research on the periphery of the nomological net is legitimate for the IS field. Relevant questions surround the study of practices and communities, organizations and institutions, family and everyday life: What makes distributed teams effective? What are the coordination struggles of global corporations? How can software implementation teams improve client satisfaction? What can home-based workers do to overcome the isolationism of work away from a central office? These may be important questions to IS researchers, even if some or all studies do not incorporate the IT artifact. The 'errors of exclusion,' as Benbasat and Zmud put it, may inform the understanding of IT in vital ways and so attract IS researchers. Indeed, if IT researchers don't ponder questions at the periphery of the nomological net, we risk building and implementing less than adequate IT!

(2) Embrace interdisciplinary participation. Some of the most exciting science going on today is profoundly interdisciplinary. For example, research in genomics is attracting decision scientists, ethicists, legal scholars, engineers, and statisticians into the field of genetics; research in behavioral finance is attracting the interests of psychologists and economists; and research on customer relationship management is attracting database specialists and decision analysts into the field of marketing. Interdisciplinary research creates migration across field boundaries and spurs opportunity for journals in multiple disciplines to address similar research questions.

If IS researchers and their journals focus closely on the IT artifact and its immediate nomological net, the field is less likely to attract the interests of those outside of the community—especially those with diminished technological concerns. It is important that IS research attracts the attention of those outside the field, especially within business schools, if it is to thrive. Since the IT artifact is not in the spotlight of managerial attention today, a retreat to this corner of concern could prove ruinous. The less relevant our research is to those in other fields, the less visible our scholarship will be, and the more isolated the field will become. We should conceive of the IS domain broadly, as Benbasat and Zmud (2003) have done so well, and keep it broad, erring on the side of inclusion rather than exclusion. We should invite and seek interdisciplinary involvement, stretching the boundaries of the community to show how we can contribute to, and draw in, research on important questions of the day.

(3) Continue to develop forums for interaction and debate. A sustainable community of practice offers multiple, informal opportunities for researcher interaction and debate (Wenger, 1998; Lave & Wenger, 1991). Learning occurs as people jointly develop ideas, interpret events,

build relationships, resolve conflicts, produce tools, and invent processes (Wong, 2002). The IS community has done well over the years in offering conferences, journals, and informal gatherings within and across universities to promote shared scholarship. Indeed, increases in the numbers of journals, special interest groups, consortia, and the like have been critical to supporting the growth (and hence the legitimacy and survivability) of the discipline.[10] For the future, it is vital that these kinds of venues continue and expand their reach. Informal forums for idea exchange are particularly valuable for absorption of newcomers seeking knowledge exchange and opportunity to gain status and reputation within the community (Wasko & Faraj, 2003). As the field grows, a wider set of opportunities for networking and recognition are needed.

Essays and general commentaries can be provocative outlets for researcher interaction, and the IS community has used these extensively over the years.[11] But as the field grows, more focused forums are likely to be more productive. For example, several years ago the *MIS Quarterly* promoted debate surrounding specific research questions and findings via publication of Notes and Replies to specific published articles. *Information Systems Research* has likewise conducted a series of discussions and debates on various topics and subfields, especially the relationship between IS research and research in other disciplines. As the field grows and becomes more multifaceted, forums for discussion of opposing models and paradigms related to specific, hot areas of research are needed.

(4) Increase communication of theory and research results. The publications within academic journals constitute an important layer of communication within a discipline (Heimeriks, Horlesberger, &Van den Besselaar, 2003). Scholarly articles can be viewed both as knowledge goods (outputs of the community of practice) and as inputs to the future social life of the community (Van Den Besselaar, 2001). Scholarly publication is a jointly constructed process, reflective of dialogue among researchers, reviewers, editors, and readers. How can we assess the scholarly communication of the IS field? There is no standard procedure for such an analysis; indeed, multiple approaches are possible (Rousseau, 2002). One simple approach is to categorize the kinds of discourse found in top journals and compare the results to discourse found in the top journals of other, related communities of practice (Garfield, 1996).[12] A thoroughgoing analysis would inventory many journals to which IS scholars contribute, both within and outside the IS community. But a more limited investigation may also be insightful. To illustrate, let us compare a sample of communication within IS journals to a sample of communication in the related discipline

of organization studies. IS and organization studies share many common interests, theoretical bases, methodologies. These two fields often reside side by side in business schools. They both pursue questions related to human behavior, groups, networks, organizations, and strategy (among other topics). They attract many of the same scholars to their communities of practice and, to some extent, compete for membership and legitimacy within academe.

To explore the relative communication patterns of these disciplines, I reviewed the articles of the last four years (1998–2002) for two leading IS journals, *MIS Quarterly* and *Information Systems Research*, and two leading OS journals, *Administrative Science Quarterly* and *Organization Science*. In the case of *MIS Quarterly*, I also reviewed the articles in the first four years following its founding (1977–1980). As Garfield (1996) notes, the significant scientific literature appears in a small fraction of journals—those routinely regarded as 'top' by the scientific community. These elite journals generate the majority of what is cited and so act as drivers to future scholarly discourse. *MISQ* and *ISR* have been regarded as top journals in IS for many years. *ASQ* and *OS* likewise are recognized for their top-tier status in the field of organization studies. The four journals represent 'matched pairs,' in the sense that *MISQ* and *ASQ* are both over 25 years old, rooted in university sponsorship, and published quarterly. *ISR* and *OS*, on the other hand, were started in 1990 and are sponsored by the INFORMS professional society; originally, both were quarterly publications, although *OS* recently moved to producing six issues per year. For each journal, I counted the total number of articles published and classified each article based on its primary contribution to the literature. Raw counts per category were converted to percentages in order to allow comparisons across journals and, in the case of *MISQ*, across time periods. I summarize the results in Table 7.1.

Note that the purpose of Table 7.1 is not to present a scientometric analysis, but rather to present simple points of contrast that can illustrate similarities and differences in the dialogue of IS scholars relative to organization studies, and to highlight changes in IS scholarly communication over time.[13] The field of organization studies is substantially larger than IS. It is difficult to estimate the size of a community of practice, but as a surrogate we can use membership in the field's dominant professional society. For organization studies the participant base is estimated as 13,478, and for IS the estimate is 3,400 members.[14] To compare across fields, we can use the total number of publications per journal as the relative base. Publications per person in a given locale or community is frequently used to compare productivity of scientists across disciplines, informal research groups, and even nations (e.g., see Inonu, 2003). A few interesting observations are as follows.

Table 7.1 *Comparison of Journal Articles by Category for Two Leading Journals in IS and Organizational Studies*

Journal articles by category[1]	MIS Quarterly				Information Systems Research		Administrative Science Quarterly		Organization Science	
	1978–1980		1998–2002		1998–2002		1998–2002		1998–2002	
	total	%	total	%	total	%	total	%	total	%
Research[2]	19	21.30	75	63.00	55	44.40	101	31.70	118	52.50
Theory[3]	32	36.00	7	5.90	25	20.20	12	3.80	71	31.40
Method[4]	4	4.50	12	10.10	22	17.70	0	0.00	3	1.30
Commentary	13	14.60	25	21.00	22	17.70	7	2.20	28	12.40
Book reviews	0	0.00	0	0	0	0	199	62.40	0	0
Executive interviews	14	15.70	0	0	0	0	0	0	0	0
System or case description[5]	7	7.90	0	0	0	0	0	0	6	2.70
Total articles	89		119		124		319		226	

Notes: [1] Categorization is based on review of Abstracts for each issue of each journal for the periods indicated. Articles are categorized according to their dominant contribution to the literature, as claimed by the author(s) in the Abstract.
[2] The paper is empirically based.
[3] The paper expounds either a conceptual or mathematical model, or both.
[4] The paper contributes a technique(s) for measuring variables or assessing a system or set of variables.
[5] The paper offers insight based in a system or case example but without theoretical exposition.

First, overall volume of publication per community member is slightly less in the IS journals, with papers per member at 3.6% for *ISR* and 4.0% for *OS*. Second, research and theory contributions in IS have grown considerably over years; 68.9% of *MISQ* contributions during the past four years were to research and theory, compared to 57.3% during the *MISQ*'s first four years. Empirical research contributions in IS now surpass those in organization studies. (*MISQ* and *ISR* average 53.7% of papers devoted to research, compared to 42% in *ASQ* and *OS*.) Third, the IS field lags the organization studies field considerably in theory production. Twenty-three percent of journal space in *ISR* is devoted to theory, with no book reviews. In contrast, *OS* devotes 31.4% of papers to theory, and *ASQ* devotes more than half its journal space to reviews of books that are largely theoretical exposition. Finally, it is notable that, overall, IS scholars devote considerably more attention to method and commentary than to research and theory. (Excluding book reviews, for the period 1998–2002, 94% of *ASQ* articles and 83.6% of articles in *OS* provided empirical research or theory contributions; this compares to 69% and 65% in *MISQ* and *ISR* respectively.)

The pipeline of scholarly communication in IS is strong. In the September 2000 issue of *ISR*, Benbasat (2000, p. i) reported 150 new submissions per year with a trend toward 'steady increase.' During the three years 1999–2001, submissions to *ISR* increased by 25% (Benbasat, 2001a), and all indications are the conference submissions and other venues are experiencing regular increases in paper submissions. Clearly, the IS community is not only active but productive. This said, it appears that greater page space in top journals is needed to accommodate the field's growth and increasing diversity. More theory contributions are needed (Benbasat, 2001b), and we would do well to devote less attention to method and commentary and more attention to substantive research output. Ultimately, the advance of the discipline depends more on discourse devoted to empirical results than commentary. Production of scientific output is not only the product of the community but the nourishment that sustains it. Compelling ideas and discoveries will serve to attract the outsider, retain the insider, and assure the future of the discipline.

CONCLUSION

Innovation processes are increasingly knowledge based and social, bringing matters such as relationship management, task sequencing, coordination, team building, conflict, project management, and so on, to the foreground. Indeed, 'communal activities surround and steer any technological innovation' (Brown and Duguid, 2000). Within this context, it is no wonder that significant research energies in the IS community are migrating to focus on matters peripheral to the IT artifact. The IT artifact may be a concern of the IS community for a long time to come, but it may not remain at the core of the discipline as the technology evolves and as the community grows and becomes more diverse.

The call for research in important areas of study, artifact or otherwise, can trigger attention and suggest possible directions for scholars. But thoughtful leaders such as Benbasat and Zmud have historically weighted—and no doubt will continue to weigh—their influence more in the research that they practice than in the guidelines they articulate.[15] Researcher actions cannot be fully determined, nor should they be.

Researchers are actors in the fundamentally social process of research creation. The social life of the IS research community is its future. How we attract and retain members, and the nature of our scholarly discourse with one another, will be the ultimate determinants of the legitimacy of the field.

ACKNOWLEDGEMENT

The comments of Detmar Straub, Sirkka Jarvenpaa, and Cecil Chua are gratefully acknowledged.

NOTES

1 Detmar Straub was the accepting senior editor for this paper.
2 An example of a smaller, informally organized conference is the Knowledge Management Symposium organized by Mani Subramani of the University of Minnesota and V. Sambamurthy of Michigan State University in March 2003. The symposium included approximately 100 participants and was held at the University of Minnesota.
3 Includes 33 'research-in-progress' papers.
4 The assistance of Professor J. David Naumann, University of Minnesota, in providing these statistics, is gratefully acknowledged. The value for the period 1999–2000 is 4000, a rounded estimate. Personal correspondence dated October 3, 2003.
5 Counts of board members include Editors-in-Chief, Senior Editors, Associate Editors, Editorial Board members, and, in the case of the founding year of the MISQ, 'Consulting Editors' who presumably helped with paper reviewing.
6 These are just a few of the many workshop and ancillary meetings associated with the ICIS and/or CIS-series of meetings.
7 For example, the DIGIT, WITS, and WISE groups were spawned as informal venues ahead of the ICIS meeting. Ten or 15 years ago, these three groups became

institutionalized around the ICIS, and newer informal groups were spawned. For example, the CCRIS group is relatively new, and more of these groups are spawned every few years as a result of researchers' interests and desire to informally interact around the larger, more formalized ICIS venue.

8 This observation could be empirically verified by counting the number of co-authors in IS journals who have different institutional affiliations and no prior affiliate contact (to verify collaboration based on informal, non-institutional ties), tracking co-authorships over time, and then comparing the results to a similar count made in another field of study.

9 The odds of an organization disbanding are strongly linked to its size and moderately related to its age (Baum, 1996). Hence, growth is a path to organizational survival.

10 To illustrate growth in exchange forums, consider the following. The Association of Information Systems reports 7 chapters, 2 affiliates and 13 Special Interest Groups (SIGs). New Chapters have been established in Italy, Morocco, Slovenia, and the Chinese-speaking world. There is a new affiliate in France, and a 13th SIG (Source: AIS Newsletter, October 2003, http://www.aisnet.org)

11 The current paper is illustrative, as is the series of Research Commentaries hosted by Izak Benbasat during his tenure as Editor-in-Chief of Information Systems Research.

12 Garfield (1996) describes this approach as a 'differentiated audit of each category of editorial material' (p. 2).

13 I do not intend my coding and analyses of these journals to meet the standards of rigorous quantitative work; rather, my goal is to gain some perspective on IS vis-à-vis a related field. Other researchers could followup with carefully wrought studies to see what these trends, if confirmed, might portend.

14 There are 13 478 members in the Academy of Management Academy (http://www.aomonline.org/aom.asp?ID=1; Dec 8, 2003) and 3400 members of the Association for Information Systems (personal correspondence from Professor Dennis F. Galletta, University of Pittsburgh, November 5, 2003).

15 The ongoing research contributions of Izak Benbasat and Bob Zmud have been enormous. As just one indicator, consider the following. At the dawn of the field, during the period 1977–1980, Benbasat and Zmud collectively contributed 6.74% of all articles published in the *MIS Quarterly*. Two decades later, with the field now in its maturity in terms of membership size and intense competitive access to journal space, these two scholars continue to be prolific. During the period 1998–2002, they collectively contributed 4.53% of articles published in the *MIS Quarterly* and *Information Systems Research*. (Note—These counts exclude editorial comments and reviews.)

REFERENCES

Aldrich, H. (1999), *Organizations Evolving*. Thousand Oaks, CA: Sage.

Aldrich, H. E. (1971), Organizational boundaries and interorganizational conflict. *Human Relations*, 24, 279–287.

Argote, L. (1999), *Organizational Learning: Creating, Retaining and Transferring Knowledge*, Boston: Kluwer Academic Publishers.

Armstrong, C. P., & Sambamurthy V. (1999), Information technology assimilation in Firms: The influence of senior leadership and IT infrastructures. *Information Systems Research*, 10(4), 328–342.

Baum, J. A. C. (1996), Organizational ecology. In S. R. Clegg, C. Hardy, and W. Nord (Eds.), *Handbook of Organization Studies* (pp. 77–114). London: Sage.

Benbasat, I. (2000), Editorial Notes. *Information Systems Research*, 11(3), i-ii.

Benbasat, I. (2001a), Editorial Notes. *Information Systems Research*, 12(2), iii-iv.

Benbasat, I. (2001b), Editorial Notes. *Information Systems Research*, 12(4), iii-iv.

Benbasat, I., & Zmud, R. W. (2003), The identity crisis within the IS discipline: Defining and communicating the discipline's core properties. *MIS Quarterly*, 29(2), 183–194.

Broadbent, M., & Weill, P. (1999), The implications of information technology infrastructure for business process redesign. *MIS Quarterly*, 23(2), 159–183.

Brown, J. S. and Duguid, P. (1991), Organizational learning and communities-of-practice: Toward a unified view of working, learning, and innovation. *Organization Science*, 2, 40–57.

Brown, J. S., & Duguid, P. (2000), *The social life of information*. Harvard Business School Press.

Brown, J. S., & Duguid, P. (2001), Knowledge and organization: A social-practice perspective. *Organization Science*, 12(2), 198–213.

Chatterjee, D., Richardson, V. J, & Zmud, R. W. (2001), Examining the shareholder wealth effects of announcements of newly created CIO positions. *MIS Quarterly*, 25(1), 43–60.

Chin, G., Myers, J., & Hoyt, D. (2002), Social networks in the virtual science laboratory. *Communications of the ACM*, 45(8), 87–102.

Garfield, E. (1996), The significant scientific literature appears in a small core of journals. *The Scientist*, 10(17), 13–15.

Heimeriks, G., Horlesberger, M., & Van den Besselaar, P. (2003), Mapping communication and collaboration in heterogeneous research networks. *Scientometrics*, 58(2), 391–413.

Inonu, E. (2003), The influence of cultural factors on scientific production. *Scientometrics*, 56(1), 137–146.

Knoke, D., & Prensky, D. (1984), What relevance do organizational theories have for voluntary organizations. *Social Science Quarterly*, 65(1), 3–20.

Kogut, B., & Zander, U. (1996), What firms do? Coordination, identity, and learning. *Organization Science*, 7(5), 502–518.

Lave, J. & Wenger, E. (1991), *Situated learning: Legitimate peripheral participation*. Cambridge: Cambridge University Press.

Leonard, D. (1995), *Wellsprings of knowledge: Building and sustaining the sources of innovation*. Boston, Massachusetts: Harvard Business School Press.

Nonaka, I. and Takeuchi, H. (1995), *The knowledge-creating company: How Japanese companies create the dynamics of innovation*. New York: Oxford University Press.

Pentland, B. (1992), Organizing moves in software support hot lines. *Administrative Science Quarterly*, 37(4), 527–548.

Price, D. J. deSolla. (1986), *Little science, big science... and beyond*. NY: Columbia University.

Ravichandran, T., & Rai, A. (2000), Quality management in systems development: an organizational system perspective. *MIS Quarterly*, 24(3), 381–416.

Roepke, R. (2000), Aligning the IT human resource with business vision: the leadership initiative at 3M. *MIS Quarterly*, 24(2), 327–354.

Rousseau, R. (2002), Lack of standardisation in informetric research. Comments on 'Power laws of research output. Evidence for journals of economics' by Matthias Sutter and Martin G. Kocher. *Scientometrics*, 55(2), 317–327.

Sambamurthy, V., & Zmud, R. W. (1999), Arrangements for information technology governance: A theory of multiple contingencies. *MIS Quarterly*, 23(2), 261–291.

Sandstrom, P. E. (2001), Scholarly communication as a socioecological system. *Scientometrics*, 51(3), 573–605.

Scott, W. R. (1995), *Institutions and organizations*. Thousand Oaks, CA: Sage.

Spender, J. C. (1996), Making knowledge the basis of a dynamic theory of the firm. *Strategic Management Journal*, 17, 45–62.

The Economist. Is big blue the next big thing? (June 21, 2003), vol. 367, no. 8329, p.56.

Van den Besselaar, P. (2001), The cognitive and the social structure of STS. *Scientometrics*, 51(2), 441–460.

Wasko, S. & Faraj, M. M. (2003), Why should I share? Examining knowledge contribution in networks of practice. Paper presented at the KM Symposium, University of Minnesota, Mar 14–15, 2003.

Wenger, E. (1998), *Communities of practice: Learning, meaning, and identity*. Cambridge, UK: Cambridge University Press.

Wittgenstein, L. (1958), *Philosophical investigations*. NY: MacMillan.

Wong, S. S. (2002), Investigating collective learning in teams: The context in which it occurs and the collective knowledge that emerges from it. Unpublished Ph.D. dissertation, Duke University.

Zuboff, S. (1988), *In the age of the smart machine: The future of work and power*. Oxford: Oxford University Press.

8
Identity, Legitimacy and the Dominant Research Paradigm: An Alternative Prescription for the IS Discipline

Daniel Robey

Benbasat and Zmud's (2003) call for a new identity for the IS field is both timely and welcome. Their message is positive and constructive, and I admire their leadership in expressing important concerns. The field of IS does need a more coherent identity with information technology at its core. Benbasat and Zmud conceive of this core as a nomological net linking key antecedents and consequences to the IT artifact. Guided by this redefinition of core properties, IS researchers may establish a stronger shared identity, avoid errors of inclusion and exclusion, and achieve greater legitimacy within our discipline's organizational field.

My own vision differs from Benbasat and Zmud's in several ways. First, I see advantages to a more flexible identity for IS, one that can be revised when needed. Second, gaining and preserving legitimacy is not simply a matter of formulating and implementing a strategic plan. We need to think cautiously about the process of changing our identity because change involves risks that may subvert our attempts to establish greater legitimacy. Third, IS needs to strengthen ties with contributing disciplines, not sever them in the rush to establish unique IS theories. Finally, I urge the IS field to avoid the lure of a dominant research paradigm.

IDENTITY AS MUTABLE AND ADAPTIVE

Organizational image and identity have been the subject of numerous empirical and conceptual articles in the management and organization sciences, including a special issue of the *Academy of Management Review* (January 2000). These inquiries are motivated by an assumed connection between organizational identity and positive outcomes such as organizational reputation and legitimacy. If a core identity can be created and shared within an organization, it might be projected externally as a positive image. Because traditional sources of identity have been lost as organizations and professions have faced economic and ethical crises, the study of identity has become more relevant and challenging. 'A sense of identity serves as a rudder for navigating difficult waters' (Albert, Ashforth and Dutton, 2000, p. 13). It is essential, therefore, that any organization or occupational field be concerned with managing its image and identity.

However, establishing an identity does not necessarily imply stability. Although identity generally connotes a stable set of core characteristics, identity may also be conceived as a mutable and adaptive property. For example, Gioia, Schultz and Corley (2000) conceive of identity as fluid and unstable, treating it as a dynamic property of organizations. Paradoxically perhaps, organizations (or occupational fields such as the IS research community) should be prepared to change their identities as they face changing conditions. Thus, a flexible identity becomes useful when the need for change arises. According to Gioia and his colleagues, organizations that are able to change their core identities are more likely to succeed than organizations that cannot. A stable identity might even become a liability that limits a professional field's ability to change in response to environmental changes.

Indeed, Benbasat and Zmud's (2003) call for a new identity is motivated by changes in the environment of IS (p. 184), and a mutable and adaptive identity for IS might permit the flexibility needed to change. For example, IS has shifted its identity from a narrow preoccupation on computer programming and application development methodologies to an identity that encompasses the social context of IS development and use. As technologies change, the IS field also needs to change to remain relevant. For these reasons, we should adopt a mutable identity that allows us to adapt to our rapidly changing environment.

In sum, I would re-interpret Benbasat and Zmud's call for establishing an identity for IS as a call for revising our identity as an ongoing practice. We have revised our identity in the past and we will need future revisions. As a field, we should adopt a strategy of 'adaptive instability' (Gioia *et al.*, 2000), one that fosters adjustment through appropriate changes in identity over time.

ESTABLISHING AND PRESERVING PRAGMATIC LEGITIMACY

Benbasat and Zmud (2003) distinguish among several types of legitimacy. They claim that IS has already achieved significant progress regarding socio-political legitimacy, which encompasses both moral and regulatory acceptance. However, they argue that IS has not yet gained 'cognitive legitimacy,' which is the state of being taken for granted by environmental constituents. They believe that a less amorphous definition of IS's core phenomenon would lead to cognitive legitimacy.

I disagree. Cognitive legitimacy is beyond the reach of IS academic research. Suchman (1995) regards cognitive legitimacy as lying 'beyond the reach of all but the most fortunate managers' (p. 583). For IS to become cognitively legitimate, alternatives to IS would have to become unthinkable. For a maturing academic field to attain taken-for-granted status in an era when centuries-old cultural, social, political, and religious institutions are being challenged would seem unlikely. Even the legitimacy of more established business disciplines like accounting and finance was challenged in the wake of corporate scandals at Enron, WorldCom, Mirant and other corporations in the early 2000's. It is inconceivable that IS could rise above such heightened social scrutiny and attain a taken-for-granted status.

It would be more sensible, in my view, for IS to pursue what Suchman calls pragmatic legitimacy, which 'rests on the self-interested calculations of an organization's most immediate audiences' (Suchman, 1995, p. 578). For IS to become pragmatically legitimate, we need to be seen as a valued partner in intellectual exchanges with our external constituents: the governing bodies, business executives, university officials, and scholars from other disciplines who are the key actors in IS's organizational field (Benbasat and Zmud, 2003, p. 185). For this to occur, we need to conform to the environment's expectations by meeting the needs of various audiences. We also need to persuade our audiences that what we do is valuable (Suchman, 1995).

These pragmatic concerns are most easily realized if we conduct our research rigorously and report it widely. However, none of these efforts is likely to result in the taken-for-granted status associated with cognitive legitimacy. Indeed, few institutions achieve taken-for-granted status, and those that do probably lack the incentive to be rigorous in their efforts to respond to environmental constituents simply because they are, in fact, taken for granted. Our efforts can, however, further strengthen our socio-political legitimacy.

If we take pragmatic legitimacy as our objective, Suchman suggests that we should perceive future changes and protect past accomplishments (1995, pp. 594–597). The key to perceiving future change is to deploy boundary spanning agents to learn about audience values, beliefs and reactions (Suchman, 1995, p. 595). Indeed, Benbasat and Zmud do an excellent job of perceiving future changes by identifying potential threats to our legitimacy. We must continue to monitor our institutional environment and not become complacent with our current level of socio-political legitimacy.

The IS field also needs to protect its past accomplishments. Suchman (1995) offers two strategies for protection that are relevant to IS: policing internal operations and 'curtailing highly visible legitimation efforts in favor of more subtle techniques' (p. 595). Benbasat and Zmud believe that internal policing (in the form of research standards and editorial practices) is effective in IS (2003, p. 185), but that our conferences and journals need to adopt practices that uphold high standards for relevant scholarship. I agree but caution that such vigilance not be so severe that the IS field 'eats its young' as a regular practice. The imposition of lofty research standards may help to establish our identity as a more rigorous and legitimate field, but we may simultaneously disable the ability of junior faculty to grow into more senior roles. Protecting past accomplishments clearly implies the preservation of established research standards, but it does not imply a rapid escalation of those standards.

It is less clear whether Benbasat and Zmud's proposal requires overt (and possibly egregious) attempts to promote IS to its constituents, or more subtle techniques for establishing legitimacy. The dangers of egregious self-aggrandizement have been articulated by Ashforth and Gibbs (1990) as the 'self-promoter's paradox,' defined as constituents' tendency to interpret self promotion as a clue that an organization is in trouble. Thus, too much self promotion can jeopardize legitimacy, an effect opposite of that intended. I strongly advise that IS avoid inflating its contributions while drawing attention to its substantive achievements.

In sum, IS should abandon any hope for cognitive legitimacy and focus instead on establishing and preserving pragmatic legitimacy.

This can be accomplished by diligent application of rigorous research methodologies and publication strategies that reach our varied audiences, both academic and practical. Pragmatic legitimacy can best be accomplished without blatant self promotion, which would be interpreted suspiciously by our audiences as a sign of weakness. If we position our contributions strategically, without inflating them, we should continue to strengthen the pragmatic legitimacy of IS research.

STRENGTHEN CONNECTIONS WITH IS's CONTRIBUTING DISCIPLINES

I attribute the phrase 'contributing disciplines' to Allen Lee (2001), former Editor in Chief of *MIS Quarterly*. Prior to Lee's clarification, we routinely discussed the importance of 'reference disciplines' in IS research. Lee's semantic distinction suggested that, on the one hand, disciplines such as economics, organization science, computer science, and management science can continue to contribute theories and methods to inform IS research. On the other hand, those disciplines provide poor models for how IS research should be conducted because they typically do not focus on technologies in their social contexts of development and use. In Lee's view, IS needs to establish an identity through research that is distinctively different from the research in other disciplines while drawing valuable contributions from them.

Benbasat and Zmud acknowledge the value of the contributing disciplines but observe that 'the current emphasis with theories from other disciplines has distracted the IS research community from developing its own theories' (2003, p. 192). Indeed, it is difficult to identify many true 'IS theories,' even after several decades of IS research. For example, most of the components of Benbasat and Zmud's proposed nomological net refer to constructs that are thoroughly researched in organizational behavior, strategic management and other non-IS fields. Should we shore up a unique identity by severing ties with contributing disciplines? Benbasat and Zmud do not advocate such a course, but I worry that their advocacy for building IS theories might be interpreted as a call for separation from contributing disciplines rather than effective integration.

In my view, it would be unwise to ignore valuable sources of theory and method in other disciplines. Although developing our own theories might increase the distinctiveness of IS, it might also lead us into an isolationism that could impoverish IS and threaten it further. I do not think that the IS field can risk severing ties with contributing disciplines. Rather, we should strengthen our connections with those disciplines and exploit them for the value they offer.

Strengthening ties with contributing disciplines increases the risk of committing Benbasat and Zmud's 'error of inclusion,' defined in terms of the causal distance between IS and non-IS constructs in a nomological net. It is appropriate, therefore, to position IS as an applied discipline. As we draw theories from relevant disciplines and employ them skillfully to inform problems specific to the IT artifact, we can strengthen our identity and earn respect from the contributing disciplines. In addition, we can minimize the risk of under-specification in IS research models (Benbasat and Zmud, 2003, p. 192) and spare ourselves the considerable effort required to construct unique IS theories.

SHARPEN THE FOCUS ON IT AS THE CORE PHENOMENON BUT RESIST THE LURE OF THE 'DOMINANT RESEARCH PARADIGM'

Finally, I disagree with Benbasat and Zmud's assessment that IS needs a 'dominant research paradigm.' The lure of the dominant paradigm is thinly masked in Benbasat and Zmud's essay. On the one hand, they say that their commentary is not about 'whether such a diversity of topics is beneficial for the IS field' (2003, p. 184). However, while accepting the intellectual diversity that characterizes the IS field, they view the lack of consensus regarding a dominant design as 'troublesome' (p. 185). This problem of diversity drives their call for a dominant paradigm, including standards and designs for research.

Benbasat and Zmud offer a glimpse of what a dominant research paradigm might be. Their nomological net is portrayed as a causal 'box-and-arrow' diagram (albeit with two-way arrows), and their concluding rules of thumb assume the use of a conventional model to guide research. Their view fails to accommodate exploratory, inter-pretive, qualitative, and critical research, which are typically not rendered in the form of causal models. Thus, their call for a new identity potentially excludes IS traditions that are skeptical of the value of positivist, causal modeling. However, Benbasat and Zmud's desire to 'clarify the IS nuances' in IS research (2003, p. 193) might be satisfied better with qualitative research that provides rich interpretations of the interplay between social systems and technical artifacts than with research that operationalizes elements of their proposed nomolog-ical net.

We do need to sharpen the focus on the IT artifact, which occupies an appropriately central position in Benbasat and Zmud's nomological net. Such positioning would ensure that IS research engages the IT artifact in the spirit suggested by Orlikowski and Iacono (2001). However, as Orlikowski and Iacono argue, the central position of the IT artifact can be addressed in many different ways that do not necessarily conform to a 'dominant' paradigm. Although the IS field might gain a new identity by eliminating valid avenues for investigating IT, such a course would only be wise if we had collectively judged some research paradigms to be inferior to others. In my view, such a judgment has not occurred.

Although I am reasonably sure that Benbasat and Zmud did not mean to exclude any particular research methodology or theoretical perspective from the dominant paradigm, I fear that readers may interpret their analysis more narrowly. Thus, I urge caution in responding to the lure of the dominant paradigm. Adopting a dominant paradigm increases the risk of silencing interesting debates and lines of research before their contributions can be evaluated. Dominance may be a characteristic of some successful fields, but I suspect that a diversity of perspectives and controversy keeps them adaptable.

In sum, I believe that we need to foster diversity rather than view it as the source of our identity problem. A diverse range of research methodologies that focus on the IT artifact in all of its complexity is likely to enhance our identity more than premature closure on a narrow range of methods associated with a dominant paradigm. As an applied discipline, we depend upon a diversity of research approaches to ensure that we learn about the IT artifact in as many ways as we can.

CONCLUSION

I have argued that Benbasat and Zmud's (2003) vision of a new identity for the IS field requires some modifications. As a field, we should view the identity issue not as a one-time adjustment but rather a continuing process of evaluation and reflection that leads to changing our identity to meet the expectations of our immediate audiences. This will not be easy, and it will demand constant vigilance. We should also not underestimate the complexity of responding appropriately to our institutional environment. Establishing and maintaining legitimacy requires a commitment to monitor our audiences and to formulate responses that are not seen as entirely self serving. In pursuing legitimacy, the IS field would be wise to continue to exploit contributing disciplines. At the risk of muddying our identity, we should not ignore their wealth of theoretical and methodological guidance available in related fields. Finally, the lure of the dominant paradigm, in whatever guise, continues to disturb me.[1] Surely we can succeed as an applied discipline by sustaining current trajectories that draw from relevant contributing disciplines. I have little hope that IS can survive by ignoring alternative paradigms and rallying around a narrower, and perhaps impoverished identity.

ACKNOWLEDGEMENT

I am indebted to Sirkka Jarvenpaa and Detmar Straub for the opportunity to contribute this commentary and to sharpen its arguments, and to Vanessa Liu for insightful discussions about the IS field and its future.

NOTE

1 For my prior arguments advocating diversity in the IS field, see Robey (1996).

REFERENCES

Albert, S., Ashforth, B. E., and Dutton, J. E., 'Organizational Identity and Identification: Charting New Waters and Building New Bridges,' *Academy of Management Review*, 25 (1) January 2000, 13–17.

Ashforth, B. E., and Gibbs, B. W., 'The Double-Edge of Organizational Legitimation,' *Organization Science*, 1 (2), 177–194.

Benbasat, I., and Zmud, R. W., 'The Identity Crisis within the IS Discipline: Defining and Communicating the Discipline's Core Properties,' *MIS Quarterly*, 27 (2) June 2003, 183–194.

Gioia, D. A., Schultz, M., and Corley, K. G., 'Organizational Identity, Image, and Adaptive Instability,' *Academy of Management Review*, 25 (1) January 2000, 63–81.

Lee, A. S., 'Editor's Comments,' *MIS Quarterly*, 25 (1), p. iii.

Orlikowski, W. J. and Iacono, S. 'Research Commentary: Desperately Seeking the "IT" in IT Research: A Call to Theorizing the IT Artifact,' *Information Systems Research*, 12 (2) 2001, 121–134.

Robey, D. 'Diversity in Information Systems Research: Threat, Promise, and Responsibility,' *Information Systems Research*, 7 (4), 1996, 400–408.

Suchman, M. C., 'Managing Legitimacy: Strategic and Institutional Approaches,' *Academy of Management Review*, 20 (3) July 1995, 571–610.

9
Design Science in Information Systems Research

Alan R. Hevner, Salvatore T. March, Jinsoo Park and
Sudha Ram

1 INTRODUCTION

Information systems are implemented within an organization for the
purpose of improving the effectiveness and efficiency of that organization. Capabilities of the information system and characteristics of
the organization, its work systems, its people, and its development
and implementation methodologies together determine the extent to
which that purpose is achieved (Silver *et al.* 1995). It is incumbent
upon researchers in the Information Systems (IS) discipline to 'further
knowledge that aids in the productive application of information
technology to human organizations and their management' (ISR
2002, inside front cover) and to develop and communicate 'knowledge
concerning both the management of information technology and the
use of information technology for managerial and organizational
purposes' (Zmud 1997).

We argue that acquiring such knowledge involves two complementary but distinct paradigms, behavioral science and design science
(March and Smith 1995). The behavioral-science paradigm has its
roots in natural science research methods. It seeks to develop and
justify theories (i.e., principles and laws) that explain or predict

First published in *MIS Quarterly* 28(1), pp. 75–106. Copyright 2004 by the Regents of the University of
Minnesota. Reprinted by permission.

organizational and human phenomena surrounding the analysis, design, implementation, management, and use of information systems. Such theories ultimately inform researchers and practitioners of the interactions among people, technology, and organizations that must be managed if an information system is to achieve its stated purpose, namely improving the effectiveness and efficiency of an organization. These theories impact and are impacted by design decisions made with respect to the system development methodology used and the functional capabilities, information contents, and human interfaces implemented within the information system.

The design-science paradigm has its roots in engineering and the sciences of the artificial (Simon 1996). It is fundamentally a problem-solving paradigm. It seeks to create innovations that define the ideas, practices, technical capabilities, and products through which the analysis, design, implementation, and use of information systems can be effectively and efficiently accomplished (Tsichritzis 1997; Denning 1997). Such artifacts are not exempt from natural laws or behavioral theories. To the contrary, their creation relies on existing 'kernel theories' that are applied, tested, modified, and extended through the experience, creativity, intuition, and problem solving capabilities of the researcher (Walls *et al.* 1992; Markus *et al.* 2002).

The importance of design is well recognized in the IS literature (Glass 1999; Winograd 1996; Winograd 1997). Benbasat and Zmud (1999, p. 5) argue that the relevance of IS research is directly related to its applicability in design, stating that the implications of empirical IS research should be 'implementable, ... synthesize an existing body of research, ... [or] stimulate critical thinking' among IS practitioners. However, designing useful artifacts is complex due to the need for creative advances in domain areas in which existing theory is often insufficient. 'As technical knowledge grows, IT is applied to new application areas that were not previously believed to be amenable to IT support' (Markus *et al.* 2002, p. 180). The resultant IT artifacts extend the boundaries of human problem solving and organizational capabilities by providing intellectual as well as computational tools. Theories regarding their application and impact will follow their development and use.

Here, we argue, is an opportunity for IS research to make significant contributions by engaging the complementary research cycle between design-science and behavioral-science to address fundamental problems faced in the productive application of information technology. Technology and behavior are not dichotomous in an information system. They are inseparable (Lee 2000). They are similarly inseparable in IS research. Philosophically these arguments draw from the pragmatists (Aboulafia 1991) who argue that truth (justified theory) and utility (artifacts that are effective) are two sides of the same coin and that scientific research should be evaluated in light of its practical implications.

The realm of IS research is at the confluence of people, organizations, and technology (Lee 1999; Davis and Olson 1985). IT artifacts are broadly defined as constructs (vocabulary and symbols), models (abstractions and representations), methods (algorithms and practices), and instantiations (implemented and prototype systems). These are concrete prescriptions that enable IT researchers and practitioners to understand and address the problems inherent in developing and successfully implementing information systems within organizations (March and Smith 1995; Nunamaker *et al*. 1991a). As illustrations, Walls *et al*. (1992) and Markus *et al*. (2002) present design-science research aimed at developing executive information systems (EISs) and systems to support emerging knowledge processes (EKPs), respectively, within the context of 'IS design theories.' Such 'theories' prescribe 'effective development practices' (methods) and 'a type of system solution' (instantiation) for 'a particular class of user requirements' (models) (Markus *et al*. 2002, p 180). Such prescriptive theories must be evaluated with respect to the utility provided for the class of problems addressed.

An IT artifact, implemented in an organizational context, is often the object of study in IS behavioral-science research. Theories seek to predict or explain phenomena that occur with respect to the artifact's use (intention to use), perceived usefulness, and impact on individuals and organizations (net benefits) depending on system, service, and information quality (DeLone and McLean 1992; Seddon 1997; DeLone and McLean 2003). Much of this behavioral research has focused on one class of artifact, the instantiation (system), although other research efforts have also focused on the evaluation of constructs (e.g., Batra *et al*. 1990; Kim and March 1995; Bodart *et al*. 2001; Geerts and McCarthy 2002) and methods (e.g., Marakas and Elam 1998; Sinha and Vessey 1999). Relatively little behavioral research has focused on evaluating models, a major focus of research in the management science literature.

Design science, as the other side of the IS research cycle, creates and evaluates IT artifacts intended to solve identified organizational problems. Such artifacts are represented in a structured form that may vary from software, formal logic and rigorous mathematics to informal natural language descriptions. A mathematical basis for design allows many types of quantitative evaluations of an IT artifact, including optimization proofs, analytical simulation, and quantitative comparisons with alternative designs. The further evaluation of a new artifact in a given organizational context affords the opportunity to apply empirical and qualitative methods. The rich phenomena that emerge from the interaction of people, organizations, and technology may need to be qualitatively assessed to yield an understanding of the phenomena adequate for theory development or problem solving (Klein and Meyers 1999). As field studies enable behavioral-science researchers to understand organizational phenomena in context, the process of constructing and exercising innovative IT artifacts enable design-science researchers to understand the problem addressed by the artifact and the feasibility of their approach to its solution (Nunamaker *et al.* 1991a).

The primary goal of this paper is to inform the community of IS researchers and practitioners of how to conduct, evaluate, and present design-science research. We do so by describing the boundaries of design science within the IS discipline via a conceptual framework for understanding information systems research (Section 2) and by developing a set of guidelines for conducting and evaluating good design-science research (Section 3). We focus primarily on technology-based design although we note with interest the current exploration of organizations, policies, and work practices as designed artifacts (Boland 2002). Following Klein and Myers (1999) treatise on the conduct and evaluation of interpretive research in IS, we use the proposed guidelines to assess recent exemplar papers published in the IS literature in order to illustrate how authors, reviewers, and editors can apply them consistently (Section 4). We conclude (Section 5) with an analysis of the challenges of performing high-quality design-science research and a call for synergistic efforts between behavioral-science and design-science researchers.

2 A FRAMEWORK FOR IS RESEARCH

Information systems and the organizations they support are complex, artificial, and purposefully designed. They are composed of people, structures, technologies, and work systems (Bunge 1985; Simon 1996; Alter 2003). Much of the work performed by IS practitioners, and managers in general (Boland 2002), deals with design—the purposeful organization of resources to accomplish a goal. Figure 9.1 illustrates the essential alignments between business and information technology strategies and between organizational and information systems infrastructures (Henderson and Venkatraman 1993). The effective transition of strategy into infrastructure requires extensive design activity on both sides of the figure—organizational design to create an effective organizational infrastructure and information systems design to create an effective information system infrastructure.

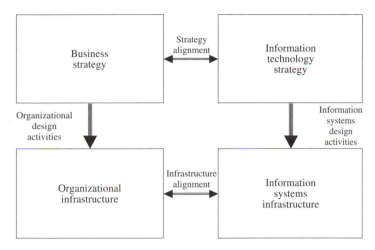

Figure 9.1 *Organizational Design and Information Systems Design Activities (Based on Henderson and Venkatraman 1993)*

These are interdependent design activities that are central to the IS discipline. Hence, IS research must address the interplay among: business strategy, IT strategy, organizational infrastructure, and IS infrastructure. This interplay is becoming more crucial as information technologies are seen as enablers of business strategy and organizational infrastructure (Kalakota and Robinson 2001; Orlikowski and Barley 2001). Available and emerging IT capabilities are a significant factor in determining the strategies that guide an organization. Cutting-edge information systems allow organizations to engage new forms and new structures—to change the ways they 'do business' (Drucker 1988; Drucker 1991; Orlikowski 2000). Our subsequent discussion of design science will be limited to the activities of building the IS infrastructure within the business organization. Issues of strategy, alignment, and organizational infrastructure design are outside the scope of this paper.

To achieve a true understanding of and appreciation for design science as an IS research paradigm, an important dichotomy must be faced. Design is both a process (set of activities) and a product (artifact)—a verb and a noun (Walls *et al.* 1992). It describes the world as acted upon (processes) and the world as sensed (artifacts). This Platonic view of design supports a problem-solving paradigm that continuously shifts perspective between design processes and designed artifacts for the same complex problem. The design process is a sequence of expert activities that produces an innovative product (i.e., the design artifact). The evaluation of the artifact then provides feedback information and a better understanding of the problem in order to improve both the quality of the product and the design process. This build-and-evaluate loop is typically iterated a number of times before the final design artifact is generated (Markus *et al.* 2002). During this creative process, the design-science researcher must be cognizant of evolving both the design process and the design artifact as part of the research.

March and Smith (1995) identify two design processes and four design artifacts produced by design-science research in IS. The two processes are build and evaluate. The artifacts are constructs, models, methods, and instantiations. Purposeful artifacts are built to address heretofore unsolved problems. They are evaluated with respect to the utility provided in solving those problems. Constructs provide the language in which problems and solutions are defined and communicated (Schon 1993). Models use constructs to represent a real world situation – the design problem and its solution space (Simon 1996). Models aid problem and solution understanding and frequently represent the connection between problem and solution components enabling exploration of the effects of design decisions and changes in the real world. Methods define processes. They provide guidance on how to solve problems, that is, how to search the solution space. These can range from formal, mathematical algorithms that explicitly define the search process to informal, textual descriptions of 'best practice' approaches, or some combination. Instantiations show that constructs, models or methods can be implemented in a working system. They demonstrate feasibility, enabling concrete assessment of an artifact's suitability to its intended purpose. They also enable researchers to learn about the real world, how the artifact affects it, and how users appropriate it.

Figure 9.2 presents our conceptual framework for understanding, executing, and evaluating IS research combining behavioral-science and design-science paradigms. We use this framework to position and compare these paradigms.

The environment defines the problem space (Simon 1996) in which reside the phenomena of interest. For IS research, it is composed of people, (business) organizations, and their existing or planned technologies (Silver *et al.* 1995). In it are the goals, tasks, problems, and opportunities that define business needs as they are perceived by people within the organization. Such perceptions are shaped by the roles, capabilities, and characteristics of people within the organization. Business needs are assessed and evaluated within the context of organizational strategies, structure, culture, and existing business processes. They are positioned relative to existing technology infrastructure, applications, communication architectures, and development capabilities. Together these define

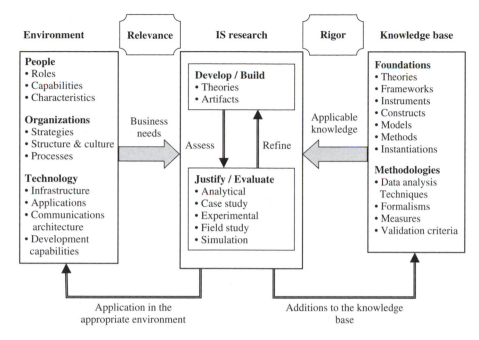

Figure 9.2 *Information Systems research framework*

the business need or 'problem' as perceived by the researcher. Framing research activities to address business needs assures research relevance.

Given such an articulated business need, IS research is conducted in two complementary phases. Behavioral science addresses research through the development and justification of theories that explain or predict phenomena related to the identified business need. Design science addresses research through the building and evaluation of artifacts designed to meet the identified business need. The goal of behavioral-science research is truth.[1] The goal of design-science research is utility. As argued above, our position is that truth and utility are inseparable. Truth informs design and utility informs theory. An artifact may have utility because of some yet undiscovered truth. A theory may yet to be developed to the point where its truth can be incorporated into design. In both cases, research assessment via the justify/evaluate activities can result in the identification of weaknesses in the theory or artifact and the need to refine and reassess. The refinement and reassessment process is typically described in future research directions.

The knowledge base provides the raw materials from and through which IS research is accomplished. The knowledge base is composed of Foundations and Methodologies. Prior IS research and results from reference disciplines provide foundational theories, frameworks, instruments, constructs, models, methods, and instantiations used in the develop/build phase of a research study. Methodologies provide guidelines used in the justify/evaluate phase. Rigor is achieved by appropriately applying existing foundations and methodologies. In behavioral science, methodologies are typically rooted in data collection and empirical analysis techniques. In design science, computational and mathematical methods are primarily used to evaluate the quality and effectiveness of artifacts; however, empirical techniques may also be employed.

The contributions of behavioral-science and design-science in IS research are assessed as they are applied to the business need in an appropriate environment and as they add to the content of the knowledge base for further research and practice. A justified theory that is not useful for the environment contributes as little to the IS literature as an artifact that solves a nonexistent problem.

One issue that must be addressed in design-science research is differentiating routine design or system building from design research. The difference is in the nature of the problems and solutions. Routine design is the application of existing knowledge to organizational problems, such as constructing a financial or marketing information system using 'best practice' artifacts (constructs, models, methods, and instantiations) existing in the knowledge base. On the other hand, design-science research addresses important unsolved problems in unique or innovative ways or solved problems in more effective or efficient ways. The key differentiator between routine design and design research is the clear identification of a contribution to the archival knowledge base of foundations and methodologies.

In the early stages of a discipline or with significant changes in the environment, each new artifact created for that discipline or environment is 'an experiment' that 'poses a question to nature' (Newell and Simon 1976, p. 114). Existing knowledge is used where appropriate; however, often the requisite knowledge is nonexistent (Markus *et al.* 2002). Reliance on creativity and trial and error search are characteristic of such research efforts. As design-science research results are codified in the knowledge base, they become 'best practice.' System building is then the routine application of the knowledge base to known problems.

Design activities are endemic in many professions. In particular, the engineering profession has produced a considerable literature on design (Dym 1994; Pahl and Beitz 1996; Petroski 1996). Within the IS discipline, many design activities have been extensively studied, formalized, and have become normal or routine. Design-science research in IS addresses what are considered to be wicked problems

(Rittel and Webber 1984; Brooks 1987; Brooks 1996). That is, those problems characterized by:

- Unstable requirements and constraints based upon ill-defined environmental contexts,
- Complex interactions among subcomponents of the problem and its solution,
- Inherent flexibility to change design processes as well as design artifacts (i.e., malleable processes and artifacts),
- A critical dependence upon human cognitive abilities (e.g., creativity) to produce effective solutions, and
- A critical dependence upon human social abilities (e.g., teamwork) to produce effective solutions.

As a result, we agree with Simon (1996) that a theory of design in information systems, of necessity, is in a constant state of scientific revolution (Kuhn 1996). Technological advances are the result of innovative, creative design science processes. If not 'capricious,' they are at least 'arbitrary' (Brooks 1987) with respect to business needs and existing knowledge. Innovations, such as database management systems, high-level languages, personal computers, software components, intelligent agents, object technology, the Internet, and the World Wide Web, have had dramatic and at times unintended impacts on the way in which information systems are conceived, designed, implemented, and managed. Consequently the guidelines we present below are, of necessity, adaptive and process-oriented.

3 GUIDELINES FOR DESIGN-SCIENCE IN INFORMATION SYSTEMS RESEARCH

As discussed above, design science is inherently a problem solving process. The fundamental principle of design-science research from which our seven guidelines are derived is that knowledge and understanding of a design problem and its solution are acquired in the building and application of an artifact. That is, design-science research requires the creation of an innovative, purposeful artifact (Guideline 1) for a specified problem domain (Guideline 2). Because the artifact is 'purposeful,' it must yield utility for the specified problem. Hence, thorough evaluation of the artifact is crucial (Guideline 3). Novelty is similarly crucial since the artifact must be 'innovative,' solving a heretofore unsolved problem or solving a known problem in a more effective or efficient manner (Guideline 4). In this way, design-science research is differentiated from the practice of design. The artifact itself must be rigorously defined, formally represented, coherent, and internally consistent (Guideline 5). The process by which it is created, and often the artifact itself, incorporates or enables a search process whereby a problem space is constructed and a mechanism posed or enacted to find an effective solution (Guideline 6). Finally, the results of the design-science research must be communicated effectively (Guideline 7) both to a technical audience (researchers who will extend them and practitioners who will implement them) and to a managerial audience (researchers who will study them in context and practitioners who will decide if they should be implemented within their organizations).

Our purpose for establishing these seven guidelines is to assist researchers, reviewers, editors, and readers to understand the requirements for effective design-science research. Following Klein and Myers (1999), we advise against mandatory or rote use of the guidelines. Researchers, reviewers, and editors must use their creative skills and judgment to determine when, where, and how to apply each of the guidelines in a specific research project. However, we contend that each of these guidelines should be addressed in some manner for design-science research to be complete. How well the research satisfies the intent of each of the guidelines is then a matter for the reviewers, editors, and readers to determine.

Table 9.1 summarizes the seven guidelines. Each is discussed in detail below. In the following section, they are applied to specific exemplar research efforts.

3.1 Guideline 1: Design as an Artifact

The result of design-science research in IS is, by definition, a purposeful IT artifact created to address an important organizational problem. It must be described effectively, enabling its implementation and application in an appropriate domain.

Orlikowski and Iacono (2001) call the IT artifact the 'core subject matter' of the IS field. Although they articulate multiple definitions of the term 'IT artifact,' many of which include components of the organization and people involved in the use of a computer-based artifact, they emphasize the importance of 'those bundles of cultural properties packaged in some socially recognizable form such as hardware and software' (p. 121), i.e., the IT artifact as an instantiation. Weber (1987) argues that theories of 'long-lived' artifacts (instantiations) and their representations (Weber 2003) are fundamental to the IS discipline. Such theories must explain how artifacts are created and adapted to their changing environments and underlying technologies.

Table 9.1   *Design-science research guidelines*

Guideline	Description
Guideline 1: Design as an Artifact	Design-science research must produce a viable artifact in the form of a construct, a model, a method, or an instantiation.
Guideline 2: Problem Relevance	The objective of design-science research is to develop technology-based solutions to important and relevant business problems.
Guideline 3: Design Evaluation	The utility, quality, and efficacy of a design artifact must be rigorously demonstrated via well-executed evaluation methods.
Guideline 4: Research Contributions	Effective design-science research must provide clear and verifiable contributions in the areas of the design artifact, design foundations, and/or design methodologies.
Guideline 5: Research Rigor	Design-science research relies upon the application of rigorous methods in both the construction and evaluation of the design artifact.
Guideline 6: Design as a Search Process	The search for an effective artifact requires utilizing available means to reach desired ends while satisfying laws in the problem environment.
Guideline 7: Communication of Research	Design-science research must be presented effectively both to technology-oriented as well as management-oriented audiences.

Our definition of IT artifacts is both broader and narrower then those articulated above. It is broader in the sense that we include not only instantiations in our definition of the IT artifact but also the constructs, models, and methods applied in the development and use of information systems. However, it is narrower in the sense that we do not include people or elements of organizations in our definition nor do we explicitly include the process by which such artifacts evolve over time. We conceive of IT artifacts not as independent of people or the organizational and social contexts in which they are used but as interdependent and coequal with them in meeting business needs. We acknowledge that perceptions and fit with an organization are crucial to the successful development and implementation of an information system. We argue, however, that the capabilities of the constructs, models, methods, and instantiations are equally crucial and that design-science research efforts are necessary for their creation.

Furthermore, artifacts constructed in design-science research are rarely full-grown information systems that are used in practice. Instead, artifacts are innovations that define the ideas, practices, technical capabilities, and products through which the analysis, design, implementation, and use of information systems can be effectively and efficiently accomplished (Tsichritzis 1997; Denning 1997). This definition of the artifact is consistent with the concept of IS 'design theory' as used by Walls *et al*. (1992) and Markus *et al*. (2002) where the theory addresses both the process of design and the designed product.

More precisely, constructs provide the vocabulary and symbols used to define problems and solutions. They have a significant impact on the way in which tasks and problems are conceived (Schon 1993; Boland 2002). They enable the construction of models or representations of the problem domain. Representation has a profound impact on design work. The field of mathematics was revolutionized, for example, with the constructs defined by Arabic numbers, zero, and place notation. The search for an effective problem representation is crucial to finding an effective design solution (Weber 2003). Simon (1996, p. 132) states, 'solving a problem simply means representing it so as to make the solution transparent.'

The Entity-Relationship model (Chen 1976), for example, is a set of constructs for representing the semantics of data. It has had a profound impact on the way in which systems analysis and database design are executed and the way in which information systems are represented and developed. Furthermore these constructs have been used to build models of specific business situations that have been generalized into patterns for application in similar domains (Purao *et al*. 2003). Methods for building such models have also been the subject of considerable research (Storey *et al*. 1997; Halpin 2001; McCarthy 1982; Parsons and Wand 2000).

Artifact instantiation demonstrates feasibility both of the design process and of the designed product. Design-science research in IT often addresses problems related to some aspect of the design of an information system. Hence the instantiations produced may be in the form of intellectual or software tools aimed at improving the process of information system development. Constructing a system instantiation that automates a process demonstrates that the process can, in fact, be automated. It provides 'proof by construction' (Nunamaker 1991a). The critical nature of design-science research in IS lies in the identification of as yet undeveloped capabilities needed to expand IS into new realms 'not previously believed amenable to IT support' (Markus *et al*. 2002, p. 180). Such a result is significant IS research only if there is a serious question about the ability to construct such an artifact, there is uncertainty about its ability to perform appropriately, and the automated task is important to the IS community. TOP Modeler (Markus *et al*. 2002), for example, is a tool that instantiates methods for the development of information systems that support 'emergent knowledge processes.' Construction of such a prototype artifact in a research setting or in a single organizational setting is only a first step toward its deployment, but we argue that it is a necessary one. As an exemplar of design-science research (see below), this research resulted in a commercial product that 'has been used in over two dozen "real use" situations' (p. 187).

To illustrate further, prior to the construction of the first expert system (instantiation), it was not clear if such a system could be constructed. It was not clear how to describe or represent it, or how well it would perform. Once feasibility was demonstrated by constructing an expert system in a selected domain, constructs and models were developed and subsequent research in expert systems focused on demonstrating significant improvements in the product or process (methods) of construction (Tam 1990; Trice and Davis 1993). Similar examples exist in requirements determination (Bell 1993; Bhargava *et al.* 1998), individual and group decision support systems (Aiken *et al.* 1991; Basu and Blanning 1994), database design and integration (Dey *et al.* 1998; Dey *et al.* 1999; Storey *et al.* 1997), and workflow analysis (Basu and Blanning 2000), to name a few important areas of IS design-science research.

3.2 Guideline 2: Problem Relevance

The objective of research in information systems is to acquire knowledge and understanding that enable the development and implementation of technology-based solutions to heretofore unsolved and important business problems. Behavioral science approaches this goal through the development and justification of theories explaining or predicting phenomena that occur. Design science approaches this goal through the construction of innovative artifacts aimed at changing the phenomena that occur. Each must inform and challenge the other. For example, the Technology Acceptance Model (Venkatesh 2000) provides a theory that explains and predicts the acceptance of information technologies within organizations. This theory challenges design-science researchers to create artifacts that enable organizations to overcome the acceptance problems predicted. We argue that a combination of technology-based artifacts (e.g., system conceptualizations and representations, practices, technical capabilities, interfaces, etc.), organization-based artifacts (e.g., structures, compensation, reporting relationships, social systems, etc.), and people-based artifacts (e.g., training, consensus building, etc.) are necessary to address such issues.

Formally, a problem can be defined as the differences between a goal state and the current state of a system. Problem solving can be defined as a search process (see Guideline 6) using actions to reduce or eliminate the differences (Simon 1996). These definitions imply an environment that imposes goal criteria as well as constraints upon a system. Business organizations are goal-oriented entities existing in an economic and social setting. Economic theory often portrays the goals of business organizations as being related to profit (utility) maximization. Hence, business problems and opportunities often relate to increasing revenue or decreasing cost through the design of effective business processes. The design of organizational and inter-organizational information systems plays a major role in enabling effective business processes to achieve these goals.

The relevance of any design-science research effort is with respect to a constituent community. For IS researchers that constituent community is the practitioners who plan, manage, design, implement, operate, and evaluate information systems and those who plan, manage, design, implement, operate, and evaluate the technologies that enable their development and implementation. To be relevant to this community, research must address the problems faced and the opportunities afforded by the interaction of people, organizations, and information technology. Organizations spend billions of dollars annually on IT, only too often to conclude that those dollars were wasted (Keil 1995; Keil *et al*. 1998; Keil and Robey 1999). This community would welcome effective artifacts that enable such problems to be addressed—constructs by which to think about them, models by which to represent and explore them, methods by which to analyze or optimize them, and instantiations that demonstrate how to affect them.

3.3 Guideline 3: Design Evaluation

The utility, quality, and efficacy of a design artifact must be rigorously demonstrated via well-executed evaluation methods. Evaluation is a crucial component of the research process. The business environment establishes the requirements upon which the evaluation of the artifact is based. This environment includes the technical infrastructure which itself is incrementally built by the implementation of new IT artifacts. Thus, evaluation includes the integration of the artifact within the technical infrastructure of the business environment.

As in the justification of a behavioral science theory, evaluation of a designed IT artifact requires the definition of appropriate metrics and possibly the gathering and analysis of appropriate data. IT artifacts can be evaluated in terms of functionality, completeness, consistency, accuracy, performance, reliability, usability, fit with the organization, and other relevant quality attributes. When analytical metrics are appropriate, designed artifacts may be mathematically evaluated. As two examples, distributed database design algorithms can be evaluated using expected operating cost or average response time for a given characterization of information processing requirements (Johansson *et al.* 2003) and search algorithms can be evaluated using information retrieval metrics such as precision and recall (Salton 1988).

Because design is inherently an iterative and incremental activity, the evaluation phase provides essential feedback to the construction phase as to the quality of the design process and the design product under development. A design artifact is complete and effective when it satisfies the requirements and constraints of the problem it was meant to solve. Design-science research efforts may begin with simplified conceptualizations and representations of problems. As available technology or organizational environments change, assumptions made in prior research may become invalid. Johansson (2000), for example, demonstrated that network latency is a major component in the response-time performance of distributed databases. Prior research in distributed database design ignored latency because it assumed a low-bandwidth network where latency is negligible. In a high-bandwidth network, however, latency can account for over 90 percent of the response time. Johansson *et al.* (2003) extended prior distributed database design research by developing a model that includes network latency and the effects of parallel processing on response time.

The evaluation of designed artifacts typically uses methodologies available in the knowledge base. These are summarized in Table 9.2. The selection of evaluation methods must be matched appropriately with the designed artifact and the selected evaluation metrics. For example, descriptive methods of evaluation should only be used for especially innovative artifacts for which other forms of evaluation may not be feasible. The goodness and efficacy of an artifact can be rigorously demonstrated via well-selected evaluation methods (Basili 1996; Kleindorfer *et al.* 1998; Zelkowitz and Wallace 1998).

Design, in all of its realizations (e.g., architecture, landscaping, art, music), has style. Given the problem and solution requirements, sufficient degrees of freedom remain to express a variety of forms and functions in the artifact that are aesthetically pleasing to both the designer and the user. Good designers bring an element of style to their work (Norman 1988). Thus, we posit that design evaluation should include an assessment of the artifact's style.

The measurement of style lies in the realm of human perception and taste. In other words, we know good style when we see it. While difficult to define, style in IS design is widely recognized and appreciated (Kernighan and Plauger 1978; Winograd 1996). Gelernter (1998) terms the essence of style in IS design 'machine beauty.' He

Table 9.2 *Design evaluation methods*

1. Observational	Case Study—Study artifact in depth in business environment
	Field Study—Monitor use of artifact in multiple projects
2. Analytical	Static Analysis—Examine structure of artifact for static qualities (e.g., complexity)
	Architecture Analysis—Study fit of artifact into technical IS architecture
	Optimization—Demonstrate inherent optimal properties of artifact or provide optimality bounds on artifact behavior
	Dynamic Analysis—Study artifact in use for dynamic qualities (e.g., performance)
3. Experimental	Controlled Experiment—Study artifact in controlled environment for qualities (e.g., usability)
	Simulation—Execute artifact with artificial data
4. Testing	Functional (Black Box) Testing—Execute artifact interfaces to discover failures and identify defects
	Structural (White Box) Testing—Perform coverage testing of some metric (e.g., execution paths) in the artifact implementation
5. Descriptive	Informed Argument—Use information from the knowledge base (e.g., relevant research) to build a convincing argument for the artifact's utility
	Scenarios—Construct detailed scenarios around the artifact to demonstrate its utility

describes it as a marriage between simplicity and power that drives innovation in science and technology. Simon (1996) also notes the importance of style in the design process. The ability to creatively vary the design process, within the limits of satisfactory constraints, challenges and adds value to designers who participate in the process.

3.4 Guideline 4: Research Contributions

Effective design-science research must provide clear contributions in the areas of the design artifact, design construction knowledge (i.e., foundations), and/or design evaluation knowledge (i.e., methodologies). The ultimate assessment for any research is 'What are the new and interesting contributions?' Design-science research holds the potential for three types of research contributions based on the novelty, generality, and significance of the designed artifact. One or more of these contributions must be found in a given research project.

- The Design Artifact—Most often, the contribution of design-science research is the artifact itself. The artifact must enable the solution of heretofore unsolved problems. It may extend the knowledge base (see below) or apply existing knowledge in new and innovative ways. As shown in Figure 9.2 by the left-facing arrow at the bottom of the figure from Design Science Research to the Environment, exercising the artifact in the environment produces significant value to the constituent IS community. System development methodologies, design tools, and prototype systems (e.g., GDSS, expert systems) are examples of such artifacts.

- Foundations—The creative development of novel, appropriately evaluated constructs, models, methods, or instantiations that extend and improve the existing foundations in the design-science knowledge base are also important contributions. The right-facing arrow at the bottom of the figure from Design Science Research to the Knowledge Base in Figure 9.2 indicates these contributions. Modeling formalisms, ontologies (Wand and Weber 1993; Wand and Weber 1995; Weber 1997), problem and solution representations, design algorithms (Storey *et al.* 1997), and innovative information systems (Walls *et al.* 1992; Markus *et al.* 2002; Aiken 1991) are examples of such artifacts.
- Methodologies—Finally, the creative development and use of evaluation methods (e.g., experimental, analytical, observational, testing, and descriptive) and new evaluation metrics provide design-science research contributions. Measures and evaluation metrics in particular are crucial components of design-science research. The right-facing arrow at the bottom of the figure from Design Science Research to the Knowledge Base in Figure 9.2 also indicates these contributions. TAM (Venkatesh 2000), for example, presents a framework for predicting and explaining why a particular information system will or will not be accepted in a given organizational setting. Although TAM is posed as a behavioral theory, it also provides metrics by which a designed information system or implementation process can be evaluated. Its implications for design itself are as yet unexplored.

Criteria for assessing contribution focus on representational fidelity and implementability. Artifacts must accurately represent the business and technology environments used in the research, information systems themselves being models of the business. These artifacts must be 'implementable,' hence the importance of instantiating design science artifacts. Beyond these, however, the research must demonstrate a clear contribution to the business environment, solving an important, previously unsolved problem.

3.5 Guideline 5: Research Rigor

Rigor addresses the way in which research is conducted. Design-science research requires the application of rigorous methods in both the construction and evaluation of the designed artifact. In behavioral-science research rigor is often assessed by adherence to appropriate data collection and analysis techniques. Overemphasis on rigor in behavioral IS research has often resulted in a corresponding lowering of relevance (Lee 1999).

Design-science research often relies on mathematical formalism to describe the specified and constructed artifact. However, the environments in which IT artifacts must perform and the artifacts themselves may defy excessive formalism. Or, in an attempt to be 'mathematically rigorous,' important parts of the problem may be abstracted or 'assumed away.' In particular, with respect to the construction activity, rigor must be assessed with respect to the applicability and generalizability of the artifact. Again, an overemphasis on rigor can lessen relevance. We argue, along with behavioral IS researchers (Applegate 1999), that it is possible and necessary for all IS research paradigms to be both rigorous and relevant.

In both design-science and behavioral-science research, rigor is derived from the effective use of the knowledge base—theoretical foundations and research methodologies. Success is predicated on the researcher's skilled selection of appropriate techniques to develop or construct a theory or artifact and the selection of appropriate means to justify the theory or evaluate the artifact.

Claims about artifacts are typically dependent upon performance metrics. Even formal mathematical proofs rely on evaluation criteria against which the performance of an artifact can be measured. Design-science researchers must constantly assess the appropriateness of their metrics and the construction of effective metrics is an important part of design-science research.

Furthermore, designed artifacts are often components of a human-machine problem-solving system. For such artifacts, knowledge of behavioral theories and empirical work are necessary to construct and evaluate such artifacts. Constructs, models, methods, and instantiations must be exercised within appropriate environments. Appropriate subject groups must be obtained for such studies. Issues that are addressed include comparability, subject selection, training, time, and tasks. Methods for this type of evaluation are not unlike those for justifying or testing behavioral theories. However, the principal aim is to determine how well an artifact works, not to theorize about or prove anything about why the artifact works. This is where design-science and behavioral-science researchers must complement one another. Because design-science artifacts are often the 'machine' part of the human-machine system constituting an information system, it is imperative to understand why an artifact works or does not work to enable new artifacts to be constructed that exploit the former and avoid the latter.

3.6 Guideline 6: Design as a Search Process

Design science is inherently iterative. The search for the best, or optimal, design is often intractable for realistic information systems problems. Heuristic search strategies produce feasible, good designs that can be implemented in the business environment. Simon (1996) describes the nature of the design process as a Generate/Test Cycle (Figure 9.3).

Design is essentially a search process to discover an effective solution to a problem. Problem solving can be viewed as utilizing available means to reach desired ends while satisfying laws existing in the environment (Simon 1996). Abstraction and representation of appropriate means, ends, and laws are crucial components of design-science research. These factors are problem and environment dependent and invariably involve creativity and innovation. Means are the set of actions and resources available to construct a solution. Ends represent goals and constraints on the solution. Laws are uncontrollable forces in the environment. Effective design requires knowledge of both the application domain (e.g., requirements and constraints) and the solution domain (e.g., technical and organizational).

Design-science research often simplifies a problem by explicitly representing only a subset of the relevant means, ends, and laws or by decomposing a problem into simpler sub-problems. Such simplifications and decompositions may not be realistic enough to have a significant impact on practice but may represent a starting point. Progress is made iteratively as the scope of the design problem is expanded. As means, ends, and laws are refined and made more realistic the design artifact becomes more relevant and valuable. The

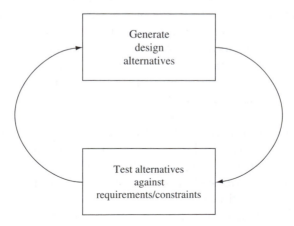

Figure 9.3   *The Generate/Test Cycle*

means, ends, and laws for IS design problems can often be represented using the tools of mathematics and operations research. Means are represented by decision variables whose values constitute an implementable design solution. Ends are represented using a utility function and constraints that can be expressed in terms of decision variables and constants. Laws are represented by the values of constants used in the utility function and constraints.

The set of possible design solutions for any problem is specified as all possible means that satisfy all end conditions consistent with identified laws. When these can be formulated appropriately and posed mathematically, standard operations research techniques can be used to determine an optimal solution for the specified end conditions. Given the wicked nature of many information system design problems, however, it may not be possible to determine, let alone explicitly describe the relevant means, ends, or laws (Vessey and Glass 1998). Even when it is possible to do so, the sheer size and complexity of the solution space will often render the problem computationally infeasible. For example, to build a 'reliable, secure, and responsive information systems infrastructure,' one of the key issues faced by IS managers (Brancheau *et al.* 1996), a designer would need to represent all possible infrastructures (means), determine their utility and constraints (ends), and specify all cost and benefit constants (laws). Clearly such an approach is infeasible. However, this does not mean that design-science research is inappropriate for such a problem.

In such situations, the search is for satisfactory solutions, i.e., satisficing (Simon 1996), without explicitly specifying all possible solutions. The design task involves the creation, utilization, and assessment of heuristic search strategies. That is, constructing an artifact that 'works' well for the specified class of problems. Although its construction is based on prior theory and existing design knowledge it may or may not be entirely clear why it works or the extent of its generalizability; it simply qualifies as 'credentialed knowledge' (Meehl 1986, p. 311). While it is important to understand why an artifact works, the critical nature of design in IS makes it important to first establish that it does work and to characterize the environments in which it works, even if we cannot completely explain why it works. This enables IS practitioners to take advantage of the artifact to improve practice and provides a context for additional research aimed at more fully explicating the resultant phenomena. Markus *et al.* (2002), for example, describe their search process in terms of iteratively identifying deficiencies in constructed prototype software systems and creatively developing solutions to address them.

The use of heuristics to find 'good' design solutions opens the question of how goodness is measured. Different problem representations may provide varying techniques for measuring how good a solution is. One approach is to prove or demonstrate that a heuristic design solution is always within close proximity of an 'optimal' solution. Another is to compare produced solutions with those constructed by expert human designers for the same problem situation.

3.7 Guideline 7: Communication of Research

Design-science research must be presented both to technology-oriented as well as management-oriented audiences. Technology-oriented audiences need sufficient detail to enable the described artifact to be constructed (implemented) and used within an appropriate organizational context. This enables practitioners to take advantage of the benefits offered by the artifact and it enables researchers to build a cumulative knowledge base for further extension and evaluation. It is also important for such audiences to understand the processes by which the artifact was constructed and evaluated. This establishes repeatability of the research project and builds the knowledge base for further research extensions by design-science researchers in IS.

Management-oriented audiences need sufficient detail to determine if the organizational resources should be committed to constructing (or purchasing) and using the artifact within their specific organizational context. Zmud (1997) suggests that presentation of design-science research for a managerial audience requires an emphasis not on the inherent nature of the artifact itself, but on the knowledge required to effectively apply the artifact 'within specific contexts for individual or organizational gain' (p. ix). That is, the emphasis must be on the importance of the problem and the novelty and effectiveness of the solution approach realized in the artifact. While we agree with this statement, we note that it may be necessary to describe the artifact in some detail to enable managers to appreciate its nature and understand its application. Presenting that detail in concise, well-organized appendices, as advised by Zmud, is an appropriate communication mechanism for such an audience.

4 APPLICATION OF THE DESIGN SCIENCE RESEARCH GUIDELINES

To illustrate the application of the design-science guidelines to IS research, we have selected three exemplar articles for analysis from three different IS journals, one from *Decision Support Systems*, one from *Information Systems Research*, and one from *MIS Quarterly*. Each has strengths and weaknesses when viewed through the lens of the above guidelines. Our goal is not to perform a critical evaluation of the quality of the research contributions, but rather to illuminate the design-science guidelines. The articles are:

- Gavish and Gerdes (1998) develop techniques for implementing anonymity in Group Decision Support Systems (GDSS) environments.
- Aalst and Kumar (2003) propose a design for an eXchangeable Routing Language (XRL) to support electronic commerce workflows among trading partners.
- Markus, Majchrzak, and Gasser (2002) propose a design theory for the development of information systems built to support emergent knowledge processes.

The fundamental questions for design-science research are, 'What utility does the new artifact provide?' and 'What demonstrates that utility?' Evidence must be presented to address these two questions. That is the essence of design science. Contribution arises from utility. If existing artifacts are adequate then design-science research that creates a new artifact is unnecessary (it is irrelevant). If the new artifact does not map adequately to the real world (rigor) it cannot provide utility. If the artifact does not solve the problem (search, implementability) it has no utility. If utility is not demonstrated (evaluation) then there is no basis upon which to accept the claims that it provides any contribution (contribution). Furthermore, if the problem, the artifact, and its utility are not presented in a manner such that the implications for research and practice are clear, then publication in the IS literature is not appropriate (communication).

4.1 The Design and Implementation of Anonymity in GDSS—Gavish and Gerdes (1998)

The study of group decision support systems (GDSS) has been and remains one of the most visible and successful research streams in the IS field. The use of information technology to effectively support meetings of groups of different sizes over time and space is a real problem that challenges all business organizations. Recent GDSS literature surveys demonstrate the large numbers of GDSS research papers published in the IS field and, more importantly, the wide variety of research paradigms applied to GDSS research (e.g., Nunamaker *et al*. 1996; Fjermestad and Hiltz 1998; Dennis and Wixom 2001). However, only a small number of GDSS papers can be considered to make true design-science research contributions. Most assume the introduction of a new information technology or process in the GDSS environment and then study the individual, group, or organizational implications using a behavioral-science research paradigm. Several such GDSS papers have appeared in *MIS Quarterly*, e.g. (Jarvenpaa *et al.* 1988; Dickson *et al.* 1993; Sengupta and Te'eni 1993; Gallupe *et al.* 1988).

The central role of design science in GDSS is clearly recognized in the early foundation papers of the field. The University of Arizona Electronic Meeting System group, for example, states the need for both developmental and empirical research agendas (Dennis *et al.* 1988; Nunamaker *et al.* 1991b). Developmental, or design-science, research is called for in the areas of process structures and support and task structures and support. Process structure and support technologies and methods are generic to all GDSS environments and tasks. Technologies and methods for distributed communications, group memory, decision-making methods, and anonymity are a few of the critical design issues for GDSS process support needed in any task domain. Task structure and support are specific to the problem domain under consideration by the group (e.g., medical decision making, software development). Task support includes the design of new technologies and methods for managing and analyzing task-related information and using that information to make specific, task-related decisions.

The issue of anonymity has been studied extensively in GDSS environments. Behavioral research studies have shown both positive and negative impacts on group interactions. On the positive side, GDSS participants can express their views freely without fear of embarrassment or reprisal. However, anonymity can encourage free-riding and antisocial behaviors. While the pros and cons of anonymity in GDSS are much researched, there has been a noticeable lack of research on the design of techniques for implementing anonymity in GDSS environments. Gavish and Gerdes (1998) address this issue by designing five basic mechanisms to provide GDSS procedural anonymity.

Problem relevance

The amount of interest and research on anonymity issues in GDSS testifies to its relevance. Field studies and surveys clearly indicate that participants rank anonymity as a highly desired attribute in the GDSS system. Many individuals state that they would refuse to participate in or trust the results of a GDSS meeting without a satisfactory level of assured anonymity (Fjermestad and Hiltz 1998).

Research rigor

Gavish and Gerdes base their GDSS anonymity designs on past research in the fields of cryptography and secure network communication protocols (e.g., Chaum 1981; Schneier 1996). These research areas have a long history of formal, rigorous results that have been applied to the design of many practical security and privacy mechanisms. Appendix A of the exemplar paper provides a set of formal proofs that the claims made by the authors for the anonymity designs are correct and draw their validity from the knowledge base of this past research.

Design as a search process

The authors motivate their design science research by identifying three basic types of anonymity in a GDSS system—environmental, content, and procedural. After a definition and brief discussion of each type, they focus on the design of mechanisms for procedural anonymity; the ability of the GDSS system to hide the source of any message. This is a very difficult requirement because standard network protocols typically attach source information in headers to support reliable transmission protocols. Thus, GDSS systems must modify standard communication protocols and include additional transmission procedures to ensure required levels of anonymity.

The design-science process employed by the authors is to state the desired procedural anonymity attributes of the GDSS system and then to design mechanisms to satisfy the system requirements for anonymity. Proposed designs are presented and anonymity claims are proved to be correct. A thorough discussion of the costs and benefits of the proposed anonymity mechanisms is provided in Section 4 of the paper.

Design as an artifact

The authors design a GDSS system architecture that provides a rigorous level of procedural anonymity. Five mechanisms are employed to ensure participant anonymity:

- All messages are encrypted with a unique session key.
- The sender's header information is removed from all messages.
- All messages are re-encrypted upon retransmission from any GDSS server.
- Transmission order of messages is randomized.
- Artificial messages are introduced to thwart traffic analysis.

The procedures and communication protocols that implement these mechanisms in a GDSS system are the artifacts of this research.

Design evaluation

The evaluation consists of two reported activities. First, in Appendix A, each mechanism is proved to correctly provide the claimed anonymity benefits. Formal proof methods are used to validate the effectiveness of the designed mechanisms. Second, Section 4 presents a thorough cost-benefit analysis. It is shown that the operational costs of supporting the proposed anonymity mechanisms can be quite significant. In addition, the communication protocols to implement the mechanisms add considerable complexity to the system. Thus, the authors recommend that a cost-benefit justification be performed before determining the level of anonymity to implement for a GDSS meeting.

The authors do not claim to have implemented the proposed anonymity mechanisms in a prototype or actual GDSS system. Thus, an instantiation of the designed artifact remains to be evaluated in an operational GDSS environment.

Research contributions

The design-science contributions of this research are the proposed anonymity mechanisms as the design artifacts and the evaluation results in the form of formal proofs and cost-benefit analyses. These contributions advance our understanding of how best to provide participant anonymity in GDSS meetings.

Research communication

Although the presentation of this research is aimed at an audience familiar with network system concepts such as encryption and communication protocols, the paper also contains important, useful information for a managerial audience. Managers should have a good understanding of the implications of anonymity in GDSS meetings. This understanding must include an appreciation of the costs of providing desired levels of participant anonymity. While the authors provide a thorough discussion of cost-benefit tradeoffs toward the end of the paper, the paper would be more accessible to a managerial audience if it included a stronger motivation up front on the important implications of anonymity in GDSS system development and operations.

4.2 A Workflow Language for Inter-Organizational Processes—Aalst and Kumar (2003)

Workflow models are an effective means for describing, analyzing, implementing, and managing business processes. Workflow management systems are becoming integral components of many commercial enterprise-wide information systems (Leymann and Roller 2000).

Standards for workflow semantics and syntax (i.e., workflow languages) and workflow architectures are promulgated by the Workflow Management Coalition (WfMC 2000). While workflow models have been used for many years to manage intra-organizational business processes, there is now a great demand for effective tools to model inter-organization processes across heterogeneous and distributed environments, such as those found in electronic commerce and complex supply chains (Kumar and Zhao 2002).

Aalst and Kumar (2003) investigate the problem of exchanging business process information across multiple organizations in an automated manner. They design an eXchangable Routing Language (XRL) to capture workflow models that are then embedded in eXtensible Markup Language (XML) for electronic transmission to all participants in an inter-organizational business process. The design of XRL is based upon Petri-nets which provide a formal basis for analyzing the correctness and performance of the workflows, as well as supporting the extensibility of the language. The authors develop a workflow management architecture and a prototype implementation to evaluate XRL in a proof of concept.

Problem relevance

Inter-organizational electronic commerce is growing rapidly and is projected to soon exceed one trillion dollars annually (eMarketer 2002). A multitude of electronic commerce solutions are being proposed (e.g., ebXML, UDDI, RosettaNet) to enable businesses to execute transactions in standardized, open environments. While XML has been widely accepted as a protocol for exchanging business data, there is still no clear standard for exchanging business process information (e.g., workflow models). This is the very relevant problem addressed by this research.

Research rigor

Research on workflow modeling has long been based on rigorous mathematical techniques such as Markov chains, queueing networks, and Petri-nets (Aalst and Hee 2002). In this paper, Petri-nets provide the underlying semantics for XRL. These formal semantics allow for powerful analysis techniques (e.g., correctness, performance) to be applied to the designed workflow models. Such formalisms also enable the development of automated tools to manipulate and analyze complex workflow designs. Each language construct in XRL has an equivalent Petri-net representation presented in the paper. The language is extensible in that adding a new construct simply requires defining its Petri-net representation and adding its syntax to the XRL. Thus, this research draws from a clearly defined and tested base of modeling literature and knowledge.

Design as a search process

XRL is designed in the paper by performing a thorough analysis of business process requirements and identifying features provided by leading commercial workflow management systems. Using the terminology from the paper, workflows traverse routes through available tasks (i.e., business services) in the electronic business environment. The basic routing constructs of XRL define the specific control flow of the business process. The authors build 13 basic constructs into XRL – Task, Sequence, Any_sequence, Choice, Condition, Parallel_sync, Parallel_no_sync, Parallel_part_sync, Wait_all, Wait_any, While_do, Stop, and Terminate. They show the Petri-net representation of each construct. Thus, the fundamental control flow structures of sequence, decision, iteration, and concurrency are supported in XRL.

The authors demonstrate the capabilities of XRL in several examples. However, they are careful not to claim that XRL is complete in the formal sense that all possible business processes can be modeled in XRL. The search for a complete set of XRL constructs is left for future research.

Design as an artifact

There are two clearly identifiable artifacts produced in this research. First, the workflow language XRL is designed. XRL is based on Petri-net formalisms and described in XML syntax. Inter-organizational business processes are specified via XRL for execution in a distributed, heterogeneous environment.

The second research artifact is the XRL/Flower workflow management architecture in which XRL-described processes are executed. The XRL routing scheme is parsed by an XML parser and stored as an XML data structure. This structure is read into a Petri-net engine which determines the next step of the business process and informs the next task provider via an email message. Results of each task are sent back to the engine which then executes the next step in the process until completion. The paper presents a prototype implementation of the XRL/Flower architecture as a proof of concept (Aalst and Kumar 2003).

Another artifact of this research is a workflow verification tool named Wolfan that verifies the soundness of business process workflows. Soundness of a workflow requires that the workflow terminates, no Petri-net tokens are left behind upon termination, and there are no dead tasks in the workflow. This verification tool is described more completely in a different paper (Aalst 1999).

Design evaluation

The authors evaluate the XRL and XRL/Flower designs in several important ways:

- XRL is compared and contrasted with languages in existing commercial workflow systems and research prototypes. The majority of these languages are proprietary and difficult to adapt to ad-hoc business process design.
- The fit of XRL with proposed standards is studied. In particular, the Interoperability Wf-XML Binding standard (WfMC 2000) does not at this time include the specification of control flow and, thus, is not suitable for inter-organizational workflows. Electronic commerce standards (e.g., RosettaNet) provide some level of control flow specification for predefined business activities, but do not readily allow the ad-hoc specification of business processes.
- A research prototype of XRL/Flower has been implemented and several of the user interface screens are presented. The screens demonstrate a mail-order routing schema case study.
- The Petri-Net foundation of XRL allows the authors to claim the XRL workflows can be verified for correctness and performance. XRL is extensible since new constructs can be added to the language based on their translation to underlying Petri-Net representations. However, as discussed above, the authors do not make a formal claim for the representational completeness of XRL.

Research contributions

The clear contributions of this research are the design artifacts—XRL (a workflow language), XRL/Flower (a workflow architecture and its implemented prototype system), and Wolfan (a Petri-Net verification engine). Another interesting contribution is the extension of XML in its ability to describe and transmit routing schemas (e.g., control flow information) to support inter-organizational electronic commerce.

Research communication

This paper provides clear information to both technical and managerial audiences. The presentation, while primarily technical with XML coding and Petri-Net diagrams throughout, motivates a managerial audience with a strong introduction on risks and benefits of applying inter-organizational workflows to electronic commerce applications.

4.3 Information Systems Design for Emergent Knowledge Processes—Markus, Majchrzak, and Gasser (2002)

Despite decades of research and development efforts, effective methods for developing information systems that meet the information requirements of upper management remain elusive. Early approaches used a 'waterfall' approach where requirements were defined and validated prior to initiating design efforts which, in turn, were completed prior to implementation (Royce 1998). Prototyping approaches emerged next followed by numerous proposals including CASE tool-based approaches, rapid application development, and extreme programming (Kruchten 2000). Walls *et al.* (1992) propose a framework for a prescriptive information system design theory aimed at enabling designers to construct 'more effective information systems' (p. 36). They apply this framework to the design of vigilant executive information systems. The framework establishes a class of user requirements (model of design problems) that are most effectively addressed using a particular type of system solution (instantiation) designed using a prescribed set of development practices (methods). Markus *et al.* (2002) extend this framework to the development of information systems to support emergent knowledge processes (EKPs)—processes in which structure is 'neither possible nor desirable' (p. 182) and where processes are characterized by highly unpredictable user types and work contexts' (p. 183).

Problem relevance

The relevance and importance of the problem are well demonstrated. Markus *et al.* (2002) describe a class of management activities that they term emergent knowledge processes (EKPs). These include 'basic research, new product development, strategic business planning, and organization design' (p. 179). They are characterized by 'process emergence, unpredictable user types and use contexts, and distributed expert knowledge' (p. 186). They are crucial to many manufacturing organizations, particularly those in high-tech industries. Such organizations recognize the need to integrate organizational design and information system design with manufacturing operations. They recognize the potential for significant performance improvements offered by such integration. Yet few have realized that potential. Markus *et al.* argue that this is due to a lack of an adequate design theory and lack of scientifically-based tools, noting that existing information system development methodologies focus on structured or semi-structured decision processes and are inadequate for the development of systems to support EKPs. TOP Modeler, the artifact created in this research effort, squarely addresses this problem. Not surprisingly its development attracted the attention and active participation of several large high-tech manufacturing organizations including 'Hewlett-Packard, General Motors, Digital Equipment Corporation, and Texas Instruments' (p. 186).

Research rigor

The presented work has theoretical foundations in both IS design theory and organizational design theory. It uses the basic notions of IS design theory presented in Walls *et al.* (1992) and poses a prescription for designing information systems to support EKPs. Prior research in developing decision support systems, executive information systems, and expert systems serve as a foundation for this work and deficiencies of these approaches for the examined problem type serve as motivation. The knowledge-base constructed within TOP Modeler was formed from a synthesis of socio-technical systems theory and the empirical literature on organizational design knowledge. It was evaluated theoretically using standard metrics from the expert systems literature and empirically using data gathered from numerous electronics manufacturing companies in the U.S. Development of TOP Modeler used an 'action research paradigm' starting with a 'kernel theory' based on prior development methods and theoretical results and iteratively posing and testing artifacts (prototypes) to assess progress toward the desired result. Finally, the artifact was commercialized and 'used in over two dozen "real use" situations.' (p. 187). In summary, this work effectively used theoretical foundations from IS and organizational theory, applied appropriate research methods in developing the artifact, defined and applied appropriate performance measures, and tested the artifact within an appropriate context.

Design as a search process

As discussed above, implementation and iteration are central to this research. The authors study prototypes that instantiate posed or newly learned design prescriptions. Their use and impacts were observed, problems identified, solutions posed and implemented, and the cycle was then repeated. These interventions occurred over a period of 18 months within the aforementioned companies as they dealt with organizational design tasks. As a result not only was the TOP Modeler developed and deployed but prescriptions (methods) in the form of six principles for developing systems to support EKPs were also devised. The extensive experience, creativity, intuition, and problem solving capabilities of the researchers were involved in assessing problems and interpreting the results of deploying various TOP modeler iterations and in constructing improvements to address shortcomings identified.

Design as an artifact

The TOP Modeler is an implemented software system (instantiation). It is composed of an object-oriented user interface, an object-oriented query generator, and an analysis module built on top of a relational meta-knowledge base that enables access to 'pluggable' knowledge bases representing different domains. It also includes tools to support the design and construction of these knowledge bases. The TOP Modeler supports a development process incorporating the six principles for developing systems to support EKPs. As mentioned above TOP Modeler was commercialized and used in a number of different organizational redesign situations.

Design evaluation

Evaluation is in the context of organizational design in manufacturing organizations, and is based on observation during the development and deployment of a single artifact, TOP Modeler. No formal evaluation was attempted in the sense of comparison with other artifacts. This is not surprising, nor is it a criticism of this work. There simply are no existing artifacts that address the same problem. However, given that methodologies for developing information systems to support semi-structured management activities are the closest available artifacts it is appropriate to use them as a comparative measure. In effect this was accomplished by using principles from these methodologies to inform the initial design of TOP Modeler. The identification of deficiencies in the resultant artifact provides evidence that these artifacts are ill-suited to the task at hand.

Iterative development and deployment within the context of organizational design in manufacturing organizations provide opportunities to observe improvement but do not enable formal evaluation—at each iteration changes are induced in the organization that cannot be controlled. As mentioned above, the authors have taken a creative and innovative approach that, of necessity, trades-off rigor for relevancy. In the initial stages of a discipline this approach is extremely effective. TOP Modeler demonstrates the feasibility of developing an artifact to support organizational design and EKPs within high-tech manufacturing organizations. 'In short, the evidence suggests that TOP Modeler was successful in supporting organizational design' (p. 187) but additional study is required to assess the comparative effectiveness of other possible approaches in this or other contexts. Again this is not a criticism of this work; rather it is a call for further research in the general class of problems dealing with emergent knowledge processes. As additional research builds on this foundation formal, rigorous evaluation and comparison with alternative approaches in a variety of contexts become crucial to enable claims of generalizability. As the authors point out, 'Only the accumulated weight of empirical evidence will establish the validity' of such claims.

Research contributions

The design-science contributions of this research are the TOP Modeler software and the design principles. TOP Modeler demonstrates the feasibility of using the design principles to develop an artifact to support EKPs. Because TOP Modeler is the first artifact to address this task, its construction is itself a contribution to design science. Furthermore because the authors are able to articulate the design principles upon which its construction was based, these serve as hypotheses to be tested by future empirical work. Their applicability to the development of other types of information systems can also be tested. An agenda for addressing such issues is presented. This focuses on validation, evaluation, and the challenges of improvement inherent in the evaluation process.

Research communication

This work presents two types of artifacts, TOP Modeler (an instantiation) and a set of design principles (method) that address a heretofore unsolved problem dealing with the design of an information system to support EKPs. Recognizing that existing system development methods and instantiations are aimed at structured or semi-structured activities, Markus *et al.* (2002) identify an opportunity to apply information technology in a new and innovative way. Their presentation addresses each of the design guidelines posed above. TOP Modeler exemplifies 'proof by construction'—it is feasible to construct an information system to support EKPs. Since it is the first such artifact, its evaluation using formal methods is deferred until future research. Technical details of TOP Modeler are not presented making it difficult for a technical researcher or practitioner to replicate their work. The uniqueness of the artifacts and the innovation inherent in them are presented so that managerial researchers and IT managers are aware of the new capabilities.

5 DISCUSSION AND CONCLUSIONS

Philosophical debates on how to conduct IS research (e.g., positivism vs. interpretivism) have been the focus of much recent attention (Klein and Myers 1999; Robey 1996; Weber 2003). The major emphasis of such debates lies in the epistemologies of research, the underlying assumption being that of the natural sciences. That is, somewhere some truth exists and somehow that truth can be extracted, explicated, and codified. The behavioral-science paradigm seeks to find 'what is true.' In contrast, the design-science paradigm seeks to create 'what is effective.' While it can be argued that utility relies on truth, the discovery of truth may lag the application of its utility. We argue that both design-science and behavioral-science paradigms are needed to ensure the relevance and effectiveness of IS research. Given the artificial nature of organizations and the information systems that support them, the design-science paradigm can play a significant role in resolving the fundamental dilemmas that have plagued IS research: rigor, relevance, discipline boundaries, behavior, and technology (Lee 2000).

Information systems research lies at the intersection of people, organizations and technology (Silver *et al.* 1995). It relies on and contributes to cognitive science, organizational theory, management sciences, and computer science. It is both an organizational and a technical discipline that is concerned with the analysis, construction, deployment, use, evaluation, evolution, and management of information system artifacts in organizational settings (Madnick 1992; Orlikowski and Barley 2001).

Within this setting, the design-science research paradigm is proactive with respect to technology. It focuses on creating and evaluating innovative IT artifacts that enable organizations to address important information-related tasks. The behavioral-science research paradigm is reactive with respect to technology in the sense that it takes technology as 'given.' It focuses on developing and justifying theories that explain and predict phenomena related to the acquisition, implementation, management, and use of such technologies. The dangers of a design-science research paradigm are an overemphasis on the technological artifacts and a failure to maintain an adequate theory base, potentially resulting in 'well-designed' artifacts that are useless in real organizational settings. The dangers of a behavioral-science research paradigm are overemphasis on contextual theories and failure to adequately identify and anticipate technological capabilities, potentially resulting in theories and principles addressing outdated or ineffective technologies. We argue strongly that IS research must be both proactive and reactive with respect to technology. It needs a complete research cycle where design science creates artifacts for specific information problems based on relevant behavioral science theory and behavioral science anticipates and engages the created technology artifacts.

Hence we reiterate the call made earlier by March *et al.* (2000) to align IS design-science research with real-world production experience. Results from such industrial experience can be framed in the context of our seven guidelines. These must be assessed not only by IS design-science researchers but also by IS behavioral-science researchers who can validate the organizational problems as well as study and anticipate the impacts of created artifacts. Thus, we encourage collaborative industrial/academic research projects and publications based on such experience. Markus *et al.* (2002) is an excellent example of such collaboration. Publication of these results will help accelerate the development of domain independent and scalable solutions to large-scale information systems problems within organizations. We recognize that a lag exists between academic research and its adoption in industry. We also recognize the possible ad hoc nature of technology-oriented solutions developed in industry. The latter gap can be reduced considerably by developing and framing the industrial solutions based on our proposed guidelines.

It is also important to distinguish between 'system building' efforts and design-science research. Guidelines addressing evaluation, contributions, and rigor are especially important in providing this distinction. The underlying formalism required by these guidelines helps researchers to develop representations of IS problems, solutions, and solution processes that clarify the knowledge produced by the research effort.

As we move forward, there exist a number of exciting challenges facing the design-science research community in IS. A few are summarized here.

- There is an inadequate theoretical base upon which to build an engineering discipline of information systems design (Basili 1996). The field is still very young lacking the cumulative theory development found in other engineering and social-science disciplines. It is important to demonstrate the feasibility and utility of such a theoretical base to a managerial audience that must make technology-adoption decisions that can have far-reaching impacts on the organization.
- Insufficient sets of constructs, models, methods, and tools exist for accurately representing the business/technology environment.

Highly abstract representations (e.g., analytical mathematical models) are criticized as having no relationship to 'real-world' environments. On the other hand, many informal, descriptive IS models lack an underlying theory base. The trade-offs between relevance and rigor are clearly problematic; finding representational techniques with an acceptable balance between the two is very difficult.

- The existing knowledge base is often insufficient for design purposes and designers must rely on intuition, experience, and trial-and-error methods. A constructed artifact embodies the designer's knowledge of the problem and solution. In new and emerging applications of technology the artifact itself represents an experiment. In its execution, we learn about the nature of the problem, the environment, and the possible solutions—hence the importance of developing and implementing prototype artifacts (Newell and Simon 1976).

- Design-science research is perishable. Rapid advances in technology can invalidate design-science research results before they are implemented effectively in the business environment or, just as importantly to managers, before adequate payback can be achieved by committing organizational resources to implementing those results. Two examples are the promises made by the artificial intelligence community in the 1980's (Feigenbaum and McCorduck 1983) and the more recent research on object-oriented databases (Chaudhri and Loomis 1998). Just as important to IS researchers, design results can be overtaken by technology before they even appear in the research literature. How much research was published on the Year 2000 problem before it became a non-event?

- Rigorous evaluation methods are extremely difficult to apply in design-science research (Tichy 1998; Zelkowitz and Wallace 1998). For example, the use of a design artifact on a single project may not generalize to different environments (Markus *et al.* 2002).

We believe that design science will play an increasingly important role in the IS profession. IS managers in particular are actively engaged in design activities—the creation, deployment, evaluation, and improvement of purposeful IT artifacts that enable organizations to achieve their goals. The challenge for design-science researchers in IS is to inform managers of the capabilities and impacts of new IT artifacts.

Much of the research published in *MIS Quarterly* employs the behavioral-science paradigm. It is passive with respect to technology, often ignoring or 'under-theorizing' the artifact itself (Orlikowski and

Iacono 2001). Its focus is on describing the implications of 'technology'—its impact on individuals, groups, and organizations. It regularly includes studies that examine how people employ a technology, report on the benefits and difficulties encountered when a technology is implemented within an organization, or discuss how managers might facilitate the use of a technology. Orman (2002) argues that many of the equivocal results in IS behavioral-science studies can be explained by a failure to differentiate the capabilities and purposes of the studied technology.

Design science is active with respect to technology, engaging in the creation of technological artifacts that impact people and organizations. Its focus is on problem solving but often takes a simplistic view of the people and the organizational contexts in which designed artifacts must function. As stated earlier, the design of an artifact, its formal specification, and an assessment of its utility, often by comparison with competing artifacts, are integral to design-science research. These must be combined with behavioral and organizational theories to develop an understanding of business problems, contexts, solutions, and evaluation approaches adequate to servicing the IS research and practitioner communities. The effective presentation of design-science research in major IS journals, such as *MIS Quarterly*, will be an important step toward integrating the design-science and behavioral-science communities in IS.

ACKNOWLEDGEMENTS

We would like to thank Allen Lee, Ron Weber, and Gordon Davis who in different ways each contributed to our thinking about design science in the Information Systems profession and encouraged us to pursue this line of research. We would also like to acknowledge the efforts of Rosann Collins who provided insightful comments and perspectives on the nature of the relationship between behavioral-science and design-science research. This work has also benefited from seminars and discussions at Arizona State University, Florida International University, Georgia State University, Michigan State University, Notre Dame University, and The University of Utah. We would particularly like to thank Brian Pentland and Steve Alter for feedback and suggestions they provided on an earlier version of this paper. The comments provided by several anonymous editors and reviewers greatly enhanced the content and presentation of the paper.

NOTE

1 Theories posed in behavioral-science are principled explanations of phenomena. We recognize that such theories are approximations and are subject to numerous assumptions and conditions. However, they are evaluated against the norms of truth or explanatory power and are valued only as the claims they make are borne out in reality.

REFERENCES

Aalst, W. 'Wolfan: A Petri-Net-Based Workflow Analyzer,' *Systems Analysis-Modeling-Simulation* (34:3), 1999, pp. 345–357.

Aalst, W. and Hee, K. *Workflow Management: Models, Methods, and Systems*, The MIT Press, Cambridge, MA, 2002.

Aalst, W. and Kumar, A. 'XML-Based Schema Definition for Support of Interorganizational Workflow,' *Information Systems Research* (14:1), March 2003, pp. 23–46.

Aboulafia, M., *Philosophy, Social Theory, and the Thought of George Herbert Mead* (SUNY Series in Philosophy of the Social Sciences), State University of New York Press, 1991.

Aiken, M. W., Sheng, O. R. L., and Vogel, D. R. 'Integrating Expert Systems with Group Decision Support Systems,' *ACM Transactions on Information Systems* (9:1), January 1991, pp. 75–95.

Alter, S., '18 Reasons Why IT-Reliant Work Systems Should Replace 'The IT Artifact' as the Core Subject Matter of the IS Field,' *Communications of the AIS* (12), October 2003, pp. 365–394.

Applegate, L. M. 'Rigor and Relevance in MIS Research—Introduction,' *MIS Quarterly* (23:1), March 1999, pp. 1–2.

Basili, V. 'The Role of Experimentation in Software Engineering: Past, Current, and Future,' in *Proceedings of the 18th International Conference on Software Engineering*, T. Maibaum and M. Zelkowitz (eds.), Berlin, Germany, March 25–29, 1996, pp. 442–449.

Basu, A. and Blanning, R. W. 'Metagraphs: A Tool for Modeling Decision Support Systems,' *Management Science* (40:12), December 1994, pp. 1579–1600.

Basu, A. and Blanning, R. W. 'A Formal Approach to Workflow Analysis,' *Information Systems Research* (11:1), March 2000, pp. 17–36.

Batra, D., Hoffer, J. A. and Bostrom, R. P. 'A Comparison Of User Performance Between The Relational And The Extended Entity Relationship Models In The Discovery Phase Of Database Design,' *Communications of the ACM* (33:2), February 1990, pp. 126–139.

Bell, D. A. 'From Data Properties to Evidence,' *IEEE Transactions on Knowledge and Data Engineering* (5:6), December 1993, pp. 965–969.

Benbasat, I. and Zmud, R. W. 'Empirical Research in Information Systems: The Practice of Relevance,' *MIS Quarterly* (23:1), March 1999, pp. 3–16.

Bhargava, H. K., Krishnan, R., and Piela, P. 'On Formal Semantics and Analysis of Typed Modeling Languages: An Analysis of Ascend,' *INFORMS Journal on Computing* (10:2), Spring 1998, pp. 189–208.

Bodart, F., Patel, A., Sim, M., and Weber, R. 'Should The Optional Property Construct Be Used In Conceptual Modeling? A Theory and Three Empirical Tests,' *Information Systems Research* (12:4), December 2001, pp. 384–405.

Boland, R. J. 'Design in the Punctuation of Management Action' in *Managing as Designing: Creating a Vocabulary for Management Education and Research*, R. Boland (ed.), Frontiers of Management Workshop, Weatherhead School of Management, June 14–15, 2002 (available at http://design.cwru.edu).

Brancheau, J., Janz, B., and Wetherbe, J. 'Key Issues in Information Systems Management: 1994–95 SIM Delphi Results,' *MIS Quarterly* (20:2), June 1996, pp. 225–242.

Brooks, F. P., Jr. 'No Silver Bullet: Essence and Accidents of Software Engineering,' *IEEE Computer* (20:4), April 1987, pp. 10–19.

Brooks, F. P., Jr. 'The Computer Scientist as Toolsmith II,' *Communications of the ACM* (39:3), March 1996, pp. 61–68.

Bunge, M. A. *Treatise on Basic Philosophy: Volume 7—Epistemology & Methodology III: Philosophy of Science and Technology—Part II: Life Science, Social Science and Technology*, D. Reidel Publishing Company, Boston, Massachusetts, 1985.

Chaudhri, A. and Loomis, M. *Object Databases in Practice*, Prentice-Hall PTR, Upper Saddle River, NJ, 1998.

Chaum, D. 'Untraceable Electronic Mail, Return Addresses, and Digital Pseudonyms,' *Communications of the ACM* (24:2), February 1981, pp. 84–87.

Chen, P. P. S. 'The entity-relationship model-toward a unified view,' *ACM Transactions on Database Systems* (1:1), 1976, pp. 9–36.

Davis, G. and Olson, M. *Management Information Systems: Conceptual Foundations, Structure and Development*, Second Ed., McGraw-Hill, Boston, Massachusetts, 1985.

DeLone, W. H. and McLean, E. R. 'Information Systems Success: The Quest for the Dependent Variable,' *Information Systems Research* (3:1), March 1992, pp. 60–95.

DeLone, W. H. and McLean, E. R. 'The DeLone and McLean Model of Information Systems Success: A Ten-Year Update,' *Journal of Management Information Systems* (19:4), Spring 2003, pp. 9–30.

Denning, P. J. 'A New Social Contract for Research,' *Communications of the ACM* (40:2), February 1997, pp. 132–134.

Dennis, A., George, J., Jessup, L., Nunamaker, J., and Vogel, D. 'Information Technology to Support Electronic Meetings,' *MIS Quarterly* (12:4), December 1988, pp. 591–624.

Dennis, A. and Wixom, B. 'Investigating the Moderators of the Group Support Systems Use with Meta-Analysis,' *Journal of Management Information Systems* (18:3), Winter 2001–02, pp. 235–257.

Dey, D., Sarkar, S., and De, P. 'A Probabilistic Decision Model for Entity Matching in Heterogeneous Databases,' *Management Science* (44:10), October 1998, pp. 1379–1395.

Dey, D., Storey, V. C., and Barron, T. M. 'Improving Database Design through the Analysis of Relationships,' *ACM Transactions on Database Systems* (24:4), December 1999, pp. 453–486.

Dickson, G., Partridge, J., and Robinson, L. 'Exploring Modes of Facilitative Support for GDSS Technology,' *MIS Quarterly* (17:2), June 1993, pp. 173–194.

Drucker, P. F. 'The Coming of the New Organization,' *Harvard Business Review* (66:1), January–February 1988, pp. 45–53.

Drucker, P. F. 'The New Productivity Challenge,' *Harvard Business Review* (69:6), November–December 1991, pp. 45–53.

Dym, C. L. *Engineering Design*, Cambridge University Press, New York, 1994.

Feigenbaum, E. and McCorduck, P. *The Fifth Generation: Artificial Intelligence and Japan's Computer Challenge to the World*, Addison-Wesley, Inc., Reading, MA, 1983.

eMarketer, *E-Commerce Trade and B2B Exchanges*, March 2002, http://www.emarketer.com/products/report.php?ecommerce_trade

Fjermestad, J. and Hiltz, S. R. 'An Assessment of Group Support Systems Experimental Research: Methodology and Results,' *Journal of Management Information Systems* (15:3), Winter 1998–99, pp. 7–149.

Gallupe, R., DeSanctis, G., and Dickson, G. 'Computer-Based Support for Group Problem-Finding: An Experimental Investigation,' *MIS Quarterly*, (12:2), June 1988, pp. 277–298.

Gavish, B. and Gerdes, J. 'Anonymous Mechanisms in Group Decision Support Systems Communication,' *Decision Support Systems* (23:4), October 1998, pp. 297–328.

Geerts, G. and McCarthy, W. E. 'An Ontological Analysis of the Primitives of the Extended-REA Enterprise Information Architecture,' *The International Journal of Accounting Information Systems* (3:1), 2002, pp. 1–16.

Gelernter, D. *Machine Beauty: Elegance and the Heart of Technology*, Basic Books, New York, 1998.

Glass, R. 'On Design,' *IEEE Software* (16:2), March/April 1999, pp. 103–104.

Halpin, T. A. *Information Modeling and Relational Databases*, Morgan Kaufmann Publishers, Elsevier Science (USA), 2001.

Henderson, J. and Venkatraman, N. 'Strategic Alignment: Leveraging Information Technology for Transforming Organizations,' *IBM Systems Journal* (32:1), 1993.

ISR, Editorial Statement and Policy, *Information Systems Research* (13:4), December 2002.

Jarvenpaa, S., Rao, V., and Huber, G. 'Computer Support for Meetings of Groups Working on Unstructured Problems: A Field Experiment,' *MIS Quarterly* (12: 4), December 1988, pp. 645–666.

Johansson, J. M. 'On the Impact of Network Latency on Distributed Systems Design,' *Information Technology Management* (1), 2000, pp. 183–194.

Johansson, J. M., March, S. T., and Naumann, J. D. 'Modeling Network Latency and Parallel Processing in Distributed Database Design,' *Decision Sciences Journal* (to appear), 2003.

Kalakota, R. and Robinson, M. *E-Business 2.0: Roadmap for Success*, Addison-Wesley Pearson Education, Boston, MA, 2001.

Keil, M. 'Puling the Plug: Software Project Management and the Problem of Project Escalation,' *MIS Quarterly* (19:4) December 1995, pp. 421–447.

Keil, M., Cule, P. E., Lyytinen, K., and Schmidt, R. C. 'A Framework for Identifying Software Project Risks,' *Communications of the ACM* (41:11), November 1998, pp. 76–83.

Keil, M. and Robey, D. 'Turning Around Troubled Software Projects: An Exploratory Study of the Deescalation of Commitment to Failing Courses of Action,' *Journal of Management Information Systems*, (15:4) December 1999, pp. 63–87.

Kernighan, B. and Plauger, P. J. *The Elements of Programming Style*, 2nd Edition, McGraw-Hill, Inc., New York, 1978.

Kim, Y. G. and March, S. T. 'Comparing Data Modeling Formalisms,' *Communications of the ACM* (38:6), June 1995, pp. 103–115.

Klein, H. K. and Myers, M. D. 'A Set of Principles for Conducting and Evaluating Interpretive Field Studies in Information Systems,' *MIS Quarterly* (23:1), March 1999, pp. 67–94.

Kleindorfer, G., O'Neill, L., and Ganeshan, R. 'Validation in Simulation: Various Positions in the Philosophy of Science,' *Management Science* (44:8), August 1998, pp. 1087–1099.

Kruchten, P. *The Rational Unified Process: An Introduction*, 2nd Edition, Addison-Wesley, Inc., Reading, MA, 2000.

Kuhn, T. S. *The Structure of Scientific Revolutions*, 3rd Edition, University of Chicago Press, 1996.

Kumar, A. and Zhao, J. 'Workflow Support for Electronic Commerce Applications,' *Decision Support Systems* (32:3), January 2002, pp. 265–278.

Lee, A. 'Inaugural Editor's Comments,' *MIS Quarterly* (23:1), March 1999, pp. v-xi.

Lee, A. 'Systems Thinking, Design Science, and Paradigms: Heeding Three Lessons from the Past to Resolve Three Dilemmas in the Present to Direct a Trajectory for Future Research in the Information Systems Field,' Keynote Address at *11th International Conference on Information Management*, Taiwan, May 2000, Available at http://www.people.vcu.edu/~aslee/ICIM-keynote-2000.

Leymann, F. and Roller, D. *Production Workflow: Concepts and Techniques*, Prentice-Hall PTR, Upper Saddle River, NJ, 2000.

Madnick, S. E. 'The Challenge: To Be Part of the Solution Instead of Being Part of the Problem,' in *Proceedings of the Second Annual Workshop on Information Technology and Systems*, V. Storey and A. Whinston (eds.), Dallas, TX, December 12–13, 1992, pp. 1–9.

Marakas, G. M. and Elam, J. J. 'Semantic Structuring in Analyst Acquisition and Representation of Facts in Requirements Analysis,' *Information Systems Research* (9:1), March, 1998, pp. 37–63.

March, S. T., Hevner, A., and Ram, S. 'Research Commentary: An Agenda for Information Technology Research in Heterogeneous and Distributed Environment,' *Information Systems Research* (11:4), December 2000, pp. 327–341.

March, S. T. and Smith, G. 'Design and Natural Science Research on Information Technology,' *Decision Support Systems* (15:4), December 1995, pp. 251–266.

Markus, M. L., Majchrzak, A., and Gasser, L., 'A Design Theory for Systems that Support Emergent Knowledge Processes,' *MIS Quarterly* (26:3), September, 2002, pp. 179–212.

McCarthy, W. E., 'The REA Accounting Model: A Generalized Framework for Accounting Systems in a Shared Data Environment,' *The Accounting Review* (58:3), 1982, pp. 554–578.

Meehl, P. E. 'What Social Scientists Don't Understand,' in *Metatheory in Social Science*, D. W. Fiske and R. A. Shweder (eds.), University of Chicago Press, Chicago, IL, 1986, pp. 315–338.

Newell, A. and Simon, H. 'Computer Science as Empirical Inquiry: Symbols and Search,' *Communications of the ACM* (19:3), March 1976, pp. 113–126.

Norman, D. *The Design of Everyday Things*, Currency Doubleday, 1988.

Nunamaker, J., Chen, M., and Purdin, T. D. M., 'Systems Development in Information Systems Research,' *Journal of Management Information Systems* (7:3), Winter 1991a, pp. 89–106.

Nunamaker, J., Dennis, A., Valacich, J., Vogel, D., and George, J. 'Electronic Meeting Systems to Support Group Work,' *Communications of the ACM*, (34:7), July 1991b, pp. 40–61.

Nunamaker, J., Briggs, R., Mittleman, D., Vogel, D., and Balthazard, P. 'Lessons from a Dozen Years of Group Support Systems Research: A Discussion of Lab and Field Findings,' *Journal of Management Information Systems*, (13:3), Winter 1996–97, pp. 163–207.

Orlikowski, W. J. 'Using Technology and Constituting Structures: A Practice Lens for Studying Technology in Organizations.' *Organization Science* (11:4), December 2000, pp. 404–428.

Orlikowski, W. J. and Barley, S. R. 'Technology and Institutions: What Can Research on Information Technology and Research on Organizations Learn From Each Other?' *MIS Quarterly* (25:2), June 2001, pp. 145–165.

Orlikowski, W. J. and Iacono, C. S. 'Research Commentary: Desperately Seeking the 'IT' in IT Research – A Call to Theorizing the IT Artifact,' *Information Systems Research* (12:2), June 2001, pp. 121–134.

Orman, L. V. 'Electronic Markets, Hierarchies, Hubs, and Intermediaries,' *Journal of Information Systems Frontiers* (4:2), 2002, pp. 207–222.

Pahl, G. and Beitz, W. *Engineering Design: A Systematic Approach*, Springer-Verlag, London, 1996.

Parsons, J. and Wand, Y. 'Emancipating Instances from the Tyranny of Classes in Information Modeling,' *ACM Transactions on Database Systems* (25:2), June 2000, pp. 228–268.

Petroski, H. *Invention by Design: How Engineers Get from Thought to Thing*, Harvard University Press, Cambridge, MA, 1996.

Purao, S., Storey, V. C., and Han, T. D. 'Improving Reuse-Based System Design with Learning,' *Information Systems Research* (14:3), September 2003, pp. 269–290.

Rittel, H. J. and Webber, M. M. 'Planning Problems are Wicked Problems,' in *Developments in Design Methodology*, N. Cross (ed.), John Wiley & Sons, New York, 1984.

Robey, D. 'Research Commentary: Diversity in Information Systems Research: Threat, Opportunity, and Responsibility,' *Information Systems Research* (7:4), 1996, pp. 400–408.

Royce, W. *Software Project Management: A Unified Framework*, Addison-Wesley, Inc., Reading, MA, 1998.

Salton, G. *Automatic Text Processing: The Transformation, Analysis, and Retrieval of Information by Computer*, Addison-Wesley, Reading, MA, 1988.

Schneier, B. *Applied Cryptography: Protocols, Algorithms, and Source Code in C*, 2nd Ed., John Wiley and Sons, January 1996.

Schon, D. A. *The Reflective Practitioner: How Professionals Think in Action*, Basic Books, New York, 1983.

Seddon, P. B. 'A Respecification and Extension of the DeLone and McLean Model of IS Success,' *Information Systems Research* (8:3), September 1997, pp. 240–253.

Sengupta, K. and Te'eni, D. 'Cognitive Feedback in GDSS: Improving Control and Convergence,' *MIS Quarterly* (17:1), March 1993, pp. 87–113.

Silver, M. S., Markus, M. L., and Beath, C. M. 'The Information Technology Interaction Model: A Foundation for the MBA Core Course,' *MIS Quarterly* (19:3), September 1995, pp. 361–390.

Simon, H. A. *The Sciences of the Artificial*, 3rd Edition, MIT Press, Cambridge, MA, 1996.

Sinha, A. P. and Vessey, I. 'An Empirical Investigation Of Entity-Based And Object-Oriented Data Modeling: A Development Life Cycle Approach,' in *Proceedings of the Twentieth International Conference on Information Systems*, P. De and J. I. DeGross (eds.), Charlotte, North Carolina, December 13–15, 1999, pp. 229–244.

Storey, V. C., Chiang, R. H. L., Dey, D., Goldstein, R. C., and Sundaresan, S. 'Database Design with Common Sense Business Reasoning and Learning,' *ACM Transactions on Database Systems* (22:4), December 1997, pp. 471–512.

Tam, K. Y. 'Automated Construction of Knowledge-Bases from Examples,' *Information Systems Research* (1:2), June 1990, pp. 144–167.

Tichy, W. 'Should Computer Scientists Experiment More?' *IEEE Computer* (31:5), May 1998, pp. 32–40.

Trice, A. and Davis, R. 'Heuristics for Reconciling Independent Knowledge Bases,' *Information Systems Research* (4:3), September 1993, pp. 262–288.

Tsichritzis, D. 'The Dynamics of Innovation,' *Beyond Calculation: The Next Fifty Years of Computing*, Copernicus, 1997, pp. 259–265.

Venkatesh, V. 'Determinants of Perceived Ease of Use: Integrating Control, Intrinsic Motivation, and Emotion into the Technology Acceptance Model,' *Information Systems Research* (11, 4), December 2000, pp. 342–365.

Vessey, I. and Glass, R. 'Strong Vs. Weak Approaches to Systems Development,' *Communications of the ACM* (41:4), April 1998, pp. 99–102.

Walls, J. G., Widmeyer, G. R., and El Sawy, O. A. 'Building an Information System Design Theory for Vigilant EIS,' *Information Systems Research* (3:1), March 1992, pp. 36–59.

Wand, Y. and Weber, R. 'On the Ontological Expressiveness of Information Systems design analysis and design grammars,' *Journal of Information Systems* (3:3), 1993, pp. 217–237.

Wand, Y. and Weber, R. 'On the Deep Structure of Information Systems,' *Information Systems Journal* (5), 1995, pp. 203–233.

Weber, R. 'Toward a Theory of Artifacts: A Paradigmatic Base for Information Systems Research,' *Journal of Information Systems* (1:2), Spring 1987, pp. 3–19.

Weber, R. *Ontological Foundations of Information Systems*, Australia: Coopers & Lybrand, 1997.

Weber, R. 'Editor's Comments: Still Desperately Seeking the IT Artifact,' *MIS Quarterly* (27:2), June 2003, pp. iii-xi.

Winograd, T. *Bringing Design to Software*, Addison-Wesley, Inc., Reading, MA, 1996.

Winograd, T. 'The Design of Interaction,' in *Beyond Calculation, The Next 50 Years of Computing*, P. Denning and R. Metcalfe (eds.), Springer-Verlag, Inc., New York, 1997, pp. 149–162.

WfMC, Workflow Management Coalition. 'Workflow Standard—Interoperability Wf-XML Binding, Document Number WFMC-TC-1023, Version 1.0, 2000.

Zelkowitz, M. and Wallace, D. 'Experimental Models for Validating Technology,' *IEEE Computer* (31:5), May 1998, pp. 23–31.

Zmud, R. 'Editor's Comments,' *MIS Quarterly* (21:2), June 1997, pp. xxi–xxii.

10
Nothing at the Center?: Academic Legitimacy in the Information Systems Field[1]

Kalle Lyytinen and John Leslie King

Turning and turning in the widening gyre,
The falcon cannot hear the falconer,
Things fall apart,
The centre cannot hold[2]

William Butler Yeats (1865–1939),
'The Second Coming'

INTRODUCTION

The Information Systems (IS) field arose from humble origins in the 1970's. The field is perhaps 30 years old, and is about as far along as might reasonably be expected in terms of size, quality and institutional status. Nevertheless, the IS field continues to be haunted by feelings of inadequacy. Such sentiments are most common in North America (Benbasat and Weber, 1996; Markus, 1999; Benbasat and Zmud, 2003), but are also found in Europe (Ciborra, 1998; Stowell and Mingers, 1997). The most common manifestation of this sentiment is the lament that the IS field lacks a theoretic core, and for that reason, is rightly seen to be academically inadequate by critics inside and outside the field.

This is a serious accusation. If well founded, it is a profound indictment of the IS field, inviting appropriate sanctions unless remedied. If groundless, it imposes needless pain on the IS field, and arguably misdirects energy that would be better spent on other matters. This paper analyzes the argument that academic legitimacy hinges on the presence or absence of core theory. It finds the argument logically weak and empirically refutable. This result does not imply that stronger theory is unwelcome in the IS field, or that such theory would not help strength the field's reputation. It merely suggests that the current fixation on legitimizing the field through pursuit of a core theory around which to center inquiry and intellectual mission is misplaced.

To move the discussion forward from the debate around the nature of core theories this paper suggests an alternative model of disciplinary legitimacy grounded in three drivers: the salience of the issues studied, the production of strong results, and the maintenance of plasticity. These principles have sustained the growth of the IS field over three decades, and established it as a legitimate actor among academic fields. If properly cultivated and enacted, they will suffice to improve the legitimacy of IS field for the foreseeable future. The needs of salience, the desire for strong results, and the quest for plasticity in the IS field preclude a center of fixed core ideas or relationships. Accordingly, the IS field must replace it with a metaphor of a center of an activity (or life form) that builds identity and legitimacy for IS field (Boland and Lyytinen, 2004).[3] This center is best seen as the free flowing give-and-exchange metaphor of IS discipline as a market of ideas in which scholars (and practitioners) exchange their views regarding the design and management of information and associated technologies in organized human enterprise. The essay conclude with an analysis of positions which IS scholars can take in relation to the market of ideas and how this institution can be strengthened as the true focal point of IS discipline.

THE ANXIETY DISCOURSE

The concern about the IS field's academic legitimacy has been described elsewhere as part of an 'anxiety discourse,' in which evidence of inadequacy (e.g., disrespect by people in other academic fields) is traced to intellectual shortcomings in the IS field itself (King and Lyytinen, 2004). This anxiety discourse weaves through the IS literature, starting before the field's founding in the late 1970's. The earliest manifestation of anxiety was not specifically directed at theory, but rather at the expected difficulty of building computer-based systems that could actually provide useful information for managers (Dearden, 1967; Ackoff, 1967). Such apprehension might be unique to the IS field. Artificial intelligence, which emerged at about the same time as IS, exuded optimism while facing challenges far more daunting. Even stranger, the IS field has sustained its apprehension in spite of undeniable triumphs in the development of complex information systems, while artificial intelligence has remained optimistic in spite of legendary failures to achieve the challenges it set for itself. There is clearly something more complex than academic legitimacy at work in the anxiety discourse.

The discourse shifted as the IS field became a more identifiable academic enterprise. It was soon recognized that the challenges of the IS field extended beyond just designing and building systems, and into understanding the organizational mission, adoption, diffusion and effects of such systems. These challenges could only be met by sourcing of ideas from a wide array of intellectual perspectives, which became justified in the discourse as adopting intellectual standards of 'reference disciplines' for IS-related inquiries (Keen, 1980, 1991). The reference discipline rubric suggested that the field lacked a coherent intellectual center, though its intellectual mission and knowledge needs did center around a shared interest in the applications of information technology to human enterprise (Kling, 1980). This initial juxtaposition of the IS field's intellectual mission and sources—a center grounded primarily in praxis, and an intellectual periphery drawing intellectual capital from without the field— formed the foundation for the anxiety discourse that was to follow. Soon, those within the field questioned the quality of the field's intellectual effort and status (e.g., Mumford, *et al.*, 1985), and doubted that the field could retain its praxis-based center when other intellectually powerful academic fields came to recognize the importance of IT in organizations (Weber, 1987). This cast serious doubts on the theoretical status of the field, and precipitated tension between the praxis oriented center and the intellectual periphery. Many came to doubt that IS could cohere sufficiently to survive (Banville and Landry, 1989; Maggi *et al.*, 1986, for a critical evaluation see Robey, 1996).

By the mid 1990s the anxiety discourse had evolved into an 'orthodox' view that the field's survival depended on substituting its praxis-based core with a theoretical core grounded in well defined intellectual constructs of theory drawing on a model of research attributed to the natural sciences (Benbasat and Weber, 1996; Benbasat and Zmud, 2003).[4] Despite careful refinement of this position over a set of articles, the 'core theory' view has not proved satisfactory in damping the anxiety. The discourse has remained stalled in a refrain that can be summarized as follows:

The central focus of the IS field is so important that other academic fields will want to appropriate it. Yet, the center of the IS field is theoretically too weak and diffused to generate sufficient solidarity as to maintain a consistent research focus that would protect the field's long term viability. This weak condition generates disrespect from the more theoretically powerful fields that surround the IS field, and that seek to appropriate the IS field's central focus. Manifestations of disrespect toward the IS field from these other fields constitute proof of the IS field's intellectual and theoretical inadequacy.

Persistent instances of perceived disrespect toward the IS field by other fields within management schools (e.g., attempts to push IS courses out of the required curriculum, efforts to deny IS faculty promotions) understandably generate feelings of inadequacy. The question arises as to whether these feelings of inadequacy should be attributed to intellectual and theoretical inadequacy, and specifically that the IS field is inadequate because it lacks a theoretical core at its center. As the following analysis shows, this is not a defensible attribution.

LEGITIMACY THROUGH THEORY?

The central question is whether the IS field's legitimacy rests on the presence of a theoretical core. In order to be convincing, the argument that legitimacy can be gained only through the possession of a theoretical core must be both valid and sound.[5] To examine this, it is necessary to establish the truth conditions for the elements of the argument, to analyze the validity of the inference involved in making the claim, and finally to determine whether the argument is sound.

Truth Conditions

Legitimacy is inherently relative and subjective: it cannot be conferred or attained through objective means. It has meaning only with respect to some socially constructed standard or expectation (Berger and Luckmann, 1967). It is very difficult to establish truth conditions for the assignment of legitimacy to any academic field. This does not mean that the concept of academic legitimacy is without meaning or import. Legitimacy reflects a field's institutional power, its problem-solving capabilities, its methodical and cognitive distinctiveness, its applicable research outcomes, its value in education, and so on. Nevertheless, it remains unclear how legitimacy is established in general among academic fields (Andersen, 2000). This raises the first serious challenge to the argument that academic legitimacy is established by the presence of a theoretical core.

This challenge is shown in the fact that none of the commentaries about the IS field's need for a theoretical core have articulated exactly what is meant by the term 'theoretical core,' a point acknowledged by Weber (2003). Benbasat and Zmud (2003) attempt to address this by defining the rules of exclusion and inclusion that define the properties of typical IS theory. However, since there is no objectively determined definition of a 'typical' IS theory, this solution must depend on a widespread agreement among the IS field as to what that term means. In fact, this solution is not a description of truth conditions, but a plea for the IS field to come into agreement on terms that can be adopted as standards against which behavior can be measured. Currently, the field is far from agreeing on such terms, and many attempts to achieve agreement have failed to affect where the field is moving. Even if such an agreement should emerge, the agreement itself would be arbitrary with respect to the truth.

The philosophy of science is replete with discussions of these problems (cf. Chalmers, 1999; Radnitzky, 1968; Habermas, 1971; Rorty, 1979). Principles deployed to argue in favor of a specific legitimating measure immediately call into question where the principles came from and how they might be justified. Principles cannot be derived analytically or empirically, which usually leads to an infinite regression of logical induction, wherein a first tier principle is justified by appeal to a second tier principle, the second tier principle is justified by appeal to a third tier principle, and so on (Lee and Baskerville, 2003). In the case of the IS field, there is no way to decide conclusively what counts as a theoretical core. The best the field can achieve is a specific, historical, inter-subjective agreement among its members as to what will count as a good theory, at any given time, backed by a set of redeemable warrants (Toulmin, 1958). The next step is to determine whether the IS field has redeemable warrants for any notion of the theoretical core.

The position most often invoked to warrant the need for a theoretical core is a version of Popperian analytic philosophy.[6] According to Popper (1968), academic fields make progress through refining and refuting theories that explain phenomena falling within the domain of the field. Theories must be subject to refutation (i.e., falsifiable) whereby they can be rejected or refined. Theories emerge as a result of an investigator's attempts to explain problems by alternative models, formulated within the scope of established theories.[7] Popper's analytic philosophy could potentially serve as a warrant for the centrality of a theory in legitimating the IS field, but it is only one

point of view, and it has been severely criticized by other philosophers for logical and empirical weakness (cf., Schilpp, 1974;
Feyerabend, 1978; Lakatos and Musgrave, 1970; Stove, 1982). It is
just as reasonable to suggest that theories across academic fields vary
significantly due to differences in social organization and prevalent
research tasks, and that no uniform relationship can be established
between a given field and a specific type of theoretical core (Whitley,
1984). Overall, the anxiety discourse is fundamentally and constantly
challenged by the absence of clear truth conditions for judging the
claim that presence of a theoretical core will produce legitimacy for
the IS field.

Validity

Assuming that reliable truth conditions could be established for the
claim that a theoretical core is necessary for legitimacy, the argument
must next be evaluated for its validity. The normal argument in favor
of a strong theoretical core flows through the following complementary syllogisms:

(1) All x :TC $(x) \rightarrow$ LF (x) *entails*   (1b) All x : $\neg$TC $(x) \rightarrow \neg$LF (x)
(2) TC (e.g., physics)   (2b) $\neg$TC (e.g., is)

_____

(3) LF (e.g., physics)   (3b) $\neg$LF (e.g., is)

Where x = Academic discipline
    TC = having a Theoretical Core,
    LF = having legitimacy as an academic field

Here syllogisms (1), (2) and (3) represent a set of logically valid
deductions. A theoretical core implies legitimacy for a discipline:
hence if a discipline has a core, it will also be legitimate. The argument thus far follows a valid form (*modus ponens*). The problem,
however, comes with the syllogism (1b), (2b), (3b), which the core
theory argument assumes, called the logical fallacy of denying the
consequent. This suggests that a lack of legitimacy results from the
lack of a strong theoretical core, and thus from the denial of the
antecedent (theoretical core, *modus ponens*) the denial of the consequence (legitimacy) can be inferred. The chain (1b), (2b), and (3b)
cannot be entailed from (1), (2) and (3), and is a logical fallacy. From
the absence of something one can derive everything, which is tanta-
mount to deriving nothing. Accusation (1b), 'The lack of intellectual

core implies the lack of legitimacy,' cannot be logically derived from accusation (1) 'A strong theoretic core confers legitimacy,' rendering (2b) and (3b) inconsistent. The claim that the lack of a theoretical core deprives IS of legitimacy is invalid, and not worth further consideration. The syllogism (1), (2), and (3) remains valid (modus ponens), and in principle, can give support to the argument for legitimacy through a theoretical core if both (1) and (2) are true.[8] However, under these circumstances, the argument that a theoretical core is necessary for legitimacy cannot be established deductively, and can be made only by induction. This raises the issue of soundness.

Soundness

Premise (1) implies an inductive generalization: all academic fields with a strong theoretic core are found to be legitimate, and that no legitimate field can be found that lacks a sound theoretic core. This is a factual accusation, depending only on the accuracy of the facts being claimed. It is difficult to demonstrate that all academic fields with a strong theoretic core are found to be legitimate: this requires a census of all fields and their theories as well as their status as legitimate. Since a single counter-example violates the induction and causes the argument to collapse, it is much easier to test the premise by finding an example of a field that is legitimate, but that has no theoretic core.

There are many legitimate academic fields that can be characterized by their focus of study, by the methods their members use, by the tendencies in their opinions or findings, and by their impacts on the thinking of those outside their field, but that have no theoretical core: classics, German literature, accounting, and history, to name a few. There are also many legitimate academic fields that have possessed numerous, fundamentally different theoretical cores across their histories. Early (Western) biology was entirely motivated by the belief that all life was created by God according to the Biblical creation story, and consisted of exploring and documenting the diversity of flora and fauna to be found in the Creation. Jean-Baptiste Lamarck provided one of the first theoretical mechanistic explanations for diversity in the early 19th century, but it was not widely accepted by practicing zoologists and botanists. Charles Darwin's monumental mid 19th century theory of natural selection slowly became an accepted organizing rubric for biology, but has undergone dramatic reconstruction since that time and is still disputed even among biologists. Psychology emerged from incoherent speculation about the nature of mind in the 18th and 19th centuries, only to be transformed in the late

20th century when instrumentation enabled closer study of the relationship between brain and mind. Geology explained morphology and stratification solely through 18th century concepts of erosion, especially those grounded in the Biblical flood, until the mid-20th century advent of plate tectonics upended all previous theory. Despite this turmoil of theory, the legitimacy of these fields has never really been questioned. The presence of a strong theoretic core can sometimes be useful in establishing or sustaining legitimacy, but it is unsound to argue that having a theoretical core is necessary for that purpose.

Legitimate academic fields have long been characterized by theoretic instability over their histories (Kuhn, 1996). Indeed, the intellectual history of the academy itself is one of instability. Universities of the late medieval period were dominated by theology and philosophy. The Renaissance university branched into the 'natural philosophy' of biology and physics. Biology differentiated into botany, zoology and bacteriology in the early 19th century, reorganized around the relative complexity of organic processes (biochemistry, molecular biology, physiology, developmental biology, ecology, evolutionary biology) in the mid 20th century, and underwent yet another reorganization focusing on mechanisms such as enzyme metabolism and molecular proteomics in the late 20th century. Physics branched into chemistry, geology and other specialties during the late 18th century and 19th century, only to be transformed in the 20th century into hybrid fields such as earth systems science (geology, atmospheric chemistry, oceanography). Most interesting, physics and biology have re-converged in structural biology (crystallography, biophysics, molecular and macromolecular biology). Despite such turbulence, the legitimacy of these fields has never truly wavered.

LEGITIMACY RECONSIDERED

The foregoing discussion deconstructs the main argument that academic legitimacy depends upon the presence of a theoretic core. If the presence of a theoretical core does not make an academic field legitimate, what does? In light of the evolution of different disciplines and analyzing mechanisms that have made them legitimate, three factors can be seen that account together for disciplinary legitimacy: (1) salience of the subjects studied, (2) the strength of results from the study, and (3) the plasticity of the field with respect to changing circumstances. While none of them separately seem to be enough for academic legitimacy, there were no legitimate fields that did not have all these characteristics simultaneously.[9] Each of these deserves a careful analysis in determining where the legitimacy of the IS field resides and what can be done about it.

Salience

The Pragmatics of IS-Related Knowledge

Research and education embodied in collegiate IS programs—as in any processional field—are dependent upon the patronage of the larger society that invests in such programs in the expectation of long-term benefits for the society. Fields that appear to be dealing with socially salient issues are more likely to be legitimized because they can claim resources given that they have what Robey (2003) calls pragmatic legitimacy. In line with this, the salience in the IS field is about pragmatic legitimacy, which 'rests on the self-interested calculations of an organization's most immediate audiences' (Suchman, 1995, p. 578).

The IS field's origins can be traced directly to the very salience of its subject matter not its theory per se. IS programs had their origins in the needs of modern business organizations for IS professionals, and in the pressures exerted by these organizations on professional schools (primarily in business administration and management) to produce such professionals. Indeed, the early anxiety found in Ackoff (1967) and Dearden (1972) can readily be interpreted as a concern that the expectations of these organizations eclipsed the abilities of both academic and practicing experts.

Salience in the IS Field Despite the Recent Downturn

Over the years these fears proved to be unfounded, and the success of information systems as practice has been demonstrated beyond question. The salience of the IS field is still evident, as seen in the rapid build up of demand for IS professionals as the dot.com boom evolved. It was obvious to organizations that the future envisioned during that boom required many more highly trained IS professionals. Recruiters went wild, salaries skyrocketed, and IS programs added rapidly faculty and courses to meet the demand. The fact that the dot.com boom collapsed demonstrates that salience can be fickle, but the phenomenon of the boom illustrates how powerful a force it can be in legitimating any academic field.

Despite the repercussions of the dot.com collapse, the salience surrounding IS remains high in the future. Investment in IT continues to rise, and the application of IT to organizational functions continues to grow. The salience of IT is seen clearly in popular

concerns in 2003–2004 about outsourcing and the offshore movement of high-value IT jobs. If these jobs were not important, and
believed to be increasingly important, no one would care that they
are moving. The Bureau of Labor Statistics estimates that job growth
in the five to ten years following 2004 will show much greater
demand for IT-related jobs than in any other area of skilled work.[10]
This does not mean that the ecology of IT-related jobs will not
change in the future. In response to this, the IS field must become
more aggressive in finding ways to match its talent pool to the newly
emerging salience at the center. Ironically, the threat that other fields
might take over the salient center of the IS field has probably been
reduced by the collapse of the dot.com boom and the perceived shift
of IT jobs overseas.

Salience as Primary Generator of Legitimacy

To summarize, the IS field cannot protect its claim on the salience of
IS by replacing the salience of its praxis with theory at the center
because theory has value only in reference to praxis. Building an
edifice of theory at the center of the IS field might please observers
from other academic fields who think that theory by itself is valuable,
but those observers are not going to support the IS field with
resources that they can just as readily claim for themselves. At most,
they can offer or withhold their approval within the academic power
structure. The question arises, then, as to why the IS field needs or
should seek the approval of those people, and whether this is the
only way to obtain their approval. They have no resources of their
own to confer on the IS field, even if they were willing to do so (and
they are not). Their resources come from exactly the same place the IS
field's resources come from: the larger society that sees value in the
work being done. To the extent that these fields have power over the
IS field, it is in their ability to wrongfully appropriate the IS field's
salience and redirect the resources raised by that salience to their
own ends.[11] The competition between the IS field and other academic
fields is ultimately not about theory at all—it is about the right to
appropriate the social salience of the work being done, and the
resources that perceived salience generates from the society at large.
Attempting to substitute theory for praxis at the center of the IS field
is actually likely to hasten the field's decline.

Strong Results

No field can capitalize on the salience of the issues it studies without
providing sustained benefits from its effects. The IS field, like all

fields, achieves this through the application of proven techniques that yield high-quality research and instruction.[12] Some of those techniques involve the generation and refinement of theory, and theory is often essential to the outcome, but the creation of theory per se is not the final game. Theory, to the extent that it has a role, is in the service of producing strong results. Strong results are the provably valuable consequences of research and instruction within the society as materialized in artifacts, behaviors and expectations. Strong results are rather easy to demonstrate on the instructional side: smart people with good IS training usually outperform smart people without good training. This, of course, was the main original motivator for establishing the field (Ackoff, 1967; Dearden, 1972; Mason, 2004) combined with the salience of how to offer systematically information for organizational activities in ways that would harness the potential of the emerging 'IT artifacts.'

Strong results are also easily seen in new artifacts that fundamentally change social behaviors (like ground-breaking computer programs or technologies like operating systems or cellular phones). The IS field abounds with examples of such artifacts, ranging from tools for decision support, and group decision support to CASE tools, development methods and large scale application systems (e.g. ERP). Some have been influential, others less so. The search for rigor and systemic criteria in assessing and developing such artifacts has gained growing interest in the 'sciences of the artificial' (Simon, 1996) through the development of design science and design theories (see e.g., Hevner *et al.*, 2004).

It is harder to demonstrate strong direct results from research ideas and models due to the nature of research itself, but when this happens the impacts on society can be deep—cases in point are the victory over Ptolemaic view of the universe, and the formulation of theories of relativity. In the IS field, demonstration of such theoretical advances are more difficult to pin down exactly as reflected in the anxiety discourse. This does not mean, however, that the impact of the IS field in the theoretical plane is negligible. It has greatly advanced understanding of the impact and role of information in any organizational activity, how it relates to design of artifacts, and how organizations as socio-technical systems operate. Such impact is also felt throughout different social sciences as citation patterns of IS research within the other fields shows (Baskerville and Myers, 2002). This does not mean, however, that strong results within IS have resulted in what Benbasat and Zmud (2003) call 'cognitive legitimacy,' i.e., that all IS theories are taken as granted by environmental constituencies and alternatives to IS have become unthinkable (Robey, 2003). At most, strong theories in IS have gained pragmatic legitimacy which rests 'on the self-interested calculations of an organization's most immediate audiences' (Suchman, 1995, p. 578).

Research that produces strong results demands long periods of sustained effort. Progress is possible only by pushing forward the frontier of the known, a bit at a time. The quality of the process for doing research is tied to the quality of results produced. Academic fields that produce strong results typically adhere to and enforce high standards with respect to knowledge claims and the ways in which those claims are redeemed. There is no inherent value in the process itself; all value accrues through the results of the process.

The quality of the process might determine the quality of the results, but it is only an input to the results.[13] In the IS field, as with any field with praxis at its center, the processes of research must be aimed at improving the strength of the results that affect praxis. Along the way, the results often inform other areas of work beyond the IS field to create generalizable knowledge. This is a good thing, and should be welcomed and even sought, but it will not legitimate the field. It can, at best, enlighten those in other fields to the fact that results useful to them are arising from research in the IS field.

There is a persistent hint in the anxiety discourse to the effect that research tied too closely to praxis is not really research at all, or at least, that it is an inferior form of research.[14] This sentiment is probably the result of a more general confusion about the nature of research, and the dysfunctional distinction between basic and applied research. This distinction rightly discriminates between research results that are immediately applicable to some problem, and those that are not, but that have the potential to affect many problems in the future when more is known. The problem with the distinction is with the political interpretation that has evolved to favor 'basic' over 'applied' as truer, purer, and more worthy of praise. The primary function of this interpretation is to direct social resources away from obviously salient applied research to less salient basic research.

As noted earlier, truth claims related to legitimacy are social constructions, and the preference of basic over applied research is no exception. The preference has roots in the legacy of the medieval and Renaissance academy that preferred thought over practice, and even over empirical study. A more immediate story is found in the mid-20th century fable of the processes by which knowledge produces economic and social welfare. This fable can be seen in many sources, but the most widely cited is Vannevar Bush's 1945 report, *Science: The Endless Frontier*. Bush's linear model of the relationships between science, technology and society is shown in Figure 10.1: scientific discovery creates technological innovation, which then produces improved welfare.[15] This model is popular among some policy makers and among many scientists, but it bears little relationship to the facts. Considerable research in the history of science and technology suggests that the lower cyclical diagram (Figure 10.2) is more accurate: technological innovation occurs largely apart from basic research, creates economic growth, and generates a surplus that can then be invested by the society in basic research that assists but seldom directly causes technological innovation (Gillespie, 1957; Hall, 1963; Mathias, 1972; Rosenberg, 1992). The examples are plentiful. Advances in sea-travel in the 15th century forced the development of better astronomical theories. Problems with steam engines precipitated Carnot's work on thermodynamics. Difficulties in development of databases stimulated Codd's work on relational theory.

The relationship between practice and theory as suggested by the cyclical model is much more complex and nuanced than assumed in simple linear models about scientific innovation. Donald Stokes has explored this issue in depth in his book *Pasteur Quadrant* (Stokes, 1997). Stokes calls basic research the 'quest for fundamental understanding' and applied research to be 'considerations of use.' Each constitutes an essential dimension of a dynamic model in which research can be high or low on either dimension (Figure 10.3). He cites Niels Bohr, a founder of quantum theory, as an exemplar of one who contributed to fundamental understanding but relatively little to use, and Thomas Edison as an exemplar of one who contributed to use but little to fundamental understanding. In his top quadrant, he cites Louis Pasteur as an exemplar of one who contributed greatly to both.

Figure 10.1 *Linear model of science, technology and society*

Figure 10.2 *Cyclical model of science, technology and society*

Research Inspired by		Considerations for User?	
		No	Yes
Quest for Fundamental Understanding?	Yes	Pure basic research (Bohr)	Use-inspired basic research (Pasteur)
	No		Pure applied research (Edison)

Figure 10.3   *Pasteur's Quadrant (Stokes, 1997. Reprinted by permission from Brookings Institution Press.)*

Pasteur's work was almost entirely inspired by practical problems, the most famous of which was the spoilage of beer. Food preservation in the early 19th century was primitive. The alcohol in beer was a preservative, making beer an important food, but beer inevitably spoiled in a relatively short time. Pasteur's development of flash heat treatment (Pasteurization, later applied to milk and other products) solved the problem by killing the yeast cells. Pasteur built upon that discovery with fundamental insights about the role of proteins in metabolism of micro-organisms that launched modern biological chemistry. The point of Stokes' book is that the most noble research is not 'basic' in the usual sense, but rather, advances both use and fundamental understanding simultaneously.

As stated earlier, there is nothing wrong with the creation of solid theory in the quest for fundamental understanding in the IS field. On the contrary, this is an important endeavor, and the IS field's success in this endeavor will certainly help legitimize the IS field in the academic circles. The critical thing, however, is to understand *how* improved theory achieves greater salience, and thereby to recognize the inherent limit of theory's contribution *per se* to legitimation. There is nothing special about theory: it is merely one component in the process of developing useful knowledge. The word arose from the Latin *theoria*, derived from the Greek *theros*, or 'spectator.' It has evolved in meaning over time to refer to a view of the world that constitutes speculation without reference to particular instances or practices. It is a 'step back' from the actual phenomena to find a broader characterization that encompasses the instances at hand. It is useful *only* because it is a cost-effective means of making sense out of many particular instances and helps orient the researcher more effectively towards the world. The value of theory resides solely in its ability to make sense of what actually happens in the world. At its best, theory covers a great many instances and many dimensions of those instances, thereby reducing the burden of understanding. In academic parlance, a good theory can cross academic boundaries and inform many different lines of inquiry.

In academic fields with praxis at their center, theory must serve praxis. For example, legal theories lay foundations for legal practice by clarifying and justifying ethical choices. In IS, theories provide ways of seeing into and intervening in socio-technical problems. Theory is only contributory to the development and constitution of the center, but it cannot be the center. Praxis-related theories sometimes arise from those working directly on the issues at the practical center, and they sometimes arise at the periphery of the field and are brought to the center. It does not matter where the theory comes from, except with respect to who gets credit for the contribution.

To summarize, the IS field's legitimacy depends on the strength of its results with respect to the praxis at the field's center. It is desirable, of course, that strong results at the center of the IS field inform other fields whenever possible, and that other fields appreciate the IS field for such contributions. It does not matter whether strong results are produced with or without theory. Most strong results are likely to be built on some theoretical components, but there is nothing necessary in this. There is no sense in presuming that theory can constitute the IS field's center and this *alone* will allow the field to remain salient.

PLASTICITY

Oscar Wilde is said to have remarked that Fashion is a vain child, but he must be humored because he dies so young. Salience can be as ephemeral as fashion, and for very good reasons. Once a major social problem is solved through research, it stands to reason that the problem will no longer be socially or technologically salient—or as Hughes (1987) states when the significant 'reverse salients' that prevent the deployment or use of large scale technological solutions have been removed in the society. For example, astronomy emerged as a key theoretical inquiry to overcome the reverse salients of the sea-fare, thermodynamics to overcome the challenges of building more efficient steam engines and so on. But none of these issues are of significant theoretical importance any more in physics research.[16] The history of the academy demonstrates that the legitimacy of academic fields lies not in holding tight to the reasons for the field's emergence, but in keeping the field's center 'plastic' by adapting to the shifting salience of the issues that might concern it. Only by keeping the field's center plastic will the field produce strong results, and with strong results legitimacy follows. This is no different with the IS discipline or any other field in management. Robey (2003), for example, promotes 'adaptative instability' as a key strategy for the IS discipline's legitimacy, while (Galliers, 2003) talks about the need for boundary spanning and the need to critically reflect on itself and range widely over related subject matter.

Plasticity is, however, only a correlate of legitimate fields, not a cause. The path to any field's legitimacy—including that of the IS field—does not lie just in becoming more plastic. Plasticity in itself does not produce legitimacy although in itself it helps keep the field salient. But when smart people work on salient issues, the field can expect to produce strong results also in the future. Likewise, the IS field cannot sustain its legitimacy in the long run without being plastic. Despite its youth, the IS field has demonstrated this many times in its evolution, and the benefits of this plasticity to the field have been significant.[17]

Plasticity does not come easy as change in the academic world is not a simple matter, given the inherent conservatism of its institutions (Kuhn, 1996). The inherent conservatism of academic institutions is well-founded and justified: the costs of building and distributing academic knowledge are high. Therefore, academic institutions furiously resist any attempt to change their current organization and associated theoretical cores. Hard-won knowledge should not simply be pushed aside by changing salience in the issues being studied. In addition, strong results require tough and painful processes for making and redeeming claims of truth. As a result, academic change is always an agonistic struggle between established and emergent views in light of growing knowledge and changing social needs. Just read a biography of any great scientist to witness this as a life world experience—the greatness of scientific heroes comes precisely from overcoming resistance and fighting against the odds and prejudice inherent in prevailing scientific knowledge. Knowledge is built through an expensive and painstaking process of argument, postulation, repetitive testing, and successive approximation. Frivolous or politically motivated assaults on new and innovative ideas can stymie progress, or even result in setbacks. At the same time it is appropriate to demand convincing arguments and evidence from upstarts: anything will not just go. If new ideas succeed in taking the leadership, they should be tested, redeemed and found excellent. Therefore, legitimate and established fields have high standards for the establishment of fundamental knowledge; but they shed older fundamentals in favor of new when the standard is met. This concept of durability of standards speaks for strong theoretical cores in the short term—but in the longer term theoretical cores do not create legitimacy.

It is the capability to change and redeem any element of the theo-retical lens that guides observation, explanation and intervention (Kuhn, 1996).

Academic change seldom results in wholesale substitution of new for old, but instead builds a layered genealogy of knowledge that sustains a coherent focus for the field. For example, quantum mechanics and plate tectonics supplemented rather than replaced classical mechanics and erosion in physics and geology, despite their contradictory models and conflicting chains of evidence. Such change has usually been gradual in the history of science, but the pace seems to be accelerating with the rapid generation of new knowledge and changes in research practice. Established disciplines have always preserved their legitimacy by being plastic and responding to the needs and opportunities at hand.

Plasticity sometimes comes only with struggle. Computer science, like IS, is a relatively recent field that grew from a variety of academic roots. Like IS, it has struggled for legitimacy. In its early years it focused primarily on two areas: computability in the traditions of Alan Turing and John von Neumann; and application to practical problems such as ballistics calculation and code-breaking. These two foci were complementary. Processing and storage constraints in early computers encouraged efforts to improve performance: analysis of algorithms, complexity theory, program correctness, and so on, often referred to as 'theory.' The revolution in semiconductors and magnetic storage relaxed the constraints, but computer science had already developed an identity and theoretical core that was grounded in the early technology constraints. Political infighting sometimes resulted in the stronger 'theory' area pushing out the so-called 'systems' area that included software and applications.[18]

This internal conflict in computer science reached a catharsis in the early 1990's with the publication of *Computing the Future: A Broader Agenda for Computer Science and Engineering*, a report of the Computer Science and Telecommunication Board of the National Research Council (Hartmanis *et al.*, 1991).[19] The report argued that computer science must re-engage applications or face demise. Orthodox computer scientists protested the report, but it subsequently shaped the agendas of the National Science Foundation's (NSF) Directorate for Computer and Information Science and Engineering (CISE) and the Computing Research Association (CRA), especially following the stunning rise of the Internet and the World Wide Web. The idea continues to gain momentum: the NSF recently issued a report from a Blue Ribbon Panel titled *Revolutionizing Science and Engineering Through Cyberinfrastructure* that calls for the wholesale transformation of science and engineering research through application of IT.[20] Plasticity has prevented computer science as a field from being left behind in the revolution that it helped to launch.

Plasticity is a complicated matter for legitimacy because it potentially threatens identity. The IS anxiety discourse tends to equate academic identity and academic legitimacy, but they are completely different (King and Lyytinen, 2004). Identity is a necessary precondition for legitimacy, and plasticity, by threatening identity, indirectly threatens legitimacy. Yet, this threat is real only if narrow constraints are put on the issues to be studied. An important kind of identity accrues to those who are consistently open to new ideas, and who look for the systematic relationships between seemingly separate things. If the IS field can be described as the study of the design and management of information and associated technologies in organized human enterprise,[21] the resulting identity is both specific enough to be recognizable and broad enough to allow for healthy plasticity. The great strength of the IS field in the past has been its boundary spanning ability. It could open the black box of information technology, and at the same time, move *beyond* the IT artifact to IT-in-application in human enterprise where the consequences of IT occur. This has remained the salient core of the IS field, and has sustained the growth of IS field for three decades. There is no reason to believe that this mission and associated plasticity will fail to sustain the field into the future.

Recent discussions about the future of the IS field reveal the strength of this tradition of plasticity. Intertwined with the call for a theoretical core has been a call for IS researchers to focus their attention on the 'IT artifact' (Orlikowski and Iacono 2001, Benbasat and Zmud, 2003; Massey *et al.*, 2001; Falkenberg *et al.*, 1999; Bergman *et al.*, 2002). This call seems to spring from the need to take the praxis at the center more seriously: to focus carefully on the artifacts that are created and have materialized in practice and the effects they have. The intent behind an increased focus on the IT artifact is laudable, as it is aimed at consolidating the work of the field and reinforcing the praxis at its center. Nevertheless, it would be a mistake to *predicate* the identity of IS field on the IT artifact. This would unnecessarily narrow the borders of the field in the direction of computer science, just as computer science is broadening its scope, and would run the risk of moving IS away from other areas that may become vital to the long-run salience of the field. Moreover, it makes no sense for an academic field to focus attention exclusively on any artifact. Because artifacts never deliver value in their own right, they are complementary assets in production, and their value cannot be understood without the context of their application.

Plasticity requires remaining flexible about the foci of study, and also about the meanings of the signifiers used to identify the field. As Wittgenstein (1953) pointed out, it is important to be careful when turning words into names because the language games that work well for a name at one point may break down later on. For example, the commonly used name 'information systems' is too broad to establish a precise identity because it can encompass a wide array of subjects that could just as easily be claimed by computer science, library and information science, communications, journalism, or virtually any field that pursues information in a systematic manner (e.g., economics, political science). Adding an adjective such as 'Management' to the front of the name could narrow the focus, but the IS field already tried that and abandoned the 'M' long ago, retaining the 'M' only in formal names such as the journal *Management Information Systems Quarterly*.

A similar story can be seen in computer science. The oldest US professional association of computer scientists, the Association for Computing Machinery, struggled for several years in the 1980's to shed its name for the hopelessly old-fashioned 'computing machinery.' The members could not agree on a new name that would produce the acronym ACM, which had become the organization's *de facto* name. They stayed with the old name and ignored the 'computing machinery.' Many leaders in computer science now regret the signifier 'computer' as too old-fashioned, preferring the broader 'computing.' Given that the names of academic fields age into placeholders for a set of plastic and fluid significations, it seems reasonable to accept the plasticity and fluidity of whatever rests at the centers of those fields.

IS THERE NOTHING AT THE CENTER?

The title of this paper can be read several ways. First, it echoes the theme of the anxiety discourse that the IS field has no center worthy of the name—the falcon has become, in fact, a pigeon. As noted earlier, this theme can take two alternative forms. In one, the only center worth having is a theoretical core that confers academic legitimacy; the falcon sees only the falconer. In another, the field needs, but does not have a consistent focus for its intellectual efforts; the falcon can see everything except the falconer. Both spring from the essential tension, observed since the inception of the field, between its praxis focused center and its intellectual periphery. The anxiety discourse makes the mistake of trying to move the periphery to the center. The IT artifact movement seeks to refocus and revitalize the field's relationship to praxis, and is at least consonant with the legitimacy requirements of salience, strong results and plasticity.

THE MARKET OF IDEAS AS THE CENTER

Another reading of the title implies that the IS field has been unnecessarily preoccupied with its concern about the center, and, therefore, the whole idea of having a center is a red herring. The wearisome and cyclical anxiety discourse makes it tempting to abandon the whole discussion. But that would be as misguided as over-investing in the search for a theoretical center. The idea that there is something at the center, or that there *ought* to be something at the center, is obviously very compelling to any member of any field (King and Lyytinen, 2004). It is only human to seek something unique and shared with those close at hand, and IS people are as human as people in any other field. The needs of salience, the desire for strong results, and the quest for plasticity in the IS field preclude a center of fixed ideas or relationships, but they do not preclude a *center based on a kind of activity*. It is necessary to give up the metaphor of a center as a set of things and their fixed relationships to ideas, and replace that with a metaphor of a center as an activity (or life form) that builds strong identity and legitimacy for IS field as time moves forward (Boland and Lyytinen, 2004).[22] This is accomplished by a free flowing give-and-exchange metaphor of IS discipline as a *market of ideas*. The real center in the IS field has been and will be constituted through a market of ideas in which scholars (and practitioners) exchange their views regarding the design and management of information and associated technologies in organized human enterprise.[23]

For some, it might seem strange to consider a metaphor of a market as a center—a way to relate people, ideas and artifacts—but there is much to recommend it.[24] The idea of a marketplace of ideas is by no means new.[25] Daniel Webster captured it beautifully in 1825 in a speech at the groundbreaking for the Bunker Hill monument in Massachusetts, wherein he focused on '...a vast commerce of ideas' consisting of '...marts and exchanges for intellectual discoveries' that brought great improvements in human welfare. His focus in that speech was the astonishing contribution of new knowledge to the human triumph '...over distance, over differences of language, over diversity of habits, over prejudice and over bigotry.' The market had indeed produced remarkable changes in the world. By 1825 steam had begun to power transport, the cotton gin had introduced mechanized agriculture, vaccination had been discovered, artificial coal gas was lighting cities, the British Parliament had overpowered the monarchy, and democratic institutions had arisen from the American and French revolutions.

The market was by no means finished. By 1875 the Bessemer process had made cheap steel the backbone of the industrial world, the railroad industry had invented operations management, the telegraph had revolutionized communication, slavery had been abolished, compulsory education had been widely established, and higher education was becoming widely available.

Markets of ideas are ephemeral, but they support concrete actions needed for salient issues. They are remarkably fluid, which makes them capable of responding to rapidly changing conditions requiring plasticity. They have the power to resolve uncertainty, necessary for establishing strong results. Markets embody the notion that any fair exchange is a legitimate exchange, which guarantees salience and plasticity in the long term. An ideal market allows people to move value around without unnecessary impediment or cost. The center of a market is not the physical or virtual place in which it occurs (i.e., academic institutions), or the rules under which it operates (e.g., editorial policies). It is not even the particular things being traded (e.g., a particular theory or results). The center of a market is *the empowerment of the participants, through due process, to place their own values on the things being traded.* Where values align, transactions between ideas occur and strong results, salience and plasticity can follow.

The idea that the market of ideas forms the *actual* center of the IS field has many additional virtues for its praxis oriented outlook. For one, it accommodates theory and praxis with equal respect, dispelling the notion that the two are exclusive. It thus reinforces the concept of Pasteur's Quadrant, legitimating *all* aspects of value in any intellectual exchange. This idea is also in line with generating a general body of knowledge (BoK) that helps address concerns about the use of IT in human enterprise (Hirschheim and Klein, 2003). Second, it also explicitly recognizes that anyone may enter or leave the market at will, which is an established tradition of the IS field (DeSanctis, 2003). Rather than lamenting this fact, as the anxiety discourse normally suggests, the IS field should embrace it as a great source of strength as diversity and intellectual quality drive strong results. By allowing and invigorating new entrants, the market can respond more quickly to fundamental changes such as rapid technological improvement and the threshold effects generated when new technologies and techniques combine in disruptive ways. Finally, by holding the market as the center each member of the IS field can seek and find value in exchanges with like-minded colleagues. If the market of ideas is at the center of the IS field, it becomes irrelevant to ask what the theoretical center of the IS field is or ought to be. The answer to this question will always be whatever the market is working on at the time, and this might call on any number of theoretical perspectives.

WHAT DOES THE MARKET OF IDEAS MEAN FOR IS ACADEMICS?

The 'market of ideas' describes the modal center of the field, but it does not necessarily help individual IS academics locate *their* work in the field, and see how they can add value to the market of ideas while pursuing their professional goals. In an ideal world, IS academics would never have to identify or justify the location of their work in the market, because the market would resolve issues of salience, results and plasticity in due time. Unfortunately, the world is not ideal, markets fail, and, therefore, each IS academic must find a reasonable place to stand when affiliating with a community of colleagues and pursuing career advancement. Given that each individual must make this choice from time to time, the question is not which choice to make but, rather, how to parameterize the options available to best exploit the market of ideas while honoring the need for security among individual scholars.

Table 10.1 provides one way for IS academics to approach this challenge. It suggests two dimensions that frame the political discourse in the conferring of academic legitimacy. The first is

Table 10.1   *Parameters of individual position in academic fields*

View of status quo	View of Self With Respect to the Field	
	Personalized	Depersonalized
Conforming	*Cell I*	*Cell II*
	Stable and established academic fields	External commentary on the academic realm
Non-conforming	*Cell III*	*Cell IV*
	Entrepreneurial innovator, not viable in the academy	Unstable and emergent academic fields

Source: Stokes, D. E. (1997), *Pasteur's Quadrant: Basic Science and Technological Innovation*. Washington DC: Brookings Institution Press. Reproduced by permission of the Brookings Institution Press.

whether to personalize one's view of the future of the field. A personalized view sees the field primarily as a vehicle for one's career advancement, and thus seeks to advance the person's career within the empowered constructs of the field. In this view, the individual sees the field as *my* field and has a personal stake in its future growth and legitimacy. In a depersonalized view, the field is seen as an incidental agglomeration of people with shared interests. In this view, the field is *a* field to which I happen to belong at the moment but I am not bound to it as a career option. The second dimension is the choice of whether to conform to the *status quo* in the field in terms of its theoretical constructs and modes of inquiry as currently constructed. A conforming choice accepts the field's established theoretical biases and traditions as legitimate and authoritative, embodying the identity of the field and contributing to the field's legitimacy. A non-conforming choice considers established biases and traditions as products of a constantly changing mix of facts, theories, opinions, and beliefs that emerge in response to the research being done and the larger conditions in the society, such as the salience of the issues at hand. In the non-conforming view, biases and traditions are temporary conditions of an inherently unstable and emergent intellectual enterprise.

Table 10.1 arrays these dimensions into a 2x2 matrix, with each cell describing the position an individual might take in relation to a field with a specific outlook how he or she might approach the 'market of ideas.'

Cell I is the position most often taken by individuals in established academic fields that are stable with respect to their focus of study. The paradigmatic example of this might be physics. It is no accident that many commentators concerned about the lack of academic legitimacy in the IS field hold physics up as an ideal exemplar of legitimacy, and use it as a paragon for a legitimate academic field (Weber, 2003). Physics exhibits academic power and pride; what other discipline would unselfconsciously refer to itself as the 'queen of the sciences?' On the other hand, physics entertains the luxury of studying something that is 'out there,' whether physicists are studying it or not. There is no danger that the physical world is going to change before physicists figure it out, and even the most self-satisfied physicist does not claim to be actually creating the physical world. Perhaps it is for this reason that the biases and traditions of physics change slowly and it has a strong and well organized body of theoretical knowledge—'core theories'—which are taught to each generation of aspiring physicists. As the noted physicist Max Born once claimed, theories in physics are never abandoned until their proponents are all dead, and the field advances 'funeral by funeral.'

Unfortunately, the models of science as applied to physics do not apply to most academic fields, and they certainly do not apply to fields that lie at the intersection of rapid technological and social change and a need to create the world anew as Whitley (1984) observed in his classical study of the organization of academic fields (King and Lyytinen, 2004). They certainly do not apply to the IS field, and, for this reason, aspiration to develop a strong core for IS does not look like a good strategy. There are, however, people in the IS field who would like to locate *all* IS research in this cell and, therefore, place strong IS theories at the center. They naturally can promote and trade these ideas in the 'market of ideas,' but in light of the earlier discussion of salience and plasticity, efforts to make the whole IS field look like physics are folly—they will not yield strong results and therefore not increase legitimacy, as a true market for ideas will not evolve.

In Cell II a scholar holds a depersonalized view of a field, but is attentive to its intellectual biases and traditions, trying to understand *how* or *why* they emerged. This cell is commonly occupied by people who do scholarly work *about* the field by following and commenting on it. Good examples of scholars adopting this position would be philosophers, sociologists, anthropologists, scientometricians, and others who focus on particular fields and their evolution as their primary intellectual interest. Often, some of these individuals may have backgrounds as practicing scholars in those fields, but for various reasons have left that work behind. Well-known examples would include Peter Medawar, a Nobel-prize winning biologist who became a philosopher and sociologist of science, and Thomas Kuhn (1996), a well-known physicist who became a still more famous sociologist of science. Individuals who pursue such work typically move towards academic programs in science and technology studies, and out of the mainstream academic areas that are the focus of their commentary. Most fields have also people who 'reflectively monitor' their own work by adopting the hat of a Cell II scholar.[26] The utility of this effort for the field being studied depends on the intention of the commentator. There is an important difference between genuinely depersonalized commentary that seeks to reveal how a field operates, and the promulgation of prescriptions on how the work of the field ought to be done. Thoughtful commentary helps those operating in the market of ideas put their activities in a larger context, with the goal of improving the quality of individual trades. Prescription, on the other hand, attempts to tell individuals what they should and should not be trading, and thus weakens the power of the market.

Cell III is populated by individuals who take personal advancement within the field seriously, but who do not conform to the biases and traditions prevailing in the field. The best examples of such individuals are entrepreneurial innovators who take the knowledge they have gained in their research and move outside the academy to exploit it. Thomas Alva Edison is probably the most famous example of this genre of intellectuals (Stokes 1997), but similar examples abound in the IS field. LEO, the first information system platform (Mason, 2004), was wholly developed by such entrepreneurs, some of whom later on became significant IS academics. People like Yourdon, Jacobson, Ross, or Scheer (one of the developers of SAP and the R3 approach) emanated from or have had close relationships with academia through their careers but did most of their intellectual work outside it. The academic realm has traditionally not felt comfortable engaging in such activity, and most countries have legal prohibitions against universities conducting for-profit activities in overt competition with private firms. An academic who wishes to run a company must usually leave the academy to do so.[27] These individuals are driven by salience and a desire for strong practical results, but they do not normally care about academic legitimacy, and they are not happy in academia. Nevertheless, they provide valuable ideas and results in the 'market of ideas' with respect to salience. This also has happened in the IS field.

The individual in Cell IV has a depersonalized view of his or her field, and is a non-conformist with respect to established biases and traditions of the field(s). Many scholars in unstable and emerging fields such as the IS field find themselves in this cell *due to the nature of their intellectual mission.* The work in such fields requires boundary spanning in order to understand, explain, and create in ways that do not fit closely with well developed theoretical models within established fields in Cell I. Cell IV scholars must accept the fluidity and unbounded nature of inquiry at the emerging frontier, and often go against the established biases and traditions that reign in well established and confined disciplines. Academic life in Cell IV is risky especially when there are no institutions to protect and legitimate the viewpoints of boundary spanners. Therefore, intellectuals in this cell face ridicule, criticism from arrogant persons, and a loss of career security. Such risks are unavoidable in unstable and emerging fields and have nothing to do with the lack of theoretical core, as the nature of the enterprise itself is about new and different contributions to the market of ideas, which accepts their indeterminacy.

Due to its youth and the nature of its intellectual mission, the IS field has most in common with Cell IV. The field arose as a rebellion against viewing the two faces of IS as separate social and technical systems. As a result, the IS field fought hard against the long-held opinion in the social sciences and management that information technology is only a minor and unimportant element in human enterprise and will continue to be so. Likewise the IS scholars have long challenged the dominant views among computer scientists that the engineering of IT artifacts does not need to take into account and understand the social and organizational issues surrounding computing.[28] As a result, the IS field has been an academic social marginal from its start. It does not have and, in fact, cannot afford the conditions of Cell I in order to prosper due to the salience and fast change in its subject grounding. Accordingly, Cell IV best characterizes the condition of most IS academics, especially those in academic programs such as management schools, surrounded by colleagues who believe it is their predetermined right to live in Cell I and to impose the expectations of Cell I on everyone else.

The Cell I politics happen always within the constraints of broader societal salience and, therefore, nothing in Cell I is sacred and cannot be influenced by changes in Cell III and IV. When the doc.com boom hit, the salience of IT changed overnight in social sciences, and the rhetoric in many of these fields changed. They became suddenly plastic towards IT related issues, and many people in those fields began to claim that IT or information was now central to their endeavors. Ergo, the IS people had potentially little to add to the discussion as they lacked the theory. This was recommended despite the fact that the history of the field witnessed a scholarly engagement on the topic over 25 years by people who had been many times educated as, e.g., economists or operations people! Suddenly IT was solely a 'marketing' issue, or an 'economics' issue.[29] Hence, theories in Cell I can be expanded and re-interpreted when salience demands one to do so. Now when the boom has gone bust, the fickle court of elite opinion is again in some of these fields that there is not much in the IT realm to worry about and the old intellectual borders, in fact, make more sense.

We see that there are several ways in which the market of ideas can be strengthened in light of differences and complementary assets that each cell has to offer. The IS field will remain mostly in Cell IV as long as technological and social change is fast and the salience remains fluid. Therefore, any drastic move from this position is likely to be dangerous for the future of the field.[30] Yet, this does not mean that the field cannot benefit from closer relationships and new ways of relating the work in all cells in 'the market of ideas.' In fact, creating such connections and arenas has been and will continue to be sources of strength for the field.

Cell I offers to IS academics an opportunity for active engagement in rigorous theoretical work in the field where its intellectual periphery is refined, extended and tested. Many of the recent statements in the anxiety discourse are constructive attempts to address the tension between the praxis oriented center, and the intellectual periphery and to improve these connections. The mistake in these attempts is that they monopolize such attempts as the sole means to make the field viable. Though the field has seen several scholars move to Cell III, there is still much to regain by forging better alliances with the visionaries and entrepreneurs. One of the authors has in the past suggested such endeavors as one means to increase the salience of the field, and its capability to respond better to the research potential offered by fast technological development (Lyytinen, 1999). The value of this activity is enormous, if it is combined within the market with the quest for sustained rigor and abstraction in Cell I.

We feel that the field could also benefit greatly with better collaboration with Cell III scholars in the research of itself. Though much has been recently published on multiple topics dealing with the status and organizations of the discipline, there is paucity of rigorous and systematic studies of the evolution of the knowledge of the field and its legitimation mechanisms. Such studies would significantly improve understanding of the mechanisms that constitute the field and its future challenges while at the same time adding to the broader theoretical discourse around technology and society. The value from such inquiries is greatly improved if used to understand how the 'ideas of market' operates and how it has evolved in the way it has as to develop new mechanisms and relationships to trade in the market.

CONCLUSION

Many in the IS field have recently observed in the words of Yeats: 'Things fall apart; the centre cannot hold.' The goal of this essay has been to show that this feeling is not because of what IS academics have done or failed to do in terms of theory; it is the nature of the work in which the field engages. IS academics are the falcons turning and turning in the widening gyre of the IT revolution. Therefore, it *is* hard to get respect and resources, as so many falconers are watching and use the theory weapon for disciplinary violence (King and Lyytinen, 2004). This analysis shows that the tendency in the anxiety discourse to conflate the problems IS people face with the putative lack of academic legitimacy due to a weak theoretical core is both misplaced and dangerous. It is misplaced because in its strongest form the theoretical core argument draws on fallacious reasoning, and in its weaker form it is not grounded in careful empirical understanding about how theoretical core and legitimacy correlate in academic fields. It is dangerous if turned into a principle because it does not make the field more legitimate and it makes the field move away from the gyre of IT revolution by stimulating behavior akin to that of a cargo cult.[31]

In light of the evolution of multiple disciplines, and by analyzing mechanisms that have made them legitimate, three factors *together* appear to account for disciplinary legitimacy: 1) salience of the subjects studied, 2) the strength of results from the study, and 3) the plasticity of the field with respect to changing circumstances. The IS field already has strength in its salience and its plasticity, both of which are driven by the gyre of technological change. Perhaps the real concern for the field is still a relative paucity of strong results. If so, the goal of stronger results is well worth pursuing, and better theory is likely to contribute to this goal. But the quest for better theory will contribute most *only* if it is understood in the context as one of many complements in the pursuit of strong results. It cannot be the sole focus as this will place it at odds with salience and plasticity.

The IS field will make progress on all fronts, and turn and turn in the gyre, if it comes to see its center as a market in the service of the 'vast commerce of ideas.' The IS field should also take pride and have self-respect in the fact that it has played an important role in making this vast commerce of ideas possible. Like any other academic field, the IS field needs intellectual discipline. But that discipline will not be achieved by creating social conventions that define what is to be excluded and what is included, or establish rules about how members of the field must do their research. Discipline can come only from IS researchers themselves, interacting in the market of ideas that includes as part of its natural function the mechanisms for discriminating between strong and weak results. If markets work well, they lower the value on anything that is not worth much to those doing the trading. At the same time, markets often permit entry of traders with unusual wares that turn out to be of great value to everyone in the market thus speeding the turn in the gyre. The IS field should treasure those cases where someone of exceptional insight persuades the community to go into territory no one previously thought of as IS. The center of the IS field should celebrate the diversity in methods *and* topics that join in the market, and let the market itself discriminate on intellectual quality. In the end this would best guarantee that the gyre expands as it turns.

NOTES

1 We are indebted to colleagues in different parts of the world where we have presented and discussed our ongoing struggle to make sense of the evolution of the IS field. These include colleagues at Case Western Reserve University, the University of Michigan, Georgia State University, the University of Western Ontario, Hong Kong University of Science and Technology, Nanyang Business School, London School of Economics, Aagdar College, the University of Colorado at Boulder, IRIS 1999, 2003, and AMCIS 2003 Philosophy track among others. We are particularly thankful to Ron Weber, Detmar Straub and Sirkka Järvenpää for their insightful comments on earlier versions of the paper.

2 We are indebted to Detmar Straub for this excellent quote.

3 This seemed to be also Keen's (1987, p. 3) idea when he wrote: 'Our backgrounds, training and interests are very different. We must take that as strength, not a cause of argument.'

4 This tension is also well documented in the endless debates over relevance vs. rigor observed as early as Keen's (1980) concept of reference disciplines and their relationship to the intellectual mission of the IS field. In this argument, rigor came from reference disciplines while relevance resided in the praxis-oriented core. This issue is beyond the scope of this essay, but it should be noted that preferring one attribute—in this case theoretical rigor over praxis-based relevance—lies at the heart of both stories.

5 A valid argument is a logical deduction of the form, derive q from $p \rightarrow q$ and p, e.g.: All men are mortal; Socrates is a man; Socrates is mortal. Validity is not enough: the argument must also be sound, meaning that both the conditional claim ($p \rightarrow q$), and the antecedent (p) must be true for the consequent (q) to be concluded. An invalid argument cannot be sound, but a valid argument can be unsound, e.g.: All men are dogs; Socrates is a man; Socrates is a dog.

6 The authors are indebted to an anonymous reader of an earlier version of this paper who explicitly used Popper to argue in favor of particular warrants, thus revealing the centrality of Popper's views to this discussion.

7 Popper's view has other problems with respect to the argument for legitimacy as a consequence of a strong theoretical core. His view captures only nomological explanations, and excludes widely accepted theories such as Darwinian natural selection evolutionary theory. Moreover, his view does not clarify whether academic fields are defined by theories, or theories by fields, although he expresses the opinion that the former *ought* to be the case.

8 We can also state that $p \rightarrow q$, $\rceil q$, therefore $\rceil p$ (*modus tollens*). This suggests that *if* a discipline does not have legitimacy it does not have theoretical core *assuming* that $p \rightarrow q$ is sound. This still requires vindication of the soundness of implication as elaborated below.

9 We are thus arguing for S&R&P→L. This naturally can be rejected by finding a counter-example like the one we demonstrated for the theoretical core argument.

10 Cf. http://www.bls.gov/emp/empfastestind.htm

11 Both authors have seen this happen as members of university committees and reviewers for research funding agencies.

12 This is similar to what DeSanctis (2003) pointed out recently when she wrote: 'Evidence of legitimacy of the IS field lies not so much in the establishment of organizations such as the Association for Information Systems (AIS), schools of information science, and university departments; instead, *the evidence of legitimacy lies in the actions of people within and between these organizations as they pursue their scholarly work*' (emphasis added).

13 This explains why scientists make public their methods in the process of producing the results. Quality control over process distinguishes science and scholarship from other forms of producing knowledge.

14 This seems to be implied when Benbasat and Zmud (2003) call for theories based on nomological nets and argue for the value of a 'dominant research paradigm.'

15 Bush had been Dean of Engineering at MIT, but was serving as an advisor to President Truman. His report is credited with creating the momentum that led to the establishment of the National Science Foundation (Bush, 1945).

16 There are however some points where these old theories may need revision and salience. For example, the first Apollo launches required much more accurate calculations than Kepler's traditional laws to predict the movement of earth and moon.

17 The often raised criticism of the IS field as being driven by 'fads' can be interpreted also as a field's attempt to retain plasticity in the face of extremely fast change in its field of study. We often see bad IS research that just follows fashion but some of the unique challenges of the field are its need for exceedingly high levels of plasticity due to the fluidity of its subject field.

18 More than one MIS group was formed in management schools by 'systems' faculty exiled from computer science during this era of purges.

19 The whole report is at http://www.nap.edu/books/0309047404/html/

20 The report is at http://www.communitytechnology.org/nsf_ci_report/

21 We use purposefully a broad definition here so that the term enterprise should be seen as a generic human activity (to conduct a way of life in a specific way)—not as a definition of an organizational form in which IT use takes place.

22 This seemed to be also Keen's (1987, p. 3) idea when he wrote: 'Our backgrounds, training and interests are very different. We must take that as strength, not a cause of argument.'

23 This is similar to Desanctis' (2003) statement that the people and their 'social life' make a field legitimate by enabling specific types of interactions on a set of chosen topics that lock in interested participants. We agree on this characterization but want to push the argument further by clarifying how dynamic, diverse and heterogeneous communities of inquiry can coalesce around the 'market of ideas.'

24 Lest this seem an unnecessary empowerment of economists, it is important to remember that economists did not invent the concept of markets, and they do not own the concept. Economists merely started studying markets along the way, and despite real progress, they are far from complete understanding of how

markets function. The markets being discussed here, which consist solely of information, are among the least understood.

25 This concept is also close to Habermas' idea of a 'public sphere' and critical discourse in public as a condition for advances in technology, politics and society (see Habermas, 1991; see also Toulmin, 1972; Rorty, 1978).

26 This essay constitutes an example of this practice.

27 These conditions vary from country to country.

28 This point is made elsewhere (King and Lyytinen, 2004), but bears elaboration. It is telling that the National Science Foundation Directorate for Social, Behavioral and Economic Sciences funded very little research on the effects of computerization between 1970 and 2000. The vast majority of good social science and management research on this subject during that period was funded from the directorates responsible for computer science where it was still regarded with suspicion and at most tolerated.

29 We are purposefully painting here a simplified account what truly happened as many people in economics, sociology, marketing etc. have now or even before the dot.com boom become our allies as new intellectual collaboration has been spawned within the IS field—an example of how it can work as a 'market of ideas.'

30 DeSanctis (2003), Galliers (2003), and Robey (2003) in their responses all suggest the same when they stress plasticity and action focus for the IS field.

31 Cargo cults emerged in the islands of Melanesia after WW II when aboriginal natives equated acquisition of riches in the form of manufactured goods with the appearance of ships and airplanes that frequented the islands during the war. The natives began erecting shrines looking like ships and airplanes in the expectation that the rich 'cargo' would materialize (Lindstrom, 1993).

REFERENCES

Ackoff, Russell L. (1967): 'Management Misinformation Systems', *Management Science*, December, 15, 6, pp. 147–156.

Andersen H. (2000): Influence and reputation in social sciences—how much do researchers agree?, *Journal of Documentation*, 56, 5, pp. 674–692.

Banville C and Landry M (1989): 'Can the field of MIS be disciplined?', *Communications of the ACM*, 32, 6, 48–60.

Baskerville R., Michael D. Myers (2002): 'Information Systems as a Reference Discipline', *Management Information Systems Quarterly*, 26, 1, pp. 1–14.

Benbasat I, and Weber R. (1996): 'Research Commentary: Rethinking "Diversity" in Information Systems Research', *Information Systems Research*, 7, 4, pp. 389–399.

Benbasat I, Zmud R. (2003): 'The Identity Crisis within the IS discipline: Defining and Communicating the Disciplines's core properties', *MISQ*, 27, 2, pp. 183–194, pp. 183–194.

Bergman M, King J., Lyytinen K. (2002): 'Large Scale Requirements Analysis as Heterogeneous Engineering', *Scandinavian Journal of Information Systems*, 14, pp. 37–56.

Berger P, and Luckmann, T. (1966): *The Social Construction of Reality: A Treatise in the Sociology of Knowledge*. Garden City, NY: Doubleday.

Boland R., Lyytinen K. (2004): 'Information Systems Research as Design: Identity, Process and Narrative', Forthcoming in IFIP WG 8.2. Conference proceedings *Relevant Theory and Informed Practice: looking forward from a 20 year perspective on IS research*, July 15–17, Manchester, U.K.

Bush, Vannevar. *Science The Endless Frontier.* A Report to the President by Vannevar Bush, Director of the Office of Scientific Research and Development. Washington, DC: US Government Printing Office, July 1945.

Ciborra C. (1998): 'Crisis and Foundations: an inquiry into the nature and limits of models and methods in information systems discipline', *Journal of Strategic Information Systems*, 7, 1, pp. 5–16.

Chalmers A. (1999): *What is this thing called science?*, (3rd edition) Hackett, Indianapolis.

Dearden J. (1972): 'MIS is a Mirage', Harvard Business Review, January–February 90–99.

DeSanctis G. (2003): 'The Social Life of Information Systems Research', *Journal of the Association for Information Systems*, 4, 6, pp. 360–376.

Falkenberg E., Lyytinen K., Verrijn-Stuart A. (eds) (1999): *Information System Concepts- An Integrated Discipline Emerging*, Kluwer.

Galliers R. (2003): 'Change as Crisis of Growth? Towards a Transdisciplinary View of Information Systems as a Field of Study', *Journal of the Association for Information Systems*, 4, 6, pp. 337–351.

Gillespie C. (1957): The natural history of industry. *Isis*, No. 48.

Feyerabend P. K. (1982): *Science in a Free Society*, London, New Left Books.

Habermas J. (1971): *Knowledge and Human Interests*, Beacon Press, Boston.

Habermas J. (1991): *The Transformation of the Public Sphere*, MIT Press, Boston.

Hall, A. (1963): 'The historical relations of science and technology'. Inaugural lecture, London, 1963, as reported in Rosenberg, N., *Inside the Black Box: Technology and Economics*. Cambridge: Cambridge University Press, 1982.

Hartmanis J. and Lin H. (eds) (1991): *Computing in the Future: A Broader Agenda for Computer Science and Engineering*, National Academy Press, Washington D. C.

Hevner A., March S., Park J., Ram S. (2004): 'Design Science in Information Systems Research', *MIS Quarterly*, 28, 1, pp. 75–106.

Hughes, T. P. (1993): The Evolution of Large Technological Systems. In W. E. Bijker & T. P. Hughes & T. J. Pinch (Eds.), *The social construction of technological systems: New directions in the sociology and history of technology* (pp. 51–82). Cambridge: MIT Press.

Keen P. (1980): 'MIS Research: reference disciplines and cumulative tradition', in *Proceedings of the 1st International Conference on Information Systems*, Philadelphia, Dec 1980, pp. 9–18.

Keen P. (1987): 'MIS research: current status, trends and needs', in Buckinham, R. A., Hirschheim R., Land F., Tully C (eds), *Information Systems Education: Recommendation and Implementation*, British Computer Society Monographs in Informatics. Cambridge, Cambridge University Press, 1–13.

Keen P. G. W. (1991): 'Relevance and Rigor in Information Systems Research: Improving the Quality, Confidence, Cohesion and Impact', in Nissen H-E., Klein H., Hirschheim R. (eds), *Information Systems Research: Contemporary Approaches and Emergent Traditions*, North-Holland, pp. 27–49.

King J., Lyytinen K. (2004): 'Grasp and reach', accepted for publication *MISQ*.

Kling R. (1980): 'Social Analyses of Computing: Theoretical Perspectives in Recent Empirical Research', *Computing Surveys*, 12,1, 61–110.

Kuhn, T. (1996): *The Structure of Scientific Revolutions*, Chicago University Press, 3rd edition, Chicago.

Lakatos I, Musgrave A (eds) (1970): *Criticism and the Growth of Knowledge*, Cambridge, Cambridge University Press.

Lee A., Baskerville R. (2003): 'Generalizing Generalizability in Information Systems Research', *Information Systems Research*, 14, 3, pp. 221–243.

Lindstrom L. (1993): *Cargo Cult: Strange Stories of Desire From Melanesia and Beyond*. Honolulu, University of Hawaii Press.

Lyytinen K. (1999): 'Empirical Research in Information Systems: On the Relevance of Practice in Thinking of IS Research', *MIS Quarterly*, 23, 1, pp. 25–28.

Maggi L., Zmud R., and Wetherbe J. (Eds) (1986): *Proceedings of the Seventh International Conference on Information Systems*, December 15–17, San Diego, California.

Markus L (1999): 'Thinking the Unthinkable: What happens if the IS Field as We Know it Goes Away?', in W. Curry, R. Galliers (eds), *Rethinking Management Information Systems*, Oxford University Press, 175–203.

Mason R. (2004): 'The Legacy of LEO: Lessons Learned from an English Tea and Cake Company's Pioneering Efforts in Information Systems', *Journal of the Association for Information Systems*, forthcoming.

Massey A., Wheeler B., Keen P. (2001): 'Technology Matters', in Dickson G., DeSanctis G. (eds) *Information Technology and the Future Enterprise*, Prentice Hall, New Jersey, pp. 25–48.

Mathias, P. (1972): *Science and Society*, 1600–1900, Cambridge: Cambridge University Press.

Popper K. (1968): *Conjectures and Refutations*, Harper & Row, 1968.

Mumford E., Hirschheim R., Fitzgerald G., Wood-Harper T. (1985): *Information System Research Methods*, North Holland, Amsterdam.

Orlikowski W., Iacono S (2001): 'Desperately Seeking the "IT" in IT research—a call to theorizing the IT artifact', *Information Systems Research*, June 2001, pp. 121–134.

Robey D. (1996): 'Research Commentary: Diversity in Information Systems Research: Threat, Promise and Responsibility,' *Information Systems Research*, 7, 4, pp. 400–408.

Robey D. (2003): 'Identity, Legitimacy, and the Dominant Research Paradigm: an alternative prescription for the IS discipline', *Journal of the Association of for Information Systems*, 4, 6, pp. 352–359.

Radnitzky F. (1968): *Contemporary Schools of Metascience*, Liber, Gothenburg.

Rorty A. (1979): *Philosophy and the Mirror of Nature*, Princeton, Princeton University Press.

Rosenberg, N. (1992): Science and technology in the twentieth century, in In Dosi, G., Gianetti, R., and Toninelli, P. A. (eds.), *Technology and Enterprise in a Historical Perspective*, Oxford: Clarendon Press, 63–96.

Schilpp P. A. (ed) (1974): *The Philosophy of Karl Popper*, La Salle, Illinois, Open Court.

Simon H. (1996): *The Sciences of Artificial*, MIT Press, 3rd edition, Cambridge, MA.

Stokes, D. E. (1997): *Pasteur's Quadrant: Basic Science and Technological Innovation*, Brookings Institution Press, Washington D.C.

Stove, D. (1982): *Popper and After: Four Modern Irrationalists*, Pergamon.

Stowell F., Mingers J. (1997): 'Information Systems: an Emerging Discipline?—an Introduction', in Stowell F, Mingers J. (eds), *Information Systems: An Emerging Discipline*, McGraw Hill.

Suchman M. (1995): 'Managing Legitimacy: Strategic and Institutional Approaches', *Academy of Management Review*, 20, 3, pp. 517–610.

Toulmin S. (1958): *Uses of Argument*, Cambridge University Press, Cambridge.

Toulmin S. (1972): *Human Understanding*, Clarendon Press, Oxford.

Weber R. (1987): 'Towards a Theory of Artifacts: a paradigmatic basis for Information Systems Research', *The Journal of Information Systems*, 1,2, pp. 3–19.

Weber R. (2003): 'Still desperately seeking the IT artifact', Editors Comments *MISQ*, 27, 2, pp. iii–xi.

Whitley R. (1984): *The intellectual and social organization of sciences*, Oxford, Clarendon Press.

Wittgenstein L. (1953): *Philosophical Investigations*, London, Basil Blackwell.

11
Reach and Grasp[1]

John Leslie King and Kalle Lyytinen

Ah, but a man's reach should exceed his grasp, or what's a heaven for?
The Faultless Painter, Robert Browning (1812–1889)

INTRODUCTION

The 16th century produced two great portrait artists. One was Leonardo da Vinci, whose enigmatic paintings remain an inspiration four centuries later. The other was Andrea del Sarto, the 'faultless painter,' whose quest for technical perfection caused him to lose touch with the deep inspiration of his art. Browning's poem about del Sarto concludes that greatness comes not from holding tight to what we can grasp, but rather from our willingness to reach beyond what we can grasp. There is a lesson in his poem for the Information Systems (IS) field as we grapple with the field's future.

The IS field's 'anxiety discourse' has been evident at least since 1972, when *Harvard Business Review* published John Dearden's 'MIS is a Mirage'—a paper that questioned the fundamental ideas behind the field. In the years that followed, Dearden's theme was repeated in various forms. At the first ICIS meeting, Keen (1980) cast the field in *reference* to other disciplines. The same year, Kling (1980) characterized the field as an arena yearning to be a discipline. In 1985, Mumford and her colleagues raised the specter of IS as a 'doubtful science' characterized by 'poor intellectual and methodical rooting.' A popular panel at the 1986 ICIS entitled, 'Back to the Future: Will there be an

First published in *MIS Quarterly* 28(4), pp. 539–51. Copyright 2004 by the Regents of the University of Minnesota. Reprinted by permission.

ICIS in 1996?' opened with the concern that IS was 'like the dinosaurs...heading blindly toward extinction' (Culnan and Huff, 1986). Banville and Landry (1989) found that the field had yet to 'be disciplined.'

The anxiety was evident even during the halcyon peak of the dot.com era. Benbasat and Weber (1996) warned of a '...miasma that spells the demise of the discipline.' Stowell and Mingers (1997) asked once again, 'is information systems a distinctive discipline?' Straub (1999) answered that IS is 'a polyglot discipline that lacks focus, centrality, and theory,' doomed to absorption by other disciplines with greater 'intellectual clarity and substance.' Finally, in May 2003, the *Harvard Business Review* reached back three decades and updated Dearden's aphorism by publishing Nicholas Carr's paper, 'IT Doesn't Matter.'

It is difficult to imagine how a field that started as a 'mirage' and doesn't really matter could be free from anxiety. Nevertheless, decades later, the IS field still rolls along. How can something so seemingly problematic survive at all? Our starting point for considering the state of the IS field is to invoke Samuel Johnson's comment about a dog walking on its hind legs—the surprise is not that the dog does it poorly, but that it does it at all.

This essay challenges the anxiety discourse and suggests an explanation for its persistence. We are not and have never been anxious about the IS field, but we know many good colleagues who are. By deconstructing the anxiety discourse, we felt we might be convinced to become anxious. Happily, the results of our efforts reaffirm our initial position and we continue to believe the IS field has a great future. We do not expect this essay to put an end to the anxiety discourse, but we do suggest an alternative view of that anxiety that may be more productive in formulating the field's strategy. In particular, we hope to show that a fixation on the issues raised by the anxiety discourse imposes serious opportunity costs on the field that it cannot afford.

We develop our analysis in three steps. First, we deconstruct the anxiety discourse, especially with respect to concerns about academic identity and legitimacy. Second, we identify the mechanisms that induce hegemony of other fields acting against the IS field and the tendency of those within the IS field to turn against each other in response to this external oppression. Finally, we recommend a set of actions for defeating the political oppression of the IS field where it exists, for expanding the field's promising instructional and research opportunities that cross traditional institutional barriers, and for pursuing a commitment to excellence based on academic criteria chosen by the IS field itself.

THE LOGIC BEHIND THE ANXIETY DISCOURSE

The foremost concern in the anxiety discourse is the perceived inadequacy of the IS field as an academic enterprise. This inadequacy is typically articulated either in referent terms (respected academics outside the field do not respect the field) or in absolute terms (the IS field does not measure up to some objective standard that other, better fields meet). Fully elaborated, the discourse typically evolves as follows: the IS field is academically weak and its only path to legitimacy is to make it academically stronger by cementing it around a theoretical core.

This argument invokes a set of 'warrants:' assumptions or beliefs that justify the movement from premises to conclusions (Toulmin, 1958). Warrants establish the connection between a writer's claims and the theoretical or empirical support used to back those claims. They often emerge from cultural experiences or personal observations and can be conspicuous or inconspicuous. They are frequently taken for granted by both the writer and the reader. Warrants often include enthymemes, which are categorical syllogisms with one unstated premise that can be reconstructed using the principles of categorical syllogism. The warrants of the anxiety-discourse argument can be stated as follows:

1. The IS field struggles because it lacks legitimacy.
2. The IS field lacks legitimacy because it lacks a clear identity.
3. The IS field lacks a clear identity because it lacks a strong theoretic core.

By extension, the IS field will acquire identity and legitimacy in good time if and only if it develops a strong theoretic core.

We find this argument unconvincing on a number of dimensions, which we discuss elsewhere.[2] A strong theoretic core might help create both legitimacy and identity in any field, but having such a core is neither necessary nor sufficient to engender identity or legitimacy. Moreover, the anxiety discourse confuses identity and legitimacy, often using the two terms interchangeably or wrongly implying that legitimacy is a precursor to identity. We must untangle these terms if we are to make progress with the objectives of our essay.

From the Latin *idem*, meaning 'the same,' *Identity* is an impression created by a set of characteristics that make a thing recognizable or known.' The essential attribute of identity is consistency in character. An iconic claim of the anxiety discourse is that identity is attained only through the exclusive ownership of a powerful, general theory. This claim is refuted by abundant examples to the contrary. English, for example, is an identifiable academic field with academic departments, journals and conferences. Yet English has no unique theories of the sort described above. English gathers its identity from the consistency of scholarly study of works written in the English language. Information Systems is an identifiable academic field with academic departments, journals and conferences. Irrespective of the IS field's theoretical status, it has an identity gathered from the consistency of its focus on the systematic processing of information in human enterprise. We therefore drop further reference to the matter of academic identity and focus attention on the sole issue of concern, academic legitimacy.

Legitimacy rests on but is not caused by identity. An academic field has to be identifiable before it can become legitimate (e.g., alchemy in the 16th century), but it may also turn out to be illegitimate (e.g., alchemy in the 18th century).[3] Legitimacy is derived from the Latin *legitimus*, or 'of the law,' and common use refers to practice that is consistent with some norm. Legitimacy defines what is regarded as appropriate or acceptable. Inevitably, it is a political issue involving the power to define and enforce the norm. Academic legitimacy usually correlates closely with the social salience of the topic being studied. Academic fields focusing on salient topics will attain legitimacy more easily than those focusing on non-salient topics, because they are of interest to the political elite who support the academy.

Another important component is the trustworthiness of the results of the work, typically established through the use of appropriate intellectual method. Method normalizes inquiry and allows scientific communities to interpret and judge claims of legitimacy quickly and effectively. Method also lends to establishing the cognitive and/or pragmatic legitimacy of the knowledge produced (Suchman, 1995). Conformance with method helps scholars approach difficult problems efficiently over sustained periods of time. Thus, method conformance indirectly assists with establishing the legitimacy of the resulting work ('the cumulative tradition'; Keen, 1980). As a general rule, academic legitimacy is the product of an identifiable and socially salient field of inquiry whose practitioners use methods deemed appropriate and rationally vindicated within the community in the execution of their scholarly work.

Academic legitimacy is not a constant. New methods emerge as new cognitive and operational capabilities are developed and identified. For example, the availability of unprecedented amounts of computational power over the past two decades has enabled the exploitation of modeling and simulation methods that support scholarly work in multiple fields of science (so called computational science).

Previously, this type of work was impossible using only theory, analytical methods, and 'strict' empirical testing. In addition, new discoveries can shift a community's attention to unexpected lines of inquiry that have no *a priori* methodological grounding. Therefore, they cannot be legitimated solely by existing method. Quantum theory in physics appeared well before the problems of classical mechanics were resolved, but it quickly became legitimate even though it had little method to support its study.

Legitimacy is also affected by changes in social salience. Artificial intelligence has persisted despite setbacks because the payoff from success would be huge; however, this is no guarantee of permanence. Alchemy's salience sustained it for two centuries before failure to deliver was recognized and the contradictions of advancing knowledge cast it out of the academy.

The anxiety discourse is about the IS field's academic legitimacy. The more dire aspects of the discourse would suggest that the IS field should have died years ago. It is clear, however, that the dog of the IS field is still walking on its hind legs. It is a stretch to suggest that the field's survival alone is adequate evidence of its legitimacy. Nonetheless, it is true that the field has been sufficiently legitimate to survive three decades in a hostile environment. This outcome cannot be due only to the salience of the topic studied, but rather is also attributable to the intellectual strength of the IS field. IS research is well conceptualized and well executed like good academic work in other legitimate fields. Thus, it can make claims of using appropriate intellectual methods.[4] The field sets and enforces appropriate norms through refereed journals and conferences with their commensurate cultures of peer review. The field has training mechanisms such as doctoral curricula and consortia to socialize its members to consistent application of method.

In addition, the IS field is socially salient. Academic IS programs were developed and supported even in hostile institutional environments because the patronage of employers, donors and research funding agencies signaled the importance of the area. Even after the collapse of the dot.com boom, the IS field remains socially essential. Its long-term salience looks undiminished in the midst of the information revolution.

Overall, the IS field seems to have much going for it. We believe the challenges it faces are seen in countless other academic fields in one form or another. Why, then, is the IS field both enduring and anxious? We suggest three causes: the youth and volatility of the field's domain of focus; academic ethnocentrism; and the institutional politics that surround many IS departments and groups. A detailed examination of the way these factors weaken legitimacy is the first step toward bypassing the anxiety discourse and achieving a more constructive discussion of the challenges the field must face.

A ROAD TO SAFETY

The Nature of IS Field

The most-powerful factor in explaining the IS field's anxiety is its relative youth.[5] New fields usually emerge in opposition to older and more-established intellectual traditions that have proven ill-equipped to deal with the emerging concerns at hand. Such upstarts are seldom welcome. The medieval academy formed around the 'letters' (e.g., philosophy, literature and theology) that still garner deep academic respect.[6] The natural sciences emerged in the late Renaissance and early Enlightenment. They struggled for decades to escape the non-scientific traditions of scholasticism that dominated the letters before emerging as a powerful order in their own right. The social sciences emerged in the early industrial age and have yet to reach the powerful status of the natural sciences. University-based professional schools are younger still and they remain subordinate to traditional academics in most elite universities.[7]

Young fields are frequently beset by internal schism. The social sciences are notoriously fratricidal, with various fields and sub-fields challenging the legitimacy of one another. The professions are worse. Academic medicine has a rich history of battles among chemopaths, osteopaths, alopaths and homeopaths. The learning-by-doing traditions of experimental engineering are locked in contest with emergent engineering science perspectives. Law schools are torn between educating for legal practice and education in legal theory. Management is fractious, with relatively young subfields such as accounting, finance, marketing and organizational behavior questioning the legitimacy of even younger sub-fields such as operations research, information systems and strategy. The IS field's relative youth seems a good candidate for the cause of the field's anxiety.

Another factor is a basic mismatch between the IS field's close ties to technology and the traditional antipathy toward technology found in management schools that are often the home of IS groups. The social sciences and the management sub-fields that derive from them have never engaged technology as a mainstream concern. They seldom have close relationships with technology-oriented programs in engineering or the sciences. Technically oriented sub-fields within management such as IS and operations management are often clumped together and marginalized by other management sub-fields.

Given that the IS field is incontrovertibly tied to technology, there appears to be no way the IS field can avoid this problem.[8] At the same time, the IS field's focus on applications alienates it from engineering and computer science, which are much more concerned with technology *per se*, are in isolation and defy everything that is not theory (i.e., formal). The fact that the essence of the IS field lies at the intersection of the technical and the social makes it inherently tense.

The IS field's youth and its shared focus on the technological and social aspects can be seen by contrasting the experience of IS faculty in management schools with those in recently created schools of information science and information technology. Those in the new schools seem less anxious about the legitimacy of their efforts.[9] These programs bring together faculty from a wide variety of backgrounds that share a coherent interest in and focus upon technology that is not present in most management schools. In addition, most of these schools are so new that their internal cultures have not yet had time to evolve class politics that use academic legitimacy as a political weapon, although they might develop such class politics as time goes on. The point here is that the new schools have a community focus on technology and relative age equality among their different sub-fields. This reduces conflict and anxiety about the legitimacy of any of those sub-fields, including IS, as all are in the same boat.

Taken together, the IS field's youth and its focus on technology are credible explanations for the anxiety discourse, at least in institutional settings. They predispose the field toward political challenges that often materialize in accusations from outside the field that the IS field is not academically legitimate. Yet neither youth nor a technology focus presents a challenge to academic legitimacy. Rather, each exacerbates endemic political tensions and precipitates political acts that arise from the problem of academic ethnocentrism.

Academic Ethnocentrism

An important clue to the political aspect of the anxiety discourse can be found in the presenting symptoms of anxiety, specifically the IS field's apparent lack of power in management schools. Recent examples include concern over the removal of key language supporting the IS area from professional AACSB accreditation criteria, laments about the exclusion of IS courses from the politically important 'core' of professional degree curricula and commentary about the relative absence of strong IS programs in some prestigious universities. Many IS academics in management schools appreciate these concerns because they have suffered the arrogance and hegemony of scholars in other fields within management schools. This kind of anxiety is easy to understand. The truly interesting question is how and why such anxiety gets systematically wound up in tales of academic legitimacy.

The simplest explanation for this confusion is the ethnocentrism of disciplines, a concept articulated in detail by Donald Campbell as the IS field was emerging (Campbell, 1969). Campbell wrote the paper following a frustrating period as head of the interdisciplinary program at Northwestern University. He postulated that interdisciplinary efforts typically fail due to the fundamental human tendency toward ethnocentrism. Broadly defined, ethnocentrism is the tendency of individuals to affiliate with those with whom they have much in common and to avoid those who appear to be different. Ethnocentric behavior need not be intentional. Those who exhibit it are often appalled when they are accused of it. The ethnocentric person need not be openly belligerent or xenophobic; it is enough simply to be anxious in the presence of those who seem 'other' or 'alien.'

Academic ethnocentrism is grounded in and paves the way for hegemonic expectations regarding intellectual foci, methods of inquiry and pedagogy, which engenders nationalistic behavior among disciplines. Simon testified beautifully about this feature in his memoirs when he wrote:

> I came to see that disciplines play the same role in academe as nations in international system. Academicians typically live out their whole careers within the culture of a discipline, rarely shaking off the parochialism this isolated existence engenders. (Still later I learned from my encounters with economics that disciplines undertake imperialistic adventures with the same zest as nations do.) (Simon, 1991, p. 173)

Ethnocentrism of this sort is certainly at work when people from other fields oppress IS professionals/researchers. We shall return to this point later. It is ethnocentrism *within* the IS field, however, that helps explain why the anxiety discourse has coalesced over the past two decades in the IS field toward concerns of academic legitimacy. A recurrent theme in the anxiety discourse is that the IS field's intellectual scope is so broad that the field will devolve to a weakly federated community in which members relate more strongly to other fields than to IS (Benbasat and Weber, 1996). Moreover, the barriers to entry for such a community will be so low that weak entrants cannot be excluded and intellectual standards will collapse.

The IS field has always been broad due to the diverse intellectual roots of its founding scholars and the equally diverse issues that, from the start, have related to the use of IT in human enterprise. In addition, the field has become increasingly broad over the years while the IT revolution has unfolded. Consequently, the field has continually struggled to identify its center. The inability to find a 'true' center is disconcerting for people who have a tendency to become ethnocentric. Therefore, the natural reaction is to *declare* a center and attempt to persuade everyone to acknowledge it. If everyone in the field acknowledges the declared center, a sense of academic solidarity and shared intellectual purpose will follow and anxieties might diminish. However, the intellectual agenda of the IS field is constantly changing for reasons noted earlier, so the center remains elusive. As a result, a feeling of inadequacy pervades the field.

The perceived inadequacy of the field is usually articulated as a shortfall against one or both of two larger ideals: 'ideal scope' (i.e., the field is too heterogeneous) and 'ideal theory' (i.e., the field does not have any theories). These are independent issues, but they are frequently conflated, resulting in deleterious consequences for the IS field. It is useful to examine these closely.

What is the Ideal Scope for Legitimacy of the IS Field?

The ideal scope argument entails the relationship between identity and legitimacy discussed earlier. Given that identity is a required condition of legitimacy (and illegitimacy), anything that confuses identity will confuse the subsequent assignment of legitimacy. The key characteristic of academic identity is seen to be consistent attention to particular kinds of problems. Too broad a range of foci by members of the field can threaten identity and therefore legitimacy. The question then is, how broad is too broad? Currently, it is impossible to come up with a definitive, identity-sensitive limit to the breadth of the IS field; there is simply too much disagreement among the field's membership to permit this outcome. It is also difficult to set up the right *parameters* that help define such limits by generalizing from the experience and success of other fields. For example, what is good for physics is not necessarily good for IS as it grapples with a different, dynamic domain composed of artifacts. The recent effort to encourage a focus on the 'IT artifact' is a good example of how the field is seeking ways to effectively identify parameters that help define adequate boundaries *for the moment*. Yet the fact that the IS field does have enough identity to be considered *illegitimate* by some proves that the current degree of breadth is sufficient to maintain identity, even if the identity is imprecise.

Elements of academic ethnocentrism can easily be mistaken for problems of ideal scope. In the IS field, as in other heterogeneous fields, scholars of one persuasion often look down on the scholars of other persuasions for the 'weakness' or 'irrelevance' of their scholarly work. Breaking the field into homogenous sub-fields, which no longer talk to one another, might solve this problem in the short run because animosity declines. This happens, however, only at the expense of collaborating on problems that cannot be understood from the perspective of any single sub-field. We believe that such negative consequences for the field have been key determinants in recent calls for more diverse and detailed research on IT artifacts (Benbasat and Zmud, 2003; Weber, 2003; Orlikowski and Iacono, 2001). This dilemma is not attributable to the scope of the field but rather to the behavior of individuals within the sub-fields for whom ethnocentric biases are more important (and easier) than the challenge of the scholarly work itself.

What is the Ideal Theory for the Legitimacy of IS Field?

The ideal-theory argument flows directly from the call for better legitimacy, as some highly legitimate academic fields have erected a set of strong theories at their center. The visible example of such fields is understandably attractive to fields that feel less legitimate. The ideal theory argument also obtains a powerful warrant from the philosophy of science in the opinions of Popper and his followers (Popper, 1968) that speak to the minds of many scholars. Popper's original claim in his 'Conjecture and Refutations' was that academic legitimacy is derived (or at least ought to be derived) only from the theoretical contributions made by a field. This view is strongly disputed by many subsequent scholars in the philosophy of science. Within the IS field, however, the warrant usually stands uncontested.[10]

Strong theory can be useful to any academic field as it can enhance a field's cognitive or pragmatic legitimacy. However, strong theory is demonstrably not necessary for academic legitimacy and there is no evidence to suggest that the creation of such theory *per se* will make legitimate a field that lacks legitimacy (Lyytinen and King, 2004). The problem with the ideal theory argument is that it takes a reasonable position with regard to the nature of academic inquiry and the value of theoretical abstractions, but then it causes trouble, however, when it directly equates theory with legitimacy, and lack of theory with illegitimacy.[11] As explained elsewhere, academic legitimacy is a consequence of the social salience of the topics studied, the presence of strong results and the ability to maintain disciplinary plasticity (Lyytinen and King, 2004) rather than the strength of the theoretical center. To the extent that a strong theory yields legitimacy, it does so primarily by contributing to the ability of a field to achieve strong results. Theory is an input to the process of getting strong results, not an outcome. Nonetheless, a strong theory is not even a necessary input for all fields and in few fields is it alone sufficient to produce or sustain strong results. Why, then, is the call for theory so powerful an argument in discussions about legitimacy?

The persistence of theory as a discriminator in obtaining legitimacy is best explained by its role in the problems of academic ethnocentrism. Theory has acquired exaggerated importance in some academic fields as many scholars live and die by the theories into which they have been socialized (Kuhn, 1996). This creates a political climate ripe for abuse. Those who can claim the mantle of theory band together to consolidate their power. They then use that power against those, whose work is not fundamentally theoretical in nature or does not concern the correct type of theory. The question of how best to do the work is subordinated to what methods are deemed politically correct for *any* kind of scholarly work. This outcome is a perversion of the original high ideals of the academy, which call on scholars to pursue, develop and defend new knowledge using whatever means are most appropriate to the task. This distortion of the value of theory readily creates another backlash. Those whose work is not best pursued theoretically respond by refuting any call for improvement in the theoretical state of the field, because they fear a subsequent attack on the quality of their work.

The problem with the ideal theory is further exacerbated when the ideal-theory argument is conflated with the ideal-scope argument. Those who criticize calls for improved theory often invoke the accusation that the pursuit of theory will necessarily narrow the scope of the field. This accusation has superficial appeal because doctrinaire, theory-wielding thugs who beat up on their colleagues for a-theoretical weakness are usually narrow-minded people. The negative reinforcement of 'theory' with 'narrow' obscures the fact that many powerful theoreticians are also broad-minded individuals who see value in a wide array of intellectual approaches to problems.[12]

On a substantive level, there is no evidence to support the claim that the pursuit of theory (or theories) *per se* narrows the scope of a field. On the contrary, the strongest of theories tend to be broadly applicable and enhance multiple lines of inquiry, as seen in many theories of economics, psychology, and social behavior. Likewise, theories of thermodynamics had great influence across a huge swath of fields, from high-energy physics to molecular biology. In addition, strong theories often have metaphorical power beyond their immediate targets. This can be observed in the profound influence of quantum theory, specifically Heisenberg's uncertainty principle, on fields as far-ranging as philosophy, religion, literary criticism and cognitive psychology or in the current buzz around complexity and chaos theory in multiple fields ranging from biology, physics, meteorology, economics and organizational behavior. Good theory does not narrow fields; people with specific interests narrow fields. Academic ethnocentrism is to blame, not theory.

Recapitulation: Scope and Theory in the IS Field

To summarize, the ideal-scope and ideal-theory arguments are not helpful to reforming the anxiety discourse. The ideal-scope argument is at odds with the IS field's tradition of being open to new ideas, as required in extremely rapidly changing fields. In fact, low barriers to entry and exit mean that smart people can feel free to come and go in this dynamic field, thus cross-pollinating IS scholarship with other fields. Similarly, the ideal-theory argument is at odds with the IS field's need for flexibility to accommodate rapid change. Strong theory is important, but not when it is used as a political weapon or stymies the need for fast cognitive change. The IS field's rambunctious behavior draws fire from incumbent powers, but that behavior is natural for a young field: it is a good thing, although it is anxiety producing. A certain amount of anxiety is by necessity built in to the IS enterprise as long as the enterprise is working well. As Hegel stated, 'without passion there is no achievement.' The challenge for the IS field is to separate healthy anxiety arising naturally from the focus of study from dysfunctional anxiety that arising from academic ethnocentrism and hegemony inherent in academic politics.

Institutional Politics and Hegemony

As we suggested earlier, IS faculty members in schools of management are particularly susceptible to the anxiety discourse. This comes as no surprise: they are surrounded by faculty in management sub-fields who have faced their own issues surrounding legitimacy. None of the management fields is much older than a century. The 'modern' management school's focus on finance, accounting, marketing and so on did not become common until the mid-20th century following the rise of professional management as practice. Moreover, the roots of management school education lie in teaching traditional professional practices that were frowned upon by other social sciences until after WWII, when management studies became more scientific (see, for example, Simon, 1991). The difference in age between the established management sub-fields and the IS field is only two or three decades, but the extra time has given established fields the ability to cultivate potent mechanisms of internal socialization and enforcement. They keep their internal fights under control in order to exert power and direct resources toward themselves through the mechanisms of ethnocentrism. In simplest terms, they simply declare that only they are ethnically pure enough to deserve resources. In doing so, they often present themselves as defenders of the academic ideal and position those who are not their peers as undeserving. They are quick to fire the deadliest shot that can be taken at any academic field: they impugn its intellectual quality. The IS field is often on the receiving end of such attacks.

It should come as no surprise that the IS field comes under attack from other management sub-fields; this is the essence of ethnocentrism. What is puzzling is the way the IS field gives in to this pressure by starting to question its own legitimacy, thus playing directly into its opponents' hands. Unfortunately, the IS field's own anxiety discourse turns back on the IS field itself, increasing concerns about the field's identity, its theoretical strength, and its academic legitimacy. By internalizing this rhetoric from without and turning it on each other, the field engages in a phenomenon called *horizontal violence* common to marginalized fields of work.[13] IS academics start to look at themselves and at each other as the primary causes of their anxiety. Unfortunately, they find much to dislike. They are harshly critical of each others' papers and proposals, they treat publications in major journals as a resource to be rationed rather than a discussion to be promoted and they grasp at efforts to define the field narrowly around their preferred interests. In so doing, they make it easy for opponents to argue that the IS field is weak because, ostensibly, even people within the field think it is weak. Ethnocentrism from without promotes ethnocentrism within.

The nature of the disciplinary game is that the IS field will never get past its anxiety discourse by improving itself so much that other fields will accept it as good. As long as other fields get to define what it means to be good, they can move the target at will. The IS field should refuse to play this game on the grounds that it fails on absolute terms (i.e., the IS field does not fall short on any absolute standard) and relative terms (the IS field is no worse than other fields in terms of academic quality). The argument is bogus, but when left uncontested, it becomes reified and powerful. The key to ending the anxiety discourse and the underlying anxiety that produces it is to find solidarity within the field and push back against the oppression from without.

ANGLE OF ATTACK

We return now to the question of whether the quest for a strong theoretic core might change the balance of power and influence legitimacy in favor of the IS field. We do not believe having such a theoretic core is necessary to achieving legitimacy; if obtained, it will not guarantee legitimacy. Still, we agree that having a strong theoretic core might help establish continuity across lines of inquiry within the field. It also might help develop a better public image of the field (symbolic capital) and thus enhance in the long run the field's ability to handle the design and use of IT in human enterprise. Unfortunately, the process of establishing such a theoretic core will probably outlast the expected careers of the many people currently in the field and thus will not relieve much anxiety in the short run.[14] Most important, the quest for a theoretic core will not reduce the oppression endemic to the institutional environments of many IS scholars. The focus on the core as the savior is misplaced and can even be dangerous. Other angles of attack will take effect more quickly. We suggest three.

First, the IS field should become more aggressive in defense of its own legitimacy by repudiating unwarranted accusations from those in other fields whenever they arise. This must occur at all levels and must be done consistently in order to establish the clear understanding that such oppression will not be tolerated. There is nothing new in this strategy; it is simply 'tit for tat,' established empirically as the quickest path to equilibrium in the theory of cooperative games (Axelrod and Hamilton, 1981). This does not mean the IS field should shy away from legitimate criticism; on the contrary, the field should embrace such criticism in the spirit of open scholarship. At the same time, the IS field must respond aggressively to politically motivated attacks masquerading as responsible assessments of the IS field's academic quality. In the end, the IS field must be the sole authoritative arbiter of academic quality for the IS field.

Second, the IS field should exploit its expanding opportunities in both instruction and research. Much of the recent anxiety discourse seems to have been triggered by a dramatic decline in IS enrollments following the crash of the dot.com boom. This echoes similar concerns that have existed for some time, most notably the fear that other management sub-fields are now competing or soon will begin to compete for students on the IS field's turf. The defensive strategy of closing ranks around a core set of IS topics and fighting for control of them is a losing proposition over the long run. The explosive growth in IT applications across many domains precludes the IS field's ability to establish such turf, much less control it. Instead, the IS field should exploit emerging instructional opportunities in the way it did once before in response to the explosive growth in administrative data processing applications in the 1960s and 1970s. As in the past, research opportunities go hand in hand with instructional opportunities. Fortunately for the IS field, such opportunities abound.

Despite the dot.com crash, enterprise-oriented applications of IT continue to grow dramatically and enrollments in related programs will continue to grow globally. Nonetheless, these opportunities pale in comparison to the rapidly growing demand for the skills of the IS field that lie outside the confines of traditional business education. These new opportunities are in the areas of manufacturing, science, health, entertainment, transportation and so on. IS academics outside management schools are already pursuing these opportunities successfully. The large IS population in management schools have much to offer to these expanding areas of IS work. Moreover, they have much to gain in both research and teaching opportunities by engaging them. Naturally, the sometimes-myopic institutional constructs of professional education create challenges in exploiting such opportunities. Yet the IS field has continually met such challenges since it began. Indeed, it has a tradition of following opportunity wherever it might lead (see, for example, Mason, 2004). This type of pioneering spirit is needed now and will continue to benefit the IS field in the future as it has in the past.

Finally, the IS field will have to work harder and be better than its critics. This requirement has always been imposed upon the young. In rising to that expectation, the young normally create progress for all. Creating a stronger theoretical grounding for the IS field is one component of this effort, but only if it is done without narrowing the focus of the field. The IS field must engage issues that are important to its members and welcome new entrants with interesting views and opinions. The IS field must embrace and exploit research strategies appropriate to the study of those issues without allowing narrow methodological orthodoxy to be imposed from without or generated from within. Contrary to the complaints of critics, the IS field has learned over time to set high expectations of itself. Those expectations should be set even higher, but they must be set entirely within the IS field, by members of the IS field and calibrated by other fields only when the work in those fields directly complements the work of individuals in the IS field.

The future of the IS field lies in being tough on the field's critics when that criticism is politically motivated, in following instructional and research opportunities irrespective of what institutional boundaries must be crossed and in setting and striving for tough academic standards on the IS field's own terms. This set of challenges is not as daunting as it might seem. The survival of the IS field over the past 30 years shows these to have been key strengths of the field all along; the same still holds true. The founders of the IS field blazed an exciting trail, but it is not the trail that lies ahead. As Whitehead rightly noted, 'A science that hesitates to forget its founders is lost.' The spirit of the field's founders provides inspiration, but the shape of the field's future lies in the efforts of a new generation of scholars who must weigh carefully the meaning of the anxiety discourse we have been discussing and what its implications are for their intellectual agendas.

A curious contradiction exists between the evident reach of the IS field's ambitions since its inception and the grasping for legitimacy that lies at the heart of the anxiety discourse. The opening quote from Browning's poem and the title of this essay, which was inspired by this quote, can be read in a number of ways. One is a call to reach out and grasp what one can. Another is an admonition to never reach for more than can be successfully grasped. We feel neither serves our purpose. Instead, we suggest that the heart and soul of the IS field's future lies in reaching beyond what can be grasped. Accepting this risk is an acceptable price to pay for aspirations of heaven.

NOTES

1 We are indebted to colleagues in different parts of the world where we have presented and discussed our ongoing struggle to make sense of the evolution of the IS field. These include colleagues at Case Western Reserve University, the University of Michigan, the University of Western Ontario, Hong Kong University of Science and Technology, Nanyang Business School, London School of Economics, Aagder College, the University of Colorado at Boulder, and IRIS 1999, 2003 among others. Several anonymous reviewers were extraordinarily helpful in making us think more carefully about what we were trying to say.

2 See Lyytinen and King (2004).

3 Alchemy (best known for its quest to turn base metals like lead into precious metals like gold) was once a mainstay of legitimate academic activity. It lost favor as scientific knowledge grew. Isaac Newton and Robert Boyle, as well as most of the founders of The Royal Society of London, were active alchemists throughout their lives.

4 We make this assertion after years of collective endeavor as reviewers and editors in academic journals in the IS field and elsewhere. We also recommend the excellent recent article by DeSanctis (2003).

5 The term 'information systems' seems to have been coined by Börje Langefors in the 1965 IFIP World Conference. *MISQ* and ICIS—the first premiere research journal and conference—started in the late 1970s. AIS was formed in the late 1980's. The field is about 30 years old.

6 As a modest example, few elite universities have closed their classics departments, in spite of vanishing enrollments, on the grounds that classics represent the ancient heart of the academy.

7 *US News and World Report* usually rates Princeton and Caltech in the 'top 5,' although neither has many professional programs.

8 The recent call by IS researchers to focus more intently on the 'IT artifact' is testimony to the close bond between the IS field and the underlying technology and the challenge this sets for the field and its research agenda.

9 These observations are anecdotal but could easily be tested using survey research.

10 There are many who disagree with Popper's philosophy of science on strictly philosophical grounds (e.g., Stove, 1982 and Bleicher, 1982), and many others from the sociology of science who claim that, irrespective of the philosophical issues, the behavior of successful scientists simply does not conform to the model implied by Popper (e.g., Latour and Woolgar, 1979; Latour, 1987; Traweek, 1992). For a more detailed discussion, see Lyytinen and King (2004).

11 It is important to note (as we demonstrate in Lyytinen and King, 2004) that 'positive' and 'negative' syllogisms of this sort are not symmetrical. The negative one (i.e., that the lack of theory implies a lack of legitimacy) is a logical fallacy (denial of the antecedent) and cannot be defended even on logical grounds.

12 The dog of the IS field is no less susceptible to Pavlovian conditioning than any other dog. The negative reaction to the calls for improved theory is a *learned response* made more powerful through the administration of negative, intermittent reinforcement by narrow-minded and wrong-headed colleagues.

13 The term arose in the study of oppressed occupational communities that internalize and redirect the oppression at each other. The original work on the subject has focused on the field of nursing and is of growing interest in the sociology of work and occupations (Duffy, 1995). It can be seen in many other fields, including computer science, environmental science, film studies, and women's studies.

14 This is based on our reading of the histories of other academic fields that have evolved strong theoretic cores (Lyytinen and King, 2004).

REFERENCES

Axelrod, R. & Hamilton, W. D. (1981): 'The evolution of cooperation', *Science* 211:1390–6.

Benbasat I. & Weber R. (1996): 'Research Commentary: Rethinking "Diversity" in Information Systems Research', *Information Systems Research*, vol 7, No 4, pp. 389–399.

Benbasat I. & Zmud R. (2003): 'The Identity Crisis within the IS Discipline: Defining and Communicating the Disciplines's Core Properties', *MISQ*, 27, 2, pp. 183–194.

Banville C. & Landry M. (1991): 'Can the field of MIS be disciplined?', *Communications of the ACM*, 32, 48–60.

Bleicher R. (1982): *The Hermeneutic Imagination: Outline of a Positive Critique of Scientism and Sociology*, Routledge and Kegan Paul, London.

Campbell D. T. (1969): 'Ethnocentrism of Disciplines and the Fish Scale Model of Omniscience', in: M. Sherif and C. W. Sherif (eds.), *Interdisciplinary Relationships in the Social Sciences*, Chicago: Aldine, 328–348.

Carr, N. (2003): 'IT Doesn't Matter', *Harvard Business Review*, May.

Culnan, M. J., and Huff, S. L. (1996): 'Back to the Future: Will There Be an ICIS in 1996?,' in *Proceedings of the 7th International Conference on Information Systems*, L. Maggi, R. Zmud, and J. Wetherbe (Eds.), San Diego, CA, p. 352.

Dearden J. (1972): 'MIS is a Mirage', *Harvard Business Review*, January–February, 90–99.

DeSanctis, G. (2003): 'The Social Life of Information Systems Research: A Response to Benbasat and Zmud's Call for Returning to the IT Artifact.' *Journal of the AIS*, Volume 4 Article 16 December.

Duffy, E. (1995): Horizontal violence: a conundrum for nursing. *Collegian. Journal of the Royal College of Nursing Australia*. 2(2), 5–17, April.

Keen, P. G. W. (1980): 'MIS Research: Reference Disciplines and a Cumulative Tradition,' *Proceedings of the First International Conference on Information Systems*, pp. 9–18.

Lyytinen K. and King J. (2004): 'Nothing At The Center?: Academic Legitimacy in the Information Systems Field', Accepted for publication, *Journal of AIS*.

Kling, R. (1980): 'Social issues and impacts of computing: From arena to discipline', In *Human Choice and Computers*, 2, A. Mowshowitz, Ed., North-Holland, Amsterdam, pp. 146–155.

Kuhn, T. (1996): *The Structure of Scientific Revolutions*, Chicago University Press, 3rd edition, Chicago.

Latour, B. (1987): *Science in Action*. Cambridge: Harvard University Press.

Latour, B. and Woolgar S. (1979): *Laboratory Life: The Social Construction of Scientific Facts*, Beverly Hills: Sage.

Mason R. (2004): 'The Legacy of LEO: Lessons Learned from an English Tea and Cake Company's Pioneering Efforts in Information Systems', *Journal of the Association for Information Systems*, forthcoming.

Mumford E., Hirschheim R., Fitzgerald G., Wood-Harper T. (eds) (1985): *Information System Research Methods*, North Holland, Amsterdam.

Orlikowski W. & Iacono S (2001), 'Desperately Seeking the "IT" in IT research—a call to theorizing the IT artifact', *Information Systems Research*, June 2001, pp. 121–134.

Popper K. (1968): *Conjectures and Refutations*, Harper & Row.

Simon H. (1991): *Models of My Life*, Basic Books, New York.

Stowell F., Mingers J. (1997): 'Information Systems: an Emerging Discipline?—an Introduction', in Stowell F, Mingers J. (eds), *Information Systems: An Emerging Disicpline*, McGraw Hill.

Stove, D. (1982): *Popper and After: Four Modern Irrationalists*, Pergamon.

Straub D. (1999): A question to Senior Editors of Leading IS Journals, *IS world posting*, July.

Suchman M. (1995): 'Managing Legitimacy: Strategic and Institutional Approaches', *Academy of Management Review*, 20, 3, pp. 571–610.

Toulmin S. (1958): *Uses of Argument*, Cambridge University Press, Cambridge.

Traweek, S. (1992): *Beamtimes and Lifetimes: The World of High Energy Physicists*. Cambridge: Harvard University Press.

Weber R. (2003): 'Still desperately seeking the IT artifact', Editors Comments *MISQ*, 27, 2, pp. iii–xi.

Commentaries

12
The Artifact Redux: Further Reflections on the 'IT' in IT Research

Wanda J. Orlikowski and C. Suzanne Iacono

We welcome the opportunity to reflect and comment on our paper, 'Desperately Seeking the "IT" in IT Research: A Call to Theorizing the IT Artifact' (Orlikowski and Iacono, 2001). In particular, we would like to use this occasion to clarify our intent in writing the paper and to reaffirm the implications entailed in the paper's conclusion, while also reflecting on some of the reactions evoked by readings of our paper.

CLARIFYING INTENT

If one looks over time, across application contexts and domains of study, a persistent theme of research in the IS community is the study of emerging information technologies. As John King put it when he was editor of *Information Systems Research*: 'What unites the information systems community is a shared interest in a phenomenal event—the rise and consequences of radical improvement in information technology' (King, 1993, p. 293). We agree with this formulation, and this is reflected in our claim that the IT artifact is a critical intellectual focus for the field (Orlikowski and Iacono, 2001). With this claim, we intend to suggest that emerging IT artifacts are the persistent meaningful forms of entrée into the research of most everyone in our community—whether the focus is decision-support systems, MRP systems, groupware, ERP systems, inter-organizational systems, email, the Internet, mobile technologies, eCommerce auctions, outsourced transaction systems, online reputation systems, etc.

We continue to believe that the IT artifact is a distinctive element of our field, binding together multiple heterogeneous elements of hardware, software, humans and institutions. However, this should not be understood as an exclusive focus on the materiality of technology. Indeed, in our paper we emphasized how the IT artifact is critically constituted by human, social, economic and historical elements. And we argued that a focus on the IT artifact entails a detailed examination of, among other things, computational capabilities, cultural meanings, human skills, social relations, economic impacts, political interests, local and global contexts, institutional influences, temporal patterns, transformational possibilities, and historical consequences (2001, pp. 131–3). Given the complex, multi-faceted and dynamic nature of emerging information technologies, we believe that the various disciplinary interests of our community—be they economic, sociological, psychological or computational—can and should be brought to bear on producing new knowledge about the IT artifact.

By focusing attention on the IT artifact, we did not suggest that activities around conceptualizing or theorizing the artifact should constitute the only work of the field or that research that did not include such a focus was somehow illegitimate or irrelevant. What we did do was point to what appears to be a blind spot in our field, and that is that despite our common interest in information technology, much of our research takes it for granted or ignores it when conducting empirical investigations or building theoretical models.

We respect the interests of all researchers to choose what they wish to focus on in their research practices. The major point of our paper was to highlight what we see as a missed opportunity for our field, to generate specific knowledge about IT phenomena—knowledge that we believe the IS research community is uniquely positioned to contribute. Our interest was, and continues to be, to encourage attention to this central, under-theorized aspect of our research, not to delimit the phenomenon of study or exclude anyone from the community.

To this end, we convened a panel on conceptualizing the IT artifact at the 2002 ICIS in Barcelona. We invited scholars representing the various views on the IT artifact articulated in our paper (i.e., tool, proxy, computational, and ensemble) to discuss how they might engage the artifact more actively in their research. The session was lively, stimulating, and generative. The four scholars (Mary Culnan, Vijay Gurbaxani, Helmut Krcmar and Dan Robey) offered both creative and valuable conceptualizations of the IT artifact from their different perspectives, effectively demonstrating that it is possible to think about and theorize the IT artifact in various meaningful and novel ways.

REAFFIRMING IMPLICATIONS

In the latter part of our original paper, we offered some proposals for how researchers may begin to engage the IT artifact more seriously in their research studies. In particular, we encouraged an opening up of the black box of technology, suggesting explicit consideration of the import and implications of the assumptions, algorithms, structures, and logics embedded in and underlying the various technological systems such as ERP, online auctions, data mining, reputation systems, statistical analyses, collaborative tools, browsers, search tools, software agents, spyware, viruses, etc. These technological contents are rarely discussed by technology vendors and are not always observed or understood by technology users. Yet their operation can have powerful intended and unintended conse-quences, affecting short- and long-term organizational, economic and societal outcomes.

A focus on embedded systems has been a feature of IS research for decades, with Rob Kling serving as one of the pioneers in developing this focus (Kling and Dutton, 1982; Kling and Scacchi, 1981; Kling *et al.*, 2003). This has been an important contribution to our knowledge of information technologies, but additional work is needed. An embedded perspective is focused primarily on the ways in which technological artifacts and infrastructures are embedded in the social realm. We believe that an equally important perspective should focus on the social preferences, choices, and policies that are inscribed into the technological artifacts (e.g., into interfaces, protocols, programs, standards, mecha-nisms, and procedures) by artifact designers, builders, and imple-menters. Thus, technological artifacts are not only embedded within social worlds, but social worlds are also inscribed into the artifacts (Akrich, 1992; Bowker and Star, 1999). And these inscriptions have real implications for such matters as human relationships and interactions, social and organizational effectiveness, economic costs and benefits, as well as issues of privacy, security, safety, reliability, legality and fairness.

While this important point has been made many times by many other scholars, its implications for IS research remain central, and relatively unexplored. Sociologists of technology have long explored the intermingling of humans and technology (Berg, 1997; Callon, 1987; Latour, 1987), while scholars such as Lucy Suchman (1994, 1995) and Batya Friedman (1997) have been writing about the categories and values built into technology designs for over a decade. Similarly, Lawrence Lessig's writings (1999, 2001) about embedded 'code' have become popular among legal scholars and lay people interested in the 'new' architectures of cyberspace and their legal and ethical entailments. For IS researchers, the implications are significant: if we are to develop and explain technologies that are useful to humans, institutions, and society, we need to better understand how the contents and contexts of technological artifacts influence their use and consequences. And vice versa.

REFLECTING ON READINGS

We have welcomed the range of reactions to our 2001 paper as we feel that deliberation about and discussion of these issues are critical opportunities for us all to reflect on our own assumptions, values, interests and identities, as well as those of the field we collectively construct. To the extent that a conversational space for such considerations has been created, we believe the field will benefit. To the extent that these conversations are used to draw rigid boundaries between appropriate and inappropriate research subject matter, we believe the field will be diminished.

Given that IT phenomena are increasingly pervasive and invasive in our everyday lives, and that they continue to exhibit unprecedented capabilities and consequences, we continue to argue that only a diversity of perspectives, methods and theories will help us make adequate sense of the development, use and implications of information technology in society. Thus, we continue to hope our paper will encourage scholars, working from multiple different points of view, to become interested in questioning the specific status, nature and influence of information technology in their studies. Or at least, to ask the question, does it make a difference that information technology is part of the story here? And if so, what is that difference, and how is it manifested materially, economically, culturally, historically and organizationally?

We further believe that a deeper engagement with information technology is important for the future of the field of IS. Engaging the artifact can enliven and enlarge the field while simultaneously stabilizing and sustaining what is—unavoidably, given the nature of information technologies—a dynamic and emergent identity. The field of IS has a particular vantage point and advantage in being able to conceptualize the IT artifact from multiple disciplinary lenses. Other fields are also beginning to focus on the intensifying socioeconomic implications of emergent information technologies. Computer science, for example, is taking some of its more social and organizational subfields, like CSCW and social informatics, more seriously than ever before. Increasingly, there are new schools of informatics that combine computer and information science with various domain sciences to engage in what some have dubbed e-science. The technologies of interest include supercomputers, middleware, grid computing, semantic webs, ontologies, visualization tools, knowledge environments for big science, and cyberinfrastructure. We hope that the field of IS will take these innovative enterprises and their technologies seriously as new domains of inquiry, rather than leaving them to researchers in other fields. Interest in the critical phenomenal event of emerging information technologies positions the IS research community to contribute significant knowledge in these new domains. We hope that the field of IS will be open to exploring and engaging these new challenges and opportunities.

REFERENCES

Akrich, M. (1992) 'The de-scription of technical artifacts', in W. E. Bijker and J. Law (eds), *Shaping Technology/Building Society: Studies in Sociotechnical Change*, MIT Press, Cambridge, MA, pp. 205–24.

Berg, M. (1997) 'Of forms, containers, and the electronic medical record: some tools for a sociology of the formal', *Science, Technology and Human Values*, 22(4), pp. 403–33.

Bowker, G. C. and Star, S. L. (1999) *Sorting Things Out: Classification and its Consequences*, MIT Press, Cambridge, MA.

Callon, M. (1987) 'Society in the making: the study of technology as a tool for sociological analysis', in W. E. Bijker, T. P. Hughes and T. Pinch (eds.), *The Social Construction of Technological Systems*, MIT Press: Cambridge, MA, pp. 83–103.

Friedman, B. (ed.) (1997) *Human Values and the Design of Computer Technology*, Cambridge University Press, Cambridge.

King, J. L. (1993) 'Editorial notes', *Information Systems Research*, 4(4), December, pp. 291–8.

Kling, R. and Dutton, W. H. (1982) 'The computing package: dynamic complexity', in J. N. Danziger, W. H. Dutton, R. Kling and K. L. Kraemer (eds), *Computers and Politics: High Technology in Local Government*, Columbia University Press, New York, pp. 136–69.

Kling, R., McKim, G. and King, A. (2003) 'A bit more to it: Scholarly communication forums as socio-technical interaction networks', *Journal of the American Society for Information Science*, 51(14), pp. 1306–20.

Kling, R. and Scacchi, W. (1982) 'The web of computing: computing technology as social organization', *Advances in Computers*, 21, Academic Press, New York.

Latour, B. (1987) *Science in Action*. Harvard University Press, Cambridge, MA.

Lessig, L. (1999) *Code and Other Laws of Cyberspace*, Basic Books, New York.

Lessig, L. (2001) *The Future of Ideas: The Fate of the Commons in a Connected World*, Random House, New York.

Orlikowski, W. J. and Iacono, C. S. (2001) 'Desperately seeking the "IT" in IT research—a call to theorizing the IT artifact', *Information Systems Research*, 12(2), pp. 121–34.

Suchman, L. (1994) 'Do categories have politics?', *Computer Supported Cooperative Work*, 2, pp. 177–90.

Suchman, L. (1995) 'Making work visible', *Communications of the ACM*, 38(9), pp. 56–65.

13
Like Ships Passing in the Night: The Debate on the Core of the Information Systems Discipline[1]

Ron Weber

On 24 March 2003, as then Editor-in-Chief of the *MIS Quarterly*, I accepted an Issues and Opinions submission written by Izak Benbasat and Bob Zmud entitled, 'The Identity Crisis within the IS Discipline: Defining and Communicating the Discipline's Core Properties.' The paper subsequently appeared in the June 2003 issue of the *MIS Quarterly* (Benbasat and Zmud 2003). In this same issue of the journal, I provided my editorial statement under the title, 'Still Desperately Seeking the IT Artifact' (Weber 2003). The title of my editorial statement was based on the title of a well-known and frequently cited paper by Wanda Orlikowski and Suzanne Iacono published in the June 2001 issue of *Information Systems Research*— 'Desperately Seeking the "IT" in IT Research—A Call to Theorizing the IT Artifact' (Orlikowski and Iacono 2001). In their paper, Orlikowski and Iacono had expressed concerns that the information systems artifact was not a central focus in much of the research that had been conducted within the information systems discipline.

Both Benbasat and Zmud's paper and my editorial were motivated by concerns we have about the scholarly status of the information systems discipline. The three of us contend that the information systems discipline lacks a 'core.' As a result, we believe the discipline lacks a distinct identity. Moreover, in the absence of a distinct identity, we believe the future existence of the information systems discipline, at least as a distinct discipline, is at risk.

Issues and Opinions papers published in the *MIS Quarterly* are supposed to communicate

> well-developed and well-articulated position statements concerning emerging, paradoxical, or controversial issues in the discipline of MIS. It is expected that such articles would open new areas of discourse, close stale areas, and/or offer fresh, insightful views on topics of importance to MIS academicians and executives.

In publishing Benbasat and Zmud's paper and my editorial, I hoped to motivate colleagues to engage in a discourse about the future of the information systems discipline. I am delighted with the outcome that has occurred; indeed, it has far exceeded my expectations. A series of papers has been published on the debate in the *Journal of the Association for Information Systems* (e.g., see Volume 4, 2003) and the *Communications of the Association for Information Systems* (e.g., see Volume 12, November 2003). More Issues and Opinions papers have also been published in the *MIS Quarterly* (e.g., Whinston and Geng, 2004). Several panel sessions have been held at the International Conference on Information Systems (e.g., Karahanna *et al.*, 2003). The debate among participants at these panel sessions has been lively and constructive. Clearly, Benbasat and Zmud's paper has touched a nerve among many colleagues within the information systems discipline. At least for the moment, my perceptions are that the debate is subsiding. I believe, however, that the nerve is still raw.

In this paper, I reflect briefly on some particular aspects of the debate that has been engendered by Benbasat and Zmud's paper. In particular, I characterize two types of argument that have appeared within the debate and comment on my perceptions of their strengths and weaknesses. Finally, if a vigorous debate is to resume again at some time in the future, I argue that it must take a particular form if long-term, productive outcomes are to occur.

CHARACTERIZING THE DEBATE

Since the publication of Benbasat and Zmud's paper, two types of commentaries have appeared. The first type I characterize as *nature-of-the-discipline* commentaries. In these commentaries, the authors articulate their views on the scope and content of the information systems discipline and the important questions they believe that research within the discipline ought to address. The second type

I characterize as *logic-of-the-core* commentaries. In these commentaries, the authors address the logic underlying the arguments made about whether having a theoretical core within a discipline lays the foundation for the discipline eventually attaining a clear identity and/or academic legitimacy.

By far, most papers published on the debate are nature-of-the-discipline commentaries. As a discipline, we seem resolute in our determination not to confront directly the argument about the relationship between building a theoretical core in a discipline and attaining a distinct identity and/or academic legitimacy in the discipline. It is interesting to speculate on why we seem reluctant to pursue this matter.

In my view, nature-of-the-discipline commentaries often provide interesting insights into colleagues' beliefs about phenomena the information systems discipline ought to address. They are singularly unhelpful, however, in resolving the issue of whether having a theoretical core is necessary if the information systems discipline is ever to attain a clear identity or academic legitimacy. The protagonists in these commentaries pass each other like ships in the night. For the most part, they make no reference or only token reference to the views of other protagonists. Instead, they focus on articulating their own views about the information systems discipline. In such commentaries, what basis exists for choosing among competing views? Is it whether the views articulated are congruent with one's own views? Is it the colorfulness or appeal of well-crafted rhetoric? Is it the justification one finds for one's own past research endeavors? Is it social pressure from one's peers or powerful colleagues within one's discipline?

Moreover, from a Kuhnian perspective, the paradigms that exist within a discipline provide the basis for defining its boundaries, not the idiosyncratic views of individual members of the discipline (Kuhn, 1970, pp. 15, 23–34). In a particular discipline, phenomena are interesting or uninteresting, depending on whether they allow a paradigm within the discipline to be further articulated or tested. An individual's own views of the nature of the discipline of which they claim membership are incidental unless they are driven by a paradigm within the discipline (although subsequently they may be important if they underpin a scientific 'revolution').

One paper that addresses logic-of-the-core arguments is Lyytinen and King (2004). It also provides a nature-of-the-discipline commentary, but it commits to a logic-of-the-core argument. I applaud Lyytinen and King's paper, because it allows us to engage directly in determining where we agree and disagree in the debate. In this regard, I disagree with a number of their arguments, but I will not articulate the details here. Rather, using Lyytinen and King's paper, I will comment briefly on some important issues in the debate that are still unresolved.

THEORETICAL CORES AND ACADEMIC LEGITIMACY IN A NUTSHELL

Lyytinen and King challenge the notion that academic legitimacy depends on the presence of a theoretical core. Leaving aside the specifics of their argument, I believe they fail to understand or articulate clearly the views of those who believe a theoretical core is important to the IS field. Some who argue for the importance of a theoretical core contend that having a theoretical core is a *necessary* condition for academic legitimacy, which is the *converse* of Lyytinen and King's key premise. Others contend that having a theoretical core is a *necessary and sufficient* condition for a discipline to have academic legitimacy, and that academic legitimacy cannot exist without a theoretical core and *vice versa*. Some (including myself) contend that having a theoretical core is neither a necessary nor sufficient condition for academic legitimacy. Rather, it is a necessary condition for having a *clear disciplinary identity*. The relationship between disciplinary identity and academic legitimacy is itself an important issue for debate.

In my view, evaluating the validity[2] of arguments about the need for a theoretical core in the information systems discipline depends on the following matters:

- Providing precise definitions of constructs such as 'discipline,' 'identity,' 'academic legitimacy,' and 'theoretical core.'
- Evaluating the validity of premises.
- Evaluating the validity of arguments.

Much could be and has already been written on each of these matters. Nonetheless, Lyytinen and King (2004, p. 223) claim: '…none of the commentaries about the IS discipline's need for a theoretical core have articulated exactly what is meant by the term "theoretical core," a point acknowledged by Weber (2003).' In re-reading the cited paper, I fail to see that I 'acknowledge' this point. What I do say (p. vi) is:

> For me, the key to identifying a core is finding phenomena where existing theories are non-existent or deficient. The key to *creating* the core is then building theory that is novel—theory that colleagues in other disciplines will acknowledge as belonging to the information

systems discipline. Conceivably, it might be a completely new theory—one that has no genesis in other disciplines. I suspect that the more-likely outcome is that the theory is a marked adaptation of or extension of a theory that has its roots in another discipline. It will be sufficiently different from its ancestors, however, that ownership will be ascribed to the information systems discipline.

To establish a core for the information systems discipline, I believe we need two creative acts. First, we need to "see" things or phenomena that are not the focus of other disciplines. Alternatively, we need to see things or phenomena that are the focus of other disciplines in new, rich, insightful ways (see the world through a dramatically different lens). Second, we need to build powerful, generic theories to account for these phenomena that are not applications of theories from other disciplines or straightforward extensions of these theories. The "value-add" associated with the theories we propose must be sufficient for other disciplines to ascribe *ownership* of these theories to the information systems discipline. In other words, we cannot establish our identity as a discipline by fiat. Instead, our identity will emerge only as the outcome of a social process—one in which members of other disciplines acknowledge that the theoretical contributions we have made are important to their own understanding and prediction of some phenomena.

In short, I believe the identity of a discipline is established through the contributions it makes to theory. The core phenomena of the discipline are circumscribed via the theories "owned" by the discipline that account for these phenomena. Disciplinary identity and ownership of theories that other disciplines deem important are linked inextricably. Likewise, the theories owned by a discipline and its core phenomena are linked inextricably.

I also canvassed the matter in Weber (1987) (although I did not use the term 'core'), and I devoted an entire chapter (Chapter 3) to the topic, 'The Core of the IS Discipline,' in Weber (1997). I have a clear idea of what I mean by 'theoretical core,' and I believe many others do, as well.

Lyytinen and King (2004, p. 226) claim that a discipline can have academic legitimacy even though it does not have a theoretical core. This observation allows us to sharpen the focus of our debate around the need for a theoretical core. Some might contest the claim made by Lyytinen and King that disciplines like classics, German literature, accounting, and history are 'legitimate' academic disciplines. Still others might argue that Lyytinen and King miss the point in their focus on academic legitimacy rather than disciplinary clarity. I believe the debate now needs to focus on what the protagonists mean by 'discipline' and 'legitimacy,' as well as the validity of premises and arguments.

SUMMARY AND CONCLUSIONS

I characterize the debate on the core of the information systems discipline as falling within two streams. Nature-of-the-discipline commentaries involve protagonists articulating their views on the scope and content of the information systems discipline and the important questions they believe information systems researchers ought to address. Logic-of-the-core commentaries involve protagonists addressing the logic underlying the arguments made about whether having a theoretical core within a discipline lays the foundation for the discipline eventually attaining a clear identity or academic legitimacy. Most papers written on the debate fall into the nature-of-the-discipline stream. These sorts of paper are useful in some respects. Unfortunately, the authors seldom confront each other directly in terms of where they agree or disagree within the debate. Instead, they pass each other like ships in the night.

Lyytinen and King (2004) provide an important opportunity to address logic-of-the-core commentaries, forcing protagonists to confront areas of agreement and disagreement directly. Denigrating logic-of-the-core commentaries by dismissing them summarily as having poorly defined or undefined terms or invalid premises and arguments is less productive than defining critical terms more precisely, articulating premises and arguments more precisely, and evaluating the validity of premises and arguments as best we can. Ultimately, protagonists might agree to disagree on the definition of terms, statements of premises and arguments, and validity of premises and arguments. The grounds on which they agree or disagree, however, would be clear. Others then could evaluate the merits of their positions more easily. Moreover, if we proceed in this way, the protagonists might find good reasons to change their stance in the debate (perhaps several times!). If they do so, they must not be denigrated if productive, open debate is to occur. Overall, I believe the information systems discipline would be the better for the resolution that occurs.

It is important that protagonists in the debate strive to state premises and arguments correctly and consistently. I believe that Lyytinen and King's (2004) paper falls short in a number of key respects that invite further discussion. It behoves us to bring a satisfactory resolution to substantive matters about the nature and future of the information systems discipline raised by senior scholars like Benbasat and Zmud. If this outcome is to occur, however, we must engage directly in logic-of-the-core arguments. On the other hand, if we persist with nature-of-the-discipline commentaries,

I believe we will regress rather than make progress with our discourse. I fear the focus will become the quality of our rhetoric rather than the validity of our arguments.

NOTES

1 I am indebted to my colleague John Crossley, Professor of Logic at Monash University, for comments on earlier drafts of this paper. All errors that exist in the paper, however, are my responsibility alone.
2 Note, Lyytinen and King (2004, p. 223) distinguish between the *validity* and *soundness* of an argument. The former refers to the correctness of the logic. The latter refers to the truth of the premises. Using their terminology, a valid argument might be based on untrue premises. In this paper, however, I use the term 'validity' in a wider sense to apply to both the correctness of the logic and the truth of the premises. More precisely, the term 'fallacy' applies only to the question of whether the logic is correct. See the entry 'fallacy' in the *Columbia Encyclopedia*, 6th edn, 2001, at http://www.bartleby.com/65/fa/fallacy.html.

REFERENCES

Benbasat, I. and Zmud, R. (2003) 'The identity crisis within the IS discipline: Defining and communicating the discipline's core properties', *MIS Quarterly*, 27(2), June, pp. 183–94.
Karahanna, E., Davis, G. B., Mukhopadhyay, T., Watson, R. T. and Weber, R. (2003) 'Embarking on information systems' voyage to self-discovery: Identifying the core of the Discipline', Panel Session at the Twenty-Fourth International Conference on Information Systems, Seattle, Washington, 14–17 December 2003.
Kuhn, T. S. (1970) *The Structure of Scientific Revolutions*, 2nd edn, University of Chicago Press, Chicago.
Lyytinen, K. and King, J. (2004) 'Nothing at the Center?: Academic Legitimacy in the Information Systems Field', *Journal of the Association for Information Systems*, 5(6), June, pp. 220–46.
Orlikowski, W. J. and Iacono, C. S. 'Research commentary: Desperately seeking the "IT" in IT research—A call to theorizing the IT artifact', *Information Systems Research*, 12(2), June, pp. 121–34.
Weber, R. (1987) 'Toward a theory of artifacts: A paradigmatic basis for information systems research', *Journal of Information Systems*, 1(2), Spring, pp. 3–19.
Weber, R. (1997) *Ontological Foundations of Information Systems*, Coopers & Lybrand, Melbourne.
Weber, R. (2003) 'Still desperately seeking the IT artifact', *MIS Quarterly*, 27(2), June, pp. iii–xi.
Whinston, A. B. and Geng, X. (2004) 'Operationalizing the essential role of the IT artifact in IS research: Gray area, pitfalls, and the importance of strategic ambiguity', *MIS Quarterly*, 28(2), June, pp. 149–59.

14
Further Reflections on the Identity Crisis

Izak Benbasat and Robert W. Zmud

To say that we were surprised by the extent of the reaction of the information systems (IS) community to our article, 'The Identity Crisis within the IS Discipline: Defining and Communicating the Discipline's Core Properties' (Benbasat and Zmud, 2003), is an understatement. Our intent was to provoke debate on what we felt to be an important issue. We very much appreciate this response (both in print and in the rich dialogues we have each enjoyed with colleagues and doctoral students), particularly the time and effort invested by so many of the field's thought leaders.

We must begin this comment by stating that we still believe strongly in the views presented in our article. That stated, we would like to take this opportunity to communicate three follow-on thoughts. First, we wish to slightly—but importantly—modify the *nomological net* used in our article to 'bound the IS discipline'. Second, we wish (1) to stress that the impetus of our article was not to draw a boundary around the IS discipline but instead to draw a boundary, however fuzzy (Whinston and Geng, 2004), around the *phenomenological domain serving as the topical basis of IS scholarly journals* and (2) to explain further why we feel such a bound is desirable. Finally, we wish to elaborate on the desirability of refocusing IS research on issues of *design*, such that research findings might lead to more actionable recommendations to practice.

THE IS DISCIPLINE'S NOMOLOGICAL NET

Figure 14.1 portrays our modified nomological net. The only difference between this figure and the original is that now the central construct is an information system, with the IT artifact highlighted as a defining element of an information system. This *does not* represent a modification of our earlier ideas.

In our article, we explicitly referred to the *application* of IT to support task accomplishment within a context (p. 186):

> We conceptualize the IT artifact...as the application of IT to enable or support some task(s) embedded within a structure(s) that itself is embedded within a context(s). Here, the hardware/software design of the IT artifact encapsulates the structures, routines, norms, and values implicit in the rich contexts within which the artifact is embedded.

Our view of an information system is essentially that expressed very eloquently by Alter (2003a, 2003b) in his discussions regarding IT-reliant work systems. We thus wish to restate our definition as:

> We conceptualize an information system...as the application of one or more IT artifacts to enable or support some task(s) embedded within structure(s) that themselves are embedded within context(s). Here, the design of an information system encapsulates the structures, routines, norms, and values implicit in the rich contexts within which the IT artifacts are to be embedded.

In fact, Alter states (2003b, p. 496), 'IT artifact verges on being a synonym for the clearer term *IT-reliant work system.*' We agree. Our emphasis on the term 'IT artifact' in the original article reflected our

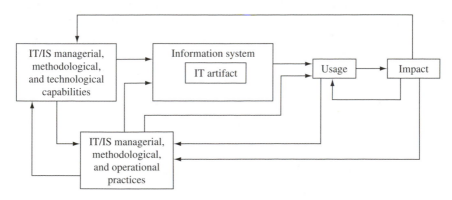

Figure 14.1   *Information systems discipline nomological net*

intent to directly link our ideas to those raised earlier by Orlikowski and Iacono (2001).

BOUNDING THE PHENOMENOLOGICAL DOMAIN OF IS SCHOLARLY JOURNALS

In defining the nomological net of the IS discipline, it was never our intention to place bounds on the nature of the research to be undertaken by IS scholars. This has been, perhaps, the most misinterpreted aspect of our article. In fact, we state (p. 190):

> We emphasize that our intention is neither to discourage IS scholars from pursuing research that excludes the constructs and phenomena depicted in . . . nor to discourage non-IS scholars from publishing appropriately focused research in IS journals. IS scholars have much to contribute to scholarship, regardless of the core issues involved (e.g., service delivery, trust among members of a collaborative group, customer or supplier relationships, organizational learning).

Instead, our concern is with bounding the phenomenological domain of IS scholarly journals.

In our article, we argued that bounding the phenomenological domain of IS scholarly journals was necessary in order to evolve an identity for the IS discipline. We still hold such a view, in particular regarding the identity of the IS discipline for IS scholars situated in business schools. A discipline's scholarly journals are a primary means through which non-IS scholars in a business school construct—typically, during institutional processes associated with assessing candidates for tenure and/or promotion—an understanding of the discipline. However, a more compelling argument for the desirability of bounding the phenomenological domain of IS scholarly journals lies with another important role of scholarly journals: that of developing the bodies of knowledge associated with the discipline.

Scholarly journals form around communities of scholars possessing overlapping research interests; and a journal's institutional structure (e.g., editorial policies, editorial governance, editorial processes, etc.) is a direct reflection of these 'forming' communities. As editorial leadership positions (editor-in-chief, senior editors, associate editors, board members, etc.) are filled in accordance with in-place institutional structures, the vast majority of incumbents are highly likely to be members of these same 'forming' communities. Consequently, the intellectual base (i.e., the knowledge held by editors and reviewers) through which scholarly contributions (i.e., journal submissions) are assessed, developed and acted on is a direct reflection of that representing these 'forming' communities.

Consider, then, what happens when an article submitted to a scholarly journal investigates a phenomenon distinct from the focal research interests of that journal's 'forming' communities but within the purview of another scholarly community:

- The editors assigned to assess the submission are unlikely to be current with leading thought regarding the phenomenon.
- These editors' intellectual networks (i.e., the scholars of whom they have strong or weak relationships) are also unlikely to contain individuals who are current with leading thought regarding the phenomenon.

As a consequence, it is unlikely that the outcome of the editorial process assessing the submission will be reflective of current thought regarding the phenomenon. When editorial assessment processes do not reflect leading thought, the development of knowledge regarding a phenomenon at best is either delayed or impaired and at worst is misdirected or deconstructed.

Drawing a boundary around the phenomenological domain of a scholarly journal thus serves the critical role of delineating the knowledge areas actively being developed by the communities of scholars associated with the journal. Submissions whose primary intellectual purpose lay within these knowledge areas are likely to be critiqued and further developed by scholars holding current thought regarding this purpose; submissions whose primary purpose lie outside this domain are not.

Finally, we must reiterate the important observation (Whinston and Geng, 2004) that the research interests of scholarly communities— and, hence, the institutional structures and phenomenological boundaries of scholarly journals—are continuously evolving. Changes to a journal's institutional structure will invariably result in perturbations to its phenomenological boundary, and new areas of intellectual investigation will continue to emerge to be subsumed within the phenomenological boundary of one or more scholarly journals. What remains critically important, however, is that the scholarly communities developing emerging areas of inquiry hold deep understandings of prior thought salient to such inquiry.

REFOCUSING IS RESEARCH ON ISSUES OF DESIGN

In the section of our original paper discussing 'errors of exclusion' we posed the following question: 'Why is it problematic to publish research excluding the IT artifact and/or elements from its immediate nomological net in IS journals?' Our answer to this question was focused solely on the implications such a course of action would have on the distinctiveness and hence the legitimacy of IS with respect to related scholarly disciplines and as a consequence the investment business schools would be willing to make in IS as an intellectual field vis-à-vis other entrenched disciplines.

There is a second important consequence that we would now like to include in our answer. In an earlier commentary (Benbasat and Zmud, 1999) concerning the relevance of IS academic research, we made the following recommendation (p. 11):

> In order for IS research to be more relevant, IS academics should portray the outputs of their research in ways such that it might be utilized by practitioners to justify and rationalize IT-related initiatives.

We believe that the absence of direct linkages to IT artifacts in IS research projects contributes to a lack in relevance for practitioners. In the IS research from earlier periods (i.e., 1970–85), many examples of work can be found where researchers focused on investigating the impact on decision making performance (i.e., decision quality, time taken and errors made) of a variety of design alternatives enabled through the application of IT artifacts, such as graphical representations, exception reports, direct manipulation interfaces, decision aids, etc. (e.g., Benbasat and Schroeder, 1977). The findings of these studies led to explicit system design recommendations that could be utilized by practitioners. More recently (i.e., 1990 and later) one of the dominant topics in IS research has been investigating the factors that influence the use and adoption of IS (e.g., Davis, 1989; Moore and Benbasat, 1991). This research has provided connections between the variables studied in earlier work, such as an effective decision aid can lead to higher decision quality (perceived usefulness) or a direct manipulation interface can lead to less time and fewer errors in both learning and using an IS (perceived ease of use), leading to higher intentions to adopt an IS.

Unfortunately, over time the focus of much IS research has gradually shifted away from the study of design (of an IS, of an IT/IS organization, of an IT/IS policy, of an IT-enabled process, of an

IS-enabling process, etc.) alternatives to variables that Orlikowsky and Iacono (1999) term 'technology as perception', namely, ease of use, compatibility, usefulness, confirmation, satisfaction, trust, enjoyment, flow, etc. It is of course worthwhile to understand the relative importance of such perceptions in influencing intentions or behaviors, across different contexts (e.g., the adoption of decision support aids, Internet-based purchasing, etc.). The observation that usefulness is more important than ease of use in influencing IS adoption, or that trust becomes more salient in certain contexts, does lead to valuable insights. However, the practitioner still needs to know what makes a design useful and easy to use (or follow, or implement, etc.). For example, why would a customer trust an online product recommendation agent? In designing an online product recommendation agent, what elements are most important for engendering trust? What is the nature of the standards, if any, that should be devised, disseminated and enforced across an enterprise regarding the design of recommendation agents? These are instances where the nature of the IT artifact comes into play and where IS scholars can make intellectual contributions that are unique to the discipline.

Hence, our suggestion to reduce the errors of exclusion is to *refocus* at least some of our attention and research investment on the front end of the 'design → solution → perceptions → intentions → behavior' continuum, identify and investigate the design alternatives that improve our application of technology, and as a consequence lead to more actionable advice for practice.

CONCLUDING COMMENTS

IS academics have periodically discussed the nature of their field for over three decades. As it is often asserted, maybe we are no different than other scholarly disciplines within business schools that have and are going through similar debates. Nevertheless, this does not diminish the importance of such soul-searching periodically. The IS community attempted to define what MIS is in the early 1970s, continued by discussing the reliance of IS on its reference disciplines at the first ICIS conference in 1980, argued that IS 'cannot be disciplined' (Banville and Landry, 1989) yet called for both a search for core theories and relevance in the 1990s, leading to current thinking. These discussions will no doubt continue in the future. They are important in that they allow the members of our community to better understand others' views, most often revealing what unites, rather than divides, the community. We are pleased that our paper has been the catalyst for an extensive and healthy debate, one that in our opinion has been more extensive and focused than ever before, culminating in the publication of this book.

REFERENCES

Alter, S. (2003a) '18 reasons why IT-reliant work systems should replace 'the IT artifact' as the core subject matter of the IS field,' *Communications of the AIS*, 12, October, pp. 366–95.

Alter, S. (2003b) 'Sidestepping the IT artifact, scrapping the IS silo, and laying claim to 'systems in organizations', *Communications of the AIS*, 12, November, pp. 494–526.

Banville, C. and Landry, M. (1989) 'Can the field of MIS be disciplined', *Communications of the ACM*, January, pp. 48–61.

Benbasat, I. and Schroeder, R. (1977) 'An experimental investigation of some MIS design variables', *Management Information Systems Quarterly*, 1(1), March, pp. 37–49.

Benbasat, I. and Zmud, R. W. (1999) 'Empirical research in information systems: The practice of relevance,' *Management Information Systems Quarterly*, March, pp. 3–16.

Davis, F. D. (1989) 'Perceived usefulness, perceived ease of use, and user acceptance of information technology,' *MIS Quarterly*, September, 13(3), pp. 318–40.

Moore, G. C. and Benbasat, I. (1991) 'Development of an instrument to measure the perceptions of adopting an information technology innovation', *Information Systems Research*, 2(3), September, pp. 192–222.

Orlikowsky, W. and Iacono, S. (2001) 'Research commentary: Desperately seeking the "IT" in IT research—A call to theorizing the IT artifact', *Information Systems Research*, June, pp. 121–34.

Whinston, A. B. and Geng, X. (2004) 'Operationalizing the essential role of the IT artifact in IS research: Gray area, pitfalls, and the importance of strategic ambiguity', *MIS Quarterly*, 28(2), June, pp. 149–59.

15
Further Reflections on the IS Discipline: Climbing the Tower of Babel

Heinz K. Klein and Rudy A. Hirschheim

INTRODUCTION

The collection of papers presented in this book provides a fascinating view of the diversity in the field. In reading them, we have come to admire the detail with which many authors were able to communicate their points of view. However, we also feel that some of the contributions take too narrow a perspective. By reaffirming the broader perspective of our own 'reflection' we might not only point to the limitations of some of the arguments presented, but also—and maybe more importantly—identify interesting and at times surprising interconnections both of a mutually supporting or contradictory nature that would prompt us to be more explicit about certain topics in our *JAIS* article if we were to rewrite it with the benefit of what we have learnt from this discussion. It was not easy for us to wrap our mind around the many divergent points of view and fight our tendencies to distort them to fit our own theoretic prejudices. We literally felt we were going round and round, climbing the many staircases of the proverbial 'Tower of Babel' to make sense of this disjointed collection of ideas. Each contribution was convincing and internally consistent, but somewhat disjointed with the others. In the end, we organized our comments that directly relate to specific parts of the article collection around three questions:

1. Where is the 'information' in the Information Technology artifact? This question relates to three papers in this book, i.e. Benbasat and Zmud; Orlikowski and Iacono; and Hevner *et al*. From their contributions, we recognize the need to be explicit about the relationship between differing conceptualizations of information, knowledge and 'information' technology and the long-term consequences of a technocratic view of the discipline.
2. What is the *potential* contribution of focusing on ontological representations as Weber's contribution suggests? In addressing this question, the issues of the representational fallacy and currently missing core phenomena emerge.
3. Why is it important for the IS research community to develop and adopt realistic views about the social structure and processes of the IS research community? This question points to a set of issues that the contributions of DeSanctis, Galliers, Lyytinen/King and Robey have raised in our mind regarding the external legitimacy of IS as an academic discipline.

WHERE IS THE 'INFORMATION' IN THE TECHNO-CENTRIST IT ARTIFACT FOCUS?

Whilst we agree that the IT artifact must not be simply ignored, it seems clear to us that only an emaciated image of the IT artifact and its embedded nature could be captured in terms of quantitative variables. Orlikowski and Iacono cogently demonstrated this claim with their classification of different ways of conceptualizing IT (productivity tool, social relationships tool, etc.). The following issues come to mind when reflecting on the critical comments that the contributions by Benbasat and Zmud; Orlikowski and Iacono; and Hevner *et al*. provoked. Their positions also caused us to reflect on the relationship between the past priorities on how IT should be used for mostly well-defined instrumental purposes and the potential threat of the outsourcing phenomenon, which has many of our colleagues worried (*cf.* Gopal *et al.*, 2002; Davis *et al.*, 2004; King, 2004; Hirschheim *et al.*, 2005).

On the Nature of Information

The principal problem with focusing primarily on the IT artifact is that it uses the ambiguous acronym 'I' for information, when in fact no artifact can produce information or its nobler cousin 'knowledge'. Information is the point of some message that helps someone, a group or individual, to reduce complexity, accomplish a purpose, or recognize that they are somehow mistaken and were about to engage in foolish or even dangerous pursuits. Often such a point is conveyed with a speech act that ultimately helps someone to see pertinent facts in a new light. Speech acts are connected to human intentions to accomplish something, i.e. to get someone to accept an assertion as true or to move someone to action with a promise, etc. No artifact can do this unless the message receiver sees the technology message source as a trustworthy 'stand-in' (or substitute) of some human agent, friend or foe. The IT artifact is at best a vehicle for symbol storage and manipulation. Therefore we would argue that most of what is truly at the core of IS as a discipline happens *after* the artifact has done its part, namely when someone, a human agent with interpretive faculties, attributes the right meanings to the reams of symbols spewed out by the artifact. Hence focusing on the artifact too narrowly would cause us the miss the information phenomenon and therefore what, in our opinion, should be the very core concerns of our discipline.

If the above is accepted as common sense wisdom, then 'IT' is at best a misnomer and at worst a purposefully misleading advertising slogan to serve the vested interests of IT-dependent industries and professions (including some academics). The IT notion is a clever propaganda slogan because with the briefest of all acronyms it signals to management and most consumers that computers can do something very sophisticated, i.e. automate away the hard work that it takes to gain information and even knowledge. However, the sober fact is that any storage and data processing technologies from Gutenberg to the so-called 'knowledge systems' have done nothing but storing and manipulating codes. Whether the codes brought to human attention assume meaning, and are thereby converted into data, depends on the human minds interpreting them. Some data may then, indeed, after some more hard brainwork, turn out to be information and knowledge for *some* users, but not all. Because IT can at best convey but not produce information and knowledge (nor even store it for that matter), the term *data technology* (DT) or even more accurately, *code processing technology* (CPT), would be much more honest labels than IT.

Nomological Net or Social Nature of IS?

In recognition of this basic fact, it is now widely accepted that information systems scholars and many practitioners deal with the human and social side of DT as well, including its hermeneutic and phenomenological dimensions (*cf.* Boland's 1978, 1979, 1985, 1987,

1989 classical contributions; also Winograd and Flores, 1980, 1986). Therefore, we should squarely put the nature of information and knowledge at the core of our discipline along with investigating the conditions that must be met so that data technology can successfully convey information and knowledge to its users. Of paramount importance is to recognize from the very start of IS research that users do not live in a social vacuum as they participate in various types of social entities, such as groups, communities of practice, organizations and others. All of these contribute to the users' ability to interpret codes as data and glean information and knowledge from the data. In other words: IS are socially embedded. Therefore, the inadequacy of the 'IS equals IT' perspective follows from Kling's (1987) web-model concept of IS even more forcefully than from the more recent Orlikowski and Iacono (2001) analysis (interestingly enough, Iacono collaborated with Kling in developing the web-model view of IS):

> ...web-models view computer-based systems as complex social objects whose architecture and use are shaped by the social relations between influential participants, the infrastructure that supports them, and the history of commitments. (Kling, 1987, p. 314)

Because the IT-centered discussion tends to ignore this basic insight, we argue that the ways in which the IT artifact concept tends to be used reveals that it is yet another reincarnation of technological determinism. We believe that the web-model view or, more broadly, the social perspective of IS connotes more than just superficial re-labeling. Therefore, it contrasts with Benbasat and Zmud's nomological net model, which puts the IT artifact as an independent variable at the center.

However, this does not mean that we would advocate ignoring technology knowledge entirely. While our earlier *JAIS* article failed to mention the IT artifact or its social embeddedness specifically, knowledge about computing and communications technologies would make up an important part of what we had termed a *Body of Knowledge* for IS in general and ISD in particular (cf. Iivari, Hirschheim and Klein, 2004). First, our classification embraced technical knowledge as a separate category, which comprises the usual spectrum of hardware and software. However, important details also surface under the headings of theoretical and applicative knowledge. This would comprise the matters which Orlikowski and Iacono outline in their article's conclusion as well as Kling's web-model research.

Therefore, we conclude that the IT artifact focus or, as it should be called more accurately, the 'code processing' artifact focus, is too restrictive because it would ultimately lead to an engineering perspective of IS accepting technological determinism as its main concept of the deep structure for explanation. This would narrow the field of IS to the point that it can be absorbed into software engineering—which the SWEBOK debate on professionalization has already proposed. Moreover, conceiving of IT in terms of variables leaves out the much richer views of an interpretive conceptualization of IS phenomena (as has been demonstrated by many researchers and is also highlighted in Orlikowski and Iacono's conclusions). The result, we believe, would be that the many insights interpretive researchers have contributed since the 1990s would at best be demoted to preliminary pilot studies or, even worse, relegated to the scrapheap of unreliable and irrelevant work.

Dangers of Techno-centrism and the Appliance Mentality

A similar consequence follows from Hevner *et al.*'s view of the nature of design science. We see this as leading to relegating any research as irrelevant that cannot be pressed into the following format: Conceptualization of variables → Model formulation → Hypothesis derivation → Data collection and test → Repeat from step 1.

The ultimate ideal behind this concept of cooperation between positivist behavioral science and engineering prototypes is what Allen Lee (undated) has called the 'appliance mentality'. Practitioners with this ideal tend to treat 'their information system as if it was something you simply buy and then plug in, like a refrigerator or washing machine' (cf. Figure 1 in http://www.people.vcu.edu/~aslee/ bitworld/sld003.htm). From this perspective, the role of IS research would simply be to create the appliance designs that can be manufactured by vendors and then sold to specific organizations or individuals. (Interestingly, this seems to be the model of ERP.) From an appliance perspective, the building and operation of IS would simply be relegated to the cheapest producer. This of course has recently happened with increasing outsourcing and offshoring. From an appliance perspective, 'IS does not matter anymore' because most of the designs have been standardized as happened to other industrial commodities. We call the link-up of behavioral IT-centered hypothesis testing with design science, the *techno-centrist perspective of IS*.

Another logical and dangerous consequence of IT artifact techno-centrism is that it would deny IS researchers the legitimacy of engaging in fundamental criticism. This issue is also clearly raised in Robey's (2003, p. 356) lucid critique of Benbasat and Zmud's dominant research paradigm preference. From our perspective, critical research is necessary to reveal vested interests, one-sided distribution of cost and benefits, and other socially damaging practices. Some examples of the need for such critical impact research are the early creation of alienating typing pools (it was a naïve reincarnation of Taylorism), online addiction syndrome, the neglect of long-term consequences of process redesign (BPR), and offshoring. Another recent area necessitating critical impact studies is the so-called digital divide or the undermining of rational choices through subliminally manipulative social ideologies (as was practiced by the tobacco industry but continues today with the gambling industry over the Internet). Techno-centrism would simply marginalize all such research in IS, which to us is a step backward in our evolution.

A CRITIQUE OF THE ONTOLOGY-REPRESENTATION PROPOSAL FOR THE DISCIPLINARY CORE

Whilst we agree that considerations of ontology are very important for the field, Weber's commentary on ontological representation provoked two issues in our mind. The first has to do with his proposal for the field to adopt a realist ontological position. In short, there are two fundamental types of ontological positions on 'representation': ontological realism and social constructivism. Weber's position is a good example of the former. It creates the attitude that human intelligence in general and AI research in particular has evolved around 'faithful representations'. Our concern with this position is that it leads to the revival of the so-called 'representational fallacy' to which early AI succumbed. The fallacy has been extensively debated in the so-called 'linguistic turn', which is often summarized with the key phrase that *'language may be the only reality that we have'*. We worry that IS researchers falling prey to this representational fallacy would lead the field down a path that is ostensibly a dead end. IS would simply repeat the AI approach to natural language processing of the 1960s and 1970s, which led to over-blown expectations of AI (e.g. Simon, 1977) and eventually to a road block for further progress. Since Winograd and Flores' (1986) analysis of the representational fallacy is easily accessible, we will focus on a second issue that Weber's commentary explicitly raises. After noting, 'how we design good or faithful representations of other systems has remained the focus of Wand's and my work', he continues (p. viii):

I fully accept that other types of information systems-related phenomena might exist for which theories borrowed from or adapted from other disciplines provide an inadequate account...For the moment, however, I am unable to identify such phenomena. Nonetheless, for two reasons I hope such phenomena exist. First, having a core that includes more than representational phenomena would likely make for a richer, more-interesting discipline...

In the following, we shall point to such phenomena which our *JAIS* paper unfortunately omitted. We feel the type of ontologies that Weber speaks of can have only temporary validity for building specific applications in a changing world of social constructions. The only exception would be ontologies for IS applications dealing with stable phenomena that are relatively well understood—such as tracking traffic patterns or inventories. However, from meteorology to particle physics, stable ontologies are rare or non-existent. Therefore, the approach to define and communicate a core identity for the IS community through ontologies is insufficient. Moreover, an overwhelming focus on ontologies is potentially dangerous because it is likely to introduce the same limitations that have already surfaced in past AI research with the representational fallacy (*cf.* Winograd and Flores, 1986).

Which Phenomena Could Potentially Serve as a Future Core for IS Research?

Our position is essentially that representation is only one of the important language functions along with the other of 'getting something done'. Language is a type of human action in which meanings are not only represented, but through which we also engage with the world and change it by influencing others, create new objects (like founding an organization and/or establishing a new law) and create new states of affairs and constraints. Hence, representations alone, even if interpreted as social constructions rooted in the lifeworld of 'communities of practice and knowing' (cf. our comments below) do not suffice for capturing the principal IS core phenomena; what must be added? We believe that we made a suggestion for this in Hirschheim, Klein and Lyytinen (1996). This suggestion is connected to Wittgenstein's 'use theory of language' and its later expansions into speech act theory (1922, 1958), which was then absorbed into a number of social action theories (e.g. explicitly into Habermas' [1984, 1987] action types; and Giddens' [1984] human agency).

To put it simply, we argued that the business of the IS discipline is to study how various technologies affect social action. Social action typologies can help to derive a broad classification of what is involved at the level of language ('structures of signification' in Giddens' terms), organizations and technology. We readily admit that the organizational level should have been broadened to other types of social entities, i.e. any type of social associations including society as a whole. Information systems are replacements for natural language communications that tend to precede social actions or are necessary to coordinate them. IS replace natural language interaction by a more limited set of predefined language constructs (cf. Hirschheim, Klein and Lyytinen, 1995). They can also serve as a mere transmission channel of natural language messages (as in email, voice mail, etc). Social actions can broadly be classified into two types. The first includes those that make a claim to power or efficiency and aim at achieving previously determined objectives with minimal effort (teleological action). They include what Giddens (1984) called 'structures of domination'. The second category involves some form of communication about facts, effectiveness and norms of social appropriateness, fairness, justice and good taste. This category also includes discourse in which the communication partners argue and negotiate their differing views on what the facts are (truth), which means are effective to achieve desired outcomes (means tests and their reliability), what is or is not socially appropriate, and what is fair and just in conflict of interest situations (omitting aesthetic discourse about questions of good taste for the sake of brevity).

Of course, the linguistic medium (terminology, symbolic functions, etc.) of different types of IS itself becomes part of the social language context. Examples of research on how the introduction of new technology provides opportunities for social structuring (e.g. Giddens' 'structures of signification') have already been published (cf. Barley, 1986; Orlikowski, 1993).

Arenas (or Spheres) of Social Interaction as Core Phenomena of IS Research

The focus on the 'language context' reminds us that the essential core phenomena for the IS discipline are the various types of interactions taking place between humans either directly or indirectly when mediated by technological (IT artifact) interfaces. This suggestion is not the same as putting the IT artifact at the center of a nomological net. Therefore, we propose that a step in the right direction of defining flexible boundaries for the IS discipline (as advocated in several other contributions) is to build on Lee's idea of focusing on the interactions between the human-social domains (or spheres) of action and the technology subsystems. In distinction to Lee (undated) we avoid the term 'social system or subsystem' as not all spheres of human interaction are easily construed as 'systems' without introducing a mechanistic bias—we realize however that in some domains the systems concept might be fruitfully applied, e.g. in the sense of Luhmann (cf. Stehr and Bechman, 2005).

In the first ICIS conference, Bariff and Ginzberg (1980) had already proposed that four levels of analysis needed to be considered: individual, group, organization and society. However, with the emergence of globalism, we need to add international organizations and intercultural systems to the mix. From this perspective it is parochial that past IS research has mostly limited itself to organizations and groups as its preferred study domains. This has, of course, begun to change as growing numbers of researchers have begun to recognize that a societal and global perspective will be indispensable for a constructive approach to the offshoring phenomenon. In light of this, our earlier framework (Hirschheim, Klein and Lyytinen, 1996) for defining core research issues needs to be broadened. Our current perspective leads us to define the following three major interaction systems that together could shape the identity of the IS discipline:

- The interactions or cross-impacts of technology with the social context of individuals, groups, communities of practice, organizations, institutions, societies and the world's global socio-cultural-political-economic constituencies.
- The relationships between different technologies that can support and enhance the creation and exchange of meanings; this includes the study and design of their interfaces and their language context of use as the latter differentiates itself along various dimensions both locally and globally. This *also* includes but is not limited to the ontological representation issues; in fact, all possible media and structures for negotiating, storing and transmitting coded meanings are to be included.
- The complete set of interactions and cross-impacts of technology between the aforementioned types of agents themselves (individuals, groups, organizations, institutions, societies, global social entities) and various types of technology. Both within category and cross-category interactions are important.

No single reference discipline looks across all three of these major interaction systems from the perspective of how information and knowledge is engaged in and created by social action. Therefore IS researchers could claim these domains or spheres of interactions as their own core phenomena, but include the results of other disciplines that may study special aspects of these domains as for example advertising effects (marketing), individual problem solving (cognitive psychology of man–machine interfaces), management–labor communications (industrial relations), control hierarchies (organizational theory), inter-government communications (political science), and so forth. Finally, if information and knowledge aspects of domains or sphere of social actions were made the core of IS research, then IS becomes a discipline of trans-organizational innovation. In this context, the outsourcing of routine functions built around canned ontological representations loses its identity-threatening character.

IS RESEARCH—IMPLICATIONS OF BEING A 'COMMUNITY OF PRACTICE AND KNOWING'

Approximately half of the articles explicitly recognize the importance of analyzing IS research as a social process of knowledge creation. We agree that this is a healthy balance. The social process view of knowledge creation has two consequences that could have been expressed more clearly in our *JAIS* contribution.

- First, it applies to the praxis of IS development and use at all levels of interaction as were indicated above. That is knowledge creation in the organization is not a technical issue but a social process issue which is the same point already made regarding limitations of a techno-centric conception of the role of IS in the field, i.e. organizations and other units of analysis.
- Second, it also applies to the nature of IS research itself and then touches on the very core and mission of the discipline. It is the second aspect that is the subject matter of the current debate. It is reflected in the keywords that emerged from this side of the debate such as community of practice, identity, unity and diversity, various forms of legitimacy, discourse with reference disciplines, boundary formation and trans-disciplinarily—to name just a few.

From this discussion, we have learned some important ideas that complement our *JAIS* comments on the paradigm discussion. There is only one important claim with which we disagree, namely that the 'community of practice' perspective supports an optimistic assessment of the future legitimacy of IS. In fact, we reach an almost opposite conclusion.

The Fundamental Importance of the 'Community of Practice (and Knowing)' Perspective

DeSanctis has offered an excellent contribution to the IS community by suggesting that the social structure of our discipline (or in fact any academic discipline) can and should be analyzed using the perspective of the community of practice (CoP) literature. Our following discussion presumes that the reader is familiar with DeSanctis' summary of five defining criteria of a CoP. It is a major shortcoming of our *JAIS* article that it failed to recognize the fruitful implications of examining the structure and processes of the IS research community as a *potential* CoP. It naturally complements Kuhn's (1970) notion of a paradigm community, on which we built. However, we hasten to add that we did cover issues that have a close relationship to the propositions and claims raised by DeSanctis albeit under somewhat differing labels. They can be found in the section on 'Internal Disconnects' (p. 255) under such phrases as 'tolerance of alternative paradigms' (and their associated communities), 'fragmentation and paradigm conflict', 'vehicles of knowledge creation', 'relevance for whom', and most importantly '*the communication deficit*'. These issues do not simply disappear by renaming the IS discipline from an 'adhocracy' to 'a community of practice'.

Why the CoP&K Concept Currently Spells Trouble for IS as an Applied Discipline

At least two issues arise from the observation that DeSanctis uncritically imports some assumptions from the CoP literature, which do not necessarily hold in the context of an academic discipline, *particularly not* for the IS discipline. These assumptions are that CoP is a community with shared assumptions on the nature of the world segment with which it is dealing and on the nature knowledge that is the foundation for its practice. A second assumption is that a CoP enjoys relatively unproblematic, outside legitimation. We feel that the current debate could be enriched and deepened considerably, if these (and possibly other) assumptions of the CoP metaphor were articulated more clearly so that the state of the discipline as a CoP can be debated more rigorously.

For this purpose, it is fruitful to note the great similarity between a community which shares a paradigm (i.e. Kuhn's paradigmatic community) and a CoP as long as we define paradigm broadly as any shared frame of reference with an associated stock of meanings taken for granted about some domain of interest. We also add that, just like a paradigmatic academic community, a CoP tends to evolve a shared lifeworld (in the sense of Schutz and Luckmann's [1974] *The Structures of the Lifeworld*; see also Berger and Luckmann's [1967] *The Social Construction of Reality*) through which newcomers become socialized into the prevailing terminology, definitions (stocks of meaning) and practices that the CoP is taking for granted. To put it in Heidegger's terms, to be a member of a CoP is a specific way of 'being-in-the-world' through continuous engagements with the (physical) entities that make up this world ('ready-to-hand-entities') and 'being-with-others' about whom we have to worry and with whom we relate to the entities of the community's shared lifeworld. From these ongoing community engagements, a common stock of meaning is built up, which is grounded on accepted practices. Along with this comes an internally recognized, but partly informal record of achievements, which enables relatively smooth and efficient communications in day-to-day affairs of common interest. If we put knowledge work and knowledge creation at the core of a CoP, we might emphasize this symbolic meaning aspect by speaking of a 'CoP *and Knowing*' or CoP&K. Boland and Tenkas (1995) presented a persuasive argument that organizations typically consist of several interacting CoP&K (cf. further discussion in Klein and Lyytinen, 2005).

In fact this is the key point. If organizations consist of *several interacting CoP&K*, in spite of having a single center of authority, the same is likely to apply to academic disciplines without a single center of authority and strong paradigmatic consensus. Therefore, the *first major issue* raised by DeSanctis' contribution is its implicit assumption that IS is *one* great community of practice. Unfortunately she does not say anything about the internal structure of the IS community (as we do in our *JAIS* contribution) nor about its boundary to the sister disciplines (computer science, software engineering, information or library science) nor about its relationship to other CoPs, which are very important for IS as an academic field, such as the professional IS practitioners and general management.

Indeed, the articles in this very book provide overwhelming evidence that paradigm conflict is alive and well. This is *prima facie* evidence that IS consists of several interacting CoP&K. Based on the literature analysis in Orlikowski and Baroudi (1991) and Hirschheim *et al.* (1996), we could argue that we have at least three major paradigms that, with their associated research literature, potentially function as the frame of reference for at least three communities of practice. Within each of these three major communities, there are important subdivisions and hence there may actually be more than three CoP&K. For example, Hevner *et al.* have claimed to bridge two paradigms, which in fact are both sub-communities of positivism—albeit different ones.

If we accept the similarity, or perhaps identity, of the paradigm (which Orlikowski and Baroudi preferred to call a 'research philosophy') and the 'CoP frame of reference' concepts, at least for the lifeworlds of academia, then the notion of paradigm conflict leads to the notion of adhocracy and this seems to support the idea that IS as a discipline may not be one but several CoP&Ks. Each of these subscribes to a different view of the (social) world, values, research methods, legitimacy criteria and mission for IS as a discipline. Yes, we have routines for global interaction like academic conferences (e.g. ICIS, AMCIS, ECIS, etc.) and shared journals; but once at a global conference, we head off to separate CoP meetings—the ones that we feel are most supportive of our current research interests. Interaction between these sub-CoP&K is very infrequent and therefore fails one of DeSanctis' critical criteria that we are all just one CoP. Similarly for journals; we tend to read those papers that share the paradigmatic lens and literature of our own research associates.

On the positive side, a CoP&K analysis of the field could yield a much richer picture of the internal community structure than the crude distinction of just three fundamental research paradigms. This monograph is one of the rare examples where papers with sharply conflicting perspectives are published together and commented on from differing perspectives—otherwise benign indifference (or silent hostility) instead of spirited cross-paradigm (cross-CoP&K) debate is the rule. To some extent DeSanctis indirectly recognizes the ongoing fragmentation of IS research when speaking of 'spawning other venues of interaction' (p. 365) and the need for continuing to 'develop forums of interaction and debate' (p. 370). Our *JAIS* article also strongly supports this recommendation with a similar call for 'Required Changes in Institutional Publication Practices' (p. 276) to overcome internal communication deficits.

The above analysis now allows us to state our arguments concerning the 'external disconnects' more succinctly with the concept of CoP&K. Our point was that the professional practitioners' CoP&K is separate from the loose intellectual federation of academic CoP&K. From this arise obvious communication deficits. To address them we called for a new research priority to create better 'under-standing of our organizational stakeholders' and to develop social boundary-spanning 'knowledge creation and transformation networks'. Of course, these networks should reach out to all stake-holders and constituencies that are of importance to IS as a discipline.

Until this happens, it is misleading to diagnose that all is well with IS as long as IS researchers form a thriving CoP&K. This is the *second major issue*. By not connecting to the outside and without outside vali-dation, *IS as an academic discipline in the longer term is at risk of losing its legitimacy* regardless of how much 'vibrancy' it signals with its internal processes (DeSanctis, p. 7). However, we do agree with DeSanctis and others (e.g. Robey) that the only way to meet this threat is to 'Resist the Lure of the "Dominant Research Paradigm"', to focus on substantive questions, to embrace inter-disciplinarity (Galliers) with the widest possible participation (DeSanctis, p. 369), improve communication and so forth. However, we are not convinced that the emphasis of substance should go hand in hand with less attention to method and commentary (DeSanctis, p. 373). In the state of differing community standards of quality, how else can we even know what substance means and where we can find it if not through commentary on results *and* the prevailing methods, which are often applied by way of fashion without proper reflection and justification.

CoP&K Summary

Given more space, we could find many quotes in the other articles supporting our conclusion that a CoP&K is a great analytical contribution to the current debate, but its application to the state of the discipline yields little reason for comfort. It reinforces our notion that IS suffers or will suffer substantially unless it finds ways to overcome its internal and external communication deficits. We do agree with DeSanctis that the internal communication deficits at this point have their positive sides—as demonstrated by this monograph—but they are still worrisome. The very fact that we have the discussion in this book shows that internal communication and reflection can be increased across CoP (paradigmatic) boundaries. The good will demonstrated by all towards this project and the widespread interest in and contributions to this debate have given us hope that IS will emerge stronger rather than weaker from this debate.

CONCLUSIONS

It should be apparent to everyone that this debate is unique (at least in IS). Never before have so many diverse and well-known voices come together between the covers of one book to debate their often conflicting views so openly and sincerely. Therefore, we consider ourselves honored and fortunate to be a part of this project. While the long-term outcome of this effort is uncertain, the hope is that this will inspire a second round of double-loop learning (Argyris) which may lift the debate to a higher level to meet the very significant challenges that await us.

We are reminded of the classical debates on the contrasting conceptions of Systems Science and hard vs. soft Operations Research. Commentators such as Ackoff and Checkland warned the Systems and OR communities of taking a too narrow view of the nature of their mission and problems, emphasizing the need for a 'soft', i.e. humanistic/social theoretic, perspective. Their calls mostly fell on deaf ears. We hope that history will not repeat itself in that the vigor of the field lies in its pursuit of diverse, trans-disciplinary trajectories (Galliers), and as Robey formulates it: 'responses that are not seen as entirely self serving...we should not ignore the wealth of theoretical and methodological guidance available in related fields' (2003, p. 357). In our minds, these fields include both philosophy and the social and cultural sciences but, at the same time, we must not forget computer science nor the practices and contributions of industry.

If the debate has shown anything, it is that '...different theoretical lenses lead to very different conclusions regarding the status and the future direction of the field' (Ives *et al.*, 2004, p. 120). Regardless of what the lenses are, we agree with Lyytinen and King (2004, p. 242) who state that the future of the field will lie with: '(1) salience of the subjects studied, (2) the strength of results from the study, and (3) the plasticity of the field with respect to changing circumstances.' In our view, disagreements about the interpretation of these three factors are not a sign of weakness, but of health.

REFERENCES

Bariff, M. and Ginzberg, M. (1980) 'MIS and the behavioral sciences: Research patterns and prescriptions', *Proceedings of the First Conference on Information Systems*, Philadelphia, pp. 49–58.

Barley, S. (1986) 'Technology as an occasion for structuring: Evidence from observations of CT scanners and the social order of radiology departments', *Administrative Science Quarterly*, 31(1), pp. 78–108.

Berger, P. and Luckmann, T. (1967) *The Social Construction of Reality*, Anchor Book, NY.

Boland, R. J. (1978) 'The process and product of system design', *Management Science*, 28(9), pp. 887–98.

Boland, R. J. (1979) 'Control, causality and information system requirements', *Accounting, Organizations and Society*, 4(5), pp. 259–72.

Boland, R. J. (1985) 'Phenomenology: A preferred approach to research in information systems', in E. Mumford, R. Hirschheim, G. Fitzgerald and T. Wood-Harper (eds), *Research Methods in Information Systems*, North-Holland, Amsterdam, pp. 193–202.

Boland, R. J. (1987) 'The in-formation of information systems', in R. Boland and R. Hirschheim (eds), *Critical Issues in Information Systems Research*, John Wiley & Sons, Chichester, pp. 363–80.

Boland, R. J. (1989) 'Metaphorical traps in developing information systems for human progress', in H. Klein and K. Kumar (eds), *Systems Development for Human Progress*, North-Holland, Amsterdam, pp. 277–90.

Boland, R. J. and Tenkas, R. (1995) 'Perspective making and perspective taking in communities of knowing', *Organization Science*, 6(4), Jul–Aug., pp. 350–72.

Davis, G., Ein-Dor, P., King, W. and Torkzadeh, R. (2004) 'IT offshoring: History, prospects and challenges', paper presented at ICIS2004, Senior Scholars Session, Washington.

Giddens, A. (1984) *The Constitution of Society: Outline for a Theory of Structuration*, Polity Press, Cambridge.

Gopal, A., Beaubien, L. and Marcon, T. (2002) 'Old wolf, new wool suit: India, IT, and the legacy of colonialism', *Proceedings of the 23rd International Conference on Information Systems*, pp. 525–32.

Habermas, J. (1984) *The Theory of Communicative Action—Volume One: Reason and the Rationalization of Society*, Beacon Press, Boston.

Habermas, J. (1987) *The Theory of Communicative Action—Volume Two: The Critique of Functionalist Reason*, Beacon Press, Boston.

Hirschheim, R., Klein, H. K. and Lyytinen, K. (1995) *Information Systems Development and Data Modeling: Conceptual and Philosophical Foundations*, Cambridge University Press, Cambridge.

Hirschheim, R., Klein, H. K. and Lyytinen, K. (1996) 'Exploring the intellectual structures of information systems development: A social action theoretic analysis', *Accounting, Management and Information Technologies*, 6(1/2), pp. 1–64.

Hirschheim, R., Loebbecke, C., Newman, M. and Valor, J. (2005) 'The new world order and its implications for the IS discipline', paper presented at ICIS2005, Senior Scholars Session, Las Vegas.

Iivari, J., Hirschheim, R. and Klein, H. (2004) 'Towards a distinctive body of knowledge for information systems experts: Coding ISD process knowledge in two IS journals', *Information Systems Journal*, 14(4), pp. 313–42.

Ives B., Parks, M., Porra, J. and Silva, L. (2004) 'Phylogeny and power in the IS domain: A response to Benbasat and Zmud's call for returning to the IT artifact', *Journal of the AIS*, 5(3), March, pp. 108–24.

King, W. (2004) 'Outsourcing and the future of IT', *Information Systems Management*, 21(4), Fall.

Klein, H. and Lyytinen, K. (2005) 'The relevancy problem', working paper.

Kling, R. (1987) 'Defining the boundaries of computing across complex organizations', in R. Boland and R. Hirschheim (eds), *Critical Issues in Information Systems Research*, John Wiley & Sons, Chichester, pp. 307–62.

Kuhn, T. (1970) *The Structure of Scientific Revolutions*, 2nd edn, University of Chicago Press, Chicago.

Lee, A. (undated) 'Five challenges to the IS field', http://www.people.vcu.edu/~aslee/bitworld/sld003.htm, last access 8/4/2005.

Lyytinen, K. and King, J. L. (2004) 'Nothing at the center? Academic legitimacy in the field of information systems', *Journal of the Association for Information Systems*, 5(6), June.

Orlikowski, W. J. (1993) 'CASE tools as organizational change: Investigating incremental and radical changes in systems development', *MIS Quarterly*, 17(3), pp. 309–40.

Orlikowski, W. and Baroudi, J. (1991) 'Studying information technology in organizations: Research approaches and assumptions', *Information Systems Research*, 2(1), pp. 1–28.

Orlikowski, W. and Iacono, S. (2001) 'Desperately seeking the "IT" in IT research', *Information Systems Research*, 7(4), pp. 400–08.

Robey, D. (2003) 'Identity, legitimacy and the dominant research paradigm: An alternative prescription for the IS discipline', *Journal of the Association for Information Systems*, 4(7), December.

Schutz, A. and Luckmann, T. (1974) *The Structures of the Lifeworld*, Heinemann, London.

Simon, H. (1977) *The New Science of Management Decision*, 2nd edn, The Free Press, NY.

Stehr, N. and Bechman, G. (2005) Introduction to the Aldine Edition, in *Risk, A Sociological Theory Niklas Luhmann, With a new introduction by Nico Stehr and Gotthard Bechmann*, Transaction Publishers, pp. vii–xxvii.

Winograd, T. (1980) 'What does it mean to understand language', *Cognitive Science*, 4(4), pp. 209–41.

Winograd, T. and Flores, F. (1986) *Understanding Computers and Cognition*, Ablex Publishers, Norwood, NJ.

Wittgenstein, L. (1922) *Tractatus Logico-Philosophicus*, Routledge & Kegan Paul, London.

Wittgenstein, L. (1958) *Philosophical Investigations*, Basil Blackwell, Oxford.

16

'Don't Worry, be Happy...'[1] A Post-Modernist Perspective on the Information Systems Domain

Robert D. Galliers

I am pleased to be able to develop some of the ideas that I presented in my *Journal of the Association for Information Systems (JAIS)* article (see Chapter 6 in this volume) that was penned in response to the earlier *MIS Quarterly (MISQ)* article by Izak Benbasat and Bob Zmud. In this, they express concern that the research community in Information Systems (IS) is responsible for the ambiguity of the discipline's (*sic*) central identity by 'under-investigating phenomena intimately associated with IT-based systems and over-estimating phenomena distantly associated with IT-based systems' (Benbasat & Zmud, 2003, p. 183). A central related argument in their article is that IS needs to focus on the core of the discipline to survive. It is an argument similar to those penned by other leading figures in our field, such as Orlikowski and Iacono (2001) and Weber (2003). My response in my *JAIS* article was to provide something of a counterpoint to these arguments by (1) questioning the stated definitions of IS as a field of study; (2) identifying a broader locus of study for IS than simply IS/IT development and use within organizations; (3) considering whether or not the field of IS *should* be viewed as a discipline; and (4) bemoaning the lack of consideration given to the inter- and trans-national nature of the IS field. I also touched on the trans- and meta-disciplinary characteristics of IS.

First, let me say how pleased I was to note the wide ranging reaction to the Benbasat and Zmud article—this in and of itself demonstrates a keen and widespread interest in our field and in its ongoing development; second, that I was interested to read the authors' response (see Chapter 14 in this volume). They provide a useful further insight into their thinking, for example, by providing a slight modification to the *nomological net* introduced in the *MISQ* article, by explaining their intention to draw something of a boundary 'around the *phenomenological domain serving as the topical basis of IS scholarly journals*', and by surfacing and clarifying their intention of 'refocusing IS research on issues of *design*'. Despite all the debate, they make it crystal clear that they 'still believe strongly in the views presented in [the *MISQ*] article'. And despite all the debate, let *me* make it crystal clear that I stick to *my* strongly held views too!

Thank goodness that we do have a range of opinion being expressed in our academy: how boring would it be were we to agree on everything. I am reminded of work by Gibbons and colleagues at the Science Policy Research Unit at Sussex University in England (Gibbons *et al.*, 1995), and also of more recent discussions in the knowledge management (*sic*) literature with regard to knowledge creation (e.g., Von Krogh *et al.*, 2000). The former argue that new knowledge will emerge from trans-disciplinary treatments of contemporary phenomena, while the latter make the case that knowledge is not simply 'out there' to be tapped and exploited, but arises from exploration (cf. March, 1991) and interaction between human beings. Related work on communities of practice (e.g., Lave and Wenger, 1991; Brown and Duguid, 1991) and knowing—as opposed to knowledge—(e.g., Kleine *et al.*, 1998) also comes to mind. Here, *our* community of practice is engaged in just such an exercise of knowledge creation—of knowing. It is an emergent and iterative process—one which will undoubtedly lead to new insights. But, this is the very point of my argument. In an attempt to crystallize and contain the IS domain, the unintended consequence (cf. Robey and Boudreau, 1999) of our actions may well be to constrain and limit the development of our field—an outcome, presumably, which we would all wish to avoid. Here, I'm reminded of the need for boundary spanning—individuals in our community who are willing to reach out into other fields (cf. Tushman and Scanlan, 1981), rather than to be more inward in their focus. Indeed, in my earlier article, I cautioned against closed systems (that exhibit entropy), and argued for innovation and emergence.

Klein and Hirschheim (Chapter 15 in this volume) deal with aspects of the argument that I would otherwise incorporate into this note (e.g., 'the techno-centrism of the IT artifact focus', and the ontological realism that underpins much of the Benbasat and Zmud argument, as against the social constructionist perspective that they—and I—take). Let me, therefore, limit my remarks in this note on two aspects of Benbasat and Zmud's rejoinder: (1) the focus on IS design within organizations, and (2) the limitations of any community of practice that restricts its focus to a prevailing orientation that finds form in journals emanating from a particular country or region. I shall conclude with a reflection on why I believe we should delight in this debate. On reflection, I realize that in some ways we may be having a debate between modernists and post-modernists (see, for example, Cahoone, 2003). The following is an attempt to summarize this conclusion, and draws heavily from Mary Klages's course syllabus on modern critical thought at the University of Colorado (see: http://www.colorado.edu/English/ENGL2012Klages/pomo.html).

> Postmodernism rejects boundaries and rigid genre distinctions. It emphasizes pastiche, parody, and bricolage. It favors reflexivity and self-consciousness, fragmentation and discontinuity, ambiguity. It places emphasis on the destructured, the decentered, and the absence of solutions. While much the same can be said of modernism, post-modernism differs in relation to its stance on these issues. Modern-ism—like postmodernism—presents this fragmented view of human subjectivity, history and the world we live in, but does so with a measure of angst. It presents this fragmentation as something tragic, something to be lamented and something to be concerned about. I see the arguments of Benbasat and Zmud, and Weber, among others, in this light. They, like many modernist thinkers, try to uphold the idea that we as a 'discipline' should accentuate the unity, coherence, and meaning that they lament as being lost in much of recent IS literature that has somehow forgotten the 'core'—which in their terms is the IT artifact. Postmodernism, in contrast, doesn't lament the idea of fragmentation, provisionality, or incoherence, but rather celebrates all this. The world is meaningless? Let's not pretend that we can make meaning then, let's just play with nonsense; let's enjoy the incongruities, the range of stances we take, and the emergence—the new knowledge that arises from the confluence of ideas emanating from our different worldviews. Let's continue to explore terra incognita. Who knows what we might find. In other words: 'Don't worry, be happy'.

But, I'm getting ahead of myself. Let me first deal briefly with the focus on IS design within organizations, and the unintended focus on US-style research that underpin the stance taken by Benbasat and Zmud. Both are aspects of their argument with which I take issue.

In my *JAIS* article (Galliers, 2003) I questioned whether the devel-opment of our field of study—and, indeed, our span of influence—should be viewed as a sign of crisis or of natural growth. I argued for the latter. It was undoubtedly the case that our primary concern within IS during the earlier years of the field's development—during the late 1970s and 1980s for example—was related to IS development methodologies. One might even argue that IS development—systems analysis and design—*defined* the field of IS in this period (see, for example, Gane and Sarson, 1979; Avison and Fitzgerald, 1988). But we have seen new topics emerge since then: decision support systems, group systems, IS evaluation, IS planning and strategy, e-commerce, security, privacy, business process re-engineering, enterprise systems, out-sourcing, knowledge management, national IT policies, off-shoring, IS governance—to name but a few. It really does fly in the face of 'reality' to suggest that *the* core of the IS field concerns IS design within organizations. Certainly, such concerns are an important *aspect* of our field—historically perhaps even more so than today— but to claim more than this does an injustice to those in our academy whose concerns relate to wider organizational, inter-organizational, management, strategy, policy, ethical, societal and global issues. In arguing in my earlier article that our locus of study is more broadly based than organizations or individuals working in organizations, I highlighted the need to include societal, policy and ethical issues within the ambit of the IS field. I invoked systems theory (e.g., Checkland, 1981, 1999) in a consideration of where to draw our boundary, noting that the very act of doing so is itself a social construction (e.g., Bijker *et al.*, 1987). I reasoned that were we not to push the boundaries, 'we may well be overly constraining ourselves and we will certainly not know whether [relevant choices have] been made', noting that alternative boundaries might be considered simultaneously.

I turn now to the question of the innate cultural bias in an argument that centers on drawing a boundary around 'the *phenomenological domain serving as the topical basis of IS scholarly journals*'. While this cultural bias is I am sure unintended, it needs to be surfaced. It is certainly the case that journals emanating from particular regions of the world, particularly North America, tend to be self-referential, focusing on particular topics and the work of members of the academy from that region, and through lenses that are commonplace in that region. This is done at the expense of related work conducted elsewhere. This is not my opinion alone; it is based on empirical evidence (see, for example, Galliers and Meadows, 2003).

In related work, Edgar Whitley and I have analyzed the papers presented during the first ten years of ECIS—the European Conference on Information Systems (Galliers and Whitley, 2002, 2005). It is clear from this analysis and from survey research conducted previously (Avgerou *et al.*, 1999) that there is a distinctive quality to European IS research as compared to that undertaken in North America. There is considerable overlap of course, but nonetheless, the distinguishing features are insightful, and might lead Benbasat and Zmud to redraw their boundary. Let me provide examples that relate to both the ontological and the epistemological dimension.

Banker and Kauffman (2004) propose ten categories for IS research in relation to their review of IS papers that appeared over the first 50 years of the journal *Management Science*. These are: decision support and design science; value of information, human–computer systems design; IS organization and strategy; economics of IS and IT; global and societal issues, electronic markets; inter-organizational issues; group decision making and creativity, and IS research. We based our review of topics considered in ECIS papers on this typology for the most part, making only minor changes to the classifications. Were we to group together the ECIS papers that covered topics focusing on IT, on IS/IT development and design, and on decision support, we would find that they account for almost 30% of the topics covered. Similarly, by grouping together papers dealing with issues concerning global and societal, organizational and inter-organizational, and electronic market concerns, we find that these account for practically 60% of the papers presented. Empirically, then, 'the *phenomenological domain serving as the topical basis*' of ECIS papers appears to be considerably broader than Benbasat and Zmud surmise, or than have appeared in *Management Science*.

We might also look at a distinction that relates to the commonly held belief that European IS researchers draw more heavily on what might be broadly classified as social theory. In order to explore this belief, we adopted a method developed by Jones (2000) to analyze the social theory content of ECIS papers. Jones's method investigates how many authors cite social theorists and how many different social theorists are cited by them. In the first ten years of ECIS, 29% of the papers (335 papers) cite at least one social theorist, with the likes of Rogers, Giddens, Latour and Polyani being cited frequently. Jones defines the social citation density (or 'Matthew Jones Index'—MJI) as the sum of the number of distinct social theorists cited by each paper, divided by the total number of papers. Using this notation, we discovered that papers presented in the first ten years of ECIS have an MJI of 0.53. We then considered the proportion of ECIS papers citing social theorists with the total number of papers presented by authors from each country and found, for the most part, that the proportions are closely correlated, with certain exceptions: the UK has provided proportionately *more* social theory papers, while the USA has provided proportionately *fewer* such papers. To provide further comparison, we compared the MJI for ECIS with the MJI of papers published during the period 1992–1999 in *MISQ* and *JMIS*. Together, these two US journals have an MJI of 0.05. Who was it who said that the USA and the UK are nations divided by a common language!

As a result of this analysis, we concluded that these data provide at least a strong suggestion that European IS research is focused more broadly, and draws far more heavily on social theory than IS research published in 'mainstream' (i.e., US-based) journals. Given the global nature of our field, I argue (cf. Galliers and Meadows, 2003) that we should be very careful in attributing global lessons from local perspectives, experience or data.

So, where is all this leading to? Well, first, I wanted to demonstrate that there *is* a range of opinion and perspective in the field of IS. These differences relate to topics of interest, research approaches adopted, and the literature cited. They *tend* to be based on schools of thought that are regionally based. Is this a good thing, or a bad thing? Benbasat and Zmud would presumably argue that it is a bad thing because we would lose academic respectability were the IS academy to be seen to be so diffuse and diverse by other academies. In my *JAIS* article, I tried to show that other academies were similarly diverse—particularly in the fields of management and the social sciences—and that many saw themselves as being trans-disciplinary. I argued that we were not alone. I argued that the broadening of our sphere of influence and interest was a good thing in terms of reputation and in terms of knowledge creation. I stick to this argument. Let me, though, try to expand on it somewhat by looking at these two opposing perspectives through the lens of post-modernist theory.

As I indicated in my introduction, on reflecting on the polarity in thinking present here—Weber describes this phenomenon (Chapter 13 in this volume) as 'ships in the night'—it seems to me that it all boils down to whether we are at one with multiple perspectives, with ambiguity, with emergence, or not. Given the complexity of the phenomena we study, I would argue that we should be at one with, or at least the inevitability of, permeable boundaries. Given the rate of change in the technology—the IT artifact of today is so very different to the IT artifact of ten years ago, let alone 30 or 40 years ago, to make it such a 'moveable feast' that it defies logic to make it the center of our focus. What is 'it' in any event, and what will 'it' be in, say, ten years' time? I therefore take a post-modernist perspective on our *domain*—note: not our *discipline*. To repeat, post-modernism does not lament, but actually celebrates fragmentation, provisionality and incoherence. Let's enjoy the incongruities and the range of stances we take in the IS academy. Let's enjoy the emergence—the new knowing that arises from the confluence of—sometimes competing—ideas emanating from our different worldviews. Let's continue to explore terra incognita. In other words: 'Don't worry, be happy'.

NOTE

1 The title is taken from the song of the same title by Bobby McFerrin on the CD *Simple Pleasures*, Capitol Records, 1990.

REFERENCES

Avgerou, C., Siemer, J. and Bjorn-Andersen, N. (1999) 'The academic field of information systems in Europe', *European Journal of Information Systems*, 8(2), pp. 136–153.

Avison, D. E., and Fitzgerald, G. (1988) *Information System Development: Methodologies, Tools and Techniques*, Blackwell Scientific, Oxford, UK.

Banker, R. D. and Kauffman, R. J. (2004) 50th Anniversary Article: 'The evolution of research on Information Systems: A fiftieth-year survey of the literature', *Management Science*, 50(3), pp. 281–298.

Benbasat, I. and Zmud, R. (2003) 'The identity crisis within the IS discipline: Defining and communicating the core's properties', *MIS Quarterly*, 27(2), pp. 183–194.

Bijker, W., Hughes, T. and Pinch, T. (1987) *The Social Construction of Technological Systems*, MIT Press, Cambridge, MA.

Brown, J. S. and Duguid, P. (2001) 'Knowledge and organization: A social-practice perspective', *Organization Science*, 12(2), pp. 198–213.

Cahoone, L. E. (ed.) (2003) *From Modernism to Postmodernism: An Anthology* (2nd edn), Blackwell, Oxford, UK.

Checkland, P. (1981,1999) *Systems Thinking, Systems Practice*, John Wiley & Sons, Chichester, UK.

Galliers, R. D. (2003) 'Change as crisis or growth? Toward a transdisciplinary view of Information Systems as a field of study', *Journal of the Association for Information Systems*, 4(6), pp. 360–76.

Galliers, R. D. and Meadows, M. (2003) 'A discipline divided: Globalization and parochialism in Information Systems research', *Communications of the AIS*, 11(5), January.

Galliers, R. D. and Whitley, E. A. (2002) 'An anatomy of European Information Systems research: ECIS 1993—ECIS 2002, *Proceedings*: 10th ECIS, Gdansk, Poland, 6–8 June.

Galliers, R. D. and Whitley, E. A. (2005) *'Vive la différence!* Distinguishing features of European Information Systems research', *European Journal of Information Systems* (under review).

Gane, C. and Sarson, T. (1979) *Structured Systems Analysis: Tools and Techniques*, Prentice-Hall, Englewood Cliffs, NJ.

Gibbons, M., Limoges, C., Nowotny, H., Schwartzman, S., Scott, P. and Trow, M. (1995) *The New Production of Knowledge: The Dynamics of Science and Research in Contemporary Societies*, Sage, London, UK.

Jones, M. (2000) 'The moving finger: The use of social theory in WG 8.2 Conference Papers, 1975–1999', in R. Baskerville, J. Stage and J. I. DeGross (eds.), *Organizational and Social Perspectives on Information Technology*, Kluwer, Aalborg, Denmark, pp. 15–32.

Kleine D., Roos J. and von Krogh, G. (eds.) (1998) *Knowing in Firms: Understanding, Managing and Measuring Knowledge*, Sage, London, UK.

Lave, J. and Wenger, E. (1991) *Situated Learning: Legitimate Peripheral Participation.* Cambridge University Press, Cambridge, UK.

March, J. G. (1991) 'Exploration and exploitation in organizational learning', *Organization Science*, 2(1), pp. 71–87.

Orlikowski, W. and Iacono, S. (2001). Research Commentary: 'Desperately seeking the "IT" in IT research—A call to theorizing the IT artifact', *Information Systems Research*, 12(2), pp. 121–134.

Robey, D. and Boudreau, M. C. (1999) 'Accounting for the contradictory organizational consequences of information technology: Theoretical directions and methodological implications', *Information Systems Research*, 10(2), June, pp. 167–185.

Tushman, M. and Scanlan, T. (1981) 'Boundary spanning individuals: Their role in information transfer and their antecedents', *Academy of Management Journal*, 24(2), pp. 289–305.

Von Krogh, G., Ichijo, K. and Nonaka, I. (2000) *Enabling Knowledge Creation: How to Unlock the Mystery of Tacit Knowledge and Release the Power of Innovation*, Oxford University Press, Oxford.

Weber, R. (2003). 'Still desperately seeking the IT artifact', *MIS Quarterly*, 27(2), iii–xi.

17
Cleaning the Mirror: Desperately Seeking Identity in the Information Systems Field[1]

Daniel Robey

Self-understanding is a profound motivation for humans engaged in almost any endeavor, from the arts to the sciences. John Coltrane, the legendary jazz saxophonist and composer, referred to his art as 'cleaning the mirror', a process through which 'we can see more and more clearly what we are' (quoted in Hentoff, 1966). Coltrane's music was characterized by a restless search for meaning, and he changed his conception dramatically within relatively short periods of his performing career. Although critics decried his radical departure from 'orthodox' methods, Coltrane's search for meaning fundamentally reshaped established forms of composition, improvisation and performance, thus changing the identity of the art form called jazz.

Academic researchers also try to clean their mirrors in a quest for their own identities. Over recent years, two sides of a debate have formed concerning the identity of the information systems (IS) field. On one side, arguments have been presented for establishing a clearer identity by narrowing our focus around a distinct, core paradigm. Aspects of this paradigm include agreement on a core phenomenon (Orlikowski and Iacono, 2001), original theory (Weber, 2003), and a dominant paradigm for guiding research (Benbasat and Weber, 1996; Benbasat and Zmud, 2003). With a clearer identity, it is argued that IS research will be regarded as more legitimate (Benbasat and Zmud, 2003).

On the other side of the debate stand the champions of diversity. Rather than viewing the absence of a core paradigm as a liability, proponents of diversity argue that greater fragmentation is appropriate for IS (Banville and Landry, 1989; King, 1993), consistent with academic values and community practices (DeSanctis, 2003; Robey, 1996), adaptable to changes in the properties of information artifacts (Whinston and Geng, 2004), and characteristic of other legitimate academic fields (Lyytinen and King, 2004). Rather than 'circling the wagons' to defend against threats, IS should become more 'trans-disciplinary' (Galliers, 2003) and regularly change its identity (Lyytinen and King, 2004; Robey, 2003). These more adaptive measures, it is argued, will ensure the IS field's legitimacy.

In our efforts to set new directions for IS as an academic field, it is important to recognize what we are now (DeSanctis, 2003). IS is currently a field characterized by both conformity and diversity. In some topic areas, IS researchers agree strongly about phenomena and how to study them, making these relatively 'tight' areas of inquiry. In other 'loose' topic areas, diversity abounds. As a whole, the IS field might be characterized as 'heterogeneous', consisting of tight areas of focused activity and loose areas of innovation. Much like contemporary jazz, we draw from established traditions while incorporating fresh ideas from outside our field and original ideas of our own. The margins of IS overlap with other disciplines, but this need not threaten our legitimacy. Indeed, innovation around traditional cores makes both IS and jazz more elastic and reflective of modern conditions.

Figure 17.1 shows a partial map of research topics in IS. The smaller shapes represent tight areas of inquiry; the larger shapes represent looser areas. Within the more tightly circumscribed topics, researchers agree on relevant theory, specific research questions, methodological issues, and standards for evaluating a study's contribution. Transaction cost economics (TCE), technology acceptance model (TAM), and diffusion of innovations (DOI) are shown as theories that have been used extensively in IS research. Although additional studies may contribute little to the overall knowledge base in these three areas, knowledge is solidified through the accumulation of findings across many studies. As a result of consensus around tight research paradigms, we might claim that we know a great deal about topics in these areas.

For example, TAM studies have repeatedly confirmed the importance of perceived usefulness and social norms on users' intentions to adopt information technologies. In similar fashion, DOI studies have identified an agreed upon set of predictors of the diffusion of IT through populations of users and organizations. There is also general agreement that IT reduces the costs of economic transactions and

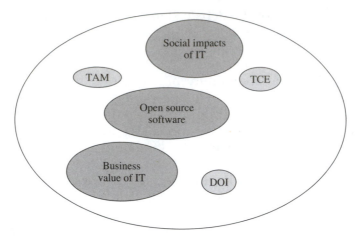

Figure 17.1   *Tight and loose topic areas in information systems*
Legend:
TAM = Technology acceptance model
DOI = Diffusion of innovations
TCE = Transaction cost economics

Tight areas are smaller shapes.
Loose areas are larger shapes.

potentially shifts economic activities away from hierarchical control and into market forms of governance.

The larger shapes in Figure 17.1 designate topic areas informed by a wider variety of theoretical approaches, research questions and methodologies. The three examples shown in Figure 17.1 are the organizational impact of information systems, open source software and business value of IT. With the exception of open source, these are not especially new topic areas. However, they have eluded paradigm consensus because researchers continue to explore contradictory findings and pursue new theoretical angles for investigating the same topic. New angles challenge older assumptions, such as the simple connection between IT and business transformation or business value. Researchers in loose topic areas are uncomfortable settling for obvious relationships, striving to explain complex phenomena with greater fidelity. Because new theoretical ideas are often drawn from other disciplines, loose topic areas maintain flexibility and adaptability.

Both tight and loose topic areas may be criticized, but on different grounds. Tight areas might be accused of wasting resources to strengthen accumulated findings about things that we already know. For example, in the presence of more pressing issues in IS, the established relationship in TAM between user perceptions and user intentions might be judged trivial and unimportant. Likewise, understanding the antecedents of technology adoption in DOI might be judged less relevant where users have less discretion to choose technologies. Loose topic areas may be criticized for failing to produce strong results (Lyytinen and King, 2004). If researchers continually challenge each other and produce new theories instead of replicating prior work, IS might achieve an agnostic state where nothing is known for certain. Loose areas of IS research may also be criticized for too much borrowing and not enough originality (Weber, 2003).

Under paradigm consensus, we clean the mirror and see researchers engaged in similar efforts. We thus create a 'school' of IS research where the rules are established and enforced through editorial policies, criteria for promotion and tenure, and other measures (in which the term 'discipline' takes on a different meaning). Small deviations from convention are tolerated but undisciplined departures are discouraged.

Under diversity, we clean the mirror to see an alarming variety of topics, theories and research methods. To some, the mirror may appear shattered, a mosaic reflecting images in multiple directions. On closer inspection, however, each facet of the field may offer something unique that is worth learning. A researcher trained in the social sciences may discover design research (Hevner *et al.*, 2004); a scholar grounded in positivist philosophy may discover interpretive epistemology; an economist may derive new insights into electronic markets by learning about social institutions; and so on. As we entertain new perspectives on complex problems, we establish a different kind of identity, one that is flexible and adaptive in response to changes in the world. In this scenario, the field's identity is constantly reshaped.

Careful reviews of tight topical areas reveal the potential to complicate and loosen them. For example, DOI studies may be complicated by asking research questions about patterns of IT use following adoption. Many technologies are adopted, but research suggests that users can appropriate similar or identical technologies in different ways. For example, theories of human agency and practice (Emirbayer and Mische, 1998; Orlikowski, 2000) have informed recent research on IS use following technology adoption or implementation (e.g., Boudreau and Robey, 2005; Schultze and Orlikowski, 2004). Likewise, TAM could be complicated by turning attention toward the patterns of usage involving ensembles of technologies that users have already accepted. Here the emphasis would shift from *whether* users accept technology to *how* users appropriate the technologies that they have accepted. By complicating the narrow focus on adoption decisions, these tight paradigm areas could be made looser and perhaps more interesting and relevant.

Careful reviews of research in loose topic areas are also needed to establish findings that are consistent across a wider range of studies. Rather than assuming complete diversity, such reviews should show regions within topic areas where a tighter consensus has emerged. For example, studies in open source software development appear to have produced a good understanding why developers contribute to open source projects when they receive no direct payment from generating public goods (Lakhani and Von Hippel, 2003). Prior to studies of this phenomenon, open source projects existed as interesting paradoxes. Reviews of loose areas should also seek areas where new research should be done. For example, Elgarah and her associates (2005) examined the theoretical underpinnings of research on EDI, identifying five conceptual gaps that required further research.

Like jazz, the IS field shares many characteristics of 'modern' social institutions. Modern social relations are plucked from other times and places and inserted into local environments (Giddens, 1990). As theories and research practices are taken from other disciplines, IS becomes more heterogeneous, in effect stretched across broader expanses of time and space. In its worst incarnations, modern institutions resemble fractured mosaics: post-modern fragments with no center. At their best, modern institutions extend their relevance and capabilities, building outward from traditions to create multiple centers of activity. This is a much different identity from the one implied by a single core paradigm. For me, it is a more attractive vision for the IS field, one that values and honors its inherent diversity.

NOTE

1 I thank Vanessa Liu for her feedback on an earlier draft of this commentary.

REFERENCES

Banville, C. and Landry, M. (1989) 'Can the Field of MIS be Disciplined?' *Communications of the ACM*, 32, pp. 48–60.

Benbasat, I. and Weber, R. (1996) 'Rethinking "Diversity" in Information Systems Research', *Information Systems Research*, 7(4) December, pp. 389–99.

Benbasat, I. and Zmud, R. W. (2003) 'The identity crisis within the IS discipline: Defining and communicating the discipline's core properties,' *MIS Quarterly*, 27(2), June, pp. 183–94.

Boudreau, M-C. and Robey, D. (2005) 'Enacting integrated information technology: A human agency Perspective', *Organization Science*, 16(1), January–February, pp. 3–18.

DeSanctis, G. (2003) 'The social life of information systems research: A response to Benbasat and Zmud's call for returning to the IT artifact', *Journal of the Association for Information Systems*, 4(7), December, pp. 360–76.

Elgarah, W., Falaleeva, N., Saunders, C. S., Ilie, V., Shim, J. T. and Courtney, J. F. (2005) 'Data exchange in interorganizational relationships: review through multiple conceptual lenses', *The DATA BASE for Advances in Information Systems*, 36(1), Winter, pp. 8–29.

Emirbayer, M. and Mische, A. (1998) 'What is agency?' *American Journal of Sociology*, 103, pp. 962–1023.

Galliers, R. D. (2003) 'Change as crisis or growth? Toward a trans-disciplinary view of information systems as a field of study', *Journal of the Association for Information Systems*, 4(6), November, pp. 337–51.

Giddens, A. (1990) *The Consequences of Modernity*, Stanford University Press, Stanford, CA.

Hentoff, N. (1996) Original Liner Notes to John Coltrane's 'Meditations', Impulse Records, 1966.

Hevner, A. R., March, S. T., Park, J. and Ram, S. (2004) 'Design science in information systems research', *MIS Quarterly*, 28(1), March, pp. 75–105.

King, J. L. (1993) 'Editorial Notes', *Information Systems Research*, 4(4), December, pp. 291–8.

Lakhani, K. R. and von Hippel, E. (2003) 'How open source software works: "Free" user-to-user assistance', *Research Policy*, 32(6).

Lyytinen, K. and King, J. L. (2004) 'Nothing at the center?: Academic legitimacy in the information systems field', *Journal of the Association for Information Systems*, 5(6), 2004, pp. 220–46.

Orlikowski, W. J. (2000) 'Using technology and constituting structures: A practice lens for studying technology in organizations', *Organization Science*, 11, pp. 404–28.

Orlikowski, W. J. and Iacono, S. (2001) 'Research commentary: Desperately seeking the "IT" in IT research: A call to theorizing the IT artifact', *Information Systems Research*, 12(2), pp. 121–34.

Robey, D. (1996) 'Diversity in information systems research: Threat, promise, and responsibility', *Information Systems Research*, 7(4), pp. 400–08.

Robey, D. (2003) 'Identity, legitimacy, and the dominant research paradigm: An alternative prescription for the IS discipline', *Journal of the Association for Information Systems*, 4(6), June, pp. 352–59.

Schultze, U. and Orlikowski, W. J. (2004) 'A practice perspective on technology-mediated network relations: The use of Internet-based self-serve technologies', *Information Systems Research*, 15, pp. 87–106.

Weber, R. (2003) 'Still desperately seeking the IT artifact', *MIS Quarterly*, 27(2), June, pp. iii–xi.

Whinston, A. B. and Geng, X. (2004) 'Operationalizing the essential role of the information technology artifact in information systems research: Gray area, pitfalls, and the importance of strategic ambiguity', *MIS Quarterly*, 28(2), June, pp. 149–59.

18
Designing Design Science

Salvatore T. March

Relevance, rigor and results are the trifecta of academic research. They are defined by the constituency that comprises and supports the discipline (Denning, 1997; Tsichritzis, 1999). In information systems (IS) this constituency includes IS academic researchers, organizations that develop and deploy information technologies (IT), organizations that procure and implement such technologies, IS managers within such organizations and, more and more commonly, general and upper level managers within such organizations. The results demanded by this constituency are (1) innovative IT artifacts that address business tasks and problems and (2) the knowledge of how to effectively choose, appropriate, implement and integrate them into the organization. Innovative IT artifacts extend the boundaries of known applications of IT, addressing important problems heretofore not thought to be amenable to computational approaches. Knowledge of how to effectively choose, appropriate, implement and integrate them into an organization unlocks their value.

Research in information systems lives at the interface of people, organizations and IT (Lee, 1999). People within organizations conduct business. Managers design organizational and inter-organizations structures within which their employees and partners develop and execute business plans, e.g., they market, produce and sell products, service customers, manage financial and human resources, and develop and manage partnerships. IT artifacts support people and organizations in accomplishing those tasks. The nature of that support is dependent upon the capabilities of the IT artifacts engaged. The success or failure of that support is dependent upon both the capabilities of the IT artifacts engaged and the designed and emergent phenomena that occur when such capabilities are appropriated within a given organizational context.

Consequently, research in information systems has developed along two lines. One is engaged in understanding the nature of the phenomena that occur when information-technology artifacts are used (or misused) by people within organizations to accomplish human and organizational goals. This research has a behavioral focus. It develops and tests theories that explain or predict human and organizational phenomena that occur within the context of specified IT artifacts (capabilities). Such reasoned explanations and predictions ultimately enable people and organizations to more effectively and efficiently use IT artifacts. The second is engaged in developing innovative IT artifacts that address tasks and problems previously thought not to be amenable to computational solution. This research has a design focus. The artifacts developed in such research demonstrate new capabilities that can be appropriated by people and organizations to achieve their goals.

Organizations implement information systems to improve performance. Business managers commonly view performance through an economic lens, defining its goals relative to maximization of firm value, i.e., the present value of the difference between revenues and expenses. Given the high cost of information technology investments managers are understandably asking questions like: 'Why do information technology investments *not* result in an increase in firm value?' and 'What can be done to maximize the likelihood that they *will* do so?' These are the fundamental questions that IS researchers must answer (Benbasat and Zmud, 1999; 2003). The first is a causal question. The second is a problem-solving, decision making question. IS researchers must address both.

Answering the first question requires an understanding of phenomena that occur at the intersection of organizations, people and information technologies—the locus of the information systems discipline (Lee, 1999). Researchers must develop and justify theories, deep principled explanations of these phenomena (March and Smith, 1995; Hevner *et al.*, 2004; Benbasat and Zmud, 2003). These are valuable in understanding what has happened and why it happened, and possibly in anticipating what will happen.

While posed theories may be explanatory rather than causal in nature their relevancy and value are determined by the degree to which they enable managers to create organizational work-systems that improve organizational performance (Alter, 2003). This is the focus of the second research question. Answering it is fundamentally a design task that requires managers to 'shape artifacts and events to create a more desirable future' (Boland, 2002). Organizations and the information technologies that support them are both artificial, designed artifacts (Simon, 1996; Bunge, 1985). Their characteristics are molded to achieve specific purposes. They are ultimately evaluated by their effects on firm value. To the degree that organizations can shape behavior, e.g., through training and reward structures, people, although certainly not artificial, also have an element of design.

Much of the IS literature has explored characteristics of organizations and people while ignoring salient characteristics of information technologies (Orlikowski and Iacono, 2001; Weber, 2003). As a result much of this research is equivocal. For example, Orman (2002) eloquently describes the folly of posing a theory to explain or predict the effects of information technology on organizational structure without including characteristics of the implemented IT artifact. Any such theory must include the combined characteristics of people, organizations and information technology.

Social scientists and organizational theorists have long studied characteristics of people and organizations. Cognitive, behavioral, organizational and economic theories that explain and predict human and organization behavior abound. It is not in the realm of information systems research to pose new theories in these areas, although certainly there are IS researchers who are also interested in the foundational disciplines such as psychology, sociology, anthropology, economics and linguistics. IS researchers use and specialize such theories in the context of extant IT artifacts that have specifically designed capabilities to further our understanding of these phenomena.

Similarly, it is the role of computer scientists and engineers to create new and innovative IT capabilities. It is not in the realm of IS research, although there are IS researchers who are also interested in computer science and engineering. However, IS researchers must engage in characterizing those capabilities and using them in the context of improving firm performance. Doing so requires a combination of design science and behavioral science paradigms in crafting a research agenda for the IS discipline.

The science of design, as posited by Simon (1996), builds upon the mathematical and computational modeling capabilities developed in applied mathematics and operations research. Fundamentally it is a modeling discipline that develops and utilizes constructs, models, methods and implementations to understand, evaluate and optimize the characteristics of a system. In IS research the system under study includes organizations, people and IT artifacts. Unfortunately IS researchers using this paradigm often ignore salient characteristics of organizations and people and focus exclusively on characteristics of the IT artifact. Furthermore, in the ken of 'Comprehensive Anticipatory Design Science' as posited by R. Buckminster Fuller (1992) this research may appear to ascribe simplistic and nearly magical capabilities to technological artifacts.

> The function of what I call design science is to solve problems by introducing into the environment new artifacts, the availability of which will induce their spontaneous employment by humans and thus, coincidentally, cause humans to abandon their previous problem-producing behaviors and devices. For example, when humans have a vital need to cross the roaring rapids of a river, as a design scientist I would design them a bridge, causing them, I am sure, to abandon spontaneously and forever the risking of their lives by trying to swim to the other shore.
>
> R. Buckminster Fuller from *Cosmography*
> (http://www.bfi.org/designsc.htm)

Introducing IT artifacts into an organizational environment may not cause people to 'abandon their previous problem-producing behaviors and devices'. One of the important IS research problems is understanding if and how well people will, spontaneously or under duress, appropriately or inappropriately, use IT artifacts introduced into an organizational environment (Venkatesh *et al.*, 2003; Goodhue and Thompson, 1995). However, the capabilities of IT artifacts enable managers to design work systems, organizational structures and job characteristics, and develop human resources to accomplish organizational goals. Managers must be cognizant of the capabilities of existing and emerging IT artifacts. Design science as a research paradigm in IS focuses on building and evaluating innovative IT artifacts that extend the boundaries of known applications of IT, addressing important problems heretofore not thought to be amenable to computational approaches (Markus *et al.*, 2002; Walls *et al.*, 1992).

IT artifacts are broadly defined as constructs, models, methods and instantiations (March and Smith, 1995). Constructs are vocabulary and conceptualizations that enable communication and description of problems (phenomena), solution components, constraints and objectives. Models use these constructs to represent problems and solutions. Methods are algorithms or guidelines that enable the construction of instantiations—computer-based systems implemented within an organization. Each may constitute a contribution to research knowledge. Constructs, models and methods are evaluated with respect to their ability to improve performance in the development and use of information systems. Instantiations or implementations demonstrate the feasibility of utilizing information technology artifacts for a given task. They often embody newly developed constructs, models and methods. They are evaluated with respect to their effectiveness and efficiency in the performance of the given task.

Artifacts are intentionally designed for a specific purpose within a specific context. The purpose defines the criteria against which the performance of the artifact is evaluated. The context or environment defines the constraints in which the artifact must operate. Artifacts have inherent constraints that define their capabilities. The process of design is adapting the internal environment of the artifact to the external environment of the task domain to achieve its purpose (Simon, 1996). Difficulties in designing IT artifacts lie in the complexity, uncertainty and evolving nature of the external environment and in the relative inflexibility of the internal environment (Brooks, 1996). Computational systems rely on software that implements specified algorithms and on data acquired from the environment. When contingencies arising in the environment are not adequately addressed by the algorithms or when data are outside the design capabilities of the artifact, the system typically fails. While fault-tolerance and adaptive-systems are areas of current research, in general, software systems are simply not reliable outside their design parameters (Leveson, 2005). They may be designed to 'fail gracefully', but fail they will.

Computational modeling and the implementation of computer programs are fundamental to this paradigm. In modeling and constructing innovative IT artifacts, researchers gain significant new knowledge and demonstrate the feasibility of the studied capability to address heretofore unsolved organizational problems. These, combined with an understanding of people and organizations, hold the promise of research contribution for the IS discipline.

Consider, for example, the AIS Special Interest Group on Agent-Based Information Systems (SIGABIS). It purpose, to advance 'knowledge in the use of agent-based IS...to improve organizational performance' (SIGABIS, 2005) has elements of both lines of research and must engage both behavioral science and design science methods. It is crucial for researchers engaged in this area of research to recognize this dual research focus.

Such research is analogous to traditional research in management science. Neither is specifically concerned with developing new computational methods or solution procedures. These are left to computer scientists and applied mathematicians. However, both are concerned with solving heretofore unsolved management problems using computational models and methods. Solving managerial problems engages both design and behavior. Managers create business strategies and design the business processes needed to implement them. The designed business processes combine people, organizational structures and IT artifacts in ways aimed at accomplishing organizational goals.

Representing the emergent behavior of inter-organizational business systems is extremely complex as is representing design decisions and evaluating their consequences. IS researchers engage behavioral and economic theories within the process of generating, predicting and evaluating the performance of alternative system designs, specifically studying the role and affects of IT artifacts.

The agent metaphor, for example, is well-suited to the representation of the varying and possibly conflicting objectives of internal and external stakeholders, enabling managers to better understand the consequences of design decisions reflected in its likely emergent behavior. These representations or models are essentially computational theories—reasoned explanations or predictions of phenomena that occur when IT artifacts are used to construct artificial worlds in support of real-world activities. However, building an agent-based model of organizational phenomena is not necessarily a research contribution. A research contribution must (1) identify the uniqueness presented by an agent-based approach for the real-world problem, (2) clearly explain why there is any question about its applicability to the problem and how the approach extends existing conceptualizations of computational capabilities, and (3) demonstrate that the approach more faithfully represents the real world and that this increased modeling fidelity significantly affects decisions taken by managers. Lacking these agent-based models become 'exercises in programming', perhaps very useful to practitioners but not constituting a research contribution. Adequately addressing these enables the researcher to formulate and address important research questions adding to the breadth and depth of knowledge in the IS discipline.

REFERENCES

Alter, S. (2003) '18 reasons why IT-reliant work systems should replace "the IT artifact" as the core subject matter of the IS field', *Communications of the AIS* (12), October, pp. 365–94.

Benbasat, I. and Zmud, R. W. (1999) 'Empirical research in information systems: The practice of relevance', *MIS Quarterly*, 23(1), March, pp. 3–16.

Benbasat, I. and Zmud, R. W. (2003) 'The identity crisis within the IS discipline: Defining and communicating the discipline's core properties', *MIS Quarterly*, June, pp. 183–94.

Boland, R. J. (2002) 'Design in the punctuation of management action', in R. Boland (ed.), *Managing as Designing: Creating a Vocabulary for Management Education and Research*, Frontiers of Management Workshop, Weatherhead School of Management, 14–15 June 2002 (available at http://design.cwru.edu).

Brooks, F. P. (1996) 'The computer scientist as toolsmith II', *Communications of the ACM*, 39(3), March, pp. 61–8.

Bunge, M. A. (1985) *Treatise on Basic Philosophy: Volume 7—Epistemology and Methodology III: Philosophy of Science and Technology—Part II: Life Science, Social Science and Technology*, D. Reidel Publishing Company, Boston, Massachusetts.

Denning, Peter J. (1997) 'The new social contract for research', *Communications of the ACM*, 40(2), February, pp. 132–4.

Fuller, R. Buckminster (1992), in A. K. Kuromiya (ed.), *Cosmography: A Posthumous Scenario for the Future of Humanity*, Macmillan.

Goodhue, D. and Thompson, R. (1995) 'Task-technology fit and individual performance', *MIS Quarterly*, June.

Hevner, A., March, S. T., Park, J. and Ram, S. (2004) 'Design science research in information systems', *MIS Quarterly*, 28(1), March, pp. 75–105.

Lee, A. (1999) 'Inaugural editor's comments', *MIS Quarterly*, 23(1), March, pp. v–xi.

Leveson, N. (2005) 'A systems-theoretic approach to safety in software-intensive systems', *IEEE Trans. on Dependable and Secure Computing* (to appear).

March, S. T. and Smith, G. (1995) 'Design and natural science research on information technology', *Decision Support Systems* 15(4), December, pp. 251–66.

Markus, M. L., Majchrzak, A. and Gasser, L. (2002) 'A design theory for systems that support emergent knowledge processes', *MIS Quarterly* 26(3), September, pp. 179–212.

Orlikowski, W. J. and Iacono, C. S. (2001) 'Research commentary: Desperately seeking the "IT" in IT research—a call to theorizing the IT artifact', *Information Systems Research* 12(2), June, pp. 121–34.

Orman, L. V. (2002) 'Electronic markets, hierarchies, hubs, and intermediaries', *Journal of Information Systems Frontiers*, 4(2), pp. 207–22.

SIGABIS (2005) AIS Special Interest Group on Agent-Based Information Systems, http://www.agentbasedis.org/, viewed 2 April 2005.

Simon, H. A. (1996) *The Sciences of the Artificial*, 3rd edn, MIT Press, Cambridge, MA.

Tsichritzis, D. (1999) 'Reengineering the university', *Communications of the ACM*, 42(6), June.

Venkatesh, V., Morris, M. G., Davis, F. D. and Davis, G. B. (2003) 'User acceptance of information technology: Toward a unified view', *MIS Quarterly*, 27, pp. 425–78.

Walls, J. G., Widmeyer, G. R. and El Sawy, O. A. (1992) 'Building an information system design theory for vigilant EIS', *Information Systems Research*, 3(1), March, pp. 36–59.

Weber, R. (2003) 'Editor's comments: Still desperately seeking the IT artifact', *MIS Quarterly*, 27(2), June, pp. iii–xi.

19
The Future of the IS Field: Drawing Directions from Multiple Maps

John Leslie King and Kalle Lyytinen

WHY THIS DEBATE, AND WHY NOW?

The foregoing papers and commentaries live up to our introductory characterization of the IS field's pluralism. An accidental observer with no prior knowledge of the IS field might find the discussion confusing, and wonder why the people in the field believe it necessary to have this discussion at this time. The discussion is not new; earlier versions of it appeared in the 1970s in concerns about the viability of the field to deliver on its promises, and around 1990 in the so-called 'rigor/relevance' debate around a presumed trade-off between intellectual quality and practical applicability. This collection captures a more recent and refined round of discussions that revolve around what Weber in this volume characterizes as debates about the *nature-of-the-discipline* and *logic-of-the-core*. The recent discussions have been more protracted and more careful than the previous rigor/relevance discussions, and reflect a greater sense of concern about the character of the IS field and its future.

We identify two broad motivations behind the recent debate. The first has to do with a deep and abiding concern in fields that attempt to straddle the realms of intellectual inquiry and practice, particularly in professionally oriented schools and colleges. As noted periodically in this collection, most IS researchers are members of faculties of management, and management as a field of study and education has a rich history of debate on these topics. The focus is the trade-off between rigor and relevance and the attempt to craft a compromise that provides sufficient scientific framing for practical knowledge while still keeping the knowledge practical so that it can be harvested for managerial practice. Despite significant attempts over the last half-century, no single compromise has succeeded in putting the concern to rest. The pendulum keeps swinging between the Charybdis of theory and the Scylla of practice. IS researchers in faculties of management are inevitably drawn into this debate, which helps to explain the intense engagement of these issues among IS researchers.

A second and more complicated motivation for the recent debate has to do with the labor market's ongoing need for professional information systems talent. The IS field was born from and has always been supported by strong external market demand. Like all professional disciplines, the IS field has been tied closely to professional labor markets. Many professional fields have created long-standing regulatory mechanisms that stabilize and smooth what might otherwise be wild swings in the match of supply to demand. For example, medicine, law and accounting have strong guild traditions, including regulation of entry to practice through qualifying examinations administered by the profession itself, and strong traditions of shaping and creating marketplace expectations of what a qualified professional should know. In contrast, the IS professional labor market in the United States and most western countries has been a roller-coaster throughout the past two decades, with the wildest recent ride being the rise and collapse of the dot.com phenomenon. Yet, there are other forces at work: the advent of outsourcing and offshore sourcing, the constant expansion of packaged software, the automation of many IS/IT functions, and so on. Professional IS talent is still needed in all western societies, but not necessarily in the quantities formerly required and not with the same skills profiles. Increasingly the talent is available in a global marketplace rather than restricted to the traditional educational networks that supported local IS education for many years.

The IS field has little refuge from the buffeting of these labor market ups and downs, and whatever buffer it has had might be declining. Other professional fields, notably some areas of engineering, have long histories of expansion and contraction in their labor markets, yet many engineering schools have been relatively stable throughout because of counter-cyclical demand profiles (e.g., jobs in electrical engineering expand as jobs in computer science decline), and many engineering schools have significant research programs that are highly funded from external sources such the US Federal Government. In contrast, a large fraction of the academic IS field is dependent on teaching in professional management programs to make its living, and declining IS enrollments is a direct threat to the field. The turbulent labor market of the past decade has coincided with a major burst of discussions about the future of the IS field, and has almost certainly heightened concerns about the field's identity, legitimacy and survivability. The outlook for the next few years seems as uncertain as the past few years, so these concerns are not likely to diminish. If the IS field is to survive and prosper, it should consider carefully the implications of its own rhetoric, and learn from the debates within its own ranks. In the process, the IS field should be cautious about confusing the short-term applicability of its disciplinary knowledge with epistemic concerns about the nature of its theories and the legitimacy of knowledge associated with the field.

WHAT HAVE WE LEARNED THUS FAR?

It is an understatement to say that there is no closure on what the IS field should be and how it should come to be that. However, there is more agreement on fundamental points than might first meet the eye. A quarter-century of discussion regarding the character, evolution and history of the field has been educational for the field. Rather than make a laundry list of agreements followed by a similar list of disagreements among participants in the debate, it seems more useful to combine the agreements and disagreements surrounding particular substantive points that define important parameters of the debate. There is no inherent order to the following; the issues appear woven throughout the discourse contained in this volume and elsewhere.

Shared Concern

To begin, there is a widespread agreement that the IS field has experienced repeated bouts of concern about the field's identity and legitimacy. However, there is significant disagreement on how concerned the field ought to be, and what, if anything, to do about these concerns. Some suggest that the IS field is in danger of disappearing if the concerns are not addressed aggressively. Others bring the concerns up in their process of suggesting that they are not really worthy of concern. Undoubtedly, there are at least some (maybe many) in the field who think the whole discussion is a waste of time and, not surprisingly, they are not joining the discussion. It is impossible to speak for them and, moreover, it is difficult to determine even the median views of the people in the field. The small fraction of the population actively writing about these issues—perhaps

20 to 40 people out of a field that routinely draws more than 1000 to its major research meetings and that globally reaches at least 5000 academics through publications—cannot be said to speak for the field as a whole. Those who speak agree that the subject is worth discussing, whether or not they agree on why it is worth discussing.

Identity and Legitimacy

There is agreement among those writing on these issues that identity and legitimacy are important in all fields of scholarship, including the IS field. Moreover, there appears to be agreement that the strengthening of identity and legitimacy is a mark of a field's growing maturity. At the same time, there is disagreement regarding what it takes to establish identity and legitimacy. More deeply, there is a rough division between two groups: those who believe that, when the nature of scientific inquiry is well established and follows particular scientific canons, identity and or legitimacy will follow; and those who believe that scientific inquiry is an emergent phenomenon that changes with scholarly challenges and the state of existing knowledge, and that identity and legitimacy are not related necessarily to specific scientific canons or positions. As long as this division persists—and it is likely to persist for a while considering that all of the authors of the commentaries in this book reinforced the points they made in their earlier papers—it is unlikely that the debate can reach consensus on the details of identity or legitimacy, or on the nature or direction of those entailments. Given that the field is still here, after many years of debate, it seems that disagreements about these fundamental issues do not threaten the field itself. In any case, such issues are under constant debate in the larger communities of philosophers, sociologists and historians of science, not to mention among scientists in many disciplinary traditions. The IS field in this sense is in good company and no exception.

The Centrality of IT

Most if not all of those in the debate agree that the IS field is closely coupled to information technology, especially technologies involving digital computers and communications. Still, there is little agreement on how this close coupling should be understood, articulated and acted upon by researchers in the IS field in order to leverage this insight. The IT focus of the field seems to be a source of strategic ambiguity that serves as both a blessing and a curse. The excitement, power and dynamism of the technology provides a strong attraction to the IS field, yet the elusive nature of the rapidly changing technology and the inherent difficulty in understanding the effects of its use on organizations, industries and society makes for daunting research challenges. Moreover, the institutional homes of many IS researchers—management schools—have not historically held technology to be very important in the larger intellectual scheme of things, which creates indifference or even hostility toward IS research agendas. In short, everyone appears to agree that the IS field is irrevocably tied to information technology, and that this brings both advantages and disadvantages, but there is little agreement on how to leverage the advantages of this research focus in environments that have little interest in grasping it. This is a particularly thorny problem for the IS field as it seeks to develop a high level of theoretical clarity and strong predictive capability.

The Role of Theory

It is almost impossible to find anyone in the debate who argues that theory is unimportant, or that strengthening the field's principal theories is undesirable. But there is considerable disagreement on the relationship between theory and the field's identity and legitimacy, and on how important theory is to the field's long-term political and institutional viability. The dispute about role of the theory in the logic-of-the-core discussion is not a schism between theory advocates and theory nihilists, as shown by the broad agreement on the general value of theory, *per se*. The disagreement centers mainly on the role of theory in identifying and or legitimating a field's intellectual work in the eyes of others. On one side are those who argue that the identity of successful academic fields is built around theories as the epistemic centers of those fields. In this view, the lack of central theories makes it difficult for any field to establish the strong intellectual identity required for academic legitimacy. The other side argues that strong intellectual identity comes from consistent, sustained and systematic attention to particular intellectual problems and challenges, and that theory plays at most a secondary role in this process. This view's primary defense is an existence proof: the claim that many clearly identifiable academic fields have no discernable theoretical core. This argument cannot be concluded with a single correct 'answer' because those in the debate have yet to agree on what they mean by theory, identity and legitimacy, how those concepts are related to one another, and what would constitute convincing theoretical or empirical proof of particular claims. This topic clearly needs and will receive further attention.

Intellectual Diversity

Everyone in the debate appears to believe that the diversity of intellectual perspectives, methods and topics is good for the IS field, at least in principle. Yet, there is disagreement regarding what diversity implies for the identity and legitimacy of the field. It is easy to mischaracterize the positions taken on this issue as bipolar extremes. In reality, the arguments are nuanced and sensitive to important academic values, including equal opportunity, intellectual openness and academic freedom. It is probably best to say that disagreements on diversity concern different individuals' views of how to characterize the 'trade-offs' involved in making decisions on intellectual diversity. Towards one end are those who believe that identity and legitimacy will only come through sustained intellectual focus. Further, such focus requires shared agenda-setting and coordination of effort to produce coherent research frameworks, better articulation of publication policies and editorial missions, agreement on what research questions count the most, and on what theoretical positions can be 'owned' by the IS field. This might restrict somewhat the scope of the field's intellectual perspectives, methods and topics, but this is a reasonable price to pay for identity and legitimacy. Those who hold this view would undoubtedly claim that their objective is not against diversity, but rather for coherent and sustained focus. Toward the other end are those who argue that the inherent nature and logic of the IS field is so turbulent and emergent that a multiplicity of intellectual perspectives, methods and topics is the only realistic way of hitting all the important research targets and reaching legitimacy. This is less an argument for diversity in itself than it is an argument against any research paradigm or position that will impractically and dangerously narrow a field whose intellectual scope covers so much territory and is changing so fast.

All things considered, the diverse parties in the debate appear to agree that the IS field is much stronger than it was when it started, and that in spite of its problems, it has been a success on all reasonable criteria. They also agree that the field focuses on an important and vibrant topic of study and practice. All the same, there remains concern over whether the field is strong *enough* to remain viable on its own recognizance, and in light of the changing fortunes of other academic fields. There is also disagreement over whether the field's importance is sustainable and controllable by people within the field as currently constituted. Although not articulated very clearly in the debate, there appears to be agreement that the IS field and its evolution is conditioned in many respects by exogenous factors such as the changing nature of the technology at the field's center, the uncertain and non-canonized character of scientific and scholarly practice presumed to guide the field's evolution, and the political complexities of the organizational and institutional environments in which IS researchers work. In a way, this is the most perplexing challenge to the IS field: to guide the field's development in spite of the field's dependence on factors that are not amenable to the choices of the people in the field.

FUTURE IMPERFECT

This volume reports on the state of the IS field as seen by a sample of participant-observers. Its primary concern is with the directions of the IS field as a world of work, asking whether those directions are desirable, what might be done differently, and how to achieve more desirable ends given limited resources. The diversity of views covered in the book raises more questions than answers about the field's future. In honor of the convoluted nature of the debates presented in this book, it is best to frame the core question about the future of the field in an equally convoluted manner using the negative interrogative of the future imperfect tense: '*Will the IS field not be OK?*' Based on the contents of the book, the nearest approximation to an answer for that question is, '*Perhaps.*'

For those who seek closure on the field's future, this is a maddening state of affairs. There is no question that the IS field would be much more tractable internally if there was widespread agreement on the field's purposes, questions, methods and standards of performance. It is worth asking, though, whether the field would be as exciting and entertaining under those conditions as it is in its current, somewhat chaotic state. And perhaps more important, it is not clear that this would make the field more secure. Security in academic fields comes from without, as a result of a receptive society agreeing that the field provides real value to the society. At the end of the day, the future of the IS field will boil down to the simple question, *Does the IS field really matter?* If so, how does it matter, and to whom? To use the contemporary business locution, what is the value proposition of the IS field at present and going forward? Most people in the IS field would probably respond that the field's value proposition centers on training IS practitioners and creating new knowledge to help guide IS practice into the future. However, as the discussions in this volume suggest, these general goals of the field look a lot less coherent when the questions of what kind of training and what kind of knowledge are joined.

The evolution of the IS field to date has been governed to a large degree by exogenous factors such as the state of technology and professional labor markets, each of which has been turbulent. And it is very likely that neither of these factors will change—the world has indeed become flatter. One big question that will face the field will be what happens to the dynamics of IT and associated services when Moore's law runs out of gas in the next decade? Will it be a boon or bane when the locus of learning shifts from improving hardware and associated software to exploiting these capabilities in a situation where significant improvements in computing power cannot be expected? It appears naïve to presume that the core value proposition of the IS field can be set by the actions of those in the field itself, but the field can operate more proactively towards shaping expectations when such fundamental shifts happen. Looking back over the history of the IS field's intellectual development, it is possible to identify three very different patterns the field might follow into the future.

The first possibility is that the IS field will prove to have been transitory, serving as midwife at the birth of the information age and becoming less vital thereafter. This might result if the exogenous factors that have been central to the field's evolution disappear or move in new directions that the people in the field do not want to travel. In this model, the most sensible future of the IS field might be to disband so that the resources of the younger field's members could be redirected toward other, more pressing needs, while older members would close out the field when they retire. Were this to happen, it should not be considered a failure: history is replete with technology-intensive intellectual discovery that was cutting-edge and incredibly important at one time, but that eventually became so routinized that it was no longer appropriate for special social investment. Perhaps the best examples of these are the ability to read, write and do simple math, but there are many others (e.g., raising plants, domesticating animals, creating metal tools, navigation). In a way, a core purpose of the academy is to turn the impossible into the real but rare, and eventually, to turn the real but rare into the valuable and routine. This is, admittedly, not a future that most people in the IS field desire, but it is wise for people in the field to consider this possibility seriously in order to put the possible futures of intellectual activity in perspective.

A second possible future is that the IS field will have re-framed itself and its purpose around the discovery and preservation of core knowledge and talent regarding application of information technology in organizational settings, irrespective of changing demand for that knowledge and talent. In this model, the core production of the field itself—the number of faculty involved, the number of students in doctoral programs, the amount of research funding—would rise or fall with demand. The field would become a repository and conservator of knowledge and skills that the opinion leadership of the field agree on. This is a highly honored tradition in the academy: classical scholarship has lived for generations on this model, despite grave threats from fiscal problems and academic reforms. Departments of classics can be found on nearly all college and university campuses to this day, although they are often small and attract relatively few students. They survive in part because they do not cost much, and they represent an important tradition in western scholarship. It is difficult to imagine just what such a model would look like for the IS field, in part because it is difficult to gauge what corpus of knowledge and skills the leaders of the field might agree on as central. If this book's content is any indication, that agreement would be a long time in coming. Nevertheless, there are probably some in the IS field who would see this as a more desirable outcome than the previous scenario.

A third possible future is that the IS field will have evolved into something new after abandoning issues and interests that became less socially relevant and adopting those that became more relevant. This would require the field to shift its focus away from some intellectual questions and toward others. Many academic fields and most professional fields have been down this path at least once. The life sciences arose from a tradition of gentleman naturalists who wanted only to better understand the glory of the creation, but the life sciences survived by turning attention toward socially valuable application of knowledge to human and animal health, agriculture and environmental sustainability. In the process, the financial support for research provided by the society at large through grants and other mechanisms went up by many orders of magnitude, and the number of people working in the field expanded dramatically. Some might claim that the life sciences today are no longer concerned with the important issues they once focused upon, and that something important has been lost, but most life scientists would probably argue that the life sciences have never been stronger. The IS field was born out of practical necessity—many organizations needed professional talent and new knowledge about the application of information technology. Such needs are likely to remain important in the future, but perhaps not in the forms seen to date. This future for the IS field is rather easy to imagine because most in the field would probably find it preferable to either of the scenarios above. However, this future is likely to require long-term acceptance of the uncertainty reflected in this book. That is not necessarily a bad outcome; to put it in IS development parlance, it would mean renaming the uncertainty from 'bug' to 'feature'. This is easier said than done, but it can probably be done.

The third model makes the most sense to the editors of this book, in part because it seems to capture the spirit evident in the contributions to this book, and in part because it is practical. Moreover, it is how the history of IS has been made. Broadly speaking, studies related to the nature and role of information in one form or another have been among the fastest growing areas of scholarship across all academic fields in the past half-century. This fact is also one of the major reasons behind the challenges the field faces in the short term. Despite continual adjustments, the US Bureau of Labor Statistics forecast of job demand still shows information-related jobs dominating nearly all other areas of work expansion over the next two decades. Whether the work these people are expected to do will fit current definitions of the term 'information systems' is another matter, but this is negotiable. Entrepreneurial people in the IS field will probably be able to tailor their research and instructional activities in ways most likely to garner support and produce useful outputs. The field under this model would evolve around what proved to work, with relatively little mourning over what was left behind.

Necessity is the mother of invention, but she is also the mother of reinvention. The discussion in this book is fundamentally about reinvention in light of different perceptions of necessity. Depending on one's point of view, the ongoing debate about the nature and future of the IS field might be seen as alarming, redundant, irrelevant or just plain baffling. It can also be seen as reassuring; as a vital form of reflective practice that continually questions presumptions about the field and forces consideration of alternatives. Irrespective of various authors' positions on the nature-of-the-discipline and the logic-of-the-core, the IS field as a whole continues to seek identity and legitimacy for its IT-centric mission, building theory and embracing intellectual diversity in the process. The disagreements are more around definitions and entailments among these issues, and around matters of degree rather than matters of kind. These disagreements form part of the refiner's fire that separates the slag from the steel. Those who bear the heat make the product stronger.

Index